EXPERIENCES

A.J.T., approaching eighty

EXPERIENCES

by
ARNOLD TOYNBEE

'Man goeth forth to his work and to his labour until the evening'

PSALM civ. 23.

1969
OXFORD UNIVERSITY PRESS
NEW YORK AND LONDON

© Oxford University Press 1969

Library of Congress Catalogue Card Number: 74-75754

Printed in the United States of America

Preface

THE PRESENT BOOK is a sequel to *Acquaintances*, which was published by the Oxford University Press in 1967. In that book my subjects are other people, and I appear there only in presenting my acquaintances to my readers. In the first and third parts of *Experiences* I am the subject as well as the narrator. In the second part I am an observer and an appraiser, but not of particular persons, as I am in *Acquaintances*. This second part of the present book is a survey of, and commentary on, the changes in human affairs within my lifetime.

Three accidents have worked together to give me the chance of living through more change than is usually experienced in the course of eighty years: I was born and brought up in England; I was born in 1889; and I was not fit for military service in the First World War, owing to a fluke that I mention in Part I, Chapter 2. Few countries have experienced so great a change of fortune as Britain has between 1889 and 1969. I am old enough to be able to remember Britain as she was at her Victorian zenith, and in August 1914 I was already doing a grown-up person's work in the antediluvian world. This first chapter of my adult life might have been the last as well if I had been a combatant in the First World War. It was the last chapter for huge numbers of my contemporaries on both sides of the front. The chances are that I should have been killed in 1915 or 1916. Actually I have lived on for more than half a century after those deadly years. Consequently I have witnessed the earlier stages of the world revolution that started in 1914 and that, since then, has been gathering momentum. It is unlikely that I shall live on to see even a partial dénouement of this historic drama, but I have already seen enough acts to make me want to try my hand at drawing up a provisional balance-sheet of human affairs in my lifetime while I am still alive and in possession of my wits.

The pieces presented in Part III of this book have been written over a period of sixty years (1907–66). The rest of the book (that is, almost the whole of it) has been written since early in 1964 when I wrote 'Janus at Seventy-five'. The first five chapters of Part I were written in the summer of 1965, at the same time as *Acquaintances*, the sixth and eighth chapters in 1966, the ninth chapter in 1966–8. Part II was begun in January 1968 and was finished in May 1968. By the intended publication-date in the spring of 1969, there will have been time for the current world revolution to pass through several more stages. In May 1968 it was still gathering speed.

23 May 1968.

Arnold Toynbee

CONTENTS

PART II: HUMAN AFFAIRS IN MY LIFETIME (1889–)
THE BALANCE-SHEET AS I READ IT

PART III: REFLECTIONS

Contents   ix

ILLUSTRATIONS

PART I

Personal Affairs

1 : Going away to School

SENDING one's children away to a boarding-school is a peculiar English custom—and only an 'upper-class' and 'middle-class' one at that. It is beyond the means of most English families; for it is expensive, unless the child manages to win a scholarship, as my wife and I each did. In Scotland, where the standard of education is higher than it is in England, to be sent away to school is exceptional in all classes, and so it is, too, in Continental European countries and in the United States. My American daughter-in-law would not hear of sending my grandson away to school. Indeed, the day-school is the standard form of school all over the World; and, for a sensitive child who takes things hard, to be sent to a boarding-school is an ordeal. The advocates of boarding-schools maintain, of course, that it is the sensitive children who need most to be sent away, because they need to be hardened if they are ever to learn to stand on their own feet.

I have never forgotten the experience of having it broken to me by my parents, when I was rising ten years old, that they were going to send me to a boarding-school from the coming summer term onwards. I can still see, in my mind's eye, the exact position of the armchair, in the drawing-room at No. 12 Upper Westbourne Terrace, in which my mother was sitting while I was standing, thunderstruck, facing her. The unforeseen and hardly credible ordeal was imminent; for, by now, this summer term was not far ahead. My parents confessed that they had put off telling me because they could not bear to give me the shock that they knew that I was bound to suffer. In truth, the Earth did suddenly give way beneath my feet. Till that moment, I had felt completely secure. I have never since recaptured that Eden-like state of existence. Perhaps it is not good for one to feel completely secure; perhaps one needs a quantum of insecurity as a stimulus if one is to learn to hold one's own in life. I doubt this, for I had entered into the life of my day-school with zest. I knew all the other boys' faces and names, and I immensely enjoyed the games in the playground. One end of the playground looked out on to the Grand Junction Canal, and the school building was one of those mid-Victorian stucco Italianate houses that still survive, here and there, between Paddington and Regent's Park.

My destiny had been settled by my mother's having received a small legacy just after the headmaster of my day-school—Warwick House—had handed the school over to his brother in order to start a boarding-school in Kent, at Wootton Court. The legacy would not cover the whole of a boarding-school's fees for two or three years; but the headmaster of Warwick House had reported to his brother that I had a fair chance of winning a scholarship at a 'public' school; if I did, this would be a good advertisement for Wootton Court; so the headmaster of Wootton Court had agreed to take me at reduced fees on spec.

The date of the beginning of term was, for me, like execution-day for a prisoner who has been condemned to death. As time rushed towards the dreadful moment, my agony rose to a climax, and this did not happen only on the first occasion. It happened three times a year for the next six years at least—in fact, till I was more than half way through the five years at Winchester that followed the three years at Wootton Court. I was on the defensive against boarding-school from first to last, and I was not enthusiastic for the University. I was not thoroughly happy again, as I had been at my day-school, till I became a student at the British Archaeological School at Athens in 1911–12. By that time I was 22–23 years old. It was in Greece, not at my two successive boarding-schools in England, that I did learn at last to stand on my own feet. I learnt it by hiking through the Greek countryside, and I was able to stand this fairly severe self-imposed ordeal because I enjoyed the experience so intensely.

Most small boys, I should guess, are more robust than I was at that stage of life. When my son Philip, for instance, was a boarder at the Dragon School at Oxford, a letter from him came one morning, which ran: 'Dear Mummy and Daddy, such a lovely thing has happened. An anti-Toynbee Society has been started.' If an anti-Toynbee Society had been organized against me at Wootton Court, I should have been distraught. I should have prayed the Earth to open and to swallow me up. Philip, however, at that age, thirsted

1   A.J.T.'s father and mother

for notoriety, even if the price was some discomfort. In the hope of making him reconsider this juvenile philosophy of his, and also out of curiosity to see what, at this age, he would make of Gibbon, I read aloud to him, one day during the next holidays, the passage in *The History of the Decline and Fall* in which Gibbon describes how the blindly ambitious senator Didius Iulianus spent his huge fortune on buying the imperial office from the praetorian guards who had just murdered the previous incumbent. The story moves swiftly to its inevitable end. The newly inaugurated emperor had only just time to eat the dinner that had been prepared for his predecessor—the food was still hot—before he was murdered in his turn. I had hoped that this story would make an impression on Philip, and it did, but it was not the impression on which I had reckoned. 'Well, you see, Daddy,' was Philip's comment, 'that emperor did quite right. He wanted to become famous, and he did. He became famous enough to make Gibbon write this story about him, and to make you read Gibbon's story now to me.' I had not thought of that, so Philip had the last word.

A child's penalty for being intellectually precocious is that he or she has to live and work and try to hold his own among children who are appreciably older on the average. Among my elders at Wootton Court, I got bullied at first; my work deteriorated; my chances of a scholarship seemed to have dwindled; and the head-master, wondering whether he had made a bad bargain over me, became unpleasantly restive. The assistant masters and my parents, together, had some difficulty in making him see that it was up to him to ensure that I should no longer be led a dog's life. He did then take the necessary steps; my work looked up again; and I was sent in for the Winchester scholarship examination, in which the competition was hotter than in any other. The date of my birthday, 14 April, allowed me to have two tries. At the first try, I failed to get on to the election roll; I came out first on the waiting-list, but, in the course of the next year, no boy in College dropped out to let me in. So I made my second try, and this time I came out third on the roll. The senior on the roll was my life-long friend E. R. Morgan, now Bishop Emeritus of Truro. The second, also above me, was R. H. Fowler, a very distinguished mathematician and cricketer. I owed my success to the highly intelligent coaching that I had been given at Wootton Court by one of the assistant masters, H. J. Haselfoot. He had taught me how to think for myself.

The scholarship examination was formidable; so much seemed to depend on how one fared in it. Here my parents showed an understanding for which I have never ceased to be grateful to them. 'Just do your best,' they said to me, as the Winchester scholarship examination date loomed up for the first time. 'None of us can do more than that. Very likely you won't win a Winchester scholarship; you will be in competition with the ablest boys from all the other preparatory schools in the country. Well, if you don't get on to the roll at Winchester, that won't be the end of the World. You know the school in the North where your Aunt Maggie is the matron. We can afford to send you there without a scholarship, and it is an excellent school, so do not worry more than you can help.' This wise and kind handling of me by my parents at this critical stage relieved my mind immensely. I could and would do my very best, and that was all that was being asked of me.

All the same, the tension was severe. It was not so bad at the first try, because I knew that I was going to have a second chance; but, at the second try, even the certain prospect of the northern school, if I were to fail at Winchester, could not completely reassure me. The examination lasted for three days, and on the second and the third morning, after breakfast, one had to scan, on the school noticeboard, the list of candidates who were still in the running for that day. A list of survivors can be as agonizing as a casualty list. At both tries, I did survive to the end. On the second occasion, on the morning after the third day, before my father and I had got up, he muttered to me from his bed: 'Your dormouse is dead.' He had been right to withhold the grievous news from me till then. I was stricken with sorrow, and, if I had known of this loss the day before, I should not have been able to give my mind to the papers. As it was, the mathematical papers, which Ralph Fowler had mastered with ease, had reduced me literally to tears. That day, my father tried to console me with strawberries, which had been under a ban for me till the last paper was behind me. Some of the best strawberry gardens in England lie between Winchester and Southampton, and the date of the Winchester scholarship examination coincided with the height of the strawberry season. I ate my strawberries without being consoled—they could not compensate me for the death of my dormouse. That term, in the carpenter's shop at Wootton Court, I had just finished making a super-cage for him, a house of many mansions; and now this would never be inhabited.

The business of scanning lists of examination results reminds me of an amusing story that Arnold Wilson once told me about himself and his father, Canon Wilson, the Headmaster of Clifton. In potency of character, the Canon was a match for his children, and this is saying much. So, when, one day, Arnold Wilson announced that he wanted to try for Woolwich, the Canon snorted: 'Woolwich? Why, Sandhurst is the place for you.' 'All the same, I want to try for Woolwich,' Arnold repeated, and, in the tussle of wills, his father grudgingly gave way. When the day came on which the Woolwich examination results were to be published, Arnold came down before breakfast, opened *The Times*, and found that he was not only in but was at the top. So he folded the paper up as neatly as if it had not been opened yet, and put it in his father's place. When the Canon came down in his turn, he opened the paper at the page containing the Woolwich list, and began to scan the list from bottom to top. 'You're not in; you're not in; I told you so,' he kept growling, almost triumphantly, as his eye travelled higher and higher up the column. Just before he reached the top, Arnold gently put his finger on his name there.

Three years at a preparatory boarding-school had only half prepared me for facing a 'public' school. At a preparatory school the gap between the youngest and the oldest ages was only three or four years; at a public school it was five or six; and, to the 'new man,' the eighteen-year-olds and nineteen-year-olds seemed like grown men— the more so because their overwhelming age was reinforced by their despotic authority. A prefect had powers over a junior that he would never have again in after-life, not even if he were to become commander-in-chief or prime minister. Moreover, a preparatory school, even a boarding one, was, to a large degree, under the rule of women—a 'regiment' which, far from being 'monstrous', was humanizing. By contrast, Chamber Court at Winchester was as exclusively male as Mount Athos. The nearest woman—Miss Stewart at 'Sick House'—was on the far side of Meads, quite out of reach after we had been locked in for the night. 'Mammy No-guts', who mended our socks by day, was no mother for any other purpose.

I remember vividly the moment when Eddy Morgan, conducted by his grown-up half-brother, and I, conducted by my father, met, for the first time, in the Second Master's study to enter on our first 'half' in College. When I went to Winchester I had not yet read any of the anthropologists' descriptions of the institutions of primitive societies, with the successive excruciating initiation ceremonies through which the rising generation is made to pass. As soon as I did read some of these descriptive anthropological works, I realized that, for five years at Winchester, I had tasted what life had been like for Primitive Man. One found oneself suddenly plunged into a world of arbitrary prohibitions and commandments (chiefly prohibitions). A boy might not wear brown boots till he had been in the school for two years. He might not wear grey flannel trousers till he had become a college prefect or an 'in loco'. He must not use the word 'think' nor, in some contexts, even the word 'the'; and this made talking tricky. He had to take off his straw hat (or top hat, if it was a Sunday) on passing through the gate leading into Chamber Court, because, before the Reformation, the middle niche, of the three niches above the gate, had contained a statue of Our Lady Saint Mary de Winton. When this boy became a prefect, he was allowed to keep his hat on, in spite of Our Lady's invisible yet abiding presence. This will give you some idea of what the status of a prefect was. In theological terms he was *isotheotókos*.

One was not thrown into this strange and complex new world without some preparation. For his first two weeks as a 'new man', a boy was not yet 'under sweat' (i.e. was not yet subject to fagging), and he was assigned a 'father' to induct him. My 'father' was Leigh Mallory, who died on Mount Everest. My 'son' was A. D. Gillespie, who was killed in the First World War. His photograph is one of those on my mantelpiece here in this room in which I am writing these words; it is just behind my right shoulder. There was a great deal to teach and to learn in that first fortnight: to begin with, a tribal language, 'Winchester notions'. A dictionary of this language had been published, so I had been able to study it in advance; but most of what a 'new man' had to know could be learnt only on the spot. What I found the most difficult to remember were the faces and names and nicknames of large numbers of people—'dons', and, still more important, grandees like 'Captain of Lords' and 'Senior Commoner Prefect'. Dons' wives had nicknames too: 'the Vulture', 'the Horse', and so on. One had to know whose wives these were. At the end of the first fortnight, the 'new man' was examined by his prefects. If the 'new man' failed to pass, his 'father' might be beaten with a wooden fives-bat. If he passed, he had to take his 'father' to School Shop and let him order, at his 'son's' expense, whatever he liked to eat and drink. I failed the first time, but, fortunately for me, Mallory was not beaten on my account— fortunately, I say, because it was understood that a 'father' was free to take it out of a 'son' who had let him down. My own 'son' Gillespie did pass. He had a first-rate mind (later on, at Oxford, he won the Ireland in a year in which we were both sitting for it). As for me, I was an industrious and anxious-minded 'father' to him.

From first to last, I was in all-out rebellion against Wykehamical institutions. The arbitrary tribal laws and lore seemed to me pre-posterous; I resented having to submit to them; and I sometimes trailed my coat. If I had been, say, a budding Masai warrior, instead of being a 'College man', I might have been put to death for this; but, in College at Winchester during the five years 1902–7, I was never made to suffer for my non-conformity. It was accepted with humorous indulgence, as the whimsies of madmen are accepted in the East.

From Winchester I brought away with me three life-long treasures: a filial relation, across a gulf of more than five centuries, with our founder, William of Wykeham, who had given us our education; a reverence, admiration, and affection for M. J. Rendall, then Second Master (which meant house-master for College) and eventually Headmaster after I had left the school;[1] and intimate friendships with a number of my contemporaries. These friendships have been as close and as lasting as the blood-relation between brothers. A few minutes after I had first met my life-long friend Eddy Morgan, I was standing in Ninth Chamber, setting eyes, for the first time, on David Davies, who was fifth on our roll, I think (but I ought not to say 'think' in a Wykehamical context; I ought

[1] See a previous book of mine, *Acquaintances* (London 1967, Oxford University Press), pp. 37–42.

to know for sure, or else stay silent). Eddy Morgan and I are still alive; David, who was a few months younger than me, is not. But, from 1902 till 1964, David and I were never parted. We went through Winchester and Oxford together; physical unfitness exempted us both from being killed in the First World War; and all through our working lives in London we used to have lunch together once a week.

About half of our generation at school and at the university did lose their lives in the First World War. Perhaps this made the bond between the survivors still closer than it already was; but between those of us who have lived out their lives and those whose lives were cut short the bond was, and is, as close as it could be.

My contemporaries at Winchester whose names are now best known are, I suppose, Stafford Cripps and D. N. Pritt, both eminent at the bar and radical in politics, though this in differing degrees. Oswald Mosley did not enter the school till after I had left. If we had not suffered fifty-per-cent casualties, the number of well-known names would now be at least double. Bobby Palmer, for instance, would today be a Conservative elder statesman; G. L. Cheesman would be the most eminent living Roman historian in the World without dispute since the deaths of Fraccaro and De Sanctis.

When I left Winchester, I wrote a Greek couplet declaring that, in spite of my education in the Classics there and my feeling for the Founder, I was glad to be leaving. Later on, at Oxford, I wrote a second couplet, cancelling the first. I was now no longer living under the rule of Winchester tribal law, and I had realized that my Winchester friendships were priceless treasures for me.

2 : Three Greek Educations

I HAVE confessed that, at Winchester, I was in a permanent state of revolt against the tyranny (so it felt to me) of the primitive tribal institutions there. My affection for Winchester is great, but it is retrospective. There was, though, one gift, out of the many gifts

given me by Winchester, that I did appreciate whole-heartedly at
the time; and this was the superb education that I was given there
in the Greek and Latin languages and literatures.

Except in 'Army Class', education at Winchester in the years
1902–7 was nine-tenths classical. The reverse side of the excellence
of the teaching of Latin and Greek was that other subjects were
starved. For instance, no time was allowed for learning French and
German simultaneously. If a boy wanted to start learning German,
he had to stop learning French, and we were taught each of them
in turn as if it, too, were a 'dead language'. It was not till later that
I realized that Latin and Ancient Greek, too, were not yet dead, considering that they were still in use respectively in the liturgies of the
Roman Catholic and the Greek Orthodox churches; and, in Hungary in 1937, I met an agèd Magyar nobleman who could still talk
non-ecclesiastical colloquial Latin. This had been the language of
the Hungarian Parliament till 1846. It was the elaborate Latin of
the post-Diocletianic Roman Imperial Chancery. For instance, my
nobleman's word for 'thou' was nothing so straightforward as
simple *tu*; it was *dominatio tua*.

At Winchester in my time, French and German were taught
mostly by the mathematics masters. The reasoning behind this was,
I guess, that the teachers of one non-classical subject might as well
be conscripted to teach another. I am not ungrateful for having been
taught to read German. Thanks to Mr. E. J. Turner's teaching, I am
as familiar with *Faust* as I am with the *Agamemnon* ; and Heine's
Reisebilder, with Mr. Turner's exposition of them, gave me an inside
view of the Napoleonic Empire and of the Metternichian reaction
that followed it. My regret is that our study of living languages was
not carried farther than that. There was no question of our being
taught to speak French and German, as well as to read them. I was
sent out into the World speechless in any language except my
mother-tongue; and I was put to shame when, in the course of the
First World War, I was sent by a war-time government department
to talk to republican German refugees in Switzerland. I found
myself tongue-tied.

In so far as I have since learnt to speak a smattering of French,
German, Italian, Modern Greek, and Turkish, I have done it by
plunging into the countryside on foot and thus putting myself under

the necessity of asking the way, buying food and drink, and finding shelter for the night. These urgent elementary needs do have a magic effect in loosening one's tongue. I once managed to ask my way along mountain-paths in Japan on the strength of a single Japanese word. This talisman word was 'ichijikan', meaning 'hour'. If I uttered the word and held up one, two, and three fingers in turn with an interrogative expression of face, I could learn how many hours' journey it still was to the next village. A traveller's needs may even make him fluent in a foreign living language; but his way of speaking it remains grotesque, and I have been put out of countenance, time and again, by the excellence of the French and German that comes out of the mouth of a member of the British Foreign Service who has been grounded in living languages as thoroughly as I have been grounded in Latin and Greek. However, at Winchester, Mr. E. J. Turner ('the Hopper') did, as I have testified, ground us in *Faust* (both parts) so admirably that, since then, *Faust*, as well as the *Agamemnon*, has been a lasting mental possession and inspiration for me.

Mathematics were taken more seriously than modern languages were. Yet, at about the age of sixteen, I was offered a choice which, in retrospect, I can see that I was not mature enough, at the time, to make wisely. This choice was between starting on the calculus and, alternatively, giving up mathematics altogether and spending the time saved from it on reading Latin and Greek literature more widely. I chose to give up mathematics, and I have lived to regret this keenly after it has become too late to repair my mistake. The calculus, even a taste of it, would have given me an important and illuminating additional outlook on the Universe, whereas, by the time at which the choice was presented to me, I had already got far enough in Latin and Greek to have been able to go farther with them unaided. So the choice that I made was the wrong one, yet it was natural that I should choose as I did. I was not good at mathematics; I did not like the stuff; and I soon discovered that it was of the essence of mathematics (no doubt this is part of their beauty and their glory) that one could never leave any step on the ascending ladder behind one. Every lower step came back at one through being involved in every higher step.

I particularly disliked trigonometry, and, from unpleasant experience, I foreboded that, if I did embark on the calculus, I should find that I had not left trigonometry behind. To this day I do not know whether this would really have happened to me, but the mere dread of it was enough to prompt me to give up mathematics as soon as I was given the chance. Looking back, I feel sure that I ought not to have been offered the choice; the rudiments, at least, of the calculus ought to have been compulsory for me. One ought, after all, to be initiated into the life of the world in which one is going to have to live. I was going to have to live in the Western World at its transition from the modern to the post-modern chapter of its history; and the calculus, like the full-rigged sailing ship, is (as Oswald Spengler has taught me) one of the characteristic expressions of the modern Western genius.

In compensation for these intellectual losses, the teaching of the Greek and Latin classics was magnificent at Winchester in my day. The education that we were then being given there was not of the kind that our founder had contemplated. William of Wykeham, Bishop of Winchester, had founded his College of St. Mary de Winton prope Winton ('prope' signified 'just outside the city walls') to feed his College of St. Mary de Winton ad Oxon, still popularly called 'New College', because, like most things in the World, it had been new once upon a time. Bishop William's purpose in founding his college at Oxford and his feeder college at Winchester had been to train peasants' sons to become parish priests. Our Founder disapproved of monks. He thought them parasitic. He himself had started his career not even as a secular priest but as a layman. He had been Edward III's principal man of business; and the King had rewarded him for his efficient services by causing him to be made a bishop. The entire process is said to have been carried out between the morning and the evening of a single day. Starting as a layman that morning, William had raced through all the orders, beginning with exorcist, till he had found himself a bishop before nightfall. The designer of his tomb in Winchester Cathedral must have known of his prejudice against monks and have therefore decided to play a practical joke on him. At the feet of the recumbent alabaster figure on top of the tomb there sit three jolly little monks, all manifestly in high spirits. Evidently they are rejoicing over the anti-monachical bishop's death.

Our education at Winchester in 1902–7 was not Wykeham's; it was Grocyn's—a Wykehamist who was one of the sixteenth-century English scholars that imported Italian humanism into England. At Winchester in the first decade of the twentieth century, we were still being given the complete humanist education of the fifteenth-century Italian Renaissance. Our 'acculturation' to the civilization of the Graeco-Roman World was so thorough that it had some quaint results, about which I have more to say in the seventh chapter of the present part of this book.

Of course, the great majority of the boys in the school did not get far enough on in the two classical languages, not to speak of the two literatures, ever to become really at home in them. For this majority, their drilling in the elements of Latin and Greek grammar was penal treadmill-work; and, after they had left school, most of what had been inculcated into them so disagreeably was quickly sloughed off again by their liberated minds. The harvest of this humanist education was gathered in only by a minority of boys who were intellectually able and whose minds also happened to have a literary bent. These necessary qualifications ruled out all but a few; and the barrenness of the humanist education for the majority of the boys who were put through its mill is the most telling of the counts in the indictment against it.

However, fortunately (so I hold) for me, I proved to be one of those for whom this classical education was not a misfit. I was never in revolt at Winchester against this. I devoted myself to it whole-heartedly; I took it altogether seriously; and indeed my rebellion against the tribal way of life, which was making me withdraw into myself, drove me to cultivate the classics with an almost demonic fervour. Private and solitary works of supererogation, going far beyond what the school curriculum required of me, were the means that I discovered for seceding from the tribal life that was so irksome to me. In the Graeco-Roman World, to which I had already gained the entry, I found a blissful city of refuge; and this was not just 'the city of Cecrops'; in Marcus Aurelius's terms, it was also the vaster 'city of Zeus'. My physical city of refuge at Winchester was Moberly Library; and it goes without saying that this was splendidly equipped for classical studies; but its range was far wider than that. In Moberly Library, I not only explored the Graeco-Roman World, to which I had the key already. Worlds on worlds swam into my ken there. To have the free run of Moberly Library was a general education in itself.

However, the Greek and Latin classics were the staple of our curriculum, and the consequences of this were quaint indeed. The objective of the Italian humanists had been a withdrawal with a view to a return. They had sought to extricate themselves intellectually and spiritually from the contemporary world in order to find their way back into the lost earthly paradise of the Graeco-Roman World. This ideal demanded of the aspirant that he should not only learn to read the Latin and Greek authors but should acquire the knack of imitating them—even reproducing the niceties of each old master's personal style. How many passages of Burke's speeches did I not translate at Winchester into Ciceronian Latin? How many passages of Emerson's essays did I not translate into Platonic Greek? We were also challenged to translate pieces of English poetry, in every genre, into Latin and Greek verse in the corresponding categories. Moreover, this arduous schooling in producing 'versions' was only preparatory. The crown of our classical education was the production of original compositions of our own in Latin and Greek prose and verse.

One consequence, for me, of this high-powered humanist education has been that, ever since I was first captivated by it, I have been alienated from my mother-tongue. In one's passage through life there are occasions on which one's feelings are so powerfully moved that they seek release and relief by expressing themselves in patterns of words. Whenever this need overtakes me, the words come out, not in my native English, but in either Greek or Latin. A non-classically-educated reader may find it hard to believe that this is not an affectation. With my hand on my heart, I can assure him that it is not. In English, I am no poet at all; so, if I were restricted to English, I should be dumb. My feelings would be bottled up without an outlet. Actually, they find vent in Greek and Latin because, in those two languages, I am a minor (very minor) poet. In the third part of this book, I have printed some Greek and Latin verses of mine, written in the course of the sixty years 1907–66. Where I have given the equivalent of a Greek or Latin poem in English, it is the Greek or Latin piece that is the original and the English piece that is the 'version'.

I have sometimes amused myself by wondering what one of the genuine old masters would make of my, and my contemporaries' and predecessors', Greek and Latin poems, supposing that he could come back to life to read them. I reconstruct his hypothetical reaction by my own reaction to works written in English by some highly cultivated and accomplished Indian man of letters. Ninety-nine per cent of the Indian man of letters' work in English is so idiomatic that I am astonished at his having succeeded in mastering a foreign language so perfectly—and then, at intervals, the residual one per cent pulls me up short and makes me smile. The effect of the one per cent of lapses from perfection is comic, just because the other ninety-nine per cent is irreproachable. The faulty one per cent convicts the writer of not being a native-born English-speaker, in spite of his amazing virtuosity in his command of his adopted language. I fancy that, if Cicero or Plato or Sophocles or Virgil could have had a pre-view of the corpus of Greek and Latin literature written by modern Western humanists since the fifteenth century of the Christian Era, their reaction would have been something like the one that I have just been describing.

The situation in which one was placed by a successful classical education in England in the first decade of the twentieth century was the position which had been taken up deliberately in the first two centuries of the Christian Era by the Neo-Atticists. These academic scholars earned their living in the Roman Empire, as I do today in the United States, by giving public lectures; but, unlike me nowadays, they never spoke about contemporary subjects. Neither they nor their audiences would have tolerated such vulgarity. They transported themselves resolutely into the age between the Battle of Marathon and the Battle of Chaeronea and impersonated one of the famous statesmen of that short-lived era—say, Pericles, arguing the pros and cons, for Athens, of going to war with Sparta in 431 B.C., or Epameinondas discussing in 371 B.C. with Pelopidas whether the Thebans should dare to risk facing the hitherto invincible Lacedaemonians in the field in the hope of taking them by surprise and overthrowing them with the new-fangled Theban shock-tactics.

At Winchester during the years 1902–7, we neo-Neo-Atticists, too, were living in the 'classical' age of Ancient Greek history. It is true that contemporary events did, from time to time, break through into our consciousness. Domestic party politics were more familiar to us than 'foreign affairs'. Domestic issues were debated in the School debating society. However, I can remember two cases in which an event in the international field was actually introduced into our curriculum.

After the outbreak of the Russo-Japanese War, Mr. Rendall cancelled one of his division's weekly compositions in Greek or Latin and told us to spend that week on studying the map of the war-zone and then, in class, to draw from memory the best map that we could—not just a map of coastlines, rivers, and mountain-ranges, but one showing ports, sea-routes, railways, fortresses, and any other features, natural or artificial, that seemed to us to be of military importance. The Russo-Japanese War meant something to us, because we knew that Russia was Britain's rival in Asia. The other case was the Anglo-French Entente Cordiale. This was set in 1906-7 as the subject for our annual Latin prize essay. The essay that I sent in still survives; and, in what I wrote, there is evidence that we were aware that the Entente was a new departure in Anglo-French relations, and that the two countries had been drawn together by a common anxiety about the rising power of Germany. But I am sure that it did not occur to us, and I doubt whether it occurred even to the master who chose the subject, that the establishment of the Entente might be a really portentous event in the world in which we were living. Still less did we forebode that it might be the prelude to a war in which our casualties would be as heavy, proportionately, as those of the Spartiate contingent on the Lacedaemonian side at the Battle of Leuctra.

The truth is that the world in which we were living—the world that was going to fall about our ears, in death-dealing ruin, only seven years later—was not, in 1907, the real world for us, any more than the world of the early Roman Empire was the real world for the adepts of 'the Second Sophistic'. The real world was, for us, the self-same one that it had been for them. It was the world that had produced those works of Greek literature that in Augustus's generation the Neo-Atticists had registered as being canonical. It was a world, as they and we saw it, that had sprung to life in the Homeric epic and had met with a sudden death after the delivery of the last of Demosthenes' speeches. For us, though not for Dio Chrysostomus or for Aelius Aristeides, that classical Greek world had had a short-lived Latin resurrection in the Augustan Age. We might dubiously countenance even 'the Silver Age' of Latin literature as well; but, at the very latest, the real world had petered out, for us, in the last line of the latest of Juvenal's satires. After that, the curtain came down on history.

This was the effect on me of my first Greek education. It had occupied twelve years of my life, the critical twelve years from the age of ten, at which I had started to learn Greek, to the age of twenty-two, at which I had sat for my final examination at Oxford in the Literae Humaniores school. I had started learning Latin at the age of seven; but, long before that, my mother had made an historian of me by being an historian herself; so the approach to the Graeco-Roman World that had attracted me the most had been, not the literary, but the historical one. Before I had taken my final examination at Oxford, my college, Balliol, had appointed me to a tutorial fellowship for teaching Ancient Greek and Roman history. I was to start on this in the academic year after the next one. Meanwhile, the college had renewed my scholarship for an additional year and had told me to spend this intervening year—the academic year 1911–12—abroad, doing whatever I thought would be most useful for equipping me for my future work in life.

I knew at once what I was going to do. I was going to complete my Greek education by spending this *Wanderjahr* on seeing with my own eyes, for the first time, the physical landscape of the Greek World that had become my spiritual home. I had realized that the descriptions, maps, and photographs with which I had made myself familiar at Winchester and Oxford were no substitutes for a first-hand view. (I have more to say on this point in the sixth chapter of this part.) So I would go first to the British Archaeological School at Rome, and would make Rome my base of operations for hiking about in the surrounding countryside for six or seven weeks. This would give me a first-hand view of the landscape which had been the setting of the formative age of Roman history. I would then go on to the British Archaeological School at Athens, and would make Athens my base of operations for hiking about in Greece for the rest of my precious free year. This year of hiking would supply the

hitherto missing element in my Greek education. I carried this programme out.

Heading towards my Mediterranean spiritual home from Dover,
I did not know, from point to point, where I was while I was
crossing France, any more than I had known where I was when I
was travelling at home in England. At an early age, I had successfully resisted an attempt to make me learn by heart the names of the
counties, rivers, and principal towns of England. I had remained
ignorant of the topography of Britain and of Gaul, and even, to
some extent, of Gallia Cisalpina too, and, worse still, I had remained
uninterested in it. But I had felt no such repugnance to learning the
topography of Peninsular Italy and of Greece and the Aegean, as far
as this could be learnt by poring over maps, plans, and books; and,
from the moment at which, on 30 September 1911, my train backed
out of Pisa station, crept past the Leaning Tower, and slid over the
River Arno, I knew, at each point-moment, exactly where I was all
the way from there to the east end of Crete, which was the eastern-
most point that I reached in my 1911–12 *Wanderjahr.*

One of the keenest intellectual pleasures in life, for me, has been
the thrill of recognition when I have set eyes, for the first time, on
some piece of the landscape of the Graeco-Roman World that has
long been familiar to me at second hand and that is highly charged
with historical associations. Τοῦτ' ἐκεῖνο: this is that. I could always
identify the mountain, island, river, plain, or city, even when it
looked disconcertingly unlike what I had expected. 'That short
sprawl of naked limestone: Why that is the Ozolian Locris', I noted,
as the *Mykáli* was steaming up the Gulf of Corinth. 'A whole
canton of Hellas. Yet it looks as if it could not provide sustenance
for even one solitary goat.' And then the thrill of the exit from the
Corinth Canal into the Saronic Gulf. Here there burst upon me,
from the reverse direction, the view described by Servius Sulpicius
Rufus in his famous letter of consolation to Cicero (*Ad Fam.*, iv, 5)
on the occasion of Cicero's beloved daughter Tullia's death. Corinth,
Aegina, Megara, Salamis, Peiraeus, Athens, all simultaneously within sight. I, too, found it hardly credible that so many historic cities
should throng together in such small compass. As we had approached
the west end of the Canal from the Gulf, the Acrocorinthus had been
unmistakable. The reality was true to the innumerable drawings and

photographs of it. But, when Athens came into view after we had rounded the southern tip of Salamis, what a surprise. I had expected to see Athens dominated by the Acropolis. Instead, I saw the Acropolis dwarfed by Mount Lycabettus; and it was the monastery on this historically undistinguished mountain's summit, and not the Parthenon, that caught and held one's eye. The British School, which was to be my headquarters for the next nine months, stands on the foot of Lycabettus's eastern slopes.

From our first sight of Acroceraunus till our disembarkation at the Peiraeus, this voyage had been, for me, the crown and completion of the intensive Greek education that had been absorbing my energies for the last twelve years. This, I felt, was the consummation to which those twelve years had been leading up; this was my long and hard Greek education's objective, now at last unfolding itself before my eyes. Yet, thrilled though I had been by the experience of setting eyes on Greece for the first time, I had not been giving quite the whole of my mind to this entrancing spectacle; for, while I had been leaning over the rail and drinking in the view, I had been talking all the time to a fellow-passenger who was standing beside me.

This passenger was a man of my own age, and he was an American; we had been comparing notes of our experience of life so far; and I had been impressed by the amount of experience that this contemporary of mine had managed to accumulate already. He had been in three or four different jobs. I can remember three of them: he had worked on a farm, in a bank, and in a bakery. Incidentally he had earned enough money in five or six years to be able now to take some months off for travelling round the World on his savings. He had already travelled through the Simplon Tunnel three times. He had doubled back on his tracks to meet his sister, who was on her travels on her own account. In his itinerary he had allotted two days to Greece before going on to Egypt. He knew practically nothing about Greece, and his two days' ration of time for filling this gap in his knowledge was, of course, derisorily inadequate. I was now allotting nine months to a stay in Greece that was to be merely the first in a series. This American's method of acquainting himself with the World was superficial, and so must have been his training for doing the successive jobs that had enabled him to pay his way.

2   Gilbert Murray, O.M.

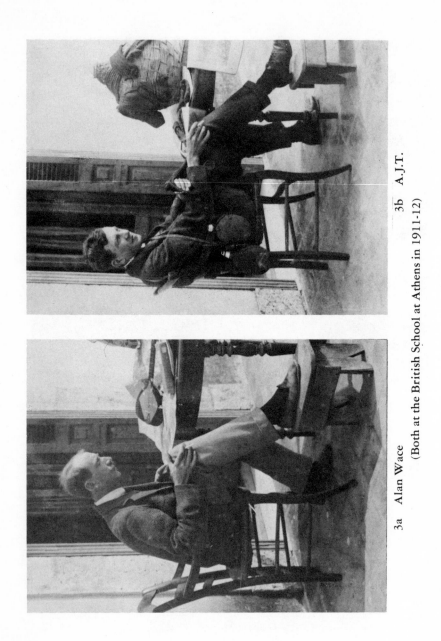

3a Alan Wace

3b A.J.T.

(Both at the British School at Athens in 1911-12)

Yet what had struck me about him most had not been his superficiality; it had been his enterprisingness.

The American's inconsequent career up to date had made my
steady one seem dull to me by comparison; and this contrast had
awakened in me my first doubts about my traditional education,
which, till now, I had taken for granted unquestioningly, as some of
my Oxford contemporaries had continued to take for granted our
ancestral religion. This American contemporary of mine had learnt,
better than I had, how to live. When we had reached the Peiraeus,
it had been he, not I, who had done the bargaining with the aggressive boatman who had rowed us ashore from the ship and with the
aggressive cab-driver whom we had hired to take us from Peiraeus
to Athens. See Greece in two days, and then go on to see Egypt!
Ridiculous! Yet I, who spent the next nine months in Greece, did
not manage to see Egypt till fifty years later. The very thoroughness
of my first Greek education had been cramping. The almost comic
superficiality of my American contemporary's education had at
least had one negative merit. It had not forced him into a rut; and I
was now deep in a rut that might have cribbed, cabined, and confined me for the rest of my life.

At both British schools, I had the good fortune to fall in with
seniors who were particularly congenial to me in their tastes and
who also made it their business to be helpful to a newly arrived
junior student. They were congenial to me in sharing my passion for
being out and about in the open country for as much of the time as
possible. To sit stewing in the School's library, reading books that
would have been equally accessible to us at home in Britain, would
have seemed to all of us a perverse misuse of time when we were in
Italy or Greece, within reach of historic scenes which we might
perhaps have only this one opportunity of visiting. Even for those
of us who had more than one year at their disposal, the number of
things to be seen in Greece and Italy was inexhaustible. The School's
role was to serve as a headquarters and as a rest-house where one
could recuperate during brief intervals between hiking campaigns.
My senior companions were as active as I was, and they were also
considerate in frequently inviting junior students to go with them
on expeditions of theirs. It was a rare chance to travel through
classical regions under such expert and experienced guidance. I feel

a lasting gratitude to the then reigning Director of the British School at Rome, Thomas Ashby, a Wykehamist of an older generation than mine, and, at the School at Athens, to A. J. B. Wace, M. S. Thompson, and F. W. Hasluck, the librarian. The Director, R. M. Dawkins, happened to be absent during the greater part of my time at the Athens School.

Alan Wace was a born archaeologist, and he was catholic in his interests — or, rather, passions; for 'interests' is too tame a word for conveying Wace's temperament. In 1911–12 Wace was working simultaneously on the stratification of Neolithic pottery, on the Mycenae of the Mycenaean Age, on the styles of modern embroidery in the Greek islands, and on the anthropology of the nomadic Vlach pastoral community whose summer village was Samarina, on the eastern slopes of Mount Smolka, one of the peaks of Pindus overhanging the upper Haliacmon basin. Wace used to accompany his Vlachs on their migrations between their summer and their winter pastures. In most of these varied pursuits, Thompson was Wace's partner. They hunted together like a couple of hounds; and, like hounds on the scent, they were indifferent, while chasing their quarry, to heat, cold, hunger, or exposure to the elements. They set one an exacting standard of physical endurance.

Ashby was as industrious a field-archaeologist as they were. His ambition, which he substantially achieved, was to identify, measure, photograph, and publish as many as possible of the surviving ancient remains along or near as many as possible of the ancient roads radiating from Rome. Ashby's way of travelling was amusingly different from Wace's and Thompson's. Those two sleuth-hounds travelled, like klephts, with the minimum of impedimenta. Ashby travelled like the White Knight in *Alice through the Looking Glass*, except that his mount was, not a wooden horse, but a bicycle. He was equipped for all imaginable contingencies. He had a sweater to put on before coasting down a hill, to make sure that he should not catch a chill from the upward-streaming draught when he was still in a muck of sweat from having pushed his bicycle up the hill behind. He also carried a camera with an ample supply of bulky heavy slides, as well as a loaf and an iron ration of cheese. Of the White Knight's paraphernalia, the bird-cage alone was missing. If you were one of Ashby's students, and he had done you the honour of asking you to travel with him, you naturally showed your appreciation and respect by carrying half of the Director's gear yourself. This tied you to him like a Siamese twin—a more compromising tie than the bond of mere comradeship that bound Wace and Thompson to each other—and an experience when I was Ashby's yoke-fellow made me aware, for the first time, that my single-track concentration on the Graeco-Roman Age had its limits.

On 30 October 1911 I was bicycling with Ashby in Umbria, down the valley of the River Clitumnus. We had lingered at the lovely little fourth-century-A.D. temple among the beautiful big white cattle; we had looked in at Fuligno; we had reached Spello; and from there Assisi was in full view, only seven miles away. At once an immense desire to push on to Assisi possessed me. As a child, I had listened to my parents reading an English translation of the *Fioretti di San Francesco* aloud to me; and I knew about Brother Elias's church, and the frescoes with which Giotto had adorned it. I now pointed forward towards Assisi in ecstasy, but Ashby could not enter into my feelings. He had been living in Italy since, I think, the age of two, and he could not remember a time when he had not already seen, to satiety, all the famous sights that Italy had to offer. He had long ago reached a stage of sophistication at which sites alone, not sights, were still exciting for him. 'Assisi? Yes, that is it; but only old ladies go there. Now there is a Roman villa foundation, over here to the right, which I have never measured yet.' What could I do? He was my Director, and I was carrying half his stuff. We measured that villa foundation and photographed it too, and by then it was time to make for the railway and entrain—loaf, sweater, bicycles, and all—since the Director had an appointment to keep in Rome at an early hour the next morning. I consoled myself for my bitter disappointment by saying to myself: 'I will get to Assisi next week.' I found myself unable to make it. I did get to Assisi in the end. By now I have been there twice; but my first visit was on 15 September 1955, so Thomas Ashby's villa foundation kept me away from Assisi for nearly forty-four years, as it turned out.

At some date in the course of this long interval, when my own interests had become almost as catholic as Alan Wace's, I read Goethe's *Italienische Reise*. With insufferable self-complacency, Goethe here describes how, at Assisi, he kept his gaze averted from

Brother Elias's barbaric church, and spent all his time on feasting his eyes on the pediment and columns of the little temple of Minerva, half way up the hill. Why not enjoy both the temple and the church? The Graeco-Roman style and the mediaeval Western style are each beautiful in its own incomparable way. Goethe had convicted himself of being, for once, a wall-eyed pedant. But, supposing that Goethe had been bicycling with Ashby and me on 30 October 1911, would he have carried his fanaticism to Ashby's lengths? Would he have opted for measuring that purely Roman villa foundation above Spello, in preference to making a dash for the temple of Minerva at Assisi—a classical building which had been robbed of its purity through having been converted into a Christian Church? I guess that Goethe would have made for the temple; for I am not convinced that Goethe was as perverse in truth as he has chosen to paint himself in this passage of the *Italienische Reise*.

My own way of travelling, when I was with Wace or Thompson or my fellow Balliol man and life-long friend Rob Darbishire, or when I was travelling by myself, was a compromise between Wace's way and Ashby's, leaning more towards Wace's. I carried a rucksack, water-bottle, and raincoat, but nothing more.

In 1911–12, travelling was technologically still rudimentary, but in some other ways it was simpler and more civilized than it is now. To get from London to Athens would take four days at the shortest, even if one went straight through by train from Calais to Brindisi and was able there to step on board a steamer that was on the point of leaving for the Peiraeus. 'Can one see the lights of your country from the top of that mountain?' a Moreot muleteer asked me one day as we were walking along together. He was pointing to Mount Erymanthus. 'Well, no. You see, it is a long way from here to my country. It is four days' journey—and this not four days on foot, but four days by ship and train.' The muleteer was not convinced. 'Yes, but it is a very high mountain,' was his comment. I dare say that today a man in a space-capsule might be able to see both the peak of Erymanthus and the lights of London at one and the same moment. Anyway, the other day, my wife and I travelled from Athens to London by jet-plane in three and a half hours. Such speeding-up of travel within a span of little more than half a century is an amazing technological achievement. The drawback is that, when one is being catapulted above the clouds, one may see nothing of the fascinating surface of the Earth. Moreover, in everything except technology, travelling conditions have deteriorated during the interval.

By 1911, Europe had been at peace for forty years, and the man-made barriers between countries had worn thin. At that date there were no formalities for crossing frontiers. If you wanted to visit a foreign country, you just bought a ticket and went, as you would do in travelling inside your own country. I did discover, though, that Turkey, which was on my programme, required a foreign visitor to produce a thing called a passport. It was one of three countries in the World that required this at that date. The other two were Russia and Rumania. Accordingly, with an eye to Turkey, I had gone, before leaving England, to my bank in Oxford and had said: 'Please get me a passport,' as I might have said: 'Please get me a gold napoleon or a gold five-dollar piece.' A day or two later the document arrived. It was a scrap of paper, engrossed: 'We Sir Edward Grey, one of His Majesty's Principal Secretaries of State, etc. etc.' No photograph to prove that I was in truth the person in whose name the passport was made out!

This exotic document nearly got me into trouble. On 29 September 1911, seven days after I had left England, Italy had declared war on Turkey, and on the evening of 16 November, as Rob Darbishire and I walked into Formia from Terracina, a carabiniere accosted us. 'I think you are Turks,' he said. He did not arrest us, but he did take the name of our hotel. Unfortunately my passport carried a mention of my intending to visit Turkey, and this might have been incriminating. For that carabiniere, the distinction between visiting Turkey and being a Turk would have been too subtle a one. I must on no account show my passport to the carabiniere, and he would not think of asking for it. He would never have heard of such things as passports in the course of his official duties up to date. We must, however, produce some exculpating document when he called at the hotel, as he evidently intended to do. When he came, I handed him my card. This had 'Balliol College, Oxford', inscribed below my name, and the word 'college' did the trick. 'Ah, collegio,' said the carabiniere, 'dunque non siete Turchi'; and, from then on, he left us in peace. His assumption that 'collegio' was incompatible with 'Turco' was incorrect, long since, in 1911, and it would, of course, be an egregious *non sequitur* today.

In 1911–12 money was simple too. The international exchanges were stable, and, between Belgium, France, Italy, and Greece, there was then a 'Latin monetary union', in virtue of which the silver coins of all those four countries were legal tender in each of them. On my expeditions from Athens into the Greek countryside, I used to carry one pocketful of Greek copper, a mixed bag of Greek, French, Belgian, and Italian silver in another pocket, and, for a reserve, a couple of gold napoleons or gold sovereigns between my stocking and my shin. I wore stockings and 'plus fours', in order to be able to change my stockings when they got wet through. Everything above them was kept dry, more or less, by my rain-coat.

This way of carrying my money once vindicated itself under a test. On 13 February 1912 I had climbed to the top of Mount Khlomós, at the meeting-point of the frontiers of Boeotia, Phocis, and the Opuntian Locris. Khlomós is not a high mountain; the altitude of its summit is only 1081 metres; but, being centrally located and overtopping its immediate neighbours, it commands a magnificent view. From its summit on that day I could see, simultaneously, Mount Geraneia to the south and Mount Olympus to the north. On an equally clear day now, one would hardly get a wider view from an aeroplane. On my way down, I wanted to find the shortest cut to the road running below, through the Opuntian plain, east-south-eastwards from Atalándi, so, seeing two shepherds on the mountain-side, I walked over to them to ask for directions.

I was taking the path that they had pointed out when I heard them shouting after me to wait for them. I did wait; we sat down together; they began to inspect the contents of my knapsack, feel in my pockets, and finally finger my watch (it was a gold one); and then I realized what I was in for. 'We want you to give us your watch,' said one of them. 'I won't give it to you,' I answered. 'It was my father's, and I value it.' The shepherd then ostentatiously put a cartridge in his gun. 'Which would you rather?' he said. 'Give us your watch, or take this?' 'I will take this (αὐτό θά πάρω),' I replied, rather nervously taking a chance on it. I had reckoned that the likelihood of his shooting me was slight. Though, at that moment, the road down below seemed to me very far away, the sound of voices and the clatter of mules' hooves did float up to us on the mountain, though faintly, and I had noticed that the other shepherd was holding together the jaws of his dog, for fear that it might bark. If they were afraid that a dog's bark might give warning that some dirty work was being done up here, they were not likely to risk the report of a shot. Happily, my reckoning proved right. When I said 'I will take that', the shepherd looked a fool. I had called his bluff, so I had won.

Moreover, these two shepherds were amateur klephts, not professionals. They had yielded to temptation on a sudden impulse; they were obviously embarrassed by the swashbuckling part that they were trying to play; and they were not hard-hearted. 'What are you?' 'A schoolmaster.' 'Schoolmasters are not rich, are they?' 'Not at all rich,' I emphatically agreed. 'Well, we will take your copper, but will leave you your silver and your watch.' As an afterthought, they suggested that we should also exchange pocket knives, and this turned out to be a poor exchange for me. But I got away with no greater loss than that. The point of the story is that they never thought of looking between my stocking and my shin, where I had two gold napoleons tucked away. I could not have carried so discreetly the present-day approximate equivalent, which would be a couple of hundred-drakhmai notes. Hidden next to my shin, notes would soon have been disintegrated by the sweat and the rain against which gold coins were proof.

This incident must have shaken me more than I had realized at the moment; for I remember how, next day, while I was walking eastwards along that road down below on the plain, my heart began to beat faster when I caught sight of a whole gang of shepherds ahead of me, with nobody else in view. This was something of a crisis. 'If I don't go forward now,' I thought to myself, 'that will mean that I have lost my nerve; and then I may not be able to face going on hiking like this by myself. What, throw away the best part of my *Wanderjahr*! Why, that is unthinkable.' So, spurred by this thought, I did walk on with a show of confidence that I was far from feeling, and, this time again, I called my opponents' bluff. As I approached the gang, it rose and flapped away. Those menacing figures had not been humans, they had been vultures. No doubt, these same vultures would have been picking my bones clean by now if the shepherd had shot me, yesterday, on Khlomós-side; but, being the carrion-eaters that they were, these birds would take no liberties with me so long as I was alive. I felt considerably relieved.

Before those nine months were over, I must have done something between 2000 and 3000 miles of walking in Greece, industriously visiting the remains of city-walls, temples, and other buildings of the Graeco-Roman Age, but, above all, measuring, in terms of walking-hours, the areas of city-state territories, observing the ratios between the extent of plain and mountain and the extent of arable and pasture, and finding, by trial and error, where, in this rugged country, one's feet could and could not carry one. This experience did substantially complete my initiation into the life of the Graeco-Roman World. One's own feet were the right means of conveyance for this purpose. In walking, I was following in the footsteps of the Ancient Greeks themselves; for they, too, had walked—even the most eminent of them—so I was travelling in the way in which they had travelled, and was moving at their pace. What other way could either they or I have found for getting about? In the Greece of Philippides the runner and of Pausanias the tourists' guide, roads capable of accommodating wheeled traffic were as rare as they still were in the Greece of 1911–12. (The efficient road-network of the Greece of 1969 is another story.)

In thus completing my first Greek education, my *Wanderjahr* went exactly according to plan. But this *annus mirabilis* gave me a second Greek education—one that had been unforeseen and unintended and that was as opportune as it was surprising. I had come to Greece to learn there from inanimate nature—fields, water-springs, rocks, and hewn stones—about the dead and buried Greek World that had become my spiritual home as a result of my humanist education in England. But, incidentally to my pilgrimage to these dumb relics of Antiquity, I found myself meeting living Greek men and women who were highly intelligent, alert, and vocal. These living Greeks had not had a Western humanist education in the Ancient Greek language and literature. They were peasants living in villages. For them Ancient Greece was not, as it had been for me at Winchester, a city of refuge from which one could keep the present-day world at bay; it was an heirloom that had value for its possible service in helping them to achieve their country's present-day national ambitions. These Greek contemporaries of mine were living—and this with characteristically Greek zest and animation—in the present-day world on which I had turned my back. I had come to Greece for the purpose of meeting, not the present-day Greeks, but the relics of their ancient predecessors. I was now meeting the present-day Greeks, and they were giving me a second Greek education. They were initiating me into the twentieth-century world in which I, too, willy-nilly, was implicated.

The Greece of 1969 is equipped with motor-roads and with motels (ξενίαι), spaced at distances from each other of about one day's journey by car. In the Greece of 1911–12 there were hardly any roads and, of course, there were no motels at all; and, even if the present scattering of motels had then been in existence, it would have been perhaps a week's journey on foot from any one of these to the next. Travelling on wheels and sleeping in motels in North-Western Greece in 1965, my wife and I covered an extent of ground in one week that would have taken me perhaps seven weeks to cover during my *Wanderjahr*. In consequence, however, we met many of our fellow foreign tourists, but not so many of the inhabitants of the country through which we were speeding. In 1911–12, I used to walk from village to village, staying in a different village each night and spending the evening, before going to bed, in the village shop, which served as a club for the men of the village after they had come home from their day's work in field or pasture. Evening after evening, I used to listen to the conversations in the village shop, and I eventually began to take part in these myself as my command of rustic Modern Greek gradually increased. It was here that I got my unexpected Greek education in the affairs of the present-day world —an education that afterwards carried me to two Paris peace conferences and qualified me for being, for thirty-three years, one of the two co-authors of Chatham House's *Survey of International Affairs*. In the Greek countryside in 1911–12, I learnt about the difference between the American language and my native Unitedkingdomese; I learnt to see the Middle West of the United States through the eyes of first-generation immigrants; and I learnt about the deadly game of international power-politics that was being played by the European great powers, including my own country.

At Oxford, I had, of course, met American contemporaries of

mine—Rhodes Scholars and others—and we had naturally been mutually aware of the difference between our respective accents; but we had not been conscious of any difference between our vocabularies. These appeared to be identical because they were the vocabularies of minorities that had been privileged to receive a higher education, and the vocabulary of book-English is approximately the same on both sides of the North Atlantic. But now, in the villages of Greece, I was meeting fellow-English-speakers whose vocabulary was limited to about a hundred basic words; and I discovered that American basic English was not the same language as the basic English of Britain. 'Sick' instead of 'ill'; 'store' instead of 'shop'; 'mail' instead of 'post': when the vocabulary had been stripped down to stark essentials, the difference between Unitedkingdomese and Unitedstatesese became apparent.

The English-speakers who were teaching me this lesson about my own language were Greek peasants who had emigrated to the United States and had saved enough money there to be able to afford to revisit their native villages. In 1911–12 the flow of Greek emigration to the United States was at its peak. The more remote the village was and the more rugged the encompassing mountain landscape was and the less work there was to do and the less money there was to be earned at home, the greater the number of the grown men who had been driven by the spur of necessity to make the formidable passage of the Atlantic into a hitherto unknown new world. I remember spending a night in one particularly remote village which at the time, so they told me, had more than half its adult male population working in America and sending welcome remittances home.

The emigrants who were back in their village on a visit were obviously enjoying themselves. On their first tour in the United States they had been painfully homesick; they had buoyed their spirits up by looking forward to the day when they would see their village again; and now here they were, with money in their pockets and with tales to tell of the wonders of America to impress the stay-at-homes. Their prestige was gratifying for them, and they had begun to wonder whether they should not stay at home for good, now that they had found their way back, when they collided abruptly with Lent. The returned emigrants had forgotten about Lent; and Lent, in Orthodox Christendom, is severe. During Lent all food containing blood is banned; and milk and eggs count as blood canonically. The most sustaining fare procurable in a Greek village in Lent was third-rate caviare from the Black Sea and octopus-tentacles chopped up in rice. The returned emigrants now began to be homesick for America; they began to dream of that substantial American food that was procurable all the year round, regardless of ecclesiastical fasts. After this experience an Americanized Greek would not face the prospect of another Orthodox Lent at home; so what did he do? He quickly asked one of the unengaged girls in the village to marry him; if she refused him, he asked another; and he persisted till he had found a wife. He was no sooner married than he took his wife off with him to America, with the firm intention, now, of making his permanent home there. He had discovered how to get the best of both worlds. With a Greek wife and children in America, he would not be lonely there again; and he and they would be enjoying the amenities of American life.

Was my mother-tongue the American language or was it not? One old lady, who had put me up for the night in her house, was sure that I did speak the American language. The next morning, when I was leaving, she made me a present of two red Easter eggs because I spoke the American language and she had two sons in America at the time. On the other hand, when I arrived, on the evening of 27 December 1911, at the village of Tsipianá, a little to the east of Mantinea, my language got me into difficulties. 'Say, John, where do you come from?' asked a man. 'From England.' 'Well, where did you learn the American language?' 'In England.' 'How did you learn the American language in England?' 'Because we speak it there.' 'Liar, I know better than that. England is not in America; England is in Europe; and they do not speak the American language in Europe.' Thereupon, my inquisitor and his fellow-villagers got together in a huddle—like an American football-huddle—to debate whether I really was lying or whether, after all, I might perhaps have been telling the truth.

After a bit, they came back to me to let me know that they had now succeeded in reconciling my statements with each other. They believed that England was, in truth, my birthplace, but that, when I had been about ten years old, my family had emigrated from Europe to the United States. This explained how I spoke the

American language so fluently, but with such a very bad accent. I did not attempt to contradict them. My veracity had been vindicated, and I was content to leave it at that. Like the Ptolemaic theory of the movements of the heavenly bodies, the villagers' emigration theory did provide a credible explanation of all the facts. Its only fault was that, like the Ptolemaic theory, it happened, all the same, not to be true. Yet I had been taught a lesson which I have taken to heart ever since. This lesson was that England was now in a minority in the English-speaking World. The majority of the people whose language was English were now living in North America; and North American English had become the standard form of the language. It was irrelevant that English had been spoken in England long before America had been heard of in Europe. History never stands still; and history had now reduced my Unitedkingdomese dialect to the status of being a bizarre provincial 'brogue'.

I also learnt about the American way of life from a standpoint that, for me, was new. Hitherto, I had seen America through the eyes of my American fellow-undergraduates at Oxford, without reflecting that undergraduates and their families are a privileged, and therefore unrepresentative, minority of society. I was now getting a view of America from below upwards, instead of being shown it from above downwards. Kansas City, Missouri, and Omaha, Nebraska, now swam into my ken. I learnt about their beautiful asphalt sidewalks, on which one could tread, with comfort, in thin patent-leather shoes—so unlike these clumsy hob-nailed shoes that one has to wear on the mountain-paths of Greece, to save one's feet from being battered to a pulp by the rocks. Fifty-one years passed before I visited these two American cities myself. Yet in 1963 my memory of the Greek villagers' descriptions of them was still so vivid that I approached each of them with glowing anticipations— to find, to my disappointment, that their sidewalks were just sidewalks. In my imagination they had come to be paved with sapphire and chrysoprase, like the sidewalks of the Heavenly Jerusalem in the Apocalypse.

But the most exciting subject of all that came up in the conversations in those village shops was the international power-game. What was the policy of Sir Edward Grey? (I knew that Grey was Foreign Secretary and that my passport had been made out in his name, but his having a policy was a point about him that had not occurred to me.) Would the war start this coming autumn? Or would it start in the following spring? (*The* war? What was that?) And, whenever it did come, what would Greece get out of it? Would she get Crete only? Or would she get Macedonia as well? For me, these questions were new, strange, startling, and instructive. They were the beginning of my initiation into the study of international affairs.

Writing a Latin *jeu d'esprit* on the Entente Cordiale at Winchester in 1906–7 had not taught me to take current international affairs seriously. Nor had I been enlightened about them at Oxford. Undergraduates had been politically-minded in my time, as they are today. But, for my generation at Oxford, politics had meant domestic politics. This had been the decade in which, in Britain, a Liberal administration had been laying the foundations of the welfare state, and the Government's measures—old-age pensions, national health insurance, and the rest—had been providing abundant controversial matter for lively debates at the Oxford Union. In the Union's allocation of its time the ration for foreign affairs had been one debate a year; and this foreign-affairs debate had been used for trying out the freshmen to discover which of them were promising speakers. Since the subject of this day's debate was an unimportant one, the debate might as well be made to serve a practical purpose. So I had come down from Oxford still a novice in international affairs. Now, in Greece, I was at last being educated in them in earnest.

I was being educated, but I was a dullard. By 1912 the river of history was racing towards a cataract; but I was still blind enough to be outraged when open-eyed Greeks took military precautions that caused me inconvenience. On 9 January 1912, for instance, at Dhomokó, Rob Darbishire was arrested on the charge that he was spying out the land. He was, of course, merely admiring the view of the snow-capped peak of Olympus apparently floating in the air —the scene described by Apuleius at the beginning of *The Golden Ass*. To pause and admire at this point is what every traveller is supposed to do. The very name Dhomokó—Thaumakoi—is a command to this effect. And now Rob had been arrested for doing just that. This seemed outrageous; and insult was being added to injury;

the gendarme who took Rob in charge was half his size and bore the, to our ears, ludicrous surname Katsoupis. Outrageous? It was not till I was back in England, not till after the start of the First Balkan War, that I recognized that the military authorities at Dhomokó had been well within their rights. Rob and I might, no doubt, have been gazing innocently, as in truth we were, at the peak of Olympus hovering white above the northern horizon. But this sky-gazing might also have been a pretext for slyly surveying the foreground; and this foreground was the strategically critical saddle, between Mount Othrys and the hill-country of the Agrapha, over which the standard-gauge railway threaded its way *en route* from Athens towards the Graeco-Turkish frontier of that date, at the exit from the gorge of Tempe.

I felt still more monstrously outraged when I was arrested, myself, on the last day of the last hike of my *Wanderjahr*. The date was 21 July 1912, and I was walking from the upper Cephisus valley to the Asopus gorge, to discover how effectively the citadel of Heraclea Trachinia had commanded this passage—an alternative to Thermopylae—between the valleys of the Cephisus and the Spercheius. When I reached the southern brow of the gorge, I saw the standard-gauge railway straddling the gorge over a trestle-bridge. By this date, I was far-gone with dysentery, and I was tired. Why make that steep descent, only 'up to re-ascend', when the railway-bridge would carry me across on the level? I crossed the bridge, and was immediately arrested by a sergeant's patrol at the far end.

The sergeant marched me to Elefterokhóri station. I announced my intention of boarding the up-train to Athens. The sergeant informed me that he was going to take me by the down-train to Lamía to be examined by his superiors. The up-train came and went, without my being allowed to take it. I was fluent enough in Modern Greek by now to be able to be vituperative, but the sergeant took this in good part. For him it was all in the day's work. He was just doing his military duty. Δέν ἤκουσα was all that he said. (Δέν ἤκουσα means literally 'I did not hear', but, constructively, 'I did hear, but I am taking no notice, as I don't wish to hold your discourtesy against you.') He put me on board the down-train, detrained me at Lamía, and handed me over to one of his men to march me round the military intelligence offices there. My soldier was even stumpier than Katsoupis had been. His fellow-soldiers, off duty, called him 'misí-oká'—'half-an-oke'—as we passed. But he had his bayonet fixed, and I was his prisoner. I was conducted up the whole ladder of military bureaux till I reached the regional command, and, at each higher rung, I became more indignant and more rude. However, they all took this good-humouredly, and the regional command quickly gave me a clean bill and let me go.

I was not placated; for the reasoning that had led the sergeant to arrest me would not have passed muster with Aristotle. The sergeant's syllogism ran: 'This man who has come off the bridge is carrying a military water-bottle; it is not a regulation Greek army water-bottle; so it must be a foreign spy's water-bottle'—as if a foreign spy would carry a badge of his profession! At Athens I made a fuss at the British Embassy. They tactfully showed sympathy, but prudently took no action. After all, I had merely suffered annoyance; I had come to no harm. It was not till after the start of the First Balkan War that I realized that the standard-gauge railway was the Greek Army's sole line of supply for the front, and that the trestle-bridge over the Asopus gorge was the most vulnerable point in this vital railway's whole course. If, while strolling across that bridge, I had laid some time-bombs that could have blown the bridge up, I should have made history. I should have blown to smithereens the appointed date for the Greek Army's D-day.

In spite of having, by now, had nine months' informed instruction in international affairs at my evening classes in Greek village shops, I was still unperceptive. That August, on my voyage up the Adriatic coast of the Habsburg Monarchy, I found every coast-town, from Cattaro to Trieste, crammed full of troops. The entire Imperial-Royal Army appeared to be mobilized there. I was enchanted by the antique cut and colour of the uniforms (these were still in the style of 1848); I did not realize, even then, what this massive mobilization signified. I did not tumble to the obvious truth—which was, of course, that the Balkan War was imminent and that the Austro-Hungarian general staff knew all about it.

Nor was I alive to the passionateness of the hatred between nation and nation which was to accentuate the horrors of warfare in my lifetime. I was not alive to it, though I had been given at least one glimpse of this hell-fire. Walking eastward along the Mesará of

Crete on 15 March 1912, I fell in with an old man driving two mules. My travelling companion was benevolence itself. He insisted on my riding (this was pure hospitality; there was no question of my paying); but, whenever we came to a steep descent, he would ask me to dismount in order to spare the mule's legs from undue strain. Towards the mules and me, he could not have been kinder; but, then, the mules and I were his fellow-Christians, and we were therefore deserving of the old man's natural human kindness. I discovered, with a shock, the sharp limits of his human feeling when I asked him, naïvely, why the villages along the edge of this fertile plain were all deserted. 'Those villages?' he cried. 'Why, the Muslims lived there. But in ninety-seven τούς ἐκόψαμεν ὅλους: we cut them all —men, women, and children—cut them all'; and he drew his hand expressively across his throat, while his voice rose to a shrill scream and his eyes gleamed as he gloated over this delicious memory.

I found myself considerably upset. Here was I, walking and talking with a human being, till now apparently benign, who had joyously taken a hand in these hideous atrocities only fifteen years back. I still did not forebode that the Cretan massacres of 1897 would be eclipsed by the Armenian deportations of 1915, and the Armenian deportations by the genocide of Jews and Slavs that I was going to live to see committed by the Nazis. Nor had I yet drawn the inescapable inference from the particular to the general. This inference is that there is a vein of diabolical evil in all human nature. Our 'Original Sin' may be overlaid by layer upon layer of civilizing habits; yet no one can go bail for the moral integrity of any individual human being or any human community. No one can guarantee that anyone will be proof against all temptations. Under temptation the volcano may suddenly erupt, even when its fires have been dormant for so long that they have been deemed to be extinct.

Meanwhile, in 1912, an eruption was already brewing. As the boat from Rethymnon, in Crete, on board which I was returning to Athens, steamed into the Peiraeus on 1 April 1912, two of my fellow-passengers ran up on deck. Ζήτω ἡ Κρήτη ('Long live Crete'), the two girls shouted; and then, emboldened by their own audacity, they shouted again, and this time Ζήτω ἡ Μακεδονία ('Long live Macedonia'). A more elderly passenger, non-Greek like me, said, smiling indulgently, Αὐτό θά εἶναι πλέο δύσκολο ('That will be more

4 C. A. Doxiadis

5   Arnold and Veronica Toynbee on Samothrace, July 1967

difficult'). This commentator was Fabricius, the eminent German scholar who had discovered the great inscription at Gortyn thirty years back, and who had been re-visiting Crete for the first time since then. Fabricius had spoken with the voice of wisdom and experience; but, before twelve months had passed from that date, the young women's optimism had been more than justified by the event. By the spring of 1913, Greece had acquired not only Crete and Macedonia but Samos, Chios, and Mytilíni into the bargain.

The First Balkan War, however, was not *the* war, nor was the Second Balkan War *the* war either. Like the Tripoli War which Italy had started just after I had set out on my *Wanderjahr*, these were just spatters of rain-drops preceding the deluge that was still to come. Within three years more, half my contemporaries had been killed in 'the Great War' as we were then calling it. But the World War of 1914–18 turned out not to be the whole of *the* war either. It turned out merely to be the first round of it. I have lived, by now, through two world wars; I have lived to feel their cumulative effect; and, in 1969, no one in the World yet knows whether the world war of 1939–1945 was the finale. Since 1945, mankind has been living under the shadow of a possible third world war which would dwarf all previous wars, since it would be waged with atomic weapons.

Why am I still alive today, to be writing these lines? If, in 1914, I had been fit for active service, the chances are that, like so many of my schoolfellows, I should have been dead by 1916. My *Wanderjahr* in 1911–12 is responsible for my survival, as well as for my having spent the greater part of my subsequent working life on writing a survey of international affairs. I owe my survival ultimately to an error on a map.

In 1911–12 only the first few sheets of the Greek staff-map of Greece had been published, and these sheets covered only the extreme north-eastern fringe of Greece within the Greek frontier of that date. For the rest of Greece, one had still to make do with an inferior appendage to the excellent Austro-Hungarian staff-map of Central and South-Eastern Europe, and, though the appendage, too, was said to have been compiled by an Austrian military cartographer, its indications were not to be trusted.

In Laconia on 26 April 1912 I had planned to walk from Káto Vezáni, where I had spent the previous night, to Gythion. Káto

Vezáni lies on the eastern fringe of the marshes through which the Laconian River Eurotas makes its way to the sea; Gythion lies on the opposite coast, with a stretch of broken country intervening between it and the western end of the coastal swamp. I had reckoned that this would be an easy day's journey, because, on the Laconia sheet of the pseudo-Austrian staff-map, a first-class road was marked as traversing the stretch of broken country, so the last lap of this day's walk promised to be smooth and swift. That deceitful sheet that I was carrying with me then is on my table, at this moment, under my eyes, with the good road indicated by a pair of shamelessly bold black lines. When I reached what should have been the road-head, after having made my way across the Eurotas by a bridge which the map did not mark, I found that there was no road at all, and that I should have to get to Gythion across country. One ravine followed another; I was now several hours behind my time-table; my water-bottle was empty; and then, to my joy, I stumbled on a swiftly-flowing stream of limpid water. Bending down, I buried my mouth in it and drank and drank again. It was only when I had drunk my fill that I noticed a man standing and watching me in front of his cottage door. 'That is very bad water', he remarked. If that man had been responsible-minded and considerate, he would have told me this before I had touched the water with my lips; but, if he *had* warned me, as he ought to have done, the chances are that I should not be alive now. Inadvertently he had saved my life; for he was right about that water being bad. It gave me dysentery; and the dysentery, which continued to plague me for the next half-dozen years, disqualified me for combatant service in the war of 1914–18.

Meanwhile, I had been aggravating my malady by refusing to give in to it. The next stage of my itinerary after Gythion was to take me to the tip of the Mani, *alias* Taenarum, which is the middle prong of the three prongs of the Peloponnese and is also the most rugged of the three. In point of ruggedness and drought the Mani is 'Hellados Hellas', 'the Greece of Greece'. The austerity of Greece is accentuated in the Mani to the point of caricature. In the whole of the Mani there is only one spring. The Maniots' drink is rainwater collected in cisterns; and, since the soil in the interstices of the Maniot limestone is red, the water in the cisterns is red too. The red water of the Mani—its κόκκινο νερό—can have done my dysentery no good. I did succeed in walking to the tip of Taenarum. I was determined to see that; for this Land's End was the site of the legendary mouth of Hades and of an historic mart for mercenary soldiers and of a famous temple of Poseidon. So I did walk to this Laconian Land's End; but I travelled back sprawling on a mule—the first time that I had indulged in this expensive luxury—and I had the sense to return from Areopolis to Athens expeditiously by steamer and train. But I did not have the sense to stop hiking after that; for it was now only the beginning of May, and I was not due in Oxford till October. How could I let dysentery cheat me of so large a slice of my *Wanderjahr*?

I went on hiking, and my dysentery grew worse as the weather turned hotter. I learnt to check the symptoms by dosing myself (no doubt, perilously) with drops of arsenic, taken in lumps of sugar. I hiked on till nearly the end of July, and then, at last, I took a passage from the Peiraeus in an Austrian Lloyd packet-boat. My plan was to stop off at Cattaro and walk up from there into Montenegro; but by that time I was so ill that I decided, grudgingly, to travel on by the same boat to Trieste, and from there I took the first through-train to Flushing. In consequence of this tardy capitulation to common sense, I have not succeeded in paying my visit to Montenegro yet, and this is now 1969. My obstinate defiance of my dysentery might have been the death of me. If it had been, I should only have got what I deserved. But, so far from killing me in 1912, that dysentery prevented me from being killed in 1914–18. When one contemplates in old age the chain of accidents that has decided one's fate, one is disconcerted. Nature seems to be incorrigibly irrational; and one is at Nature's mercy—at one's own human nature's mercy, not least. My Uncle Arnold was killed by meningitis at the age of thirty, while I have been preserved by dysentery to reach my present age of eighty.

In the autumn of 1907, just before the beginning of my first term as an undergraduate at Oxford, I had been paying a call on my mother's old friend Eleanor Jourdain, the Vice-Principal (later, Principal) of St. Hugh's. I had known Miss Jourdain since as early as my memory went back, and I felt entirely at home with her; she was like a member of the family. On this occasion, I must have been pouring out to her all the things that I planned to do, and have been lamenting the shortness of life; for I remember her saying with a smile: 'You have forty years.' Reckoning from the date of that conversation, I have now had nearly sixty-two years so far, and have not yet lost either my physical strength or my wits. I have needed all that time—more than half as much time again as Miss Jourdain had allowed me—to carry out my agenda. In 1907 neither Miss Jourdain nor I had suspected that the time at my disposal might be only seven years. Yet, only seven years after that, my contemporaries were joining the army—half of them to meet their deaths before the First World War was over. This would have been my destiny too if, in the meantime, I had not drunk the contaminated water of that treacherous stream in the Vardhounia. If, in 1907, I had had an inkling of the catastrophe that was bearing down on us, I should not have been reassured by Miss Jourdain's estimate that I had forty years of working-time still ahead of me.

My first Greek education—the one that I had received at Wootton Court, Winchester, and Oxford in 1899–1911—had followed old-established traditional Western humanist lines, and it had worked itself out exactly according to plan. My second Greek education—in Greece in 1911–12—had been a surprise. It had not been planned and not been expected; it had been a windfall, a bonus. For forty-one years—1915–56—I was working, on the strength of this second Greek education of mine, as a temporary civil servant in two world wars and, in between and again afterwards, as one of the two writers and editors of the Chatham House *Survey of International Affairs*. During that long time, I never dreamed that this unexpected second Greek education was not going to be my last. Yet in 1969 I find myself receiving an unexpected third Greek education after a nominal 'retirement'.

My third Greek education started at Karachi in Pakistan in 1960. My most recent previous visit to Karachi had been in 1957, and I had then found Karachi changed out of all recognition from the Karachi that I had visited first in 1929. In 1929 Karachi had been a second-class port and rail-head. The only notable object of interest there had been the tropical zoo. Since then, however, the British Indian Empire had been partitioned; Karachi had become the capital of one of British India's three successor-states, the new-born

Pakistan, and the place had been invaded by hordes of Muslim civil servants and by vaster hordes of Muslim refugees. For refugees, Karachi in its state of nature was an inhospitable asylum. The choice for the sites of their shanty-towns was between mangrove-swamp and gravel desert. In the Indo-Pakistani sub-continent in 1956–7, the misery of Karachi had been equalled only by the misery of Calcutta, with its millions of Hindu refugees from Eastern Bengal. And now, in 1960, I found Karachi transformed, out of all recognition, once again.

The miserable shanty-towns had vanished. They had been replaced by a string of simply but decently built and skilfully designed new settlements. Over the face of what had formerly been the desert, these settlements stretched away, one beyond another, to the horizon. They had to be numerous; for, while the number of refugees who had needed re-housing had been huge, each of the new settlements had been kept within human dimensions: that is to say, it had been limited to a size that made it possible, in five or ten minutes, for the children to walk between home and school and for the housewives to reach the shops and the community wash-house. Each unit was, in fact, small enough to allow the people housed in it to know each other personally; and it was evident that the physical framework for a new community-life which the planner had provided was producing its, no doubt, intended psychological and social effects.

In the shanty-towns round Karachi in 1957 the refugees had been human flotsam and jetsam. Uprooted, as they had been, from their ancestral homes on the other side of the new frontier, they had been unable to strike root in the forbidding new physical environment into which they had been flung, pell-mell. In the new settlements that I was visiting in 1960, the re-settled squatters were manifestly striking root again. Their ancestral communities had been lost to them for good; but they were now no longer in the wilderness, as they had been in 1957. Their lost community-life had been replaced by the new one that they had now found, and they had found it thanks to the genius of somebody who had planned for them these new human-sized settlement units. Who was this genius who had not only entered imaginatively into the refugees' human needs but had known how to provide for these needs in material form by marshalling bricks and mortar in an exciting new pattern? The planner, I was told, was a Greek named Konstandínos Doxiádis. He was also planning a new capital for Pakistan, Islamabad, in the northern Panjab.

What, exactly, was Dr. Doxiádis's profession? My Pakistani informants found it difficult to define this. Architect? 'Oh, more than that. Doxiádis does not just plan a building in isolation from its setting. He plans a group of buildings to form a settlement.' (We were standing in one of his settlement units as we were talking.) Then is he a town-planner? 'Well, he is something more than that again; for he does not plan in isolation a settlement or a city either. He plans it in the setting of the landscape. But he does not stop there. His field of thought and action is nothing less than the whole habitable area of the Earth's surface. In short, his planning is global; and his space-scale is matched by his time-scale. He looks into the future through telescopic sights. He is planning for at least a century ahead—planning for a time when the habitable part of the Earth's surface will be one big city. Doxiádis foresees a time—and this not so far off; it is rushing to meet us—he foresees a time when all the World's present sprouting cities will have coalesced into a continuous conurbation, "Ecumenopolis". He points out that the traditional relation between town and country is going to be reversed. From the date of the foundation of the first city of Jericho till our own age, the normal coverage of the globe's land-surface was field, pasture, and waste. The cities were rare plums in the cake; and their exceptionalness was symbolised in their ring-walls, which they needed to protect them against the ever-present threat that they might be reabsorbed into the countryside. It is only two centuries ago that the explosion of the Industrial Revolution burst open the constricting city-walls and sent the industrialised city sprawling out over what had hitherto been the open country. Already the open country is dwindling into patches of "green belt", and it is these that are now having to be fenced in, to save them from being engulfed in Ecumenopolis. Doxiádis has re-housed the Karachi refugees for us and he is building Islamabad for us; but his heart, we guess, is in something bigger and less immediate. His ultimate mission is to plan how to make life in Ecumenopolis tolerable.'

I had already been deeply impressed by my first sight of Dr. Doxiádis's works; I was still more impressed and excited by my

Pakistani friends' description of the planner himself. I headed for the site of Islamabad, to see how there Dr. Doxiádis was handling a different problem from that of re-planting refugees—the problem of laying out a new capital city. I soon learnt that Pakistan was only one of many theatres of his activity. He was laying out a new port-town in Ghana; he was reconditioning the slums of Philadelphia, Pennsylvania; he was being called in by the municipal authorities of Detroit, Michigan, to advise them how to cope with the mushroom-like proliferation of their city, and by the Brazilians for advice on the corresponding problems of Rio de Janeiro and São Paulo. In fact, his operations were world-wide. I was eager to meet Dr. Doxiádis; and, a couple of years later, my wish was fulfilled. At the end of a lecture that I had been giving in Athens for the British Council, he came up to speak to me; and he then introduced me to the faculty and students of his Institute of Ekistics in the Athens Technological Center on the southern slope of Mount Lycabettus, on a level with the summit of the Acropolis. Of course Dr. Doxiádis designed this remarkable building himself, as well as the block of flats, farther along the same street, in which he has his home.

Now that I found myself in Dr. Doxiádis's presence, I quickly put to him a question that I had been longing to ask him ever since I had seen and admired his work at Karachi. 'How,' I asked, 'did you get your insight into the needs of refugees? How did you arrive at a re-settlement pattern that would enable these uprooted human beings to strike root again?' 'Well, partly perhaps,' Dr. Doxiádis answered me, 'because, in my own life, I have had the same experience. I my-self am the child of a refugee family.' Dr. Doxiádis's father had been a doctor in the former Greek community in the town of Steni-mákhos in Bulgaria, and the family had had to leave its Bulgarian home for Greece during the exchange of populations in that part of the World after the First World War.

But what is 'Ekistics'? Well, it is a new name for a new subject of study—the subject that my Pakistani informants had given me a hint of. Ekistics is the study of human settlement. It embraces the whole history of human settlement, since the date—not so long ago on the time-scale of mankind's age up to date—at which some pro-gressive human communities raised themselves to a level of eco-nomic efficiency that made it possible for them to become sedentary

without starving. Ekistics, like all other approaches to the study of
human affairs, has to be studied in the time-dimension—studied,
that is, historically. But it is also no accident that Ekistics is a new
study, launched in our generation; for Ekistics is not just a theoretical
'discipline'; it is also a practical response to an imminent need
—the need, already mentioned, to make life tolerable in Ecumenopolis.

Ecumenopolis? No one, now alive, who is already as old as I now
am is going to live to see Ecumenopolis for himself. My grandchildren, though, may live to be enveloped by Ecumenopolis. For
their generation, life in Ecumenopolis is going to be a matter of
practical concern; and, since my grandchildren's concerns are mine
too, Ekistics is a subject in which I take the liveliest interest. When
~~I was sixteen, I let slip my opportunity of getting a taste of the~~
calculus. Now, sixty-four years later, at urgent eighty, I do not in-
tend to lose my present unexpected new opportunity for expanding
my mental horizon. It lies in the very nature of Ekistics that this new
study widens the outlook of anyone who enters on it from whatever
approach. Ekistics cannot be narrowed down into just one more
specialized 'discipline'; for it cannot be studied at all without taking
account of every side of human activity; and therefore any student
of Ekistics is bound to meet, and to profit greatly by meeting,
fellow-students whose fields are excitingly different from his own.
At the third of Dr. Doxiádis's Delos symposia on Ekistics, which
met in July 1965, there were biologists and anthropologists as well
as architects and town-planners; and, for an historian, their contributions were illuminating. So now I have embarked on my third
Greek education—one in Ekistics under Dr. Doxiádis's auspices
—and I propose to pursue this one so long as I keep my life and
wits.

My first Greek education initiated me into the past, and my
second one into the present. My third one promises to initiate me
into the future. I owe all three educations to the mental vitality and
vision of about a hundred generations of my Greek fellow human
beings. Of course, Greece is not all the World. Though I started as a
single-track Hellenist, my field has broadened out into the com-
parative study of civilizations; and this approach to human affairs
has the merit of developing one's sense of proportion. Yet—three

Greek educations! What people in the World besides the Greeks could have done as much for me as that? My gratitude to my Greek instructors is of a corresponding order of magnitude.

3 : August 1914

AUGUST 1914: 'the very word is like a bell'; and the dead to whom it tolls us back are the men of many nations, on both sides of the front,[1] whose lives were taken in the course of the four following sacrificial years. August 1914: Why is it that, at least for English people of my generation, the naming of this date still moves us so deeply? August 1914 has receded, by now, more than half a century into the past, and in the meanwhile there has been a second world war. Why does not the mention of the date September 1939 have the same effect on us? One reason is, I think, that one cannot feel the same shock for the second time with the same intensity. In 1939 the outbreak of a world war was no longer a new experience for us. In some ways the second experience was the more excruciating of the two; for, this time, we had seen the coming war bearing down on us far ahead of its outbreak; it did not burst upon us out of the blue, like a thunder-clap. Moreover, our experience of the First World War had told us, in advance, what tribulations we had now to expect to undergo once again. Yet, just because of this excruciating fore-knowledge, the shock, on the second occasion, was not so violent.

Another reason why the date August 1914 is graven on our hearts is that, for Britain, more perhaps than for any other country that has been engaged in either of the two world wars, the outbreak of the First World War marked a portentous break in her history. By August 1914 Britain had been exempt from engagement in any great war for almost a century. For us the last great war had ended on 18 June 1815, at Waterloo. In the school curriculum of my generation, Waterloo was also the end of history. It is true that,

---

[1] See a previous book of mine, *Acquaintances*, pp. 23-4, for a notable tribute paid in one of the belligerent countries to the war-dead on the 'enemy' side.

during the intervening ninety-nine years, Britain had fought a number of 'little wars'—a larger number than most other countries. But these minor hostilities had not touched us on the quick. Go to Winchester College chapel, look at the brass plate inscribed with the names of the Wykehamists who lost their lives in the Crimea, and compare that with the columns of names round the four sides of the new cloisters built in memory of those who died in 1914–18. This will give you the measure of the difference; and, in this exemption from any crushing toll of war-casualties for nearly a hundred years, Britain had been exceptional among the countries of the Western World. The Continental European countries had had a mid-century bout of violent revolutions and wars that had racked them from 1848 to 1871. The United States had had her civil war of 1861–5, the biggest war of any in the World within the ninety-nine years ending in August 1914 and also the costliest war of that century in the toll that it took of life, happiness, and wealth, with the one big exception of the T'ai P'ing rebellion in China. By August 1914 the Continental European countries had had only forty-three years of exemption from a great war, and the United States only fifty-two years by April 1917, before they were plunged, successively, into the First World War. Britain's period of exemption had been approximately twice as long as that; and our psychological unpreparedness made the violence of the shock, when it came, proportionately great.

I myself belong to the last generation of middle-class English people who had finished their education and had started on a professional career before August 1914 overtook us. People of my generation who are still alive were just old enough in August 1914 to have seen the pre-war world with grown-up eyes. The break that August 1914 made in history therefore cuts more clear and sharp for us than it does for people, only a few years younger, who in August 1914 were still in their teens.

My experience of the outbreak of war in August 1914 was, in its small way, rather dramatic. I had completed my second academic year as a don at Balliol; and, after an expedition to Winchester in July to examine Senior Sixth Book for the Goddard scholarship, I had just returned to Castle Howard, where I was spending the long vacation, and had settled down to write a Home University Library volume on the history of the Ancient Greek civilization. I was one of the host of people in the World whose plans for that summer were abruptly cut short. At Winchester, after my fellow-examiner, Livingstone, and I had awarded the Goddard scholarship to C. A. Macartney, I asked Macartney how he was going to spend his summer before going up to Oxford. 'I am going to walk to Vienna,' he said. Though Macartney had won Goddard by prowess in the Greek and Latin classics, his mind was already turning towards contemporary Central Europe. My next meeting with Macartney was after the war. 'And did you walk to Vienna?' I asked him. 'Well, not that summer, and I did not go there on my feet, but I have been serving there, since the war, as a passport officer.' As for my Home University Library volume, August 1914 came down on it like a guillotine before I had finished writing the second chapter; and, after that, two world wars and their consequences went on keeping me at arm's length from this particular piece of work. More than forty years passed before I was able to start writing it again; but, this time, I managed to write it to a finish. I finished it in the end because my heart was set on it, as Macartney's heart was set on Central Europe. Even world wars, if one survives them, will not prevent one from carrying out one's cherished plans eventually, however long may be the delay that these barbarous upheavals impose.

The assassination of the Archduke Franz Ferdinand and his wife had taken place between my settling in at Castle Howard and going to Winchester. It had shocked the World; but its private aspect, as a a hideous common crime of violence, had in most people's minds been more to the fore than its public aspect as a spark that might cause a terrific explosion. Before the First World War, diplomacy was even more secret than it is today, and the public was content to have it so. The public did not realize that its own lives and fortunes were going to be affected by the international power-game; and, since diplomacy was an esoteric art, it was a boring subject for the uninitiated majority. No doubt the small initiated minority in the cabinets and foreign ministries of Europe had appreciated the gravity of the Sarajevo assassination immediately and fully. But they had kept a discreet silence; and, as the weeks passed without any overt developments in the international arena, the public's attention reverted to its normal private pursuits.

Travelling back from Winchester to Castle Howard towards the end of July, I had entered into conversation with the man sitting opposite to me in the train from King's Cross to York. Our talk touched upon the international situation. My fellow-traveller turned out to be a Quaker, and his hereditary dedication to the cause of peace had kept him more alert than I had been to the course of international affairs. Talking over the political aspect of the Sarajevo crime, we found ourselves agreeing that logically it must be going to lead to a general war between the European powers; but we also agreed that it was inconceivable that logic would prevail. A general European war was something beyond the pale of probability; and indeed the weeks that had passed since the commission of the crime had not produced any very alarming public political developments up to date. We were soon to be undeceived.

Though in July 1914 Britain was not at war yet, Castle Howard had been at war for some time already. It was under siege by the militant suffragists. The owner, Rosalind Countess of Carlisle, was not an anti-suffragist, as my Aunt Charlie[1] was. Lady Carlisle was a suffragist, and a convinced one; but she was also a convinced anti-militant; and, as she was a conspicuous and potent personality and a redoubtable combatant, she had drawn upon herself the militants' hostility, and they had served notice on her that they were going to burn down her magnificent house. Accordingly, Castle Howard had been put in a state of defence. A policeman from Malton, Mr. Keown, had come into permanent residence; and the house had been engirdled with a continuous line of string, stretched tight on tent-pegs and festooned with little bells. The calculation was that when the maenads, petrol-can and matchbox in hand, came surging to the attack in the dark, they would stumble over the string and would sound the alarm in time to bring Mr. Keown out to dispute their farther advance. Mr. Keown was not being kept entirely idle. The alarm was sounded occasionally—not by militant women, but by browsing rabbits—and, at each of these false alarms, Mr. Keown dutifully turned out at the ready. On the whole, however, he seemed to be having an easy time.

On the day on which Britain went to war, events at Castle

[1] See *Acquaintances*, pp. 21–36.

Howard suddenly moved swiftly. Two telegrams were delivered simultaneously. One of them was for Lady Carlisle from the militant suffragists. 'Our war with you is off for so long as the war with Germany is on,' this telegram read. The other telegram was for Mr. Keown. He was a reservist in the Guards, and his telegram read: 'You are mobilised. A dog-cart will call for you at midnight.'

As long as I live, I shall never forget Mr. Keown's face and voice just before he climbed into that dog-cart. It had arrived exactly on time. Lord Haldane's organization of the British Expeditionary Force had been very efficient. 'Three million Germans,' Mr. Keown was saying, half to himself, 'and I am in the front line.' He was, and he fought right through the war, but happily he survived to become Superintendent of Police at Malton in the inter-war years.

4 : Two Paris Peace Conferences

I AM not the only person in my generation who has attended two Paris peace conferences. There were several of us who shared with each other this uncanny and disquieting experience. I have called the experience disquieting; but to leave this word unqualified would be parochial. It might not be disquieting for a Hellene or for a Hindu; for to find things coming round again in recurrent cycles is just what his theory of the rhythm of the Universe would have led a Greek or an Indian philosopher to expect. It is disquieting for a Muslim or a Christian or a Jew; and it upsets us, 'the People of the Book', because it suggests that, after all, the cyclic theory may be nearer the truth than our own ancestral faith that history moves, not in circles, but in a straight line which is running from a starting point towards a goal. As we see it, a goal gives the Universe a meaning, whereas cyclic history reads to us like 'a tale told by an idiot, signifying nothing'. Yet, though we may find our Judaic teleology inspiring, we might be hard put to it if we were called upon to demonstrate that it, and not the cyclic theory, fits the facts; and the experience of recurring Paris peace conferences makes it difficult not to become convinced that recurrence is the way in which the Universe really works.

Yes, this is the platform at Victoria Station from which the British Delegation's special train for the Paris Peace Conference always starts. Here is the familiar special steamer waiting at the dock; and, now that we have reached Calais, they will, as usual, be giving us lunch, before we entrain for Paris, in the dining-room over there. Over there? But, this time, the dining-room isn't over there any more. There is nothing at all over there. There is no Calais. Calais, this time, is in ruins. So at this point the cycle is not running true to form. Last time, Calais was still standing. This time, it has been laid flat. Does this change invalidate the cyclic theory? If it does, this is not an indication that, after all, we are forging straight ahead towards the millennium; it indicates, rather, that we are still circling, but circling in a descending spiral.

Well, now we are in Paris for the peace conference. Our last attendance at it was in 1919, and this is 1946; so it has come round again in twenty-seven years. Is twenty-seven years the Paris-peace-conference wave-length? If it is, we shall be back again in 1973; and that is a horrifying thought; for, in order to have a Paris peace conference, one has first to have a world war. Shall we live to see world war and peace conference come round again? Manifestly there may be another world war. Who can guarantee that there will not be one? But, if there is one, it is highly improbable that any of us will live to see the end of it, and it is certain that there will not be another peace conference after it. This is certain because the atomic weapon was achieved—and was used—last year. So another world war would be an atomic world war; and, after an atomic world war, it would not be just Calais that would be laid flat. A Paris peace conference after an atomic world war? Who could be so credulous as to believe in the possibility of that? No, an atomic revolution of history's wheel would spiral us all down, next time, to perdition. Such nightmare fancies kept flitting, like bats, through my mind while I was repeating in 1946 the journey that I had made in 1919.

The Paris peace conferences of 1919 and 1946 displayed, of course, differences as well as likenesses. But the likenesses predominated, and most of the apparent differences turn out on analysis to be likenesses distorted by an excruciating extra turn of the screw.

In the set-up of the two conferences the salient likeness was that there was no representation of the defeated enemy powers. Indeed, this time, defeated Germany could not have been represented even if, this time, the victors, remembering Hitler's exploitation of 'the Versailles Diktat', had wished to parley with a German delegation. In 1946, Germany, like Calais, was flat. There was no government of Germany in existence for the victors to meet. An apparent difference for the better in 1946 was the presence, this time, of the Western victors' Russian ex-ally. This time, Russia was not prostrate, as she had been in 1919. Once again she was bleeding from grievous wounds; but this time she was still erect and was, indeed, now overshadowing half the Earth. Then did not her presence at the conference-table give the proceedings a greater reality, to this extent, in 1946 than they had had in 1919? Unfortunately not; for, though the Russians and their Western ex-allies were confronting each other, this time, across the table, there was virtually no intercourse between them. About as much business might have been transacted if they had been meeting, as in 1919, on Prinkipo Island.

In 1946 the atmosphere of the conference was not stormy, as it had sometimes been in 1919, but this was not the improvement that it might have been expected to be. In fact, it was a bad sign; for the reason why it was not stormy was that it was glacial. In 1919 the principal representatives of the powers had been in a human enough relation with each other to be able to quarrel; and they had commanded the necessary means of linguistic communication for quarrelling vocally, thanks to Clemenceau's being able to speak English. The Italian delegates' only foreign language was French; Lloyd George's only one was French as French was spoken by Lord Grey; and President Wilson was not a ready linguist either; so Clemenceau was an indispensable go-between, and this gave him an appreciable diplomatic advantage.

In 1946 all interchanges between the principal delegates were channelled through interpreters; and the life was taken out of the proceedings by the lengthiness and boringness of the process of translation. The principals were also at their interpreters' mercy; for, though the interpreters may not have ventured to distort the meaning of their principals' words, they still could, and sometimes did, misrepresent the spirit of the words by their intonation. I saw

this being done again and again by the French delegation's interpreters into Russian, who were French citizens of White Russian
origin. The French delegation's policy was to try to mediate
between the Russian delegation on the one side and the pair of
English-speaking delegations on the other side. I have listened to
Monsieur Bidault making, in French, some suggestion that was as
conciliatory in tone as it was in substance, and I have then listened
to his interpreters firing off their translation at Molotov like a pistol
shot. I know no Russian, so I could not tell whether the interpreters'
words were a fair rendering of Monsieur Bidault's words; but their
tone certainly did not reproduce Monsieur Bidault's tone, and
apparently there was nothing that Monsieur Bidault could do about
it.

In each conference I had only a minor job, but it got me on to the
back benches of the conference-room, clutching papers that might
or might not be needed by the delegates in the front row; and, since
my responsibility for action was slight, my opportunities for observation were good. The many hours that I spent, at both conferences,
listening in, have been a pricelessly valuable part of my education.

Of the celebrated statesmen whom I was thus able to watch in
action, Molotov stands out in my memory as having been the most
entertaining. In my childhood I had once seen, at the zoo in London,
some mischievous people trying to tease a hippopotamus who was
lolling imprudently close to the edge of his tank. One mischief-
maker was poking him with the tip of his umbrella; another had
dropped a lighted cigarette on to his back. The hippopotamus's
would-be tormentors were doing their worst, but they were being
frustrated. They were provoking no reaction whatsoever. One
could not even tell whether the hippopotamus was aware of their
presence. Well, Molotov reminded me of that hippopotamus when
I was watching him in Paris in 1946. Mr. Byrnes or Mr. Bevin
might say the most frightful things about him, or even to him, and
their interpreters would pass these broadsides on with gusto. But
Molotov always remained formidably bland. I noticed that there
was not a wrinkle on his lofty forehead, though one knew that he
had gone through personal ordeals that would have broken any
ordinary human being's nerve. Molotov's self-control would have
been the envy and admiration of a Stoic, Epicurean, or Buddhist.

Molotov's invulnerability (ἀπάθεια) and imperturbability (ἀταραξία) —the austere ideals of the Greek and Indian philosophies of detachment—were practical, and apparently effortless, accomplishments; and this serenity of Molotov's was, of course, a winning card.

Again and again, in 1946, I had the enjoyment of watching Molotov play his hand. The game always went the same way. For the first hour or two, or indeed for as many hours as the treatment might require on each occasion, Molotov would obstruct all Byrnes's and Bevin's efforts to get some business done. Had Molotov read Goethe's account, in the *Italienische Reise*, of the English nobleman interviewing Goethe on the steps of the cathedral at Naples for precisely ten minutes, watch in hand? Anyway, Molotov was aware that Anglo-Saxons are exasperated by being made to waste their time; and, of course, wasting it for them was no waste of time for him. From Molotov's point of view, his time was being thoroughly well spent in getting Bevin and Byrnes into the state in which he wanted to have them. You could tell when that state had been reached by the physical symptoms. Byrnes's face would begin to twitch; Bevin would begin to bark out furious ejaculations. When Molotov had observed these indications that he had won the psychological match, he would at last consent to talk. At this stage he possessed a decisive psychological advantage. But what did this profit him?. His tactics had been masterly, but they had won no appreciable ground for him from his opponents. These entertaining sessions never resulted in any agreements of any importance.

The weakness of the Russian style of diplomacy is that it overreaches itself. Holding out, as the Russians are apt to do, for total victory, and this over trifles as well as over points of substance, they often fail to attain an important objective that they might perhaps have attained if they had not provoked the other side into showing an obstinacy to match the Russians' own. Mutual obstinacy stultifies negotiation. The purpose of negotiation is to try to reach agreement between parties who have not the power, on either side, to impose their wills. Agreement requires reciprocal give and take, and, when this is not forthcoming, negotiations grind down to a standstill.

However, this impasse at the conference table did not prevent the members of the contending delegations from making friends with each other; and, for me, one of the few agreeable features of the

Paris peace conference of 1946 was the acquaintance that I made with the Russian representative on the committee on which I was serving. Like me, this Russian colleague of mine was not a professional. His career was in the field of higher education, and his peace-time life included what, in Western countries, would have been thought of as being middle-class amenities. For instance, he and his wife had a flat in Moscow, a dacha in the countryside nearby, and a month's holiday in the summer. He liked swimming, so he used to spend his month on the Crimean or the West Caucasian riviera.

While he was on his temporary diplomatic job, he was given treatment that struck his Western colleagues as being generous—as is illustrated by a true story that had a happy ending. At one morning's session of our committee, we persuaded him to join the rest of us in addressing five questions to our immediate superiors. At lunch-time the rest of us were congratulating ourselves on the success of our morning's work; for those questions promised to lever our business an inch or two forward. When we re-assembled after lunch, our Russian colleague quickly remarked that, in the morning, he had got the impression that we fancied that he had agreed to our sending these five questions forward. If this impression of his was correct, then he was sorry to have to inform us that we had mis-interpreted what he had said. He had agreed to no such thing. Inevitably this annoyed us, but we had come to feel an affection for him (he was indeed lovable), and our annoyance changed to concern when, before our barren afternoon session had ended, a telegram arrived for him from Moscow, saying: 'Your wife has just had her baby; a plane for Moscow is at your disposal at the Paris airport, to bring you to visit her and your new-born child. Come at once.'

To us, with our Western *idées fixes,* this sounded ominous; and we were conscience-stricken. In persuading our colleague to agree those five questions that morning, had we been unintentionally getting him into trouble? Those two inches of progress—a progress that had now, anyway, been cancelled—were certainly not worth that. Our friend disappeared; and his place on the committee was taken by a taciturn young man. During the next three weeks we were continually asking for news of our absent colleague from his young *remplaçant*; and, each time, the young man was noncommittal. Perhaps he really had no news. Perhaps all that he cared about was to impress us by appearing to know more than he chose to tell. And then, one morning, our colleague himself reappeared at the committee again, and it turned out to have all been true. His wife *had* had a baby; a plane *had* been placed at his disposal for taking him to Moscow to see her. Talking it over together afterwards, my American colleagues and I agreed with each other that, in corresponding circumstances, our respective delegations might perhaps have granted us compassionate leave of absence, but that our respective treasuries would certainly have made us pay out of our own pockets for the extravagance of a special plane.

The one amenity at the Paris peace conference that somewhat consoled this Russian friend of mine for being kept kicking his heels there was the opportunity for seeing the historical sights when off duty; and, being highly cultivated and extremely industrious, he did his sightseeing very thoroughly.

One Sunday, when he was having lunch with me, I suggested that we should spend the afternoon together at Versailles, and he agreed with alacrity. I signalled to my British Army Service Corps driver, and off we went. When we arrived, I found that the driver had not only never been to Versailles before but had never heard of it; so I told him to park the car and come along with us. Our progress was slow; for my companion was anxious not to miss any detail; so it was nearly six o'clock p.m. by the time when we found ourselves approaching Marie-Antoinette's *hameau*. Marie-Antoinette? The driver had never heard of her either. So I said 'she was a queen', and my companion said 'she was beheaded'. Then he turned to me and addressed me in a now familiar impersonal style. 'You know', he said, 'the Russians treated the imperial family more humanely than the French treated the royal family. The French tormented the royal family with a cat-and-mouse trial; the verdict was a foregone conclusion. And then the French broke the royal family up. They separated the Dauphin from his parents, and, to this day, no one knows what became of the poor child. Now, the Russians were more considerate. They did not break the imperial family up; and they did not tell them that they were going to be shot till three minutes before the execution.' Wishing to be polite, I said, falling in with this impersonal style: 'Well, I suppose the English began it by cutting off King Charles's head'. 'Oh, but they did nothing to his family', my Russian colleague quickly took me up.

If we had been members of the eighteenth-century French Court, our mutual courtesy could not have been more exquisite. At that moment a nightingale began to sing, and simultaneously it came on to rain; but my friend did not notice the rain, nor the time either. The magic sights and sounds had thrown him into an ecstasy, and he was standing there enraptured, oblivious of everything else. Meanwhile, my Anglo-Saxon mind was busy with characteristically prosaic thoughts. 'I am getting rather wet, and the driver may be getting restive; by now he will have had more than his fill of history lessons, and he will be fretting to get home to his tea.' I managed to get my Russian companion away before the driver started to make a scene.

Even peace conferences have light-hearted interludes. On that Sunday at Versailles in 1946 I was recollecting a visit to Versailles on another Sunday afternoon—the first Sunday of the Paris peace conference of 1919. On that winter's day the long ponds below the palace had been frozen over, and they had been covered with lively skaters, arrayed in all the military uniforms of all the Allied and Associated Powers. What animation! What a rhythmical pattern! It had been as graceful as the best Russian ballet. Suddenly I had realized why my pleasure in contemplating this scene was so intense. This was the first time for more than four years that I had seen human beings set free again to surrender themselves whole-heartedly to pure enjoyment.

However, in spite of such occasional alleviations, peace conferences are painfully depressing on the whole. They are depressing because they are frustrating; and they are bound to be frustrating; this is inherent in the nature of the circumstances in which they take place.

A peace conference is an attempt to put the World together again after the World has been shot to pieces in a war. But to be called upon to try to settle all the World's affairs at one go is a veritable Psyche's Task. It would still have been that, even if there had been no previous war to throw the parties to the conference into a pugnacious mood, and even if they had had any amount of time at their disposal for negotiations that are too laborious and too delicate to allow of their being conducted successfully in a rush. Actually, the parties are not in a calm and conciliatory mood, and they have to work under a mounting pressure on them to conclude. The primary task that is laid upon the parties to a peace conference is to make peace, and to make it quickly, even at the price of not making it well. The pressure to conclude is severe, because, until a peace-treaty has been signed, the World remains in a state of war, and, so long as that continues, the World's ordinary day-to-day peace-time business continues to be half paralysed. The majority do not know or care about the niceties of the public questions at issue, but they do know that their private affairs are still suffering, though hostilities have now ceased. This makes them impatient and resentful; and their official representatives at the peace conference feel the chilly breeze.

Another reason why peace conferences are frustrating is because the parties are apt to succumb to the temptation of warping justice for the sake of gaining advantages in the sordid game of power-politics.

There will be international power-politics as long as there are local sovereign states. Wars are power-politics heated up to above boiling-point; but, even at times when no fighting and no killing is going on, power-politics will still be active, and the effects of the game will still be vicious. The holding of a peace conference signifies that the latest bout of power-politics has ended in the defeat of the enemy of yesterday; and the enemy of yesterday has no sooner been eliminated than the allies of yesterday, whom the not yet defeated enemy had held together, become opponents of each other and resume the power-game among themselves, with a new alignment of the players. This is unfortunate, not only for the prostrate ex-enemy, but for anyone else whose fate happens to lie in the peace conference's hands. The decision of an issue on its merits will now be subordinated to a calculation of the decision's probable effects on the respective national interests of the competing parties. I have watched—indignant but impotent—while justice was going by the board at Paris both in 1919 and in 1946. I will cite a couple of flagrant instances.

In 1919, Italy was trying to exact from her allies all that they had promised her, under duress, in the secret London treaty of 1915.

Italy was now demanding Fiume besides. The United States was resisting these unjust demands that were being made at the expense of self-determination for Tirolese Austrians and for Jugoslavs, and France and Britain were supporting the United States half-heartedly. Whether they revoked on their treaty-commitments or committed injustice, they would be putting themselves in an invidious position on either alternative. Italy then withdrew from the conference in a calculated huff—she calculated that her withdrawal would bring her three partners to heel. To spite Italy, the three then sanctioned Venizelos's adroitly-timed request to be allowed to land Greek troops at Smyrna, next door to the zone in South-Western Turkey that had been earmarked for Italy in the secret treaty of Saint-Jean-de-Maurienne. This counter-retaliation against Italy was an irresponsible act. The decision was taken after telegrams had been received in Paris from the British, French, and American naval, military, and consular authorities in Western Turkey, unanimously imploring their principals in Paris not to let Greek troops land at Smyrna, whatever other action against Italy they might or might not see fit to take. The result of this irresponsible move in the inter-ally power-game, in defiance of professional advice, was the Graeco-Turkish war and the uprooting and expatriation of the Greek minority in Turkey and the Turkish minority in Greece.

In 1919 President Wilson, concentrating his efforts on saving as many Jugoslavs as he could from Italy's clutches, threw the South Tirol to the Italian wolves. The South Tirol was the country in the upper basin of the River Etsch (*alias* Adige) whose inhabitants were German-speaking Austrians. This was one of the pieces of the Habsburg Monarchy that, in the secret treaty of 1915, had been promised to Italy by Britain, France, and Russia. President Wilson left the South Tirol to its pre-arranged fate. This was one of the most inexcusable of the violations of the principle of self-determination in the 1919 peace settlement.

When, in 1946, I went to the next Paris peace conference, I confidently expected to see this particular injustice redressed. In entering the war on Germany's side, Italy had surely forfeited her 1919 treaty-rights, even though she had changed sides at a stage of the Second World War at which it had become clear that the anti-German coalition was going to win once again. As for Austria—

now no longer the old Austrian Empire but the diminutive German-speaking state that had issued from the peace settlement of 1919—she, too, had been in Germany's camp in the Second World War, but she had been in it as a result of Hitler's having previously annexed her by force. Surely her compulsory belligerency would not be held against her. Surely, so far as the Tirol was concerned, the Paris peace conference of 1946 had a free hand for righting the injustice that had been done at the Paris peace conference of 1919. Surely the victors of 1946 would jump at this chance of doing the good deed that it was in their power to do now without let or hindrance.

The victors did nothing of the kind. One and all, they reasoned about the Tirol, not in terms of justice, but in terms of power-politics. 'I, the United States, in pursuit of my rivalry with the Soviet Union, and I, the Soviet Union, in pursuit of my rivalry with the United States—I need to draw into my camp as many of the second-rate and third-rate powers as possible. I cannot hope to win the allegiance of *both* Italy *and* Austria, because these two countries are at loggerheads with each other over the South Tirol, and, over this issue, I shall have to come down on one side or the other, no doubt at the cost of driving into my rival's camp the country that I am going to offend by taking her opponent's side in the South Tirol dispute. So it is a choice between Austria and Italy. Which of the two shall I conciliate, and which shall I alienate? Well, which of the two will make the more valuable satellite for me? In other words, which of the two is the bigger and the stronger? Why Italy, of course. So here I have my answer to the question of what my policy about the South Tirol is to be. The question answers itself. My policy is to maintain Italy's rule over the South Tirol and to reject Austria's demand for a revision of the settlement made in 1919.'

On this power-politics point in 1946, American and Russian thinking ran parallel to an identical conclusion. Both super-powers supported Italy against Austria, each of them for fear that, if she had supported Austria and had thereby vindicated justice, Italy would have gone over to the rival super-power's side. This was one of the few issues on which, in 1946, America and Russia agreed, and they agreed on it readily and promptly. Britain and France, of course, followed suit.

What a tragedy that, when, for once, the rival victors did agree, the identical motive should have been so unworthy. I was shocked; but, having been at another Paris peace conference before this one, I was not surprised.

Well, I am glad that the date of my birth and the invention of the nuclear weapon have given me, between them, a double guarantee that, even if the cyclic theory is the truth about human affairs, I shall never have to attend a Paris peace conference again.

5 : Thirty-three Years at Chatham House

ONE evening in Paris in 1919, at a stage of the Paris peace conference of that year at which its end was in sight, I turned up to attend a meeting in the Majestic Hotel, the British delegation's quarters, to which all the temporary officials in the American and British delegations had been invited. The permanent officials would have been invited, too, if they could have obtained permission from their superiors to accept.

I found the room crowded. The moving spirit had been one of the British temporary officials, Lionel Curtis. Lionel had a genius for action, and he had sensed that, in convening this meeting, he had anticipated a wish that had been taking shape in the minds of the rest of us. We were all conscious that our spell of war-work in government service was now drawing to a close. Some of us had been offered permanent official careers. I had been one of these; but, after much heart-searching, I had declined; and all but a very few of us were going back, when our governments released us, to our interrupted non-official careers. Our years of war-work had been a queer experience—queer because it did not seem to be part of our normal lives; it felt more like a fragment of some other life that was incommensurate with normality, as war-time had been incommensurate with peace-time. Yet, though this experience had been strange and was going to be transitory, we were not reconciled to the idea of closing the door on it and forgetting about it.

We were unable to forget about our war-time experience because it had been illuminating. We had learnt that world wars, which in pre-August-1914 Britain and America had appeared to be 'ancient history', were after all a terrible living reality. Of our British contemporaries who had been combatants, at least half had lost their lives; and there was no guarantee that the terrible catastrophe of 1914–18 would not recur. That would depend on how well or how badly the governments and peoples of the World were going to handle the international problems of the post-war period; and we temporary officials could not be indifferent to this; for, after the war, it was no longer a tenable thesis that international affairs were the concern of state departments and foreign offices exclusively. We had learnt, from the toll of war-casualties, that international affairs concerned everybody; and it was obvious that we were not going to be able to contract out of the consequences of the governments' foreign policies just by returning, for our own part, to our pre-war non-official avocations. Our own fate and our children's fate was at stake, and therefore our personal, as well as our civic, responsibility was involved. We needed still to be able, after our return to private life, to do something about these international affairs which had now proved to be one of the most barbaric and most dangerous fields of contemporary human action. What provision for meeting this need of ours could we make? This was the question that the present meeting had been convened to discuss.

The agenda for the meeting was a practical proposal. It was being proposed that we should found an Anglo-American private society for the scientific study of international affairs. By 'scientific' the draftsmen of the motion meant 'objective, unbiased, unpartisan, un-emotional'. No doubt, these were ideals which could be realized only imperfectly, human nature being what it is. But the closer that the proposed society's activities could approximate to being 'scientific' in the sense in which the word was intended to be taken, the more effective they would be likely to be for their purpose. The purpose would be to make as accurate a study as possible of the course of current international affairs. It was submitted that sound study was the indispensable basis for statesmanlike action;

and statesmanlike action was what mankind needed if a repetition of the catastrophe of 1914–18 was to be avoided. It was urged, however, and this emphatically, by the sponsors of the proposal that the activities of our society, if we did found it, should be confined to study strictly. The action for which, one might hope, the results of such study might prove useful would have to be taken by governments that would be responsible to electorates. International action is politics, and scientific work will not be genuinely scientific unless politics are kept out of it. Therefore the first article in the constitution of our society should provide that the society was not to have any policy corporately, though this would not, of course, restrict the freedom of its members, individually, to favour and promote this or that policy in their political capacity as citizens and voters.

The proposal pleased us. It promised to meet a need of which many of us had been conscious, and its suggestion for defining the scope of the future society's activities struck us as being wise. We decided to found a society for the scientific study of international affairs on the suggested lines. I had, of course, no idea, at the time, how greatly my own life, personal as well as professional, was going to be affected by that evening's decision. I was one of many among those present who put in an application for membership.

Later on, the original Anglo-American society was divided into two—the Council on Foreign Relations, with its headquarters in New York, and the Royal Institute of International Affairs (Chatham House), with its headquarters in London. The reason for this change was not any divergence of opinion as between the American and the British members of the original society; it was simply a question of what was practically feasible; experience had soon shown the difficulty of administering, as a single unit, an organization whose membership was divided between two continents. The two sister-institutions, the Council and the Institute, have always maintained the closest and most cordial relations with each other.

The Foreign Office in Whitehall did not, at the time, look with favour on the outcome of that evening's meeting in Paris. They had been willing to take outsiders into their fold temporarily as an emergency measure in war-time. What else could they have done when the war had increased the volume of their work so enormously? Yet, even during the First World War, 'the War Depart-

ment' of the Foreign Office had consisted of just four clerks, all of
them officers on the permanent strength, and the junior member of
the quartet had done the department's typing. All along, the Foreign
Office had been bent on returning, as soon as the Paris peace conference was over, to its traditional way of working. Traditionally the
Foreign Office had been managed like a family business. The number
of first-division Foreign Office clerks had been kept small enough to
make it possible for them all to be in a personal relation with each
other. A monopoly of the conduct of foreign affairs was this Foreign
Office family-circle's historic prerogative. Chatham House had ex-
pressly debarred itself even from having views about policy, and
it had never thought of attempting to trespass on the actual policy-
makers' preserve. Yet at this date the authorities in the Foreign
Office still felt that it might prove a nuisance for them, and might
perhaps to some extent cramp their style, if outsiders were to begin
making a scientific study of the Foreign Office's jealously-guarded
field of operations.

Until after the First World War the Foreign Office was, in fact,
still about zero per cent public-relations-minded and one hundred
per cent security-minded. Like liberty and equality, publicity and
security pull in opposite directions. The Foreign Office knew this,
but it had not yet recognized that security need make any concessions at all to publicity. The Foreign Office was conscious of the
dangerousness of the field of human relations with which it was
concerned, and it was convinced that the only safe way of doing its
delicate work was to do it behind a curtain of secrecy.

The handling of relations between local sovereign independent
states that have the right and the power to go to war with each other
is indeed a dangerous game, and it is going to become more and
more dangerous so long as this antiquated political system survives
while the accelerating advance of technology is continuing to put
more and more deadly weapons into the local governments' hands.
In the Atomic Age the incompatibility of the World's petrified
political structure with its revolutionary technological equipment
has become terrifyingly extreme. In 1969 we still have no idea
whether we are going to succeed in releasing this tension before we
are overtaken by some annihilating resolution of forces; and this
accentuation of the dangerousness of international relations would

be an argument for tightening up official secrecy proportionately if governments were living in a political vacuum. This is, however, on longer practical politics in countries which have a democratic franchise, and in which an increasing percentage of the citizen-body is constantly becoming better-educated and better-informed.

In a democracy the government cannot go far beyond the point to which it has managed to carry public opinion with it; and this is true, above all, in the jealously-guarded preserve of the World's ministries of foreign affairs. (In 1969 there are about 125 of these.) In the field of international relations in the Atomic Age, decisions taken by governments are literally matters of life and death for the entire population. If the government of a democracy loses touch with public opinion, a policy that it has elaborated in secret may be indignantly rejected by the press and the public when, on the eve of being put into effect, the secretly-hatched policy has to be brought out, at last, into the light. An illustration of this truth is the rejection of the Hoare–Laval plan by the press and public of the United Kingdom in 1935. In a democracy, this is official secrecy's inherent risk. Publicity is the only possible insurance against this risk; and therefore publicity has to be given its due, even though some relaxation of security may be the unavoidable price of this. In the striking of a compromise between these two considerations, where is the line to be drawn? No doubt, in a relatively civilized field of public activity such as the field of education, publicity can be given wider scope than it can in the barbaric field of international relations; but, here too, complete secrecy is no longer a practicable ideal. However, the Foreign Office's negative first reaction to the foundation of a British Institute of International Affairs was no surprise to me, because, not long before the start of the Paris peace conference of 1919, I had had a fantastic personal experience of the Foreign Office's then still persisting allergy to public relations.[1]

In the course of the inter-war years the Foreign Office's attitude towards public relations changed radically. At Chatham House we could register the Foreign Office's progress in public-relations-mindedness by the successive modifications of its original stand on the question of its permanent officers' participation in our work. At the beginning they were forbidden to become members of the

---

[1] For this, see *Acquaintances*, pp. 203-4.

Institute. Later they were given leave to become members and to attend meetings, on the understanding that they would not take part in the discussions. Finally they were given leave to speak if they wished. I imagine that the Foreign Office had discovered that some acquaintance with the state of public opinion was indispensable for the effective performance of their officers' work, and that Chatham House had been found to provide a forum in which public opinion on international affairs could be sampled. The Foreign Office must eventually also have realized that the best way to elicit opinions is to take part oneself in the debate. Before the outbreak of the Second World War a press department—still unthinkable in 1918—had become a key part of the Foreign Office's works, and the department's press conferences were being attended by the newspapers' diplomatic correspondents.

Five years after the foundation of Chatham House, I found myself joining its staff. (The job that I had been commissioned to do was to launch a Chatham House *Survey of International Affairs*.) I stayed at Chatham House till I reached retiring age thirty-three years later. This was something new in my professional career. I had held my Balliol fellowship for only two years and a bit, and then, after the First World War, I had held for five years the Koraes Chair of Byzantine and Modern Greek Studies in the University of London. After these relatively short tenures, I had resigned from each of these previous posts—from my fellowship, of my own will; my resignation from the Koraes Chair had been only formally voluntary. At Chatham House I stayed on. What held me there?

This question presents itself because, at Chatham House at the age of thirty-five and upwards, I had a status that was inferior to my status at Balliol at the age of twenty-three. At Chatham House I was an employee from first to last; and, though I had access to the Research Committee, to which I was immediately responsible, I did not have a vote on the committee, and, until near the end of my time, I did not have access to the Chatham House Council, which had the last word on questions relating to my work. By contrast, at Balliol I had been a guildsman. The fellows of the college were the college itself incarnate. We not only picked the undergraduates and directed their education; we owned and administered the college's property, and we made its policy. In short, we were our own masters. As far as status goes, the position of a fellow of an Oxford or Cambridge college is first-rate; so, if status had been the paramount consideration for me, I should presumably have tried to work my passage back to one or other of those two universities. My own college, which I had chosen to leave, might not, perhaps, readily have reopened its doors to me. (Later, Balliol generously elected me to an honorary fellowship—an honour that I prize.) However, I did not try to take the road back. Status was not, for me, the determining consideration, though there were times at Chatham House when I was painfully conscious that my status there was not what it had been at Oxford. What, then, were the pros and cons that determined my constant decision to stay on at Chatham House nevertheless?

The advantage of being one's own master, which the fellow of an Oxford or Cambridge college enjoys, was outweighed, for me, by some disadvantages in the university don's career that, according to my reckoning, were grave.

The gravest was one that is intrinsic to the educator's job at all levels. The rhythm of educational work is, and seems bound to be, cyclic. Each year the conveyor-belt brings to a teacher, for him to educate, a new annual batch of pupils of the same age as the batches that have passed and the batches that are still to come; and the teacher has to give each successive batch the same instruction. For each generation of pupils in turn, this instruction is novel, but, for the teacher, it inevitably becomes staler and staler with each accumulating year. In my second year as a don I was already catching myself repeating the same forms of words in discussing with my pupils an essay on some stock subject; and there were some subjects that were so essential that one could not avoid setting essays on them to every pupil who passed through one's hands. I now made a count; and I found that, if I were to stay at the college as long as the present Master had been there already (he was then turned seventy, while I was still only twenty-four), the number of times that, by then, I should have set, listened to, and criticized the unavoidable essay on, say, Solon or on Peisistratus would run into four figures. This disconcerted me.

The rhythm of every educator's professional career is unquestionably cyclic, whether the rhythm of the Universe is cyclic or not. The university don's job is the plum of the profession in the sense that the age-group of pupils that passes over the don's conveyor-belt is the oldest, and therefore presumably the most mature, of all the successive age-groups of young people who are still *in statu pupillari*. Just because of this, however, the don's relation with his pupils is a more delicate and difficult one than the schoolmaster's or schoolmistress's.

At the school stage the teacher does not only belong conspicuously to an older generation than his pupils; this difference in generation is of the essence of the relation between him and them. By contrast, the university student is in the transitional stage between being juvenile and being grown-up. Unlike both the schoolchild and the adult, the university student is an unclassifiable creature—neither fish, flesh, nor fowl—and this makes the relation between him and his dons ambiguous. The art of handling university students is to make oneself appear, and this almost ostentatiously, to be treating them as adults, while keeping them in invisible harness and even, when necessary, giving them a flick of the whip. This is a tricky job, and at Oxford and Cambridge the dons have developed a way of their own for performing it.

The 'image' (to use Madison Avenue language) that they try to give of themselves in their relations with undergraduates is that of being older contemporaries rather than being representatives of an older generation. The don tries to appear and to behave like his pupil's elder brother, not like his dominie. If the don can sustain this role, it is evidently the ideal role for him to play. But, from the start, it is something of a *tour de force*, and it inevitably becomes more artificial, and therefore less facile, with each additional year in the don's career. As the years pass, the gap between 'image' and reality widens inexorably; and this exposes the don to the prospect of a cumulative process of frustration. There are, of course, some men and women who are to the manner born, and these can stay dons for half a century without losing touch or going stale. These natural-born dons can do wonders for successive generations of pupils, and, in achieving this, they will be fulfilling their own natures. They are blessèd, but they are also rare. I knew, revered, and loved some dons of this rare kind; but I did not feel that I myself had either the gift or the vocation.

Cyclic motion is the nearest kind to stationariness. Circling and standing-still resemble each other in ruling out, as they both do, the possibility of directional movement from some starting-point towards some goal. If life has no direction, nothing happens in it; but, when nothing happens in life, time does not stand still; time flows on, but flows imperceptibly. One finds that it has gone before one knows where one is.

This feature of the don's career was brought to my attention within a few weeks of the beginning of the first university term in my short career as a don. This was the Michaelmas term, 1912. The Master of the college, J. L. Strachan-Davidson, had reached his seventieth birthday; the fellows were giving a dinner in his honour to celebrate the happy occasion; the senior fellow, A. L. Smith, known for short as 'A. L.' to distinguish him from 'J. A.', was proposing the Master's health; and, in 'A. L.'s' speech, the *pièce de résistance* was the information that, during the fifty-two years that had now passed since the Master had first come up to Oxford at the age of eighteen, he had never been away from the college for as long a time on end as twelve months.

This was a revelation of a feature of the Master's personal history that 'A. L.' was rightly presenting to us as being characteristic. 'A. L.' was also presenting it as being something delightful; but, for me that evening, the revelation was shattering. I, too, had come up at the age of eighteen; I, too, had not been away from the college for more than a single academic year since then; and, while it was true that, as yet, I was only twenty-four, I suddenly saw the next forty-six years passing in a flash and the same speech being made about me that was now being made about Strachan. Only a few weeks back, I, in my turn, had been formally elected to a fellowship of the college, and on this occasion a document had been drawn up and agreed which certified that, if I did not go bankrupt, did not commit any other immoral act, and did not marry, my fellowship was—subject to these three conditions—to be mine from now on, without any time-limit. With this in mind, I found that the celebration of the Master's seventieth birthday had loosened my seat in the coveted saddle on to which I had so recently been elevated.

I was the more upset when I recalled Alfred Zimmern's story, told in another book of mine,[1] of the directive that he had been

---

[1] In *Acquaintances*, pp. 53–4.

given by Warden Spooner when Alfred had been starting on his
third year as a fellow and tutor of New College. Alfred was a school-
fellow of mine in an older generation. As an undergraduate I had
found his lectures immensely stimulating; and I had a warm affection and regard for him as a friend; so his example had a powerful
influence on me. Alfred's disturbing encounter with the Warden of
his college had loosened his seat in his saddle to the point of eventually moving him to dismount. He had resigned from his fellowship
after having held it for six years. My recollection of Alfred's experience reinforced the effect, on me, of the dinner in honour of the
Master of Balliol's seventieth birthday.

The cyclic rhythm of the don's profession was formidable; the
requirement of celibacy was forbidding. In that document relating
to my election to my fellowship, marrying was named as one of the
three offences that would automatically terminate my tenure.
Marrying was here put on a par with a couple of 'immoral' acts.
Did this implicitly stigmatize marriage as being immoral too?

The next Master of Balliol but one after J. L. Strachan-Davidson
was A. D. Lindsay. (A. L. Smith held the office in between.) One
day, when Strachan-Davidson was still Master, while Lindsay was
the senior 'Greats don' in the college and the two junior fellows
were Bob Gibson and I, Lindsay came up to the pair of us with a
grin on his face. 'The Master said an amusing thing to me just now,'
he told us. 'The Master said: "I hope that Gibson and Toynbee will
be crossed in love. I have always found that fellows who have been
crossed in love become very faithful servants of the college ever
afterwards."' Lindsay could afford to laugh at this; he was safely
married already. He had, I suppose, forfeited his fellowship in consequence, but, if so, he had been reinstated. Bob Gibson and I, however, did not think Lindsay's story funny. We must have looked
glum; for Lindsay went off grinning more merrily than ever. The
Master had failed to prevent Lindsay not only from marrying but
also from joining the Labour Party. He had contended, without
success, that, while dons were free to be either Liberals or Conserva-
tives, the Labour Party was, for dons, a *religio non licita*. Strachan-
Davidson was both a don and an authority on Roman Law, so this
was the formula that came natural to him. A famous couplet in one
of W. S. Gilbert's lyrics would have made Strachan-Davidson's

point more effectively; but, though these verses had been written, and had then been sung repeatedly on the stage, within Strachan-Davidson's own lifetime, he may have been unacquainted with them. I cannot picture him in the audience when one of Gilbert and Sullivan's operas was being performed at Oxford.

A few months afterwards I had become engaged to be married. I had waited till I had made sure, by experiment, that I was competent to earn my living in my present profession at any rate; but I had taken action as soon as I had delivered my first lecture without coming to grief. The morning after my engagement, I called on the Master to make an appointment with him for that afternoon. I did not tell him what my business was, and I looked forward to the interview with trepidation. Meanwhile my news had quickly gone the round of the Senior Commonroom, and the senior fellow, A. L. Smith, had taken my affair in charge. 'Don't break it to him yourself; I will break it to him,' he had said, and he had decided, on the spot, that, after lunch, he and I should go for a walk together and that, at the appointed hour, he, instead of me, should knock at the Master's door.

When we set out, 'A. L.' told me that he was taking me to a wood where he had heard a nightingale sing at this season the year before. Listening to the nightingale would put us in an auspicious mood for transacting our subsequent business. The nightingale's haunt, supposing that the bird was regular in its habits, proved to be some distance out of Oxford, and, while we had no guarantee that the nightingale had come back to the same place this year, it soon became certain that we should be late for the appointment with the Master if we did not shorten the itinerary that 'A. L.' had mapped out. The appointment was intimidating enough in itself; the thought of aggravating a difficult situation by keeping the Master waiting was almost more than I could bear. I suggested that we should turn back. 'Quite unnecessary,' was 'A. L.'s' answer. 'Don't want to keep the Master waiting? Why, it will do him good.' 'A. L.'s' nonchalant attitude increased my uneasiness; and, when we did at last reach the nightingale's presumed haunt, we lost more time again by waiting in vain for the bird to make its appearance and to strike up. By the time we were back at the college we were very late indeed. 'A. L.' now went to the Master's lodgings, while I lurked unhappily in the garden quad. After a bit, 'A. L.' reappeared, still looking jaunty. 'What did the Master say?' I asked, with my heart in my mouth. 'Oh,' 'A. L.' answered, 'he said: "Damn! I knew the fellow had something disagreeable to tell me when he made that appointment with me this morning."'

'A. L.' had gone out of his way to be kind to me. It is true that he would have been an incongruous champion of celibacy; for he himself was a married man of many years standing, and by now he had a long family of daughters, with one son at each end. To contain them the college had built for them a big house, 'The King's Mound', on the Master's Field (the Balliol playing-field). When I went round to the King's Mound next morning to thank 'A. L.' again, Mrs. Smith took a commission for her husband's good offices to me. She made me take a swarm of bees that had settled on a tree in her garden. In anticipation of my call, she had a bee-keeper's veil and gloves all ready for me to put on, and in my state of exaltation I hardly felt the stings that penetrated these defences.

I was reinstated in my forfeited fellowship, and this was handsome behaviour on the college's part. The Master and fellows would have been entirely within their rights if they had given the vacated place to someone else. However, marriage does not entirely solve the problems of a don's life. Being a don is not just a profession; it too, like marriage, is a way of life. A college is not a business office; it is a fraternity. But it is no easier to have two homes than it is to serve two masters. There is bound to be a tug-o'-war between them, and wife and family are bound to win in their competition with the secularized form of monasticism that is the nature of collegiate life. To take and keep a vow of celibacy is not beyond human powers if it is done for the glory of God; but, for most people, the service of education is not an adequate motive for evoking this degree of self-devotion. In a tug-o'-war between secular collegiate life and marriage, collegiate life will come off second best; but I guess that, for most married dons—though there are conspicuous exceptions, such as 'A. L.'—the dual allegiance, even if unequally distributed, sets up a tension that adds appreciably to the difficulties of life. My own experience of this had moved me to resign from my Balliol fellowship, of my own volition this time, in 1915, after I had left Oxford for London to do war-work there.

These were the considerations that ruled out, for me, all thought of trying to become a don again, even at moments at which I was finding my status at Chatham House irksome; and such *contretemps* were not very frequent. Even so, my objections to a don's life might not, perhaps, have prevailed if the positive attractions of Chatham House had not been numerous and powerful.

The immediate attraction of the job that Chatham House had offered me had been a highly practical one. At that moment I had been out of a job, and, with children to educate, I had needed to find a new job without delay. I had just had to resign from the chair of Byzantine and Modern Greek Studies in the University of London. Soon after my appointment to this post, I had obtained a summer term's leave of absence for studying current Greek affairs on the spot. The Graeco-Turkish war after the war, which had been precipitated by the Greek Army's landing at Smyrna, with Anglo-Franco-American sanction, in 1919, had then still been going on. At Athens, Venizelos had unexpectedly fallen, and King Constantine I had returned from exile. Greek affairs had thus been in flux. I had wanted to study them at first hand, and I had financed my expedition by going to the Levant as war-correspondent for *The Manchester Guardian*. On this temporary job I had witnessed atrocities being committed by Greeks against Turks, and I had, of course, reported them. This had been awkward for the Anglo-Greek founders of the Koraes Chair, for the University of London, and for me. My position had become untenable, and I had resigned. This incident is now 'ancient history', and I feel no inclination to try to apportion the blame. Moreover the *culpa*, at whatever door it may have been lain, turned out, for me, to have been *felix*. It brought me to Chatham House, and there it put me into partnership with Veronica, *quod mihi felix erat faustumque*.

Meanwhile, I had been 'up against it' when, before my last term at the university had run out, I had received a letter one day from Sir James Headlam-Morley, who had been one of my senior colleagues in the Political Intelligence Department of the Foreign Office. 'A job must, and indeed shall, be found for you,' this benevolent letter had said. I had been overcome with relief and, still more, with gratitude; for I had had no claim at all on Headlam-Morley's good will, that he should concern himself on my account.

I had no doubt that he would be as good as his word. By then, I already knew him well enough to feel sure that he would not promise more than he was sure that it was in his power to perform.

I was the beneficiary of a lucky coincidence. Just at the time when I had resigned from the Koraes Chair, the Council of Chatham House had decided to begin producing an annual *Survey of International Affairs*, to follow on to the Chatham House *History of the Peace Conference of Paris*, which was now nearing completion. After the foundation, in Paris, of the original Anglo-American society for the scientific study of international affairs, it had been decided that the publication of objective works, dealing with the society's field of interest, must be one of the society's activities. We had decided to begin by producing a history of the peace conference in which the founding members of the society had been participants; and Mr. Thomas Lamont, a partner in the New York banking firm J. P. Morgan and Company, had undertaken to finance the production of this. Thanks to Mr. Lamont's princely act, *The History of the Peace Conference of Paris* had been produced, under Chatham House's auspices, in six volumes. The work was a symposium. Very many of the contributors were former members of the American and British delegations who were recording transactions in which they themselves had had a hand. The editor was a former member of the British delegation, Professor H. W. V. Temperley, of Cambridge, who was an extremely distinguished historian.

The History of the Peace Conference is a monumental work, and, thanks to the quantity of the first-hand knowledge that is embodied in it, it will retain its value even when all the contemporary official archives have been made public. History, however, did not come to an end with the conclusion, in 1920–21, of the five peace-treaties. Long before Volume VI of the *History of the Peace Conference* of 1919 had been published, the flow of post-war events had become a flood. For instance, one of the five peace-treaties themselves—the brittle treaty of Sèvres that had been imposed on Turkey—had already manifestly become a dead letter. It had been repudiated by a resistance movement led by a great man, Mustafā Kemāl. If Chatham House's intention to produce a record of international events was to be sustained, the *History of the Peace Conference* must be supplemented by a history of its sequels.

The Council of Chatham House recognized the need to meet this demand; but it was hard put to it to find ways and means. The projected *Survey of International Affairs*, like the *History of the Peace Conference*, required an endowment, and none was forthcoming till after the first three volumes of the *Survey* had been published out of funds temporarily diverted from their destination, which was the building of a lecture-hall. Then, in the nick of time, Lionel Curtis elicited Sir Daniel Stevenson's endowment with the *léger de main* with which a conjurer produces a rabbit out of his hat. In 1924, however, when the Council took the decision to launch the *Survey*, no endowment for this undertaking was yet in sight; so it had to be planned with the minimum possible outlay. It was decided that the *Survey*, unlike its predecessor the *History*, must be produced by a single writer with only one part-time assistant, supplemented by a girl who, single-handed, was to read, mark, cut, and classify the contents of the World's press. Headlam-Morley, now Historical Adviser to the Foreign Office, was, outside his official duties, the Chairman of Chatham House's Publications Committee. It fell to him to find a writer for the projected *Survey*. His kindly wish to help me thus chimed in with his difficult task of providing for the needs of Chatham House. On Headlam-Morley's recommendation —based, I suppose, on his personal knowledge of me and my work during the First World War—the Council authorized Headlam-Morley to offer me the job of launching the *Survey* and carrying the narrative down as far as I could within the period of twelve months which was then the limit of the time for which the Council could guarantee its ability to find the money for paying me.

Would I have accepted the invitation if I had not been in dire need of a job? Since I was in dire need, this question did not arise for me. I jumped at the offer; yet I accepted it with trepidation. Headlam-Morley and I did not know in advance whether the information that was public would prove adequate for producing a current history of international affairs that would be sufficiently accurate, precise, and detailed to be of some value to prospective readers. Nor could we foresee what the scale of a precise narrative would have to be, or how much of the ground could be covered on the right scale in twelve months. We did foresee that this year's work would be a labour of Hercules; and we did know that I should not have

access to the files in the British Foreign Office and in the ministries
of foreign affairs in other countries. We were both conscious of the
value of this secret information; for we had both had access to it for
our work during the war and the peace conference, and Headlam-
Morley was enjoying access to it still—though he was, of course,
debarred from sharing this access with me now that I had ceased to
be a temporary Foreign Office clerk. Besides being conscious of
having to attempt to write the *Survey* without being able to draw
on this prime source of information, I was conscious of the inadequacy of my own intellectual equipment. The history with which I
was (and still am) best acquainted was Graeco-Roman history; and,
though, thanks to my *Wanderjahr* in Greece and my subsequent war-
work, I had since won a footing in contemporary history, this footing was confined, so far, to the current affairs of the Near and
Middle East, and I was now undertaking to write a global survey of
current international affairs.

To help me out, Headlam-Morley suggested that, if the financial
means could be found, I should farm out to regional experts certain
fields that, from Headlam-Morley's Europo-centric standpoint,
seemed peripheral. He mentioned Eastern Asia and Latin America.
My reaction to this helpful offer was that, having undertaken to
write a global survey, I should like to keep the whole of it in my
own hands. If means were found for lightening my load, I should,
of course, gratefully accept them; but, instead of trying to divide
the job on a regional basis, I should prefer to farm out some technical topics—mainly financial and economic—which I did not feel
myself qualified for trying to tackle. My reason for this counter-
suggestion, which Headlam-Morley accepted, was a pair of
'hunches'. I guessed that Europe was now soon going to lose the
dominant, and therefore central, position in the World that she had
been holding for the last four centuries; and I also guessed that we
were moving into a stage of mankind's history in which the whole
World was going to coalesce, whether for good or for evil, into a
single society in which each of the hitherto virtually self-contained
geographical regions would interlock and interact with every other
region. If these guesses of mine hit the mark, the history of a coalescing World could not be written intelligibly unless it were
written as a unity in which neither Europe nor any other region

would be given pride of place. To bring this point home to my readers, I included, in the first few volumes of the *Survey*, a map showing the World centred, not on Europe, and not on the North Atlantic, but on the Pacific.

I did carry out my original twelve months' assignment. But why did I want to go on writing the *Survey* after that? When the twelve months had elapsed and I had delivered my batch of volumes, Chatham House's and my reciprocal obligations lapsed. Why did I want to keep the job when, thanks to Lionel Curtis and to Sir Daniel Stevenson, it was now put on a permanent basis? I had had time, meanwhile, to turn round. I could have looked for, and probably have found, some other job if I had chosen. What held me?

One consideration that, for me, counted for a good deal may perhaps sound trivial. A job at Chatham House was a job in London, and my roots were, and still are, there. I had been born and brought up in London, and so far there have been only three years of my life (1912–15) during which I have been living in England without having a London home. During those three years I had a feeling of being in exile. I was homesick for Kensington Gardens, which, in my childhood, had been the centre of my universe, and I missed the London buses and the Underground. My mind then dwelled wistfully on early memories: that chocolate-coloured horse-bus in which I had loved to ride, from Queen's Road (now Queensway) Metropolitan station to the Zoo; that trace-horse that used to be hitched on to the Islington bus to help it up the hill; those pails of bran-mash that an ostler once brought out of the stables of an inn to refresh the bus-horses at the mid-point of the long-distance drive to Cricklewood; and the builds—both of them peculiar yet each peculiar in a highly distinctive style—of the steam-locomotives on the Metropolitan Railway and on the District Railway. (The change of locomotives between the two segments of the Inner Circle used to take ten minutes.) I was even homesick for the choking blue-black smoke that used to pour up from Gower Street Station into the street through a grimy grating.

Of course, even by 1912, the outward shape of London transport had changed out of all recognition. My father had often taken me to watch the two-wheeled horse-carts removing the spoil from the shafts that were being sunk for the construction of 'the Twopenny Tube' (the Central London Railway); and he had laughed at my terror when the first motor-bus that I had yet seen took me by surprise in Piccadilly Circus as it hurled itself round the corner of Swan and Edgar's. By 1912, London was fast changing, and in the twenty-four years that have now passed since the end of the Second World War it has undergone further changes that surpass those of the whole half-century before that. In 1969, travelling about London is less agreeable and more fatiguing than it was in 1899. Yet, if I were to stop riding in London's present-day capricious buses and crowded tubes, I should, I am sure, feel a sharp sense of loss. Are such life-long attachments to local colour really trivialities? My guess is that a psychologist would pronounce that they have their psychological importance. One cannot be expatriated with impunity; and, so long as I stayed at Chatham House, I was going to be living and working in my native city.

Another attraction of Chatham House for me was the world of men and women with whom I found myself in touch there. Many of the members of Chatham House were people whose careers had been excitingly un-cyclic. They were people whose personalities had been ripened by stimulating experiences and great responsibilities. To meet them and to consult them and to get them talking was, for me, a continual addition to my education.

In this company of outstanding personalities that were contributing to the work and life of Chatham House, two figures stand out for me: Lionel Curtis and Headlam-Morley. These two, between them, had created Chatham House *ex nihilo*. They co-operated most effectively; their abilities were complementary, and they knew it; so they could afford, in jest, to affect a contempt for each other's limitations. Lionel, the man of action (he was a matchless promoter of good causes), professed to write off Headlam as being an incurable academic, knowing well that he was dependent on Headlam for developing the intellectual side of Chatham House's work. Headlam, the scholar, professed to write off Lionel as a crank. He used to make a point of teasing Lionel by never using Lionel's new-fangled term 'British Commonwealth' in place of the traditional 'British Empire'. Yet once, when Chatham House was particularly hard up, Headlam said to me: 'When the Irish question has been settled, Chatham House will begin to get some money. Do you understand what I mean?' 'Yes, you mean,' I said, 'that, when the Irish question has been settled, Lionel will be able to give up his present temporary work in the Colonial Office; and then, when he turns his attention again to his hobby of raising funds for Chatham House, the money is certain to begin coming in again.' To work for Curtis and for Headlam-Morley, and to have their friendship as well as their guidance, was a big bonus that I received as a reward for joining the staff of Chatham House and remaining on it.

When I had been told that I was to have an assistant for the job of producing the *Survey*, I had also been given a choice. I might, if I wished, bring in someone from outside, or alternatively I might take on someone who was already on the Chatham House staff. I had no outsider in view, and I reflected that, if I did bring an outsider in, I could not be sure how the newcomer would get on at Chatham House with the people who were already there. I therefore asked to have, for my assistant, someone who was already on the staff, and there turned out to be only one who could do the job. At that time (it was in 1924) the staff of Chatham House consisted of three people, apart from me, who, to begin with, was only a temporary officer, working, under contract, on a particular job. The three were Margaret Cleeve, Veronica Boulter, and Jessica Westley. Miss Cleeve was chief executive officer; Miss Westley was Miss Cleeve's secretary; Miss Boulter was working on the research, rather than on the administrative, side. I was therefore asking for Miss Boulter to be deputed to work with me on the *Survey*, and this was agreed by Miss Cleeve with alacrity. It was, I knew, the choice that Miss Cleeve had been hoping that I would make.

How were Veronica and I to organize our working partnership? I knew from the first what I did not want. I did not want a colleague of mine to play permanently the part of 'research assistant'. From what I had seen of 'research assistance' in some of the 'provincial' universities (there was no such thing at either Oxford or Cambridge), it seemed to me to be a device for making a woman do work for which a man took credit. This seemed to me unfair to the 'research assistant' and uncandid towards the public. I should have a bad conscience if I were to publish, under my own name, a finished product that had not been my own work at all stages of production, from start to finish. I did not, and do not, see how, on any other terms than these, one can do an honest job. However, for some time —indeed, until after I had produced the first two volumes of the *Survey*—Veronica did work part-time as my 'research assistant'; but, after that, I asked her to become my co-author. I could not have worked permanently with a colleague on any other basis, and by this time I knew all about Veronica's ability. It was my good fortune that I had found a colleague who was capable of taking on the partnership on this footing. Our minds proved to match each other. To this day, if I open some volume of our *Survey* at random and glance at the page, I am unable, as often as not, to tell whether that page was Veronica's work or mine.

When the proofs of the first of the *Surveys* on which Veronica and I had collaborated in this new way were on my table and I was drafting the title-page, as a matter of course I put both our names on it, to let the reader know that there was two persons' work between the covers. When I passed my draft to Veronica, she struck her name out; I put it back again; she struck it out once more. Being the sub-editor of the volume as well as one of the two authors, she might claim to have the last word on a point of form, and I feared that, out of modesty, she had now committed me to perpetrating a fraud on the public when the printer saved the situation for me. He restored Veronica's name on the title-page and printed it off without sending a further proof to us. When the volume came out of the press, Veronica had to capitulate to the *fait accompli*, and, after that, her name appeared, along with mine, on every volume that we produced together till our retirement. I am grateful to that printer, and I still should be, even if it turned out that his correction of our title-page was a random shot. I prefer to believe that he was acting on an intuition of what was true and right.

To work in partnership was a new experience for me. Ever since I had withdrawn into my shell at Winchester, in reaction against the pressure of tribal life, I had tended to work as a lone wolf, and my *Wanderjahr* in Greece and my subsequent war-work in Whitehall and in Paris had only partially humanized me; but I had now learnt to appreciate a different way of working. My partnership in work with Veronica at Chatham House continued after she had become my second wife in 1946, and, since our retirement, she still continues to make the indexes for all my books.

In human life, the *summum bonum* is human fellowship. There is no substitute for that. Yet even the happiest personal life would have something lacking in it if it were not supplemented by a satisfying vocation; and, in this impersonal field as well, I owe much to Chatham House. I found my work there satisfying both intellectually and morally, and it also gave me scope for other work, outside its limits. From 1927 to 1954, I was able, thanks to my partnership with Veronica, to drive the Chatham House *Survey of International Affairs* in double harness with a private venture of my own: *A Study of History*. There was no disharmony between these two pieces of work. Each of them benefited from the other.

I found the writing of the *Survey* intellectually satisfying because this job did not have the intellectual drawback that I had come up against in a don's work at Oxford. The work of tutoring successive generations of undergraduates had a built-in cyclic rhythm. On the other hand, there could be nothing cyclic about the writing of a *Survey of International Affairs*. The subject was a guarantee of that. One never knew in advance, as one did know, only too well, in the tutor's job, what the morrow was going to bring forth; but one could be sure that it was not going to reproduce the events of yesterday. Unlike the don's annual round, which, by repetition, would become more facile, but also more boring, with each new year, the survey-writer's job could never cease to be laborious because it could never become monotonous. The exchange of jobs was a welcome one to me, and I did not repine at the price of it. I had soon been irked by the monotony of a repetitive annual round, but I did not, and do not, shrink from hard labour.

What do I mean by saying that I found the writing of the *Survey* satisfying morally as well as intellectually? How could there be moral satisfaction in work that was intended to be 'scientific' in the sense of making an objective impersonal approach to the study of international events? In writing the *Survey*, I did my utmost to keep my personal hopes and fears, and my judgements of right and wrong, from colouring my narrative; and, where I was conscious that I had not achieved this aim, I did my best to put my cards on the table, to help the reader to note and to discount my prejudices. Any student of human affairs who imagines that he can study these without being subject to any personal bias is deceiving himself; the best that a student of human affairs can do is to detect his own bias and to declare it.

I was, and am, a whole-hearted believer in the value of an approach to human affairs that is as 'scientific' as is humanly possible. I was therefore whole-heartedly in favour of the founders' decision that Chatham House should limit its activities to 'scientific study' and should debar itself from having, and from promoting, any corporate policy. 'Scientific' study, however, by its very nature, cannot be an end in itself, even though it may be an indispensable instrument for the pursuit of an end beyond it. The reason why scientific study can be a means only, not an end, is because the ultimate purpose of life is not study but action. Chatham House's 'scientific' work, for the sake of which Chatham House debars itself from taking corporate action, will have practical value only in so far as it helps the users of its products to take individual action that is wiser and more enlightened than this action might have been if it had not been taken in the light of the objective information that Chatham House tries to provide.

Speaking now *ad hominem*, after having survived two world wars and lived to see the invention of the atomic weapon, I have no doubt about the action that the study of international affairs in my lifetime has enjoined upon me. I am speaking now as a human being, a great-grandparent, and a citizen, not as an historian dedicated to the pursuit of objectivity in his professional work. As a human being, I cannot be content to contemplate the World as I find it. *Tantâ stat praedita culpâ.*[1] My study of the World will have been barren and irresponsible if it has not equipped me and spurred me to do what I can—infinitesimal though the effect of my action may be—to help mankind to cure itself of some of the evil that, in my lifetime, I have seen human beings inflict on each other. I must do all that I can to save my grandchildren and great-grandchild from being overtaken by the fate that has criminally cut short the lives of so many of my contemporaries.

---

[1] 'The faultiness of the nature of the Universe is gross, flagrant, and intrinsic' (Lucretius, *De Rerum Naturâ*, Book II, line 181). The rest of the passage of which this is the last line, and the climax, is quoted on p. 150.

Living when and where I have lived, and having had the education and the experience that I have had, I have been concerned above all, since August 1914, to do what I can in my lifetime towards bringing about the abolition of war. This is the wickedest of all living human institutions, and it is also an institution to which human beings cling with obstinate tenacity. In 1914, war could take lives only by the million. Since 6 August 1945 it has been on the way towards becoming deadly enough to wipe out the human race and perhaps even to make the surface of our planet no longer habitable for any form of life. *Écrasez l'infâme.*

Though a freak of chance disqualified me for combatant service in the First World War, I have been brought face to face with the wickedness of war from August 1914 onwards. Before August 1914, most people in Britain, with the signal exception of the Quakers, were morally obtuse to this wickedness, though we had been engaged in enough 'little wars', and aggressive little wars at that, to have had our eyes opened if we had so willed. If we had not still been blind, my parents would never have let me play murder by knocking over toy soldiers with shots from toy cannon, and I myself should never have taken pleasure in this unpleasant game.[1] Since August 1914 we can no longer plead invincible ignorance.

Before the end of the First World War, half my contemporaries had been killed; but I was not an eye-witness of their deaths, and it is what one has seen with one's own eyes that impresses one's imagination the most deeply and haunts one's memory the most persistently. Accordingly, the two visual memories that stand out in my mind the most vividly whenever I think of war are not the faces of my dead friends; they are the faces of three people who were strangers to me.

In 1915, soon after I had left Oxford for London to do war-work there, I was sent on some errand to the War Office in Whitehall. As I was entering, I saw, facing me, a notice-board on which there was posted a list of officers recently reported killed, and, at the same moment, two women passed me. They had just read on the board the announcement of a death. One of the two was weeping bitterly; the other was talking rapidly and emphatically—as if her hurrying words could overtake and perhaps retrieve the cruel loss that had

[1] See pp. 214-15.

been suffered by her companion. I can see those two poor women's faces as clearly today in my mind's eye as, on that day, I saw them in the life. While I still have life and strength, I must work for the abolition of the wicked institution that was the cause of that terrible sorrow.

My second visual memory is of the dead body of a young Greek soldier, killed in March 1921 at the second battle of Inönü. The body was rigid; the face was waxen; the tiny perforation-mark in the forehead seemed too insignificant a cause to have extinguished a life instantaneously. The dead boy was lying a few yards below the Turkish trenches on the crown of the ridge which the boy's unit had been storming. In the trenches there were the bodies of Turkish peasants—brave 'embattled farmers'—that had been horribly mutilated by Greek shell-fire. These young men, Greek and Turkish, had all been brought into the World by the birth-pangs of mothers; they had been nurtured with love; and now they had been taken to be slaughtered on the threshold of manhood. I must work for the abolition of the wicked institution that was the cause of this criminal destruction of the most precious thing on Earth.

There are ways of working for the abolition of war that are more direct than my way has been. Instead of spending thirty-three years on the writing of the Chatham House *Survey of International Affairs*, I might have applied for a post on the staff of the League of Nations or the League of Nations Union. Believing, as I do, that intellectual work is a necessary basis for action, apart from its intrinsic value in itself, I have always felt that, in persisting with the *Survey*, I was not merely helping to expose the major evil of our time (and, indeed, of all times since war began); I have also always felt that I was helping to try to suppress this wicked institution before it annihilated us, its makers.

In my private warfare against war, I am a total abolitionist. I am not a total abstainer from alcohol. I have seen too many cases of teetotalism defeating its own purpose. In this field, Prohibition has, I believe, proved to be the worst enemy of voluntary moderation; and, for combating the social evil of alcoholism, the longer road looks to me more promising than the short cut. War, on the other hand, **is**, in my judgement, like slavery, a social evil with which there can be no compromise. I do not believe in the efficacy of abolishing the atomic weapon while retaining conventional weapons, or of reducing the quantity of armaments without renouncing the use of the residue. My objective is the total abolition of war, and nothing short of that. Yet I am an abolitionist who is not a pacifist. If I had been given a chance of voting for war with Japan over Manchuria in 1931 or with Italy over Ethiopia in 1935 or with Germany over Czechoslovakia in 1938, I should have voted for war on each of these three agonizing occasions.

I should have voted for war because I believe it is neither right nor politic to offer no military resistance to a militarist on the war-path. The dilemma here is an agonizing one because, on the one hand, non-resistance to military aggression gives the World over into the militarists' hands, while, on the other hand, when one engages in a 'holy war' against aggression, one cannot foretell how long one's war will stay holy. In making war, even if one is making it in the cause of ending war, one is using evil as an antidote to evil; and in this game the dice are loaded in Beelzebub's favour. Nor can one tell how many 'wars to end war' may have to be waged on mankind's long *via dolorosa*. My contemporaries who gave their lives to end war in the First World War died believing that this was the last war that the survivors and their descendants would ever see. Thus, in seeking to abolish the ancient institution of war, one finds oneself entangled in inconsistencies and frustrations.

This experience is daunting, but it has to be faced; for it is a facet of one of the hard facts of life. The fact is that each generation carries a load of *karma* that has been bequeathed to it by its predecessors. The living generation does not start life free; it starts life as a prisoner of the past. Happily the prisoner is not helpless; he has it in his power to break the fetters of inherited custom; but he can break them only by a mighty effort, and he can never break them all. Human freedom is not illusory, but it is never total.

In the case in point, we do have the freedom to abolish war by a pacific political act. The institution of war between states is a parasite on the institution of local sovereignty; a parasite cannot survive without its host; and we can abolish local sovereignty pacifically by voluntarily entering into a world-wide federal union in which the local states would surrender their sovereignty while continuing to exist as subordinate parts of the whole. This is the positive solution

(Radio Times Hulton Picture Library)

6 A Chatham House committee meeting. Left to right: G. M. Gathorne-Hardy, Miss Margaret Cleeve, Sir Roderick Jones (back to camera), Lord Snell (behind table), Lionel Curtis, Arnold Toynbee

(National Monuments Record, London; taken in 1923)

7   Chatham House from St. James's Square

of the problem of war that Lionel Curtis advocated. One need not, and should not, be dogmatic about the details of a federal constitution for the World. But one should work for the achievement of this in some form or other. In the Atomic Age, this looks as if it were mankind's only alternative to mass-suicide.

During the first three years of Veronica's and my work on the *Survey*, we had to get it moving and also had to catch up with the arrears of events that had been accumulating since the terminal date of the *History of the Peace Conference*. At that stage we were having to work on the *Survey* for twelve months in the year. By the summer of 1927, however, we had drawn abreast of current events, and, from that summer onwards, I was able to combine my share of the writing of the *Survey* with the writing of *A Study of History*. I used to divide my time between these two pieces of work in an alternating rhythm. At the beginning of November, each year, I would start planning the contents of the *Survey* volume for the preceding calendar year. It was not possible to see the shape of what had been happening in a given year till within about two months of its ending. From November onwards, through the winter, spring, and early summer, I would sit in London, working with Veronica on the *Survey* at Chatham House. In June I would go into the country, finish off there my work on the current *Survey* volume that I had still to do, and, at the same time, put in a long vacation's work on the *Study*, breaking off from this and returning to London and the *Survey* when the beginning of November came round again. I could not have done this if Veronica had not stayed in London far into the summer, year after year, as she did, to see the current volume of the *Survey* through the press and to compile the index. Her splendid indexes have doubled the *Survey*'s practical usefulness, and the *Study*'s usefulness too.

Keeping two large pieces of work going simultaneously was, of course, hard work, but the combination was stimulating and—what was more important—the *Survey* and the *Study* each gained by this. It would, in my opinion, have been impossible to write the *Survey* intelligently or even intelligibly if one had been engrossed in the study of current events to the exclusion of the more distant past. Life is lived in the time-dimension; human beings act in the light of memory; and the collective memory of communities and societies embraces spans of hundreds and thousands of past years. Any past event that is remembered may influence current action; so, in writing about the events of the immediately preceding calendar year, we never knew in advance how deep down we might have to delve into past history in order to explain why, during the past twelve months, people had acted as they had. If the historical background of the present is not kept in view, the present is likely to become an insoluble puzzle, and, in trying to cope with this unknown quantity, an unhistorical-minded man of action may get bogged in a rice-field or lost in a jungle.

This truth was being illustrated, in 1968, by the quandary in which the American people had landed themselves by that time in their dealings with Vietnam and with China. In talking to Americans in 1968 about these two sore subjects, I found that, for some Americans —including some who had had, or were having, a university education—China and Vietnam had to become satanic in order to become historical. For Americans who had this outlook, the histories of Vietnam and China had begun at the respective moments at which a Communist régime had come into power in each of these two countries. Yet how can one expect to be able to deal success-fully with present-day China and Vietnam if one ignores their past? How can one understand the reason for China's present truculent temper if one is not aware that, from 1839 to 1945, China was being stamped on by the British, French, Russians, and Japanese? And how can one appreciate the shock and the humiliation that the Chinese people suffered from being then suddenly treated as 'natives' if one is not aware that, before 1839, China had been, in Chinese eyes, 'the Middle Kingdom' or even 'All that is under Heaven'—had, that is to say, been the centre of the civilized world and been as much of the World itself as was of any importance? How, again, can one understand the reason for the Vietcong's tenacity in fighting to rid Vietnam of America's presence if one is unaware that, before the United States intervened in Vietnam, the Vietnamese had been struggling for a century to rid their country of France's presence there, and had been struggling for two thousand years before that to save their country from being absorbed into the body politic of China, as so many regions, north of Vietnam, had been engulfed in China already? These illustrations perhaps make the point that, without bringing the historical background into the picture, it would be impossible to make sense of current events. In writing the *Study*, I was providing myself with this indispensable historical background for the *Survey*, and providing it on the *Survey*'s own global scale.

Conversely, the *Survey* benefited the *Study*. When one is studying the history of generations that are no longer alive, one has to resurrect these dead generations mentally by an act of imagination. One can only imagine what they were like in life by analogy with our knowledge of the living; and the only living people whom we know are our contemporaries. For this reason, it is indispensable for every historian to have a foot in contemporary history, whether the historian's own special field of work is the Victorian Age or the Pyramid-Builders' Age or the Lower Palaeolithic Age. However far sunk in the past the age that the historian is studying may be, he will have the same need to bring it to life by breathing into it the life of human beings whom the historian has caught, not yet dead, but still alive. If I had not been writing the *Survey* while I was writing the *Study*, I should have lacked the most effective instrument that I have possessed for conjuring up the long-ago extinct societies of which I was trying, in the *Study*, to take a synoptic view.

Thus it was fortunate for my work in all fields that I was able to carry on the *Survey* and the *Study* side by side for twenty-one years (1927–54, less seven years of war-work in 1939–46). I could not have done this if I had not been, for thirty-three years (1924–56), a member of the staff of Chatham House.

6 : Why and How I Work

(i) WHY

WHAT has made me work? When I was a child at school, the spur that I was first conscious of was anxiety. I was anxious always to be well ahead in puzzling out the meaning of passages of Greek and Latin that I might be called on to construe in class. I am still anxious to arrive well in time for catching trains and planes. This has its disadvantages. It uses up a lot of nervous energy that might be put to more positive use; and sometimes I carry my beforehandness to a point at which it catches me out. When I arrive at the station forty minutes ahead of my train's departure-time, the porter will not wait till the train comes into the station; so I have to put my luggage on board myself. Something like that happened to me once when I was called on to construe a difficult passage of Thucydides. I had prepared it carefully; but that had been several weeks ago; I had now far outshot the point that we had reached in class, and my mastery of this passage had grown rusty. If the master had not known my ways, he might have thought that I had not done my homework. I think he guessed the truth—which was that I had done it too far ahead of the date at which it was being required.

Anxiety can be a bad thing if it goes to these extremes, and it is never a good thing in itself. It is, though, a powerful driving-force; so its drawbacks may be outweighed by its results.

A second spur that has pricked me on has been, and still is, conscience. In a previously published book,[1] I have mentioned that my grandfather on my father's side came off a farm within sight of the tower of St. Botolph's church at Boston, England. The puritan conscience was perhaps part of my father's family's social heritage. In my attitude towards work I am American-minded, not Australian-minded. To be always working, and this at full stretch, has been laid upon me by my conscience as a duty. This enslavement to work for work's sake is, I suppose, irrational; but thinking so would not liberate me. If I slacked, or even just slackened, I should be conscience-stricken and therefore uneasy and unhappy, so this spur seems likely to continue to drive me on so long as I have any working-power left in me.

Anxiety and conscience are a powerful pair of dynamos. Between them, they have ensured that I shall work hard, but they cannot ensure that one shall work at anything worthwhile. They are blind forces, which drive but do not direct. Fortunately, I have also been moved by a third motive: the wish to see and understand. I did not become conscious of this motive till some time after I had become aware of the other two; but I think that, before I became conscious of it, it must have been moving me, and this since an early stage of my life. Curiosity is a positive motive for action. It is also one of the

[1] *Acquaintances*, p. 2.

distinctive characteristics of human nature as contrasted with the natures of non-human animals. All human beings have curiosity in some degree; and we also all have it about things that are of no practical use—or that seem, at least, to be of no practical use at the time when our curiosity is first excited by them. However, this universal human quality is stronger in some people than it is in others. This is one of the points in which human beings differ from each other markedly. The charge of curiosity with which I have been endowed happens to be high. This is a gift of the gods, and I am heartily grateful for it.

At school the anxiety that drove me into preparing my class-work far ahead of time had the fortunate effect of liberating my time for the pursuit of my curiosity. Just before a lesson in class for which I had prepared long ago, I would be free to work at what I liked, when some of the other boys were preparing for this next lesson at the last moment. 'What I liked' means 'what I chose', 'what I had set myself to work at.' The anxiety that had enslaved me to my work had also freed me to make myself my own director of studies. The prescribed work had become subordinate to the work that I mapped out for myself. In doing the prescribed work far ahead of time, I had taken it in my stride and had got it out of the way.

When I am asked, as I sometimes am asked, why I have spent my life on studying history, my answer is 'for fun'. I find this an adequate answer, and it is certainly a sincere one. If the questioner goes on to ask whether, if I could have my life over again, I would spend it in the same way again, I answer that I would, and I say this with conviction.

But why study history in particular? Curiosity is omnivorous. There are innumerable other things in the Universe, besides history, that can and do arouse curiosity in human beings. Why has my curiosity focused itself on history? The answer to this question is one that I know for certain. I am an historian because my mother was one. I cannot remember a time when I had not already taken it for granted that I was going to follow my mother's bent. When I had turned four, my father said that they could no longer afford a nurse for me. My mother asked if she might keep the nurse for a year longer, supposing that she earned the nurse's twelve-months' wage by writing a book; and my father agreed. I can remember vividly the excitement of seeing the proofs of *Tales from Scottish History* arrive. The fee was twenty pounds, and that was a nurse's wage for a year in England in 1893–4. When the year was up and the money was spent, the nurse went and my mother took over the job of putting me to bed. She kept me happy and good at bedtime by telling me the history of England, in instalments, from the beginning to 1895.

Certainly it was my mother who inspired me to become an historian, but I have followed my mother's bent in this rather general sense only. My mother, I think, loved the concrete facts of history for their own sake. I love them, too, of course. If one did not love them, one could never become an historian. Facts are an historian's stock in trade, and he has to acquire them in quantities that would be repellent if the facts did not fascinate him. I love the facts of history, but not for their own sake. I love them as clues to something beyond them—as clues to the nature and meaning of the mysterious Universe in which every human being awakes to consciousness. We wish to understand the Universe and our place in it. We know that our understanding of it will never be more than a glimmer, but this does not discourage us from seeking as much light as we can win.

Curiosity may be focused on anything in the Universe; but the spiritual reality behind the phenomena is, I believe, the ultimate objective of all curiosity; and it is in virtue of this that curiosity has something divine in it. Thanks to my mother's bent, my approach to this ultimate objective happens to be through the study of human affairs. Physics, botany, geology, or any other study that one can think of, offer alternative roads towards the same human goal. However, in the Jewish–Christian–Muslim *Weltanschauung*, history is set in a framework of theology. This traditional Western vista of history has been rejected by many Western historians—and by their non-Western disciples too—during the last two centuries and a half. Yet I believe that every student of human affairs does have a theology, whether he acknowledges this or not; and I believe that he is most at the mercy of his theology when he is most successful in keeping it repressed below the threshold of his consciousness.

Of course I can speak only for myself. I am sure that the reason why the study of human affairs has the hold on me that it has is because it is the window on the Universe that is open for me. A geologist or a botanist, travelling through a landscape that has not been the scene of any important events in human history, will see in it the hand of God, as vividly as I see this at, say, Bodh Gaya or Jerusalem. But, since my own approach to the presence behind the phenomena happens to lie in the field of human affairs, unhumanized non-human nature does not speak to me movingly. I am moved by Mount Cynthus more than by Mount Everest, and by the Jordan more than by the Amazon.

Why work, and why at history? Because, for me, this is the pursuit that leads, however haltingly, towards the *Visio Beatifica*.

(ii) HOW

Between the ages of ten and twenty-two, I was preparing, most of the time, for sitting for successive examinations. I have already described the experience of competing in the scholarship examination at Winchester.[1] Preparing for examinations, which was my main business for those twelve years, is educative in some ways. It makes one responsible for putting oneself to work. Though an able and sympathetic master can help the child to learn how to do that, he cannot do it for him; and no one except the examinee himself can help him when he has taken his seat in the examination-hall with an examination paper before his eyes and three hours, but not one minute more than that, allowed to him to spend on answering the questions.

H. J. Haselfoot, the master at my preparatory school who gave me special coaching for the Winchester scholarship examination, was the best teacher that I have ever had. He taught me how to work, and I have been benefiting by his teaching ever since. Though I recognized, at the time, what an exceptionally good teacher he was, my gratitude to him has continually increased as I have found his advice hold good for tackling one intellectual job after another. Mr. Haselfoot's first and best piece of advice was: 'Don't panic because the time given for answering the questions is limited. Don't plunge in without previous thought. The best-spent time out of your three hours will be the time before you put pen to paper, if only you give yourself this time at the beginning to think of your problem as a

[1] See pp. 5-7.

whole. This is the right method, whether the problem you are faced with is a subject for an essay or a piece of Greek or Latin to be translated into English or, conversely, a piece of English to be put into Greek or Latin prose or verse.' Mr. Haselfoot taught me to try always to be articulate; to try always to see the wood, without letting myself get lost among the trees; to proceed from the known to the unknown; and to take it for granted that a passage of Greek or Latin must make sense, and to recognize that, so long as it did not seem to make sense, one had certainly not yet got on the right track.

The three-hours' essay is a splendid education for journalism and for the civil service and for the law. If one has learnt the art of essay-writing at any early age, one will know how to write an article or a minute, or how to digest a brief, against time—and one is always working against time in practical life. Scholars who have not schooled themselves to work against time are putting themselves in danger of remaining unproductive, and they cannot vindicate their unpracticalness by contending that work done against time will be imperfect. It will, of course, be imperfect; all human work is imperfect, because human nature is; and this intrinsic imperfection of human affairs cannot be overcome by procrastination. In work of every kind, including intellectual work, there comes the right moment for taking action. There is no instrument that will tell one when the moment has arrived; one has to sense it by intuition, and the right timing will be different in each case. But to find and hit the right timing is indispensable for success; and to delay too long can be just as fatal as to act precipitately can be. The effect of wrong timing, either way, will be to aggravate the imperfection that is inherent in any human activity.

Thus education through preparing for examinations, and through taking these when the time comes, can have some good effects. It can, however, also have the very bad effect of inducing a habit of passivity in one's attitude towards the acquisition of knowledge. The examination, in which one is going to have to take action eventually, is, for most of the time, apparently far off; and, when it does overtake one, the action is short and sharp. One is engaged in the preparation over far longer stretches of time, and this may therefore have a greater effect on one than the examinations themselves. In preparing for an examination, the prospective examinee does not have the initiative. The examiner has that. He dictates to the examinee, at the last minute, the action that the examinee has to take. During the long-drawn-out preparatory period, all that the examinee can do is to accumulate as much knowledge as he can of the whole of the field in which he is going to have to stand fire. The examination system may thus put it into the examinee's head that the ideal objective in intellectual work is to acquire an exhaustive knowledge of a precisely delimited field.

The field that was delimited for me at Oxford was that of Greek and Roman history; for, before I took my final examination as an undergraduate in the Honours School of Literae Humaniores, I had been appointed to a tutorial fellowship at my college for the teaching of this subject. By the time I had finished with that final examination for qualifying for a degree, I had become sick of being examined, and I had determined that I would never sit for an examination again. I did not take up a suggestion that I should sit for the examination for an All Souls fellowship, which, had I won it, I could have held concurrently with my Balliol fellowship; and, during the fifty-eight years that have passed since I sat for 'Greats' at Oxford, I never have sat for any other examination—with the single exception of one on poisonous gases on the eve of the Second World War. I did pass this examination, too, successfully, but I immediately forgot what I had learnt up for it, because my mind refused to retain a knowledge of so hateful a subject. To make and keep a resolve never again to submit to be examined is not difficult. It is more difficult, as I discovered, to liberate oneself from the examinee's characteristic state of mind.

In the summer of 1911 I had a long vacation at my disposal between taking my final examination and going abroad to travel for a year in Italy and Greece. I spent that summer on continuing to prepare for the Literae Humaniores examination retrospectively. I had taken the 'first period' of Greek history, which broke off at the year 404 B.C. I now went on to study, with the same thoroughness, the original sources and the modern literature for the non-overlapping part of the 'second period', which broke off at the year 323 B.C. I read the relevant books of Xenophon and Diodorus and the relevant lives in Plutarch's series, with a mass of relevant modern literature as well—annotating the margins of my Greek and Latin texts, like a Byzantine scholiast, in minute handwriting, for which I used a triple-H pencil.

One might have thought that this was a limited task; and, in fact, before leaving England that autumn, I had mastered most of what I should need to know for taking pupils in the second period of Greek history, as well as in the first. However, even the field of Graeco-Roman history is not finite; for, though the corpus of original sources, including inscriptions and archaeological evidence, is fairly concise, the modern secondary material was and is still growing at the same prodigious and ever-accelerating rate in this field as in most other fields of knowledge. I soon realized that I should never catch up with all the books and papers that were being published on Greek and Roman history, even if I were to keep my post of ancient history don at Balliol for the rest of my working life. For me, however, the situation was more serious than that; for I had long ago made up my mind not to confine my intellectual curiosity within the bounds of the field of Greek and Roman history, as this field had been delimited in the Oxford School of Literae Humaniores.

My scholar-uncle, Paget Toynbee, had made me aware of my intentions about six years back. I had been staying with him in his house at Dorney Wood and had been eagerly exploring his library. He noticed my omnivorousness, and, as I was leaving, he said to me, gravely: 'Your Aunt Nellie and I (Aunt Nellie, in self-defence, had become a scholar too) have come to the conclusion that you are spreading your interests too wide. You ought to specialize now.' I thanked him for his advice politely, but also hypocritically, for I had instantly resolved that I was not going to take it. I have adhered to this resolve ever since, and, looking back, I am profoundly glad that my uncle's prestige did not intimidate me into following what has been the intellectual fashion in my generation, as well as in his. My own line was, and is: 'Homo sum, nihil humanum a me alienum puto';[1] and I was following this line in the summer of 1911. Long before reaching the bounds of the Oxford field of Greek and Roman history, I had been planning to break my way out. I had been planning to explore the Hellenistic Age of Greek history, which the Oxford School of Literae Humaniores ignored. I had been planning

---

[1] 'I am a human being, so there is nothing human that I do not feel to be my concern' (Terence, *Heautontimorumenus*, line 77).

to make myself a Byzantinist. I had been planning to learn Arabic, Persian, and Turkish, and to master these languages and the literatures written in them as thoroughly as I had already mastered the Greek and Latin languages and literatures. In the summer of 1911 all these further objectives were on my agenda, as soon as I should have disposed of Greek history between the years 404 and 323 B.C. This was a dangerous moment, for me, in my intellectual history, and the danger arose from my having acquired the examinee's habit of mind. It was no wonder that I had acquired this, considering how great a part my successive examinations had been playing in my intellectual life. It is true that I had kept myself free from one of the examinee's occupational infirmities. I had refused to allow myself to be cooped up within an arbitrarily delimited field of knowledge. Mr. Haselfoot had saved me from that by teaching me, once for all, to look at a problem as a whole; and, since the problem that I had made mine was human affairs, nothing short of a study of human affairs as a whole would satisfy me. This was good in itself, but it did not combine well with another of the examinee's infirmities—one to which I had succumbed—and this was the bad habit of accumulating knowledge for passing examinations, and not for use. In expanding the field of my curiosity to embrace all human affairs, I had been doing to myself what the giants in Jötenheim had once done to the god Thor when they had covertly connected up with the sea the drinking-horn that they had challenged him to drain. Thor was a mighty drinker, and, in a long draught, he had swallowed one-third of the waters of the sea before he had been forced to confess himself beaten. Even a god could not drain the sea dry; and even a young man of twenty-two, with the whole of his working life still ahead of him, could not have mastered the whole of human affairs, however hard he might work and however long he might keep his wits. Without realizing it, I had pitted myself against infinity; and in a contest between a mortal and infinity the mortal is bound to lose, unless he can extricate himself in good time from this unequally-matched duel.

In the summer of 1911 I was intent on pressing on with the endless agenda that I had set for myself. In effect, I was preparing myself for an examination after death; and this was inconsequent, now that I had decided never to let myself be examined again in my lifetime.

Unwittingly I was condemning myself to inevitable frustration; but
now I was saved from this self-imposed fate by a new kind of
activity that took hold of me against my will and that annoyed me at
first, because it slowed down my progress in mastering the materials
for the study of Greek history after the year 404 B.C. I found myself
comparing passages in Xenophon with passages in Thucydides that
gave information about the organization of the Lacedaemonian
army. Were these passages consistent with each other or were there
discrepancies between them? And, if there were discrepancies, were
these due to errors on the part of one or other of the two authorities,
or had the Lacedaemonian army been reorganized between the dates
with which Thucydides and Xenophon were dealing respectively?

My mind was running on these questions instead of getting on
with the stint of reading that I had set for it to carry out. I had supposed that I had disciplined my mind, long ago, to do what I told it
whether the task was agreeable or not. Why was my mind rebelling
now? It was rebelling, as I eventually realized, because it was starting
to make something; and, when a human mind is once engaged in an
act of creation, it will refuse to let anything or anyone stand between
it and the achievement of its enterprise. It will not let even its owner
thwart it to that extent.

These workings of my mind in the summer of 1911 did eventually
result in an article that was published in *The Journal of Hellenic
Studies*,[1] the first piece of work of mine to be published, except for a
short note in *The Classical Review*. I had now found a way of my
own for banning infinity. Instead of going on acquiring knowledge
ad infinitum, I had started to do something with the knowledge that
I already possessed, and this active use of knowledge gave direction,
for the future, to my acquisition of knowledge. I had refused, and
was still refusing, to set limits to my acquisition of knowledge by
confining it within an arbitrarily delimited field, but I had now
found a better way of setting bounds to the boundless (setting a πέρας
to τὸ ἄπειρον, in Greek terms). I would limit infinity by directing
my acquisition of knowledge to meet the demands of action. The

[1] 'The Growth of Sparta' (*J.H.S.*, vol. xxxiii, Part II (1913), pp. 246–75). This
article is the germ of Part III, 'The Rise and Decline of Sparta', of a book of mine,
Some Problems of Greek History, that went to press in the summer of the year
1968.

knowledge was there, at my disposal, stored on the shelves of libraries and in the galleries of museums. I need not, after all, be in such a hurry to master it, for it would not run away. I could and would take as much of it as I wanted, when I wanted it, for use in making something with it. In other words, I would acquire knowledge, henceforward, for use in projects of my own, not for the sake of satisfying an imaginary post-mortem examiner.

I have been thankful, ever since, that I have eluded the fate of becoming a life-long examinee. I realized how melancholy this fate might be when, years afterwards, I re-met a distinguished but unproductive Oxford scholar whose scholarship I had admired when I had been an undergraduate. This scholar told me now, in his old age, that he was ploughing his way through the Byzantine historians and was finding them repulsive. They were repulsive for him because he thought of them as decadent and ineffective imitators of classical literature, instead of thinking of them as informants about Byzantine life, in which he was not in the least interested. He was reading the Byzantine historians now, to his own chagrin, because he had formed an unbreakable habit of reading, every day, something in Greek that he had not read before, and by this time he had lived long enough to have read already everything in Greek that could give him any satisfaction. He was an examinee who had outpaced his imaginary post-mortem examiner, and who had therefore lost his lifelong occupation even before losing his life or his wits.

After I had started to make something out of what I knew, the meaning of the word 'work' underwent, for me, a significant change which was also, I feel sure, a salutary one. Work now came, for me, to mean writing or making preparations to write. It no longer meant reading. Since 1911 I have allocated no working time for reading, and, in particular, I have reserved exclusively for writing the hours between breakfast and lunch—the time of day at which my mind is the most active. I have left my reading to take care of itself, and this policy has justified itself, to my mind, by its results. I have read what I have needed to read for use in my writing, though I have written far more than I had dreamed of writing at the start, and though I have interpreted my needs broadly. I have always succeeded in reading a good deal more than has been strictly necessary for my successive practical purposes.

This change in the purpose of my reading led me to make a corresponding change in my way of taking notes. I had begun, as I have mentioned, by making notes on the margins of my Greek and Latin texts, and this scholiast's way of note-taking had been the most convenient so long as the interpretation and understanding of texts had been, for me, an end in itself. Now, however, I had learnt to use texts as materials for making something of my own, and for this new purpose I needed to have my notes in some handier and more accessible repository. From about 1922 onwards I started to take notes in notebooks on points, in books that I was reading, which seemed likely to come in useful for something that I was going to write. Usefulness for writing had now become my criterion, so I took my notes of this new kind, not only on Greek or Latin texts, but on modern books as well. By this year 1969 I have more than thirty of these notebooks, full to the brim. They have, long since, become my most relevant immediate source of the information that I need for writing. From a note, in a notebook, of a passage in some book that I have read, I can always refer back to the original.

Since 1911 I have managed to write a good many books of my own; and, of course, any achievement has to be bought at a price. The price that I have paid for having become a fairly productive writer has been a failure to achieve my early ambition of mastering Byzantinology and Oriental languages up to the standard of my mastery of Greek and Roman history and the Greek and Latin languages and literatures. I have read most of the Byzantine historians. Their works were accessible to me, thanks to their having written in the pseudo-classical Greek that set my old Oxford acquaintance's teeth on edge. I have acquired a smattering of Arabic and a rather better knowledge of Turkish, and these reconnaissances into the field of Islamic studies have been of inestimable value for me. However, in this field I am still only on the threshold; I have not made the field mine, as I have made the Graeco-Roman field. I am sure that I should have learnt Arabic and Persian and Turkish thoroughly if I had continued to think and work like an examinee. I regret keenly that I have not mastered these fascinating languages— especially Arabic and Turkish, which carry an inquirer whose mother-tongue is an Indo-European one beyond the range of the innumerable Indo-European languages, with their boring uniformity of structure. But then I ask myself: What would it have profited me to have become an Arabic scholar and a Turkish scholar if I had found no use for these additions to my knowledge? Would I be willing, if I could be given the choice, to have become proficient, after all, in Arabic and Turkish at the price of having produced no books? Of course I would not be willing to make this exchange. It would be like the Homeric exchange of a golden suit of armour for a brazen one.

In giving priority to writing I have renounced any considerable further acquisition of knowledge in the field of languages. But there is another field of knowledge—the first-hand knowledge of countrysides—in which I have always been eagerly adding to my stock whenever I have had the opportunity. Till after my retirement, I was starved of travel, to some extent, by lack of time and funds. But ever since 1911 I have always travelled as often and as long and as far as I have been able. This is the one activity to which I have given precedence over my otherwise paramount activity of writing. Whenever I have had a chance of intellectually profitable travel, my writing has had to wait. As I see it, travel ought to come before everything else for a student of human affairs. Human beings and human societies cannot be understood apart from their environment, and their geographical environment cannot be apprehended at second hand. One may pore for years over descriptions and photographs and maps of a country without getting a true notion of its character; and, then, one glimpse of the landscape with one's own eyes will give one the essential information which the secondary sources had failed to convey.

One sees and learns the more from a landscape the more slowly one travels through it and the closer one keeps to the ground. The best way of all is to walk over it with a rucksack and a water-bottle and an unlimited fund of time to spend. Thus equipped, the unhurried pedestrian is independent. He can go where he pleases, and can satisfy his curiosity in detail. Mule-back, horse-back, or ox-cart are next best to one's own legs as one's means of conveyance. Next best to these is a landrover or a jeep. An ordinary car with a low clearance narrows the possibilities drastically. The traveller is now confined to roads of the kind that are first-rate from the driver's technical standpoint but are third-rate from the standpoint of the traveller whose purpose in travelling is, not to reach a destination, but to see what there is to be seen on the way. A helicopter or a planelet with a low ceiling—for choice, a Cessna—is not a bad vehicle for enabling one to see the World. A giant jet-plane is almost useless. Within a few moments after taking off it carries you above the clouds and keeps you in that dull layer of the Earth's air-envelope till a few moments before it lands. For a traveller who is travelling for curiosity's sake, and not for the purpose of being cata-pulted, *quam celerrime*, from one Hilton hotel to the next, jet-plane travel is exasperating. Yet even this least useful of all forms of con-veyance so far invented does occasionally yield visual information by accident, thanks to some fleeting rift in the Earth's cloud-coverage. Tobruk, Lake Avernus, the Golden Gate at San Fran-cisco: I have had an entrancing glimpse of each of these from a point in the sub-stratosphere. Each time, though, the glimpse has made me repine at not being down to earth, on foot. So my advice to any traveller who is travelling in order to learn would be: 'Fight tooth and nail to be permitted to travel in what is technically the least efficient way.'

I will also offer five pieces of advice to intellectual workers who agree with me that the right and healthy purpose of acquiring know-ledge is to make out of it some work of one's own.

My first piece of advice is Mr. Haselfoot's golden counsel: 'Don't plunge in precipitately; think before you act; give yourself time, first, to see your subject or your problem as a whole.'

I myself found that this counsel stood me in good stead when I was starting out on each of the two largest enterprises on which I have embarked so far, the Chatham House *Survey of International Affairs* and *A Study of History*.

In the *Survey*, which I had the happiness of writing, from first to last, in partnership with my wife, our task was to carry on the story of international affairs from the points at which the Chatham House *History of the Peace Conference* of 1919 had broken off. The field of the *Survey* was to be the whole World; and, for reasons that I have mentioned in the preceding chapter, I was unwilling to farm out to specialists the surveying of the affairs of some allegedly 'outlandish' regions. To take the whole World for one's province was an exciting task, but it was also a big one and a formidable one. Where to begin? I began by writing a small volume, *The World after the Peace Conference*, in which I tried to give a cross-section picture of the state of the World in or about the year 1920. This gave me a base-line for starting a narrative that my wife and I eventually carried down to the year 1946.

In approaching *A Study of History*, I began by making a false start. In the summer of 1920, when the idea of the book was already simmering in my mind, I tried to write it in the form of a commentary on the second chorus (πολλὰ τὰ δεινά) in Sophocles' *Antigone*. This Greek poem does convey, superbly, the strangeness, the grandeur, and the pathos of human life; all these three qualities of it are implicit in the 'portmanteau-word' δεινά; but my mediaeval-minded approach to my subject by reference to a Greek masterpiece was too indirect to be practicable, as I soon discovered. Sophocles could not find my way into my subject for me. I had to find it for myself, and I did not find it till a year later, when I was in the train —somewhere in Western Bulgaria—*en route* from Istanbul to London after having been observing the Graeco-Turkish War in Anatolia as *The Manchester Guardian's* special correspondent. I then found myself jotting down, on half a sheet of notepaper, a dozen headings which turned out to be the subjects of the principal divisions of my future book. This time, I did not rush into action. My first considerable stretches of free time, after that, were the summer long vacations of 1927 and 1928; and I spent these, not on trying to start writing the first part of the book, but on expanding each of my headings into sets of detailed notes. I did not begin writing till the summer of 1930; and meanwhile, in 1929, I had taken the longest journey that I had made yet. I had travelled to China and Japan, going out overland to the head of the Persian Gulf and thence by sea, and coming back overland via the Trans-Siberian Railway. It was after this that I found myself ready to start writing the book.

My second piece of advice is: 'Act promptly as soon as you feel that your mind is ripe for taking action. To wait too long may be even more untoward in its effects than to plunge in too precipitately.'

I have already mentioned that, when my wife and I were starting to write the *Survey*, we were working under the direction of an older and more experienced scholar, Sir James Headlam-Morley, the Historical Adviser to the Foreign Office, who was also Chairman of the Publications Committee of the Royal Institute of International Affairs. When, some time after our starting-date, I produced my little volume on *The World after the Peace Conference*, Headlam-Morley became worried. 'This essay that you have produced is all very well,' he said; 'but your real job is to write a narrative, recording what happened next. I recognize that the job is a vast one. What you need to do now is to make a start with some piece of it. When once you have done that, you will find that the rest will come. In starting, you will be feeling your way; for a survey of current history is a new *genre* of history-writing. My advice is that, for your first piece, you should choose some topic that is not very large and also not very important. Probably you will not be satisfied with your first draft, and will find that you want to work over it again. Never mind; the point of getting down now to the writing of this first piece is that it will help you to get the whole thing moving.' Headlam-Morley suggested that I should begin by writing the history of the post-war dispute between the Netherlands and Belgium over the navigation of the Scheldt. I followed his suggestion, and it all turned out as he had said that it would.

My third piece of advice is one that is good, I believe, not only for writers of historical works, but for writers in every field. 'Write regularly, day in and day out, at whatever times of day you find that you write best. Don't wait till you feel that you are in the mood. Write, whether you are feeling inclined to write or not. What you write when you are feeling out of sorts will not be so good, of course, as what you write when you are in your best form. You will be dissatisfied with your first draft, as I was dissatisfied with my first draft on the dispute over the navigation of the Scheldt. However, you can revise your first draft, and, though, even after that, this piece will not be so good as a piece that you wrote originally with zest, it will nevertheless probably pass muster, and meanwhile you will have made progress with the carrying out of your project. If you were to wait till you had achieved perfection, you would be waiting for the rest of your working life; for nothing made by human hands or minds is perfect. If there are any perfect works, they are not Man's but God's; and, when a mortal assumes that he can achieve perfection, he is being guilty of the sinful pride that goes before a fall.'

For learning not to wait for the mood, the examination system is a good training; for in examinations the time allowed is so short, and the time-limit is so strictly imposed, that it must be obvious to any examinee that for him to wait till he felt in the mood would be disastrous. During the twelve years 1901–11 during which examinations were the crucial events in my working life, I was fortunate in never once being incapacitated at the time when an examination came on. I was, however, sometimes under the weather. I might be labouring, for instance, under a heavy cold. But an examination is like a battle. While it lasts, one must exert oneself to the uttermost, even if one happens at the time to be physically below par. The practice of sitting for examinations trained me to keep myself at work even under adverse conditions; and, for getting work done, this is a valuable habit.

My fourth piece of advice is: 'Don't waste odd pieces of time. Don't say to yourself: "There, I have finished that piece of work, and it is really not worth beginning this next piece till tomorrow morning or till after the week-end. So for the rest of today or for the rest of this week I might as well let myself relax and take things easy."' The truth is that you might not as well do that; for the right moment for starting on your next job is not tomorrow or next week; it is *instanter*, or, in the American idiom, 'right now'. It is significant that 'right now' is an Americanism; for Americans are pre-eminently men of action.

On 16 December 1911 I arrived in the Peiraeus from Megara with several hours of daylight still to run. So, instead of taking the metro to Athens straight away, I walked round the walls with which Conon had fortified the Peiraeus in 393 B.C. and waited to take the train till night fell. At supper at the British Archaeological School that evening, the Librarian, F. W. Hasluck, asked me what I had been doing since I had gone off on this expedition, five days back. I told him my itinerary, and, when I got to the last lap of it, he said: 'Well, you have guts.' This took me by surprise and made a great impression on me, because Hasluck was a veteran hiker through Mediterranean lands. On reflection, I saw what he meant. On a hike in a hard country, fatigue is cumulative. On this last day of the hike that I had just completed, I had left Megara at an early hour in the morning, crossed by ferry to Salamis, walked across the island, crossed by ferry to a point near Xerxes' Throne, and walked on to the Peiraeus from there. At the Peiraeus by that time I had certainly been physically tired; 'suddenly very weary; glad to arrive at the School', are the last words of the entry in my diary for that day; but this weariness had not taken the edge off my zest for spending every minute of my time on seeing as much of Greece as I could. Hasluck's casual word of commendation has constantly been in my mind ever since. I have always felt that I must live up to the reputation that Hasluck has given me, and this has been a spur to me. Never dally. 'Work . . . while it is day; the night cometh, when no man can work.'[1]

My fifth piece of advice is: 'Always look ahead. Look far ahead, as a racing motorist looks, through his telescopic sight, at the horizon which he will have reached before he knows it.'

Since before the outbreak of the First World War, I have had an agenda stretching ahead of me through an incalculable number of future years. In the autumn of 1965, for instance, I published a book called *Hannibal's Legacy* whose germ was a course of lectures that I had given at Oxford for the School of Literae Humaniores in the academic year 1913–14. While I was writing my notes for those lectures, I was planning to turn them into a book. Event after event, beginning with the First World War, then intervened between me and this particular objective. But I never lost sight of the subject, which was the effect of the First and Second Romano-Carthaginian Wars on Roman life. I always kept a look-out for relevant books and articles, and made notes on these, in my growing series of notebooks, for use when, some day or other, I should get down, at last, to carrying out this particular project. I did get down to it in the summer of 1957, and, in writing the book, I have used notes that I had taken five, ten, or twenty years before the opportunity came for using them.

My wife says that I have a peculiar faculty—a 'sixth sense', she calls it—for scenting, years in advance, what I am going to need for carrying out some project which, on my agenda, is still a long way down the list. She also says that I have a gift for recording, in a brief

[1] John ix. 4.

note, just what I am going to want later on. The use that I have made of my notebooks certainly shows that this has been my way of working; but I am not sure that it indicates any special capacity. Probably any intellectual worker who thought of using this method could use it successfully. No doubt, it requires some ability, but, above all, it requires practice and persistence.

Τῆς δ' ἀρετῆς ἱδρῶτα θεοὶ προπάροιθεν ἔθηκαν.[1]

7 : Janus at Seventy-Five
(14 APRIL 1964)

I AM now seventy-five. Half my contemporaries at school and at the university were killed before they had turned twenty-seven. Ever since 1915 I have been surprised at being still alive, and rueful that my friends whose lives were then cut short have been deprived of the opportunity that I have had. In my seventy-fifth year I delivered to the Oxford University Press the manuscript of a book, *Hannibal's Legacy*, which I had been contemplating since I had lectured on the subject for the Literae Humaniores School at Oxford in 1913–14. I did not get down to working on this book till 1957. An historian needs time—more time than seems to be needed by poets and mathematicians. If my contemporary G. L. Cheesman of New College had had as much time as I have now had, he would have done very great things in Roman history. But Cheesman was killed at the Dardanelles in 1915.

Every human being is a Janus. 'We look before and after.' When one is young, it is easy to look forward; one has not yet accumulated much of a past to draw one toward the backward-looking view. As one grows older, the temptation to dwell on the past and to avert one's eyes from the future grows. This tendency is well known, and

[1] 'Achievement? It has to be sweated for; the gods have made sweat the sole way' (Hesiod, *Works and Days*, line 289). For once, the Olympians and Yahweh were of one mind. 'In the sweat of thy face shalt thou eat bread, till thou return unto the ground', was the sentence passed by Yahweh on Adam (Gen. iii. 19).

it has to be resisted. If one were to fall into this backward-looking stance, one would be as good (I mean as bad) as dead before physical death had overtaken one. Lord Russell is reported to have said, when he was already far on in his eighties, that it is important to care immensely about things that are going to happen after one is dead. All ageing people ought to make this saying their own, and to act on it, as Lord Russell has done. Our minds, so long as they keep their cutting edge, are not bound by our physical limits; they can range over time and space into infinity. To be human is to be capable of transcending oneself. Compared to the range of the mind, the longest lifetime is brief. One can accomplish very little in one life-time, even if one's life is not cut short. Anything that an individual does accomplish has meaning and value only in the larger context of society and history in which the individual plays his tiny part.

As I was born in 1889 and am still alive in 1964, I have lived to see what looks like a transition from one age of world history to another. I grew up during the later years of the forty-three years of peace in Europe that had begun in 1871. I never dreamed that this state of peace was not permanent until I was overtaken by August 1914; and on armistice day 1918 I never dreamed that I should live to see a second world war in my lifetime. I grew up in an age of stability and security for the middle class in Britain. One's family might have very little money; but, if one was moderately able, hard-working, and well-behaved, one could count on having a satisfying middle-class career. At my college in Oxford, Balliol, before 1914, any freshman who had no clear idea of what he wanted to do after he went down was put down for the Indian Civil Service by the dons as a matter of routine. An I.C.S. career was assured to any Balliol man who could not do better than that. And the contract that a successful candidate for the I.C.S. concluded with the Government of India gave the new recruit security for the rest of his life.

The mental world in which I was brought up was equally stable. It was still the mental world of the Italian Renaissance. The Greek and Latin classics became one's spiritual home; and on me, at any rate, this had the curious effect of partly detaching me from the living Western World into which I had been born. I came to look on this modern Western World with alien and unadmiring eyes. History, for me, was Greek and Roman history; mediaeval and

modern history were an irrelevant and rather impertinent epilogue
appended to history proper by the North European barbarians. This
epilogue was not even in the main line of succession. It was a side-
line. The main line had run on from the Roman Empire through the
Byzantine Empire and the Ottoman Empire to the present-day Near
and Middle East. This is a region of the present-day world that was
alive for me. The Turkish revolution of 1908 interested me so much
that it turned me into the regular reader of *The Times* that I still am
today.

My spiritual home in the Graeco-Roman World has, as things
have turned out, been of great practical help to me. It has been a
haven of stability in the midst of a welter of change. In the living
world into which I have been born, a placid phase of history has
been swept away by a turbulent phase within my lifetime, but my
footing in my Classical World has moderated for me the shock of this
violent transition. In the barbarians' postscript to history, one paragraph has been followed by another. But history itself—that is,
Greek and Roman history—still remains what it always has been.

The drawbacks of a classical education in the modern age are
obvious. A traditional concentration on the Greek and Latin classics
prevented me from making myself at home in the marvellous
physical universe that had been opened up to view by the progress
of physical science during the three centuries before the time at
which I was at school. Science, and the higher mathematics that are
the key to science, have remained a closed book to me. There is no
adequate compensation for this loss in the faculty that I have
acquired, from my drilling in Latin and Greek composition, of
expressing my feelings in Greek or Latin verse when something
moves me. I have never been able to write poetry in my vernacular
mother-tongue; and this consequence of having taken a classical
education seriously is a quaint one.

On the other side of the account, however, my classical education
has given me two benefits which, to my mind, are of inestimable
value. It has given me a mental standing-ground outside the time
and place into which I happen to have been born; and this has saved
me from over-estimating the importance of the modern Western
civilization. While I do care—and care very much—about the future
of the present-day world, 'my' world, in the sense of the world in

which I have the greatest intellectual and emotional stake, is not this present-day Western-style one. It is the Aegean and Mediterranean World of two thousand years and more ago—of, say, Polybius's time (he lived from about 208 to about 128 B.C.). The second great benefit that I have gained from my classical education is a life-long conviction that human affairs do not become intelligible until they are seen as a whole, and a consequent life-long effort that I have made to arrive at a comprehensive view of human affairs. By the time when I was being educated, Western scholars were already shredding the seamless web of human affairs into morsels that were as minute as they were numerous, and they were examining each of these morsels under the microscope as if each of them were a self-contained universe instead of being, as it was, an inseparable part of a larger whole. I am thankful that my old-fashioned classical education saved me from being instructed in human affairs in this nineteenth-century German way. The fifteenth-century Italian way seems to me to be a much better one, because it seems to me to give a vision of human affairs that is much truer to life. The humanist student of the Classics is taught to see Graeco-Roman life as a unity. In his eyes, the languages, literature, visual arts, religion, politics, economics, and history of his Classical World are not so many separate 'subjects', insulated from each other in thought-tight compartments; they are facets of a unitary way of life, and neither this nor they can be seen properly unless the parts are seen synoptically as contributions to the whole.

Twentieth-century science, as well as fifteenth-century humanism, can give one this 'holistic' view. At the moment when—feeling my way toward 'holism' through humanism—I was setting out to write the first batch of volumes of my book *A Study of History*, General Smuts's *Holism* was published; and I was excited and encouraged to find that the goal at which I was aiming had already been reached along a quite different mental road which I myself had not succeeded in exploring. As I have mentioned in an earlier book,[1] I had done some work for General Smuts at the Paris peace conference of 1919, and he had seemed to me like someone who had stepped straight out of 'my' Classical World into the present-day world. What was classical about him was his versatility. Farmer,

[1] *Acquaintances*, chapter 13.

lawyer, soldier, statesman, philosopher, man of science: Smuts was like one of the characters in Plutarch's *Lives*. 'All-roundness' was the key to Smuts's greatness; it was the key to Einstein's greatness too. Einstein made his epoch-making discoveries by putting together things that lesser minds had left asunder. Sir Winston Churchill is another great man in the same un-modern vein. These three great men's comprehensiveness is a bond between them which transcends the differences in their personalities and in their careers. All three would have felt at home if they had been born into the world of Polybius and Cato the Censor and Archimedes.

These three are not my only modern Western heroes. Among the modern Western historians, I am vastly indebted to Clarendon, Gibbon, Freeman, Bury, Theodor Mommsen, and Eduard Meyer. They have all appealed to me and have inspired me because each of them, in his own way, has something in him of Churchill's and Smuts's un-modern comprehensive-mindedness. The statesman-historian Clarendon was Smuts's and Churchill's seventeenth-century counterpart. Gibbon illuminated the piece-meal researches of the seventeenth-century scholars, as Einstein illuminated those of the nineteenth-century men of science, by conjuring a unity out of them. Freeman had a vision of the unity and the universality of history; and, like the fourteenth-century Islamic philosopher of history Ibn Khaldun and the eighteenth-century Western philosopher of history Vico, Freeman had the gift of 'seeing the World in a grain of sand'. The time and place in which he lived limited his horizon to the western end of the Oikoumenê; yet, from this narrow field of observation, he divined the truth that human affairs are an indivisible whole. He saw this as clearly as if the histories of the civilizations of Egypt, Asia, and the Pre-Columbian Americas had been as accessible to him as they are to historians of my generation. Eduard Meyer combined a mastery of the Greek and Latin sources for the pre-modern history of the western end of the Oikoumenê with some first-hand knowledge of the Sumerian, Akkadian, and Egyptian languages and scripts. He pushed his mental horizon as far eastward as the Bactrian Greeks pushed their conquests in India.

As for Mommsen and Bury, what I admire in them is their eighteenth-century practice, not their nineteenth-century principles, to which, I am glad to say, they failed to live up. My Mommsen is the early Mommsen of the *Römische Geschichte*, not the later Mommsen of the *Corpus Inscriptionum Latinarum* and of the *Gesammelte Schriften*. Mommsen's *Roman History* is a work of literary art which ranks, to my mind, with Gibbon's *Decline and Fall*. Mommsen is said to have lived to look back upon his authorship of the *History* as a youthful indiscretion which he hoped to have redeemed by his editorship of the *Corpus*. If this was really Mommsen's final judgement on his own work, I dissent, and, in dissenting, preserve Mommsen as one of my intellectual heroes. I dissent as emphatically from Bury's dictum that history is a science, nothing less and also nothing more. Bury tried hard to match these words of his in his works. He did not succeed, and it is this that gives Bury's works the high value that they have for me. In spite of his principles, Bury, too, was a humanist in practice.

I have been happier than Bury and Mommsen in escaping the mental conflict from which each of them suffered. Thanks to the effect on me of my classical education, the nineteenth-century cult of specialization has meant nothing to me. I have never even been tempted to bow down in the House of Rimmon. I have never made the choice between being an historian of politics, economics, religion, the arts, science, or technology; my conscious and deliberate aim has been to be a student of human affairs studied as a whole. I have rebelled against their being partitioned into the so-called 'disciplines'. In taking this line, I hope I have jumped clear out of the eighteenth century into the twenty-first without having got my feet entangled in the nineteenth century or in the twentieth. I feel confident that the tradition of the past is also 'the wave of the future'. We are now moving into a chapter of human history in which our choice is going to be, not between a whole world and a shredded-up world, but between one world and no world. I believe that the human race is going to choose life and good, not death and evil. I therefore believe in the imminence of one world, and I believe that, in the twenty-first century, human life is going to be a unity again in all its aspects and activities. I believe that, in the field of religion, sectarianism is going to be subordinated to ecumenicalism; that, in the field of politics, nationalism is going to be subordinated to world-government; and that, in the field of the study of human affairs, specialization is going to be subordinated to a comprehensive view.

This has been my own objective in my own work. My education taught me to see the Graeco-Roman civilization as a unity; I have tried to expand my historical horizon systematically. I have aimed at bringing within my range of vision, and my range of action, all the other societies, of the same species as the Graeco-Roman society, that have come and gone up to date. I have tried to do the same with the philosophies and the higher religions. I have tried to gain a foothold in the Buddha's and Confucius's philosophies, as well as in Plato's and Aristotle's and Epicurus's and Zeno's. I have tried to feel my way into Islam as well as into Judaism, and into Hinduism and the Mahayana as well as into Christianity. And, in spite of my slight distaste for the modern Western civilization which has now pervaded the whole surface and air-envelope of our planet, I have tried to gain a footing in current human affairs, besides keeping my footing in the past.

As I have mentioned already, I originally broke my way into current affairs by following up the main line—that is, the Levantine line—of the sequel to the Graeco-Roman civilization till this mental journey brought me to the living civilizations of the Near and Middle East. Between 1911 and 1923, I was, I think, in danger of letting myself become imprisoned in a couple of specialisms. I was then heading for becoming a combination of 'Balkanist' with 'ancient historian'. Fortunately I was saved from being caught in this blind alley by a personal mishap. I became personally involved in a conflict between two Near Eastern nationalisms. I had, in consequence, to resign the Koraes Chair of Byzantine and Modern Greek Studies in the University of London; and, in taking another job, I found that I had committed myself to expanding my study of current affairs from the Near and Middle East to the contemporary world as a whole. I had undertaken to produce a *Survey of International Affairs* for the Royal Institute of International Affairs, and the commitment required me not to leave any region of the present-day world out of account. I must try to follow current events not only in the Near and Middle East and not only in Europe and the United States but in Latin America, the Soviet Union, and China as well.

From 1924 to 1956 I was producing the *Survey of International Affairs* at Chatham House in partnership with my wife. From 1927 to 1954 I was producing the first ten volumes of *A Study of History*. From all points of view this was, for me, a most happy combination of activities. I do not believe that I could have produced either the *Survey* or the *Study* if I had not been at work on both of them simultaneously. Together they gave me the widest horizon that I was capable of attaining and the most comprehensive field of work that I was capable of handling. And this was a fulfilment of my aim. For my aim was to expand my horizon and my field up to the limits of my capacity.

> Ἐτρέχομέν ποτ᾽ ἐγώ τε βροτῶν τ᾽ ἀκόρεστος ἀμητήρ.
> ὠκὺς ἐμός, κείνου πούς βραδύς· ἔφθασ᾽ ἐγώ.
> Νῦν δ᾽, ἀΐδηλ᾽, ὀλέσαις μ᾽ ὅτε βούλεαι· ὀψὲ γὰρ ἔρδεις.
> οὐκέτ᾽ ἀμαυρῶσαι ἔργ᾽ ἐμὰ σοὶ δύναμις.

> I was running a race with the Reaper.
> I hastened; he lingered; I won.
> Now strike, Death! You sluggard, you sleeper,
> You cannot undo what I've done.

8 : Other Business

(i) THE END OF AN AGENDA (22 FEBRUARY 1966)

IN January 1966, when I gave the manuscript of *Some Problems of Greek History* to be typed, I had finished all the business that was then on my agenda. This was a new experience for me; for I had had an unfinished agenda constantly in mind for more than half a century, ending at that date. Two of the now finished items—*Hannibal's Legacy*, published in 1965, and *Hellenism*, published in 1959—had been on my agenda since before the outbreak of the First World War; others, of which the biggest was the Chatham House *Survey of International Affairs*, had been added in the meantime. My wife and I had worked together in writing the *Survey* over a period of thirty-three years.

The completion of this agenda is like the completion of my children's education. A business that, for years on end, seemed to stretch away *ad infinitum* has suddenly come to an end. I still have my health and my wits, and, so long as my wits do not fail me, my curiosity will not. The number of the books that I still want to read, and of the countries that I still want to visit, remains unlimited; but, for the moment at least, the satisfaction of this general curiosity is no longer being directed towards the accomplishment of definite projects for pieces of creative work. Thus I find myself back again where I was while my mind was opening up during the years when I was being educated and was learning to educate myself. But at that stage I was unconsciously preparing myself for carrying out the agenda that began to take shape in my mind as soon as my education was over. In 1966 this agenda is behind me, not ahead of me, and I am rising seventy-seven, not twenty-three. At this age I cannot be preparing for a second agenda of the same kind as the one that I have now completed. Are my curiosity, and the energy of which it is a symptom, going to run out, this time, into the sands, without producing any effective results? Or am I preparing for an agenda of some different kind?

I am finding my present situation disturbing, and even painful. Yet, in so far as I can jump clear of myself and can look at myself from outside, I can see that my state of mind is also ridiculous, because it is self-contradictory.

So long as my agenda was unfinished, I was being perpetually goaded by anxiety into getting on with it. I have described how, already at school, anxiety led me to prepare my lessons weeks and months ahead of the date at which the point that I had reached in my preparation was going to be reached in class. Throughout the half-century during which I was carrying out my grown-up agenda, I would start work on the next item on the very day on which I had finished work on what had now just ceased to be the current item. I never paused to take breath, and this anxious eagerness to finish has increased as I have grown older. Since I have turned seventy I have seen in each additional year of life a bonus which could not be taken for granted and which might not be repeated.

My son Philip hit off my temperament in his first novel, *The Savage Days*. He represents me there as being tormented by feeling

{" "}

that I had not enough time to do all that I wanted to do. This has, in truth, been my usual state of mind until only the other day. As time went on, and as one item after another on my agenda was disposed of, I became more and more conscious that time was a *sine qua non* for achievement, at any rate in my line of work. This made me also conscious of the preposterously unfair inequality of fortune. I thought, more and more, about the unfinished—and never to be finished—agenda of contemporaries of mine at Winchester and at Oxford or at both who had been killed in the First World War: G. L. Cheesman, L. W. Hunter, Wilfrid Langdon. Their agenda had been at least as substantial and as promising as mine. Yet only a few fragments of their projected work had been harvested, while here was I living on to finish one item of my agenda after another. This inequality became more and more intolerable to me—and the more so because it was the consequence of an irrelevant accident.[1] My fortune and my prematurely dead friends' opposite fortune were, both alike, undeserved. At the same time, I was thankful for those years of life which had been granted to me but not to them (granted to me by whom? thankful to whom? Was I in debt to blind chance or to some divine power that was purposeful but, if so, was not just, since it had dealt out good and evil capriciously to my dead friends and to me?).

The more grateful I came to be for the gift—or the windfall—of time, the more eager I came to be to make the most of this precious time for getting on with my agenda. Yet now, when it is completed at last, I am distressed at having a blank sheet under my eyes, with no further unfinished items to keep me on the run. Not having an agenda any longer has turned out to be more distressing for me than it ever was to have an unfinished one. When there are only two alternatives and when each of them is distressing in some measure, there must be something wrong with the distressed spirit. Since the blank sheet is proving more difficult for me to cope with than the full sheet was, it looks as if my half-century-long agenda must have been, among other things, an opiate. Am I distressed now because I no longer have a compulsive occupation to distract me from facing something from which I shrink and have always shrunk hitherto? This Martha-like anxiety to be preoccupied with practical busi-

[1] Recorded on pp. 37–38.

ness looks like a spiritual infirmity. If it is one, is it one that is peculiar to me? Or is it one that is characteristic of the prevalent habit of mind in the modern Western society in which I happen to have been born and brought up? No doubt my compulsive wish to keep myself busy is part of my personal temperament. This temperament would still have asserted itself if I had happened to be born and brought up in India. In India, however, my temperament would have been counteracted by the traditional spirit of Hinduism, whereas in England it has been confirmed and reinforced by the *Zeitgeist* of the modern Western World. Our present-day Western *Zeitgeist* impels all Westerners—even those whose temperament is introvert and contemplative—to provide themselves with a non-stop agenda of extrovert activities to occupy all their waking hours. Time not filled by work has to be filled by 'recreation', which is sometimes very like more work under another name. When the present-day Westerner is off duty, he has to play golf or to turn on the radio or the television.

'Recreation' in the present-day Western sense has always seemed to me to be an unhealthy regression to childishness. I have therefore despised it, and I believe I have been right. But does not this judgement commit me to condemning, with it, my own trick of keeping myself preoccupied by a continuous agenda of work all round the clock? The discomfort that I am feeling now that my half-century-long agenda is at an end suggests that, for me, this was serving the same perverse purpose as the infantile philistine's radio and television. It was making it possible for me to avert my mind from 'other business' from which I shrink—shrinking partly because I am myself and also partly because I am a Westerner.

This current Western state of mind has been depicted poignantly by Lucretius. He was able to draw it from the life, because it was also rife in the Roman governing class in the generation in which their political handiwork, the republican regime, was manifestly coming to grief.

People seem to feel that there is a load on their minds that is wearying them with its weight. If only they could be as clearly aware of the causes of this and of the source of this massive malady in their hearts. If they could, they would not lead the kind of life that is so common a spectacle today. We see someone at a loss to know what he wants, and therefore perpetually seeking to be on the move, as if that would enable him to cast off his burden. Bored at home, he keeps on sallying out from his grand mansion, and then suddenly returns, having found that he feels no better out of doors. Driving his cobs, he rushes precipitately to his villa out in the country, with the urgency of a fireman going to the rescue of a house on fire. He has no sooner reached the villa's threshold than he yawns; or he goes off into a heavy sleep and seeks relief in oblivion; or perhaps he heads hurriedly for the town and revisits that. In this way everyone is on the run from himself—a companion from whom he cannot escape in reality. He is his own unwelcome yoke-fellow, and he hates his inseparable self because he is a sick man who does not grasp the cause of his disease.[1]

Lucretius then gives his own diagnosis of the disease in words that might have been written by a Christian Father.

If he recognised the cause correctly, he would leave everything else and would concentrate on studying the nature of the Universe. He would, because what is at stake is the question of the state after death in which human beings are destined to remain, not for a passing hour, but for all eternity.[2]

Death is indeed a hard fact for every human being to face; I shall be coming to this shortly. Yet I do not believe that the problem of facing death—formidable though this is—is the fundamental cause of the spiritual malady that Lucretius describes and that we, in the present-day West, are experiencing so acutely. The malady is, I should say, a shrinking from facing ultimate reality, and I do not believe that death is the most crucial of the sovereign realities, though I do not believe, either, in the reality of immortality in the sense of a post-mortem everlasting prolongation, in another world, of the life that we live and know in this world.

Here the Indian attitude and outlook seem to me, if I understand them right, to be better founded and more penetrating than the Western. For me, who have been brought up in the Western tradition, the end of my agenda is disconcerting because, to my Western vision, it looks ominously like the end of effective life. If I had been brought up in the Indian tradition, on the other hand, the blank sheet might look like an announcement, not of the end of life, but of its true beginning. A Brahman, like a Westerner, has a practical

[1] Lucretius, *De Rerum Naturâ*, Book III, lines 1052–70.
[2] Ibid., lines 1071–5.

agenda. He too is expected to marry, beget children, and bring his children up. This is his duty to society; but, when the Brahman has discharged his duty, he is free to pursue what, for him, is the true end of Man, and, for the Brahman, Man's true end is the 'other business' that is waiting for him after all the items of practical business on his agenda have been transacted. When the Brahman's children are grown-up and out in the World, the Brahman is at liberty to withdraw from the World into the forest and to spend the rest of his life there in contemplation. For him, it is this spiritual activity, in this late stage of life, that gives the whole of life its purpose and its meaning.

I believe that in this point—and it is a point of supreme importance—the Indian ideal is the right one. Can I act on it? If I try to, I shall have to contend with two obstacles: my personal temperament and the present-day spirit of the Western society, which is the social milieu in which I have been living and doing my work. The present-day Western spirit is just a habit, and not even a very old one. In the mediaeval stage of Western history the West was not an adverse social environment for contemplation, though it may not ever have been as favourable a one as India.

My personal temperament is going to be more difficult to contend with; yet I believe that the faculty of contemplation, and the impulse to use this faculty, are innate in human nature. These common human faculties must be latent in me too, however thickly they may have been overlaid in me by the anxiety to distract myself with extrovert activities. It must be possible to break through this crust and to release the flow of the waters of spiritual life.

(ii) DEATH

Lucretius holds that fear of death, and fear of the state that follows death, is the chief single cause of human anxiety. I have known intimately two people who did suffer from a painful fear of death in their old age. One was my Great-Uncle Harry;[1] the other was Gilbert Murray. Their feeling about death was the same, though their beliefs about the nature of Man and the Universe were very different. My Uncle Harry was an orthodox Evangelical Episcopalian Protestant Christian; G. M. was an ex-Roman Catholic

---

[1] See *Acquaintances*, chapter 1.

agnostic rationalist. These tenets, different though they were, ought, logically, each to have made death easier to face. Uncle Harry held the official Christian view that right theological belief, as well as right moral conduct, is an indispensable condition for salvation in an after-life. He was also sure that he himself was included in the small minority of human beings whose theological position was impeccable. In theory, he believed himself to be sure of salvation after death; in practice, he dreaded the prospect of having to die on his way to salvation. As for G. M., his *Weltanschauung* was substantially the same as Lucretius's; so, logically, his fear of death ought to have been allayed by Lucretius's argument that, since the sequel to death is everlasting oblivion, death liberates us from all possibility of post-mortem suffering. Presumably G. M. did believe this with his mind, but his rationalist belief could not dispel the irrational anxiety in his heart.

I myself am now nearly seventy-seven, so the date of my own death now cannot be far off. At the longest, I cannot expect to live for more than fifteen years more, and, in one's seventies, a span of fifteen years is no more than the twinkling of an eye. It is more probable that I shall die much sooner than that. So far, however, I have not been troubled with the fear of death that tormented Uncle Harry and G. M. Is this immunity of mine, up to date, due just to a lack of imagination? I have never yet been face to face with my own death as an immediate certainty or probability or even possibility. When I do find myself up against my own imminent death, shall I be as much afraid of death as Uncle Harry and G. M. were for a considerable time before death eventually overtook them? I cannot foretell what my reaction at that stage will be.

The deaths that make an impression on us are the deaths of our contemporaries. We are apt to discount the deaths of people of an older generation as being in the normal course of nature, and, in most generations, we take it for granted, as long as there is an older generation left to do the dying, that it is normal for ourselves and our contemporaries to go on living. I myself, however, happen to belong to a generation in the Western World in which for a man, though not for a woman, an early death in his middle twenties has been the normal lot, while survival for a further half-century, which has been my lot, has been exceptional enough to feel abnormal.

About half my contemporaries at school and at the university were killed in 1915–16. It was only an irrelevant accident, mentioned above, that saved me from sharing the fate of my contemporaries who died young.

Moreover, as early in my life as I can remember, and long before I had any inkling that the young men of my generation might be going to be immolated in a massive human sacrifice, the fact of premature death was familiar to me. I had been named after an uncle who had been killed—by bacteria, not by human beings—at the early age of thirty. This tragedy had naturally made a deep impression on our family, and the abiding shock that it had given to my near relatives in my father's generation was part of the atmosphere in which I grew up. Later, I learned from my Aunt Gertrude of the premature death of my Great-Uncle George Toynbee. He, too, had been a young man of great intellectual power and promise, but he had died of galloping consumption at the age of twenty-nine—one year younger than his nephew Arnold, whose life did not overlap with George's, as mine has not overlapped with Arnold's.

Thus early death has been familiar to me from cases, at close quarters to me, in three successive generations, including my own. Since 1915–16, I have always felt it strange to be still alive myself; and, the longer that I have gone on living since then, the stranger this has come to feel. Death seems normal to me; survival seems odd. Of course, familiarity does not necessarily act as an antidote to fear; yet, short of that, it might be expected at least to diminish fear when the test comes. In my own case, I shall not know the answer to this question till my turn comes to undergo the experience.

Within the last ten or fifteen years, contemporaries of mine who, like me, survived the First World War have begun to die 'natural' deaths from old age. The first of them to die was Jack Denniston, and, no doubt, his death was hastened by the permanent after-effects of the three wounds that he had received in the First World War. There was no such cause for the death of David Davies, my junior by several months, who died two years ago. David was always physically infirm. Before he was seventy, both his body and his mind were beginning to wear out and to run down. For David, death, when it came, was a release. Then John Stainton, my senior by several years, was killed by cancer in his early seventies. In the summer of 1957, when, a few days before his death, I saw John for the last time, I was just starting work on *Hannibal's Legacy*, and I have lived on to publish this large book last autumn. I now find myself feeling exceptional among that exceptional contingent of my contemporaries who survived the First World War. I have survived long enough to finish a half-century's agenda. For me, therefore, to repine at death would be preposterous. What business have I to have stayed alive—and this with my physical health and my wits still intact—for these last two or last nine or, indeed, these last fifty years?

Moreover, to be mortal is not by any means wholly disadvantageous. When I catch myself resenting not being immortal, I pull myself up short by asking myself whether I should really like the prospect of having to make out an annual income-tax return for an infinite number of years ahead. Should I also really like the prospect of having, *ad infinitum*, to suffer the pressure of the ceaselessly turning screw of inflation?

Death does eventually release each of us, in turn, from the burdens and injustices of this life. Death is, in fact, our eventual saviour from the tyranny of human society in this world—a tyranny that is tolerable, if at all, only because it has an inexorable time-limit. At the moment of death the Inland Revenue authorities and the inflaters will suddenly become impotent to afflict me any further. I now put out my tongue at them anticipatorily on behalf of my corpse. I am grieved that these human oppressors will still be able to afflict people, loved by me, who will survive me; but death is going eventually to come to the victims' rescue—and to the oppressors' rescue too. Death limits life's liabilities. This boon that death confers is supremely valuable, and ought therefore to be immensely consoling, as has been pointed out, manfully, by Lucretius and, plaintively, by Housman.

However, when one has acknowledged this service of death's—and it is a signal service—one is still brought up sharply by death against one of those incongruities in our human condition which make it awkward and painful to be human. A human being is endowed with some godlike spiritual and intellectual capacities. He has the capacity to commune and co-operate with the spiritual presence behind the phenomena of the Universe, and the capacity to explore the Universe itself intellectually through any number of light-years. At the same time he is as short-lived and as insignificant physically as a midge; and the planet that, for a moment, is this human midge's habitat is, itself, a speck of dust in the gigantic cosmos—an ephemeral speck in a cosmos that may also have had a beginning and be going to come to an end. By comparison with our physical stamina, our spiritual and intellectual capacities are colossal. But why should there be this misfit in the make-up of the psychosomatic combine that a human being is? Death raises this question, but does not give the answer.

(iii) INCAPACITATION BEFORE PHYSICAL DEATH

I may be deceiving myself in thinking that I am not afraid of death, but I know, without any doubt, that I am afraid—and very much afraid—of being incapacitated before physical death overtakes me. Mental, more than physical, incapacitation is the possibility that frightens me. I have gone in fear of this fate since 1908, when I was confronted by mental incapacitation at close quarters. The victim was then forty-seven, and I was nineteen. The victim lived on, physically, after that for another third of a century. This was not life; it was death-in-life. It appalled me, and its shadow lowered over me oppressively till I had passed the menacing age of forty-seven myself.

To be incapacitated in the prime of life is unusual; and probably, if the victim known to me had been born in his children's generation, and certainly if he had been born in his grandchildren's, he would have been cured and salvaged. One of the few bonuses from the two world wars has been the sudden rapid advance in psychotherapy, thanks largely to the abundant and revealing information that was provided for its pioneers by war-time cases of shell-shock. Normally, mental derangement is a malady of old age. It has become a fairly common old-age malady now that the progress of medicine has prolonged the expectation of physical life.

Like death, senility has its compensation. It releases a troubled soul from chafing and a loving soul from grieving. Yet, so long as one is physically alive, one would wish for a survival of mental awareness, even at the price of continuing pain. To suffer does not deprive one of one's humanity; senility does deprive one of it; and perhaps the worst malady that can befall a human being is to cease to be humanly *compos mentis* while remaining alive physically. Even a partial loss of mental capacity is excruciating for someone who has been endowed with great intellectual power and vigour, and who has distinguished himself by prowess in turning these gifts to good account. One of my acquaintances whom I have mentioned in a previous book was overtaken by a stroke before death released him. I was told that he recovered sufficiently to be fully *compos mentis* again, but not sufficiently to be able to do any more serious intellectual work. He had to while away the time that remained to him on reading light literature. Being the man that he was, he must have found this mental frustration distressingly distasteful and humiliating.

I think, too, of Lord Samuel, who was unusually fortunate in retaining, to the end, not only the full clarity of his lucid mind, but also all his physical faculties except his hearing. At the party with which his family and friends celebrated his ninetieth birthday, he stood up to make a speech without notes. He appeared to be speaking with all his former ease, and what he said was as pointed and coherent as ever. Yet this wonderful old man, too, lived to illustrate the truth of verse 10 of the 91st Psalm.

The days of our age are threescore and ten; and, though men be so strong that they come to fourscore years, yet is their strength then but labour and sorrow—so soon passeth it away, and we are gone.

The last words of this passage are the one consolation for the failure of our powers before physical death. Affliction with these infirmities is, like life itself, a limited liability. The time-limit set by death makes even mental derangement bearable. Yet, to my mind, this is a far more formidable affliction than death is, and, like death, this failure of our powers brings us up against the startling misfit between our capacities and our limitations.

(iv) BEREAVEMENT

The greatest happiness in life is mutual love, and therefore the greatest sorrow, next to sorrow for one's sins, is not for anything—not even for the worst thing—that can happen to oneself; it is sorrow for the suffering of the people whom we love, and it is sorrow over our parting from them if we outlive them. Yet this is a sorrow from which one must not shrink if one's love is whole-hearted. When two people who love each other are parted by death, the suffering falls on the survivor; the one who has died is being saved from suffering by oblivion; and, if the survivor is truly loving, he cannot wish that the drinker of the cup should have been his mate and not himself.

In the Christian—or ex-Christian—world the happiest ending for a husband and wife who are deeply attached to each other is to die simultaneously, as may happen in an air accident. This casual remission of bereavement for both parties is, however, rare. It cannot be had for the asking. A simple and rational release for the sufferer from bereavement is, of course, to put an end by his own act to his or her own life too, and so join his or her dead mate in the peace of oblivion that death brings with it. This way of release by suicide can be taken without disapproval in present-day China and Japan by anyone who has come to the conclusion that, for him, to go on living has become an unwarrantable burden for himself or for other people. Suicide in the same circumstances carried no stigma in the pre-Christian Graeco-Roman World either. The ex-Christian Western World of my generation is still governed by the traditional Christian superstition on this point. Christians condemned suicide as an impious usurpation of the Creator's prerogative of deciding the date at which a creature of his should die. Suicide still shocks ex-Christians who no longer believe in God's existence. This continuing prejudice is illogical, but it is still strong enough to deter those who do not share it from causing the dismay that suicide still creates in Western countries. The Graeco-Roman and East Asian practice is more rational and more humane.

(v) FACING ONE'S SELF

It is formidable for a human being to face himself. Facing himself means taking to heart the record of his moral failures, and every human being will have many moral failures to regret. The saints will have fewer and less grave sins on their consciences than the rest of us, but the saints' consciences are so tender, and their moral standards are so exacting, that they are more conscious of their sinfulness, not less conscious of it, than we are.

It is not easy to examine one's own conscience objectively. One is likely to let oneself off too lightly or, alternatively, to lean over backwards in one's effort to make sure that one is judging oneself severely enough. The sins to which one is most sensitive are unlikely to be one's worst sins, because every human consciousness is a past master of the art of tricking itself into seeing itself in too favourable a light. Facing one's self is therefore a still more formidable ordeal than bereavement or incapacitation or death. Yet Lucretius is speaking the truth when he says that one's self is a companion from whom one cannot escape; and, if one did succeed in escaping from it, one would be cutting oneself off from what lies within the self, according to an Indian view. On this view, a human being who has penetrated to the innermost recesses of his self will there find himself face to face with ultimate spiritual reality.[1]

(vi) FACING OLD AGE

I am writing this as I approach my seventy-seventh birthday, and within the last few months I have become conscious of having grown old. I have now to contend with the problems that old age brings with it. I have been fortunate among my contemporaries in having reached this age without having, so far, lost either my health or my wits, so I must not repine at the price of length of life. My friends who were killed in the First World War would gladly have paid this price, or a higher one, for the boon of living as long as I have lived by now.

Every stage of life has its own ordeals and own rewards. My reward for having reached my present age is that this has given me time to carry out more than the whole of my original agenda; and an historian's work is of the kind in which time is a necessary condition for achievement. The ordeal of which I am most conscious at this stage is that of having to draw in my horns. To do this is an admission that one is not superhuman; and, for a human being, this recognition of his limitations is painful, though no doubt it is also salutary. How far am I to go in a progressive withdrawal from the more strenuous activities of life? If I try still to go on doing all that I have always done, I can do this now only at the cost of an excessive tax on my reserves of strength both physical and psychological. On the other hand, I feel sure that, if I were to let go my grip, and if, for instance, I were to flinch from continuing to do unpleasant but bracing chores such as the checking of my bank statements and the

[1] See further pp. 140, 159, 177, and 369.

making of my income-tax returns, I should quickly become incapable of action. I am having to grope my way towards finding a passage between the Symplêgades.

A living creature is beset by self-centredness so long as it is alive. The passage through the successive stages of life does not alter that. But the experience of the final stage, on which I have now entered, does bring home to me, more forcibly than I have ever felt this before, the vanity of putting one's treasure in something so inadequate as a human being's self-hood. I have begun to realize that the 'other business' at the foot of my agenda may be the most important item on the agenda and also the hardest to carry out. My business now is to try to detach my treasure from myself in order to place it somewhere that will be nearer to the true centre of spiritual reality.

9 : Religion: What I Believe and What I Disbelieve

(i) THE SUBJECTIVITY OF RELIGIOUS EXPERIENCE

RELIGION means for me a human being's relation to an ultimate reality behind and beyond the phenomena of the Universe in which each of us awakes to consciousness.

In this one sentence I have raised at least four debatable issues. My definition of religion is disputable. Indeed, there are people who hold that religion can be defined only as an illusion, because they hold that there is no such thing as an ultimate reality. People who hold that religion is illusory can hold that the illusion is bona fide, or can hold that it is induced subconsciously, or even deliberately, as a psychological opiate to alleviate the painfulness of being human. The existence of human beings is, of course, a datum of experience. Each of us is aware of his or her own existence and of other people's existence, but the conception of human nature that each of us has is as open to dispute as our views about religion are. Finally, those who hold that there is such a thing as ultimate reality can also hold that this has nothing in common with the element in human nature—I will call it the spiritual element—that moves a human being to seek communion with ultimate reality and harmony with it. On this view of the nature of ultimate reality, the quest that we call religion is foredoomed to failure, however sincere this quest may be. Alternatively one may hold that ultimate reality is akin to the spiritual element in human nature that is a datum of consciousness and an accompaniment of it. If a person holds that there is an ultimate reality and that the spiritual element in human nature has an affinity with it, his concept of the spiritual element in human nature—a phenomenon of which each of us does have experience—will be his key to his concept of ultimate reality. Ultimate reality itself is an unverifiable hypothesis, though there are human beings who believe that they have had experience of this, as well as of themselves and of their fellow men and women.

A human being's views about the nature of the species of which he is a specimen are derived, like all his views, from his experience. This is the only source of information that he has about any phenomena. His experience of non-human nature is a 'public' experience which he shares with his fellows, and in this field there is a consensus in every human society, though the common picture will differ as between one society and another, and will change within one and the same society if there is scientific progress in the observation of the phenomena and in the interpretation of the results of this. Our experience of human nature, too, is of this 'public' kind in so far as it is experience of our fellow human beings; but a human being's experience of human nature is also partly derived from his experience of this in himself, and here he is in the realm of subjectivity. He can report what he finds in himself and can compare his findings with his neighbours' reports of their findings about themselves; but, if the reports disagree, the truth is not verifiable. A human being cannot enter into another human being's psyche to ascertain whether the other human being's report of what he has found there is correct in the opinion of an independent observer from outside. There is no way of ascertaining that one man's report about himself is correct and that another man's report about himself is erroneous. All these reports of self-observation are on an equal footing with each other, and none of them is on sure ground.

In this inconclusive situation, the best that any one of us can do is to put on the table as many of the cards in his hand as his consciousness reveals to him. Psychological discoveries, made in my life-time, tell me that the subconscious layer of my psyche may be holding other cards—perhaps key cards—hidden from my sight.

My own subjective view of human nature is, no doubt, partly the peculiar product of my personality, but it is certainly also partly the product of my social and cultural and religious background. I happen to have been born in 1889 into a middle-class family in England. My father was a professional man, a social worker. My mother, before her marriage, had also been a professional woman. She had earned her living by teaching—for which she was qualified by having been a student at Newnham College, Cambridge, and having won first-class honours in the Cambridge history tripos. Her father had been a manufacturer in the Midlands; my father's father had been a London doctor brought up on a fen farm in Lincolnshire. Both my parents were members of the Episcopalian Protestant Church of England. Both of them, as far as I know, believed this Christian Church's doctrines, theological as well as ethical, without fanaticism but also without reservations. At any rate, they brought me up—I am sure, in good faith—as an orthodox Church-of-England Christian. I did have reservations from an early age. For instance, I disbelieved instantaneously in the assertion that Jesus had been brought to birth without having had a human father. When I was an undergraduate at Oxford I became an agnostic, and at first I concluded, from my loss of traditional orthodox Christian belief, that religion itself was an unimportant illusion. Now, more than half a century later, I am still an agnostic, as the sequel will show, but I have come to hold that religion is concerned with a reality, and that this reality is supremely important.

It is obvious that my interpretation of my experience of human nature is conditioned by my own history. I am a product of my Christian upbringing and my Christian historical background, which, reckoning from today, is perhaps eleven hundred years old on my father's family's side in the Danelaw and perhaps two hundred years older than that on my mother's family's side in Mercia. My being an ex-Christian counts for more, I should judge, in my *Weltanschauung* than my having become an agnostic. The weight and momentum of a human being's cultural heritage are immense.

How far am I justified in equating my subjective picture of human nature with the objective reality? I suppose this depends on the extent of the consensus that I can fairly claim. If I knew that the picture in my mind was, is, and will be present identically in all other human minds too, this complete consensus of subjective views would approach as close to objective certainty as is possible. I do know that my picture is not just my individual fancy. In essential points it is the Christian picture; so, if it is partly or wholly an illusion, it is an illusion that has been shared by all believing Christians and by all ex-Christian agnostics of my kind — and I am, I should say, a typical agnostic of my generation in the Western World. More than that, the essential points in the Christian picture of human nature are to be found, I believe, in the picture of it as seen by the followers of all other religions, higher and lower. If so, my picture is corroborated by a consensus of almost all the human beings who have lived so far.

Is not this enough to warrant the claim that this picture is a faithful rendering of the objective truth? No, I should not be justified in making this claim, and this for two reasons. In the first place, I cannot speak for the still unborn generations; and, if mankind refrains from liquidating itself, the number of representatives of the species 'homo sapiens' who will come into being during the next two thousand million years is likely to be immeasurably greater than the number of those that have been born during these first million years of our species' existence. In the second place, I cannot be sure that I have the consensus of every human being now alive.

In Western Christendom during the last three hundred years there has been a progressive falling-away from belief in traditional Christian doctrines. An example of this is my own secession from Christian orthodoxy to agnosticism. The spread of the West's ideas over the rest of the World has started a similar secession from the other living historic religions. All over the World, this secession has now gone to a length at which a generation is arising for whom the traditional beliefs and precepts of its ancestral religion—whichever of the historic religions this may be—are either unknown or else, if known, are nonsense that makes no appeal to either heart or head.

Here, already, is a breakaway from the consensus of previous generations down to mine.

I and those who think and feel like me might, of course, retort to our nihilist-minded juniors that they are under a delusion. Our own view of human nature is, we might still claim, the truth, however violently the nihilists may kick against the pricks. This claim, however, would surely be presumptuous; and even if it could be substantiated—and it cannot be—it would still have an Achilles' heel. Let us suppose, for the sake of the argument, that the essence of human nature truly is what it has been pictured as being by a consensus of all the adherents of all the religions. Then we could conclude that every human being has been, is, and will be born with this nature. But we cannot guarantee that a human being will not have the will and the power to sterilize elements in his nature that seem to us to be essential—such elements, for instance, as conscience and love—if the pricks of conscience and the calls of love are dismissed as nonsense by an overwhelming consensus of opinion in the time and place at which this human being grows up.

I shall have these chastening considerations in mind in painting my picture of human nature as I see it. I am, I believe, on sure ground in claiming that this picture is shared with me by hundreds of millions of my fellow human beings, but I cannot claim more than this. I cannot claim that it is unquestionably the true picture. Nor can I claim that, if it could be demonstrated to be the true picture, it would be proof against being wilfully defaced by human beings who had the will and the power to dehumanize themselves. These reservations apply to everything that, in what follows, is stated baldly, as if it were universally recognized matter of fact.

(ii) MY INABILITY TO PASS THE TESTS OF RELIGIOUS ORTHODOXY

My ancestral religion, Christianity, requires the acceptance of the following tenets among others. The ultimate reality is God. There are no other gods. God is a person, in the sense in which a human being is; or, it might be more accurate to say: our knowledge of human personality, whose nature we know by experience, is the closest approximation possible, for a human mind, to a comprehension of the nature of God's personality, which can be known to us only by analogy. God is both infinitely powerful ('omnipotent') and infinitely loving. He is the creator of the Universe, and the Universe, as he created it, was a monument of both his love and his power. 'God saw everything that he had made, and behold, it was very good.'[1] However, the Universe as we human beings know it from our own experience is not very good. The good in it is mixed with, and marred by, evil. Christianity accounts for this discrepancy between the Universe as God is held to have made it and the Universe as man finds it to be by seeing in the discrepancy the consequences of 'the Fall' of the first human beings whom God created. But Christianity does not—and indeed cannot—explain how a God who is both infinitely powerful and infinitely loving came to create a universe which has turned out not, after all, to be very good, considering that it was a universe in which a Fall, that introduced evil, could and did occur. Christian theology has to try to vindicate an infinitely powerful God's infinite lovingness in face of the undeniable presence of evil in a universe that God is held to have created. The facts have compelled Christian theologians to acknowledge that God has refrained from exerting his alleged omnipotence to save his originally unblemished creation from falling into evil courses. The theologians have sought to save God's lovingness by claiming that God has sacrificed himself for the sake of redeeming his fallen creation. They have sought to save God's power by claiming that his self-sacrifice has achieved its loving purpose.

This tenet of Christianity's rests on the further tenet that God has incarnated himself in Jesus. I have to believe in the Incarnation if I am to believe in the Redemption, and the truth of the Incarnation is not demonstrable. Moreover, the doctrine of the redemption of the World through God's incarnation in human form on this planet requires the assumption, made in Christian doctrine, that mankind on this planet is the *chef-d'œuvre* of God's creation. In the age in which this assumption was originally made, its makers believed that the Earth is the centre of the physical universe; and the subsequent discovery of the plurality of worlds impugns the Christian belief in the unique importance of Man in God's eyes. The authorities of the Roman Church had this point in mind when they put Giordano Bruno to death. But they could not silence science or arrest its pro-

[1] Gen. i. 31.

gress; and Bruno himself might have been staggered by the scale of the physical universe as we now picture it. In a virtually infinite number of solar systems in a virtually infinite number of galaxies there may be a virtually infinite number of planets inhabited by beings like ourselves. Quantities of this order of magnitude reduce the human population of our own planet to insignificance. If God has sacrificed himself for redeeming us, he will have done as much for the fallen human-like inhabitants of all other habitable planets. Is it credible that God has been incarnate and been crucified on every one of these?

Christianity debits God with the Fall in order to credit him (O, *felix culpa*) with the Redemption. It is difficult to believe that such a dispensation has been the work of a god who is both loving and omnipotent. This is difficult to believe, even if one also believes that the episode on this planet has been unique. But, supposing that the scale of the physical universe is what science now holds it to be, we have to believe that, if the Fall and Redemption have occurred, they have occurred a virtually infinite number of times. I do not find this credible.

Christianity's account of Man's position in his universe is, of course, peculiar to Christianity; but Christianity is not peculiar among the historic higher religions in seeking to account for Man's position in one way or another. Each of the religions of this species gives its own account of this; and, though the several accounts differ widely, the motive for seeking to account for Man's position has been the same in every case. The common motive is a benign desire to help human beings to make their rough passage from birth to death. Life is formidable for a living creature that has awakened to consciousness. A human being is aware of the blemishes and the misfits in the universe in which he finds himself and from which there is no escape for him on this side of death. More disturbing still, Man is aware of his own sinfulness. He therefore longs for an assurance that, in spite of appearances and experiences, his universe is fundamentally and ultimately rational and good, and that he himself, in spite of his sinfulness, is redeemable.

Each of the historic higher religions offers just such an assurance. It offers this bona fide, and therefore confidently, and it also speaks authoritatively, in the sincere belief that its explanation of things is a discovery, or a revelation, of ultimate truth that is true beyond question. This offer of knowledge that is deemed to be certain about issues that are recognized as being crucial for Man promises to meet one of the most deeply-felt of all human needs. Moreover, the report is not just a report; it is also a programme for action. It does not stop short at giving Man an account of his place in the Universe; it tells Man what to do in order to be saved in the situation in which he finds himself; and the need for salvation is felt by human beings even more deeply than the need for truth. This is why the hold of the historic higher religions has been so widespread and so long-lived. But their hold depends on the fulfilment of one condition: if human beings are to adhere to them, their tenets must be credible; and each of the higher religions has tenets that are fundamental from its point of view but that are not credible for me.

Among the fundamental tenets of my ancestral religion, the Virgin Birth of Jesus, his Resurrection, and his Ascension are incredible for me because I cannot reconcile these tenets with my mental picture of the nature of the Universe.

My mind rejected the doctrine of the Virgin Birth for this reason at an early age. I remember my mother's telling me about the Virgin Birth, and I also remember that, in explaining it to me, she showed embarrassment. I am not sure what it was that embarrassed her. She may have been shy of asking me to believe a hardly credible story. It is more likely, I think, that she was shy of giving me an explanation of the story that required a reference to the facts of sexual reproduction. I was entirely ignorant of these facts at the time and, indeed, for many years afterwards. I did know already, however, that every child has a father as well as a mother; so, when my mother told me that Jesus had had no human father, I did not believe it. I remember clearly that my disbelief was instantaneous and unqualified. Looking back on this episode now, I see that I was rejecting the doctrine of the Virgin Birth because I could not reconcile it with an already established belief of mine in 'the uniformity of Nature'. Of course, at the time, I did not realize that my reason for disbelieving a traditional Christian doctrine was its incompatibility with the then current *Weltanschauung* of modern science. At the time, I was as much in the dark about science as I was about sex.

My knowledge of science is still rudimentary; and I am conscious that, in this field, I am taking my beliefs on trust, as believing Christians are taking theirs in the field of religious doctrine. My knowledge of Nature is all at second hand; and I am aware that, as scientific research continues, the scientists' own first-hand views about Nature are constantly changing. Within my lifetime, their concept of 'the uniformity of Nature' has, so I understand, been modified. This supposed 'law' of Nature is now hedged with qualifications, and these are perhaps even held to be limitations of the field in which the 'law' holds good. It is, I suppose, theoretically possible that, one day, the scientists may pronounce that virgin births, resurrections, and ascensions are regular parts of the order of Nature. If this were to happen, I should then have to revise my own second-hand views about Nature to correspond with the scientists' latest first-hand views. However, if this actually did happen, the Virgin Birth, the Resurrection, and the Ascension of Jesus would thereby forfeit the value that they had had till then in the Christian scheme of things, because their value for Christianity has lain in their being, not fulfilments, but breaches, of the recognized order of Nature, i.e. in their being 'miracles'.

I find the notion of a 'miracle' intrinsically illogical. If God is the omnipotent creator of Nature, including the 'laws' that natural events normally obey, then a 'miracle' would be a breach, by God, of laws that had been made by God himself; and this would seem to me to be an exhibition, not of the divine power that is already exhibited in the 'laws', but of a divine caprice that would diminish my respect for divine power. 'Miracles' would be pertinent exhibitions of divine power only on the assumption that the laws that God is breaking are, after all, not of God's own making. My view about the character of so-called 'miracles' has been put, better than I can put it, in a passage of the Hippocratean treatise on the effects of varieties of atmosphere, water, and location on human life (περὶ ἀέρων, ὑδάτων, τόπων). 'I, too, hold that these phenomena are divine; but then I also hold that all other phenomena, also, are divine and that nothing is either more divine or more human than anything else. All phenomena are uniform—and are therefore uniformly divine, if you like to call them that. At the same time, each of them has its own nature, and every phenomenon has a natural explanation.'

If I find incredible everything in the creed of Christianity that requires belief in something 'miraculous', what is left? I do not believe in the historicity of the Virgin Birth, the Resurrection, and the Ascension; I do believe in the historicity of the Crucifixion. There could have been no motive for Christians to invent an account of their founder's death that would be 'for the Jews a stumbling-block, for the Greeks folly'; and the adoption of the sign of the Cross as Christianity's visual symbol is convincing material evidence that the Crucifixion is an historical fact. This fact is the basis of Christianity's affirmation that God is love. The writer of the First Epistle General of Saint John believed that Jesus was the son of God (whatever meaning the word 'son' may be held to have in this *ex hypothesi* super-human context), and this writer also held that Jesus submitted himself voluntarily to suffering death on the Cross out of love for his fellow men. The same belief has been declared, in deeply moving words, by Saint Paul in his Epistle to the Philippians.[1] I can believe that, if I knew all the facts, I, too, should hold that Jesus gave his life for love. Can I also believe that Jesus was the son of God?

The meaning of the term 'son of God' is difficult to define, because, in this context, the words 'son' and 'father' are being used analogically. The only son-and-father relation of which we have experience is the one between human persons who are son and father in the physical sense; and in Christology the relation is certainly not conceived of as being physical. Indeed, Christianity holds that Jesus was unique among human beings in having no physical father, human or divine. The relation between Jesus and God is conceived of as being a spiritual relation analogous to the ideal spiritual relation between a human son and father. I can believe that Jesus was God's son in the sense that Jesus was inspired by love more whole-heartedly than any other human being of whom we know. But, if being God's son is interpreted in this way, then Jesus was not God's only human son, though his sonship may have come nearer to the ideal than anyone else's. Sonship of God, in this sense, would be a matter of degree; and, while it is possible that no other human being has been God's son to Jesus's degree, it might also be true that one could find few human beings who would not also be God's sons in some

[1] Phil. ii. 6–8.

degree, however minimal. On the evidence of the Gospels, this was one of the truths about human nature which Jesus saw and prized. Jesus had the insight to detect the hidden spark of love in a sinner's breast; more than that, he had the spiritual power to kindle the spark into flame.

If it is true, as I believe it to be, that love transfigures human beings into 'children of God' in this metaphorical sense, and if it is also true that the touchstone of love is self-sacrifice, Christianity's recognition and proclamation of this truth is Christianity's distinctive contribution towards explaining Man's situation and towards providing, for Man, the means for his salvation. The Christian belief that, in the crucifixion of Jesus, God was sacrificing himself for mankind's sake seems to me to be incompatible with the Christian doctrine that God is omnipotent, but to be reconcilable with my own unorthodox belief that God's love is unlimited but that his power is not.

Christianity's fundamental tenet is, as I see it, a belief that self-sacrificing love is both the best and the most powerful of all the spiritual impulses that are known to us. I believe that this is true, and I also believe that the grasp of this truth is the essence of Christianity; but my holding of this essential Christian belief does not make me a Christian; for Christianity is the religion of the Christian Church, and the Church is an institution. I cannot call myself a Christian unless I know that I shall be recognized by the constituted authorities as being one; and I know that I should not pass the most elementary tests of Christian orthodoxy. Besides failing to pass on the Virgin Birth, the Resurrection, and the Ascension, I should fail on God's omnipotence. Though I hold the Christian belief that God and love are identical, I do not share the Christian certainty that the god who is love is also all-powerful. On this crucial issue, I see eye to eye with Marcion, not with Irenaeus.

I should also fail to pass the tests of the other higher religions. For instance, I do not believe that the Jews are God's 'Chosen People'. I believe that every human being is in some degree a child of God in a sense that I have already tried to define. I cannot believe that a god who is both loving and omnipotent would make an invidious discrimination between some of his children and others. Such discriminations are made, not by God, but by us human beings ourselves; in making them, as we usually make them, in our own favour, we are succumbing to the sin of self-centredness; and self-centred-ness is the antithesis of the love in virtue of which we have God for our father. To believe that one's own tribe is God's Chosen People is the error of nationalism. It is a moral error as well as an intellectual one. Other peoples besides the Jews have fallen into it. I do not believe that either the Jews or the British Israelites are the Chosen People; and, *a fortiori*, I do not believe that the repatriation of the Jews to Palestine is the consummation to which all human history has been leading up since the second decade of the sixth century B.C.

I could not pass Islam's tests either. I believe that Muhammad was a prophet who ranks with Jesus and with Zarathustra. The Prophet Muhammad's moral infirmities—for instance, his warlikeness and his uxoriousness—are merely evidence that he was human; they are not evidence that he was not also spiritually great. But I do not believe that this, or any, particular prophet can have been the last of the prophets. The human race has still an expectation of about 2000 million years more of existence on this planet. If it is true that 'where there is no vision, the people perish',[1] how could a God who is deemed to be loving and omnipotent leave his children to perish at the dawn of their history?

One test of Buddhist orthodoxy that I could not pass is the belief in re-birth (metempsychosis; the transmigration of souls). This belief is Buddhism's primordial tenet. If the Buddha had not believed in the reality of 'the sorrowful round of re-birth', he would not have dedicated himself, as he did, to the spiritual enterprise of seeking a way of breaking out of the vicious circle. He appears to have believed in re-birth unquestioningly; and this uncritical acceptance of that belief was common to him and to contemporary Indian philosophers of other schools who differed from him sharply on other questions—for instance, on the question whether or not there are such things as souls. Yet I know of no convincing evidence for the reality of re-birth. The belief in it perhaps originated in the experience of North Asian Shamans when they were in a state of trance. They had the impression that, in this state, their souls dis-engaged themselves temporarily from their bodies and ranged over the Universe. But, even if this psychic experience had been an

---

[1] Prov. xxix. 18.

objective psychosomatic reality, it would not have proved that souls could or did pass from one body into another.

I do not believe in re-birth, and I also have a moral objection to the Buddha's prescription for winning release from it. The Buddha's counsel to his fellow-creatures is that they should purge themselves of desires of all kinds—not only of egotism and greed, but of love and pity as well. I should feel it utterly wrong to purge myself of love and pity, and I am totally unwilling to try. If the price of this refusal is the forfeiture of the possibility of entering Nirvâna, I would rather pay this price than extinguish in myself all desire for the welfare of my fellow-creatures. The Buddha himself gave this desire priority over his own entry into Nirvâna; and, in this, his practice was nobly inconsistent with what he preached.

Moreover, what the Buddha preached seems to an outsider to be inconsistent with itself. What the Buddha sought to inculcate in his disciples was not, and could not be, an effort to get rid of *all* desires. The Buddhist was directed to concentrate on a single master-desire— the desire to get rid of desires that generate self-centredness. But this very concentration on escaping from self-centredness is—paradoxi- cally, yet undeniably—an exercise in self-centredness, and this in an extreme form. This stumbling-block in the path of primitive Buddhism has been detected, not only by outsiders, but by critics within the Buddhist fold. Buddhist criticism of Buddhism on this score led to the secession of the Mahayana and emboldened the followers of this new sect to call it 'the Great Way', though, in the eyes of the adherents of primitive Buddhism, the 'Mahayana' is a deviation from the authentic path.

Among the historic higher religions, Zoroastrianism presents per- haps the fewest stumbling-blocks to me. Zoroastrians see life as the arena of a warfare between good and evil; and this picture seems to me to correspond to what we know of the spiritual structure of human nature. Man's endowment with consciousness and will en- ables and compels him to make choices; and some of the choices that a human being has to make are choices between life and good on the one hand and death and evil on the other. Thus I share the Zoroas- trians' principal belief. At the same time, I do not share their inci- dental beliefs that the warfare between good and evil is destined to be waged only for a season, and that it is also destined to end, at its terminal date, in a definitive victory for the good. My own belief is that Original Sin—i.e. the sin of self-centredness, which is built into the psyche of every living creature—is born afresh in every child that is brought into the World. 'Never has a sinless child been born to its mother.' This way of putting the Christian doctrine is Archbishop William Temple's, but the words that I have used to convey his meaning are not his. They come from a Sumerian precursor of the Book of Job.[1] I believe that the continual conflict in each human being's soul will be perpetuated as long as mankind itself survives. I do not believe that Man, either individually or collectively, will ever be able to afford to rest on his oars in the belief that his spiritual battle has been won once for all. This belief is surely proved illusory by the moral fall that has been its invariable nemesis.

Thus I disbelieve some of the obligatory dogmas of most of the higher religions; and in most cases the dogmas that I disbelieve are fundamental in the eyes of the religious authorities. This disbelief has been my settled attitude of mind since I began, sixty-one years ago, to study philosophy in the school of Literae Humaniores at Oxford. Convictions that I have held for that length of time are my settled convictions, and the holder of them is my true self. I cannot guarantee that I would not abjure my settled convictions with my lips if I were to be put to the torture or were to become senile or were to keep my wits but were to lose my nerve at the imminent approach of death. Drowning people sometimes catch at straws, and I, among others, might behave in this pathetic but ignominious way if I were put to a severe enough test. I therefore testify now, at a time when I am still thoroughly *compos mentis* and am not yet at death's door so far as I am aware, that my true convictions are those that I have held for the last sixty-one years. I repudiate, in advance, any recantation of these convictions that I might make at some future date when I might no longer be my true self.

The point at which I part company with all the historic higher religions is the point at which they attempt to give exact and definitive answers to the riddle set to Man by the situation in which he finds himself. The would-be exactness and definitiveness of these answers are no evidence that the answers have been verified or are

[1] Quoted by S. N. Kramer, *History Begins at Sumer* (New York 1959, Doubleday), on pp. 107 and 117.

verifiable; it is, as I see it, merely evidence of mankind's impatient eagerness to have its ambiguous situation clarified for it.

Man's situation is, indeed, paradoxical. Man has a mind that can comprehend infinite time and space, and he has a conscience that can pass moral judgements; yet prima facie it looks as if these spiritual faculties are dependent for their survival on their association with the life of a short-lived physical body. If certain parts of the body have been generated with a lack or an insufficiency of certain physical ingredients, the human being's spiritual faculties never come to flower, or at least never fully; and, if certain parts of a normal person's body run down before death, the person's spiritual faculties automatically fail. In any case at death the spiritual faculties disappear from this phenomenal world; and the widely and tenaciously held belief in the immortality of the soul after death is not borne out by any cogent evidence. Moreover, our bodies, though 'fearfully and wonderfully made', are, in physical terms, specks of dust on the surface of a speck of dust called the Earth which is a satellite of another speck of dust called the Sun; and our sun is a speck of dust in our galaxy, which is a speck of dust in a universe that may be infinite in terms of space-time.

However, the dust of which a human body is composed, quantitatively trivial though it is, is an integral part of the inconceivably vast physical universe; and, when, after death, the body dissolves into its physical elements, these elements themselves are not annihilated. Death has destroyed the organism that, for a brief time, had succeeded in maintaining itself as a puny counter-universe; but the physical materials of which the dissolved human body was composed at the moment of death have not been destroyed through ceasing to be incorporated temporarily in an organic physical structure. They are continuing to exist as parts of the physical universe, though this no longer in an organic form.

Science has been able to ascertain this, because science's earliest researches, and its greatest successes so far, have been in the field of reality in its physical aspect. In our own day, science has made a start with the exploration of reality in its psychic aspect as well; but psychological science is still in its infancy, and, though the possibilities, opened up by it, of an increase in our knowledge and understanding of the Universe are potentially enormous, it is still too early for us to be able to foresee whether these possibilities are going to be converted into achievements of anything like the same order of magnitude as science's already accomplished achievements in the physical field. Meanwhile, the study of the spiritual aspect of human nature, on which modern Western science has embarked only recently, has been pursued, by now, for at least 2500 years, in the Indian practice of contemplation.

Already by the Buddha's day the school of Indian philosophy to which the Buddha himself was opposed had reported that the essence of a human being's spiritual aspect is identical with the ultimate spiritual reality behind and beyond the phenomena of the Universe.[1] If the intuition on which this report is based has penetrated to the truth, this signifies that the spiritual aspect of a human being, like his physical aspect, is an integral part of a universe that, in its own dimension, may be as 'vast' (an unavoidable loan-word from our vocabulary for describing physical reality) as the physical universe is; and from this it would seem to follow that, at death, the aspect of a human being that we call his spirit or his soul ceases to be the ephemeral separate personality that it has been during the now dead human being's lifetime, but continues to exist as the ultimate spiritual reality with which, even in bodily life on Earth, it has never ceased to be identical in the spiritual vision of observers who have had the inward eye to see.

If this is the truth, 'matter' and 'spirit' may each be infinite in its own dimension; and every human being will be a point at which these two perhaps infinite entities intersect each other. We do not understand what the relation between them is. I suspect that their apparent duality may be an illusion produced by some feature in the structure of our minds that diffracts an indivisible reality into fractions which we do not know how to re-combine.

Human nature presents human minds with a puzzle which they have not yet solved and may never succeed in solving, for all that we can tell. The dichotomy of a human being into 'soul' and 'body' is not a datum of experience. No one has ever been, or ever met, a living human soul without a body, though, as I have noted, we do meet living human bodies in whom the soul has been virtually extinguished or has never come to flower. The partition of the

[1] See pp. 124, 159, 177, and 369.

human personality between two supposedly different and incommensurable orders of being is a mental act of human intellects, and it is a disputable one. Present-day medical and psychological research seems to agree in indicating that a human personality is an indivisible psychosomatic unity. The psychic aspect of its life cannot be properly understood if this is artificially isolated from the physical aspect, nor, conversely, is the physical aspect intelligible in isolation from the psychic aspect. This is not a new discovery; it is a rediscovery of a once widely recognized truth. It is the assumption implied in the stories in the Gospels of acts of healing performed by Jesus. The same assumption is implied in the Christian Church's belief that Jesus rose from the dead physically as well as spiritually, and that all human beings who have ever lived and died are destined to experience a bodily, as well as a spiritual, resurrection on the Day of Judgment. Someone who accepts—as I myself do, taking it on trust—the present-day scientific account of the Universe may find it impossible to believe that a living creature, once dead, can come to life again; but, if he did entertain this belief, he would be thinking more 'scientifically' if he thought in the Christian terms of a psychosomatic resurrection than if he thought in the shamanistic terms of a disembodied spirit.

Yet there is evidence that an embodied human spirit can be *en rapport* with another embodied human spirit by a means of psychic communication that does not make use of the physical apparatus of the senses of either of the two persons who are *en rapport* or of any of the physical media, outside human bodies, that are used in our indisputably physical means of communication such as wireless radio or wire-conducted telephone and telegraph. I myself have been a first-hand witness of numerous successful experiments in communication between Gilbert Murray and his daughter Rosalind, my first wife, in which G. M. described scenes, some from real life and some from the fictitious world of plays and novels, which Rosalind had previously chosen and had described to the other people in the room while G. M. was not only out of the room but was far enough away for it to have been impossible for him to have picked up these messages by even a hypersensitive accentuation of the physical sense of hearing—an accentuation of it to a degree that would surpass any case of which there is any credible record.

This first-hand evidence has convinced me that extra-sensory perception is a reality. Gilbert Murray, who possessed this faculty in an unusually high degree, held that, in varying degrees, it is possessed and is used by all human beings. His view was that, in a conversation, something more passes between the parties than is conveyed by the spoken words. Our words, he suggested, are supplemented, on the fringe, by communication through extra-sensory perception. He also suggested that, before our ancestors acquired the power of articulate speech, which employs the physical apparatus of parts of the human body and the physical medium of waves that we hear as sounds, these speechless pre-men or proto-men had already been able to communicate with each other (as any social animals must be able), and that, at this previous stage, extra-sensory perception, which has since been pushed out by language into the fringe, had been the central means of communication to which cries and gestures were supplementary. If this was true of Man's ancestors before they acquired the power of articulate speech, it must be true, *a fortiori*, of the social species of non-human animals.

If extra-sensory perception is a proven reality (and I am convinced by first-hand evidence that it is), its existence indicates that a human being may, after all, not be the psychosomatic monolith that he appears to be in the light of present-day medical and psychological research. Human nature is still mysterious, and the mystery extends, beyond human nature, to the whole Universe, in both its spiritual and its physical aspect, and to the ultimate reality in and behind and beyond the phenomena.

For a human being, the mystery of existence is baffling and tantalizing. It is therefore natural that we should be impatient to see this mystery elucidated, and hence natural, too, that we should be tempted to take short cuts to elucidation that are offered to us in the form of unverified and perhaps unverifiable dogmas. Our consequent readiness to accept dogmas uncritically is human, but that does not necessarily mean that it is expedient. There are situations in which it is better to ride out a storm on the high seas than to make for the nearest port. At sea in a storm the sailor is risking shipwreck; but, so long as he remains at sea, he has open water ahead of him. On the other hand, the nearest port may prove not to be the haven where he would be. Man's constant yearning to seek rest and security is an infirmity against which he should be on his guard.

I find myself in the position of a hermit crab who has shed one alien shell and may be tempted to clothe himself in another. The temptation must be resisted, because the chances are that the second shell will fit no better than the first. The crab will do better to stay in the open, naked and unprotected, but, at this price, free to go forward on his way. As I am not a crab but a human being, my way is a voyage of exploration. My aim is to have the maximum of religion with the minimum of dogma.

I have now set out, as honestly, frankly, and clearly as I can, the standpoint at which I have arrived in the course of nearly eighty years since the date at which I was baptized. Baptism in an Anglican church has made me a Christian of the Anglican persuasion officially; and I have never repudiated my membership in the Church of England. Yet, if any of the Anglican ecclesiastical authorities were to read this chapter as far as this present point, they would certainly rule that I was now no longer a member of their communion. Nor am I *extra Ecclesiam Christianam* only. I am also ineligible for membership in most of the other living higher religions as well. The only major living higher religion to which I might conceivably gain admittance is Hinduism; for Hinduism is catholic in the sense of being comprehensive, not catholic in the Catholic Christian Church's original sense of being a particular religion's universally recognized standard form. Hinduism might admit me. In the hierarchy of castes, I should rank below the sweepers.

To be ineligible for membership in any, except perhaps one, of the historic living religious communities is unfortunate for me, because religion is not just a personal affair between a human being and the ultimate spiritual reality; it is also a social affair in which, in communicating with ultimate reality, human beings enter into communion with each other. The three crucial events in a human being's life—his birth, his marriage, and his death—are celebrated, in the liturgies of the higher religions, in rites in which our fellow human beings express their—and God's—participation in the personal fortunes of each one of us. To forgo this consecration of the major events of life is a high price to pay for having fallen out of tune with one's ancestral religion's doctrines. In the present-day world, I am a representative of a large and increasing fraction of the human race that has lost its attachment to its ancestral religious community; and 'displaced persons' are a menace to society on the religious plane, as they are on the political. There is a conservation of religious, as well as physical, energy; and in our time the energy that has ebbed out of the historic higher religions has been decanted into Nationalism and the other post-Christian ideologies. These are all varieties of the worship of human power, and this is one of the worst forms of lower religion that mankind has hit upon so far. It would be to our benefit, both individually and collectively, if the historic higher religions could manage to open their doors wide enough to enable their ex-members to re-enter without damage to either party's intellectual and spiritual integrity.

In my family on my father's side, it is possible that I am the first Toynbee to find himself right out in the cold since my ancestors came over to Lincolnshire from Denmark and were received into the Christian Church about a thousand years before I myself was born. My father was a still unquestioning middle-of-the-road Christian; my Great-Uncle Harry was a fanatical low-church Protestant; I am not sure about the position of my Uncle Arnold and my grandfather and my Great-Uncle George; I should guess that none of those three was one hundred per cent orthodox, but that none of them was definitely outside the Church, as I am; and I have no doubt that, throughout the previous nine hundred years and more, their ancestors in Lincolnshire had been assenting members of the Christian community as a matter of course.

Is re-entry into the Church a practical possibility for me and for the increasing number of my fellow ex-Christians whose position today is the same as mine? My expectation is that the Christian Church, along with the other historic higher religious communities, is eventually going to open its doors wide enough to re-admit ex-members who stand where we stand. Most branches of the Christian Church, and most of the other religious communities too, have now begun to liberate the essence of their faith and practice from the non-essential accretions that have accumulated in the course of time. This, however, is a delicate task, and therefore it is likely to be a slow one. It seems improbable that I shall live to see the door open to a width that will make room for me to find my way back through it without my having to jettison my intellectual liberty and honesty. I am not willing to pay that price for the sake of regaining religion in its social aspect.

I and my contemporaries who have a religion but not a religious community are not the only generation that has ever found itself in this position. It is a position that is characteristic of times of transition such as is the time into which we happen to have been born. Times of transition are uncomfortable to live through. In compensation, they are interesting. My Great-Uncle Harry lived and died at a time that, for middle-class English people, was stable. He was born four years after the date of the Battle of Waterloo, and he died five years before the outbreak of the First World War. I have lived through two world wars by now, but I should not feel tempted to take Uncle Harry's lifetime in exchange for mine.

There have been ages—some of them, long times on end—during which human minds have been passive and submissive, not venturing to think for themselves, but taking their mental furniture at second hand, and untested, from canonized authorities. At the western end of the Old World an eighteen-hundred-years-long age of this kind came to an end in the seventeenth century. In that century, Western minds began to dare once again to think for themselves for the first time since the second century B.C.; and, although, in our time, ex-Christian and ex-Confucian ideologists (Nationalists, Communists, Individualists) have relapsed into dogmatic slumber, ex-Christian agnostics still preserve the intellectual independence that our seventeenth-century path-finders have bequeathed to us. I am not willing to betray this precious heritage of intellectual freedom. As I see it, this would be a betrayal of mankind's future.

(iii) THE LIMITS OF MY AGNOSTICISM

I have put it on record in this chapter that my disbelief in some of the obligatory dogmas of the historic higher religions has been steady for more than half a century; but my attitude towards religion has not been static throughout that time. My rejection of religion was sudden; my re-conversion has been gradual, but it has been lasting, because it has been a response to successive challenges of experience. I have come to believe that religion itself—as contrasted with its historic outward forms—is an intrinsic faculty of human nature. I believe that being human involves having religion, and that human beings who declare that they have no religion are deceiving themselves through failing to search their own hearts. More than that, I believe that religion, besides being present in all human souls, is the most distinctive and most fundamental element in human nature. Religion is a search for the ultimate spiritual principle in the Universe; and the purpose of this search is not just the intellectual one of learning the ultimate truth; beyond that, it is the spiritual purpose of learning the truth in order to try to put oneself into harmony with it. This is, of course, what each of the historic higher religions is trying to help its adherents to do; and I am at one with the adherents of all the higher religions in this common endeavour.

(iv) LOVE IS GOD

In a couplet of Greek verses printed in the third part of this book, I have declared that I believe that love is God. I have not arrived at this belief unaided. I might never have arrived at it if I had been ignorant of the First Epistle General of Saint John, in which it is affirmed that God is love; and this affirmation, by itself, might not have been convincing to me if I had not had personal experience of love and had not witnessed mutual love in other people and in some of our non-human fellow living creatures. I know by experience what love is, but I have not any evidence that love is God. In adopting, without evidence, the belief that love and God are identical, I am following the writer of the First Epistle General of Saint John by making an act of faith.

We human beings know love from experience, but we do not know God from experience. Human beings do have experiences which may feel like encounters with God to someone who has been brought up in a theistic religion. I have had two such experiences in my life so far. But the theistic interpretation of these experiences is not verifiable and not demonstrable. The existence of God is an hypothesis, and our conceptions of God's nature vary widely in the tenets of the different religions. My creed consists of a single article: 'Deus est mortali iuvare mortalem': 'For a human being, God is the act of helping another human being'. I believe that the true end of Man is self-sacrificing love; that love is divine; that it is the only god that we know from experience; and that Man should devote himself to this god without any reservations, whatever the consequences may be.

(v) LOVE IS NOT OMNIPOTENT

The three Judaic religions—Judaism, Christianity, and Islam—hold that God, at least in one of his aspects, is merciful, compassionate, and loving; but they also hold that God is omnipotent. The orthodox Christian thesis has been given a memorable expression by Tennyson in two quatrains of *In Memoriam*.

> Strong Son of God, immortal Love,
> Whom we, that have not seen thy face,
> By faith, and faith alone, embrace,
> Believing where we cannot prove:
>
> Thine are these orbs of light and shade;
> Thou madest Life in man and brute;
> Thou madest Death; and, lo, thy foot
> Is on the skull which thou hast made.

The thesis is that death, like everything else, has been created by God, and that God has demonstrated his mastery over death in Christ's resurrection.

I learnt that passage of *In Memoriam* by heart at Winchester; but my visual memory holds the imprint of a picture that used to hang in my mother's bedroom. It was a photograph of a painting by Tennyson's contemporary Watts. This allegorical picture is called 'Love and Death', and, instead of endorsing the Christian thesis, it challenges it. Watts's Love is a god, but he is not omnipotent. He is being defeated in a despairing struggle to defend some beloved person, outside the picture, against the approach of Death; for Watts's Death is a god too, and he is the stronger. Death is not going to be denied. He is advancing with a gesture that is serenely authoritative. He is conscious that he is stronger than Love, and he is confident that he is also wiser; and, in truth, Death is Nature's effective device for insuring that she shall not be committed irrevocably to any of her hit-and-miss experiments in evolution. As Watts sees it, Love is not omnipotent, and this view is supported by the findings of our experience and by the conclusions about the nature of things that follow from these findings.

One of the most poignant human experiences is the sorrow at being parted by death from a beloved fellow human being. The greater the love, the greater the grief. I have cited two sad cases, which came home poignantly to me, in a previous book.[1] In the poem from which I have quoted, Tennyson arraigns Nature for the heartlessness with which she sacrifices individuals for the sake of preserving the species, and then discards the species itself to join its specimens on a scrap-heap that is the monument of Nature's prodigal incompetence. Is it credible that, if love were omnipotent, love would have solved Nature's problem for her by creating death, considering the price that death exacts from love in the coin of grief?

Man's spiritual powers are incommensurate with Man's mortality. A human being's capacity, not only for loving but for thinking, learning, knowing, teaching, acting, making, is vastly greater than the performance that his feeble physical stamina allows him to achieve within the short space of a human lifetime. Yet in this world, which is the only world that we know, a human spirit does not outlive its physical body. Indeed, the ageing of the body deprives some human beings of their wits even before their physical death. There is a misfit here which human beings have found frustrating, humiliating, and agonizing ever since mankind first came to consciousness. Is it credible that, if love were omnipotent, love would have created this misfit?

Then, too, life preys on itself. Animals prey either on plants or on animals of other species. The order of evolution may be an ascending order when judged by the intellectual criteria of intelligence and efficiency, but the same order looks like a descending one if we judge it in the moral terms of behaviour. Man is the most efficient species, in virtue of being the most intelligent species, of life on this planet; but he takes advantage of his superiority in efficiency to prey on all other species; and mankind is also the only species that preys on itself too. We are unique among the mammalia in fighting fratricidal wars to the death. The mother's breast, which has given its name to the order of living creatures to which Man belongs, is a symbol of love. War is the deliberate repudiation of love. Man's institution of war brands him as a delinquent member of the order in which he claims to rank the highest.

[1] See *Acquaintances*, chapters 8 and 19.

(vi) THE INCONCEIVABILITY OF OMNIPOTENCE

Love is not omnipotent. Watts's picture, not Tennyson's poem, tells the truth. Does this conclusion discredit the act of faith in which love is identified with God? Is omnipotence of the essence of godhead? We human beings have no experience of God apart from love, and we have no experience of omnipotence either. Omnipotence signifies power without limits; this implies power to do what is impossible, as well as what is possible, and, for human minds, 'power to do what is impossible' does not make sense. In attributing omnipotence to God we are implicitly denying God's reality without making any intelligible addition to our acknowledgement of God's power. If we divest God of an epithet that is meaningless, we shall not be derogating from his majesty; we shall be enhancing it.

This is the case against omnipotence as a matter of fact. There is also a case against it as a matter of morals. Jesus is said to have said: 'With man, this is impossible; but with God all things are possible.' If this is the truth, it was possible for God to create life without self-centredness, love without bereavement, consciousness and freedom of choice without sin; and, since sin and bereavement and self-centredness exist, they must have been brought into existence deliberately by the God whose omnipotence could have done without them if he had so chosen. In deliberately choosing to afflict his creatures with these unnecessary evils, the omnipotent God would have convicted himself of being a fiend, if human reason had not saved God's goodness by finding that omnipotence is impossible.

Marcion and Blake, who shared the orthodox Christian belief in the reality of an omnipotent creator-god, identified him with the dark side of Yahweh the god of Israel and Judah, as this god is portrayed in the Old Testament. Blake nicknamed his and Marcion's creator-god 'Nobodaddy' (Nobody's Daddy), to indicate the unlovingness and unlovableness of his character, in contrast to Jesus's vision of 'God the Father'. Considering the evils of the World as we know it, an omnipotent creator must have that amount of evil in himself. Marcion was logical in distinguishing his evil creator-god from the god who, in the New Testament, is identified with love. In Marcion's vision, the god who is love is a stranger in the creator-god's universe, and mankind, in virtue of its capacity for loving, is also a stranger there.

Marcion's myth is, to my mind, more convincing than the orthodox Christian myth which, in opposition to Marcion, was given its
classical expression by Irenaeus. We could make Marcion's myth
more convincing still by eliminating the creator-god and leaving,
as the only known divine presence, a non-omnipotent love and
righteousness that are doing their best within the limits of their not
unlimited power. To do his best is the most that can be asked of
anyone, man or god.

(vii) THE FAULT IN THE UNIVERSE

These considerations suggest, not only that love is not omnipotent,
but that there is no omnipotent power governing and guiding the
universe in which we human beings find ourselves.

> Ex ipsis caeli rationibus ausim
> confirmare aliisque ex rebus reddere multis
> nequaquam nobis divinitus esse creatam
> naturam mundi: tantâ stat praedita culpâ.[1]

I feel the force of Lucretius's argument. Our common experience
of the Universe in which we find ourselves does inform us that the
Universe has a fault in it. It is a fault in both the physical and the
ethical meaning of the word. We do not know whether it is true or
not that the Universe 'ails from the prime foundation', as Lucretius's
echo, Housman, maintains. We have no evidence about that; but
the fault is manifest at the level of the emergence of life on this
planet. Every living creature known to us has two relations with the
rest of the Universe which are not only different but are also dis-
cordant. On the one hand a living creature is an integral part of the
Universe. In its physical aspect it is demonstrably part and parcel of
the Universe's material fabric; and in its psychic aspect we may guess
that it partakes in a spirit that is present in everything that exists. On
the other hand a living creature is attempting, so long as it is alive, to
maintain itself as a counter-universe, separate from, and indeed in
opposition to, the Universe of which it is in truth an inseparable

[1] 'There is a truth which I can affirm with confidence because I find it written into
the structure of the heavens (I can also deduce it from a mass of other evidence):
it is out of the question that the Universe can have been created for our benefit by
divine providence. The faultiness of the nature of the Universe is gross, flagrant,
and intrinsic' (Lucretius, *De Rerum Naturâ*, Book II, lines 178–81).

part. Every living creature behaves as if it were the Universe's centre and *raison d'être*. In so far as it has the power, it exploits the rest of the Universe, including its fellow living creatures, in its own interest.

This act of secession and declaration of independence is one of the symptoms of coming to life; and life—including pre-human life— seems to us human living creatures to be a better and a higher state of existence than pre-animate nature (if there is such a thing). At the same time, we feel that the fault, in the geological sense, through which a living creature asserts its separateness from the rest of the Universe is a fault in the spiritual sense as well, and this in more than one way. In asserting its separateness, its centrality, and its para- mount importance, a living creature is flying in the face of the truth. It cannot truly disengage itself from the rest of the Universe, and it is certainly not the Universe's true centre or true *raison d'être*. Every living creature is asserting an identical claim to be the centre and the *raison d'être* of the Universe; only a single one out of these myriads of claims could conceivably be well-founded; and every such claim, without exception, is fantastically incompatible with all that we know about the Universe's structure; so we may conclude that no single one of these claims is valid. A living creature's self-centredness is also a negation of morality. There is no possibility of morality in a world of living creatures each of which is pursuing its own self- interest and nothing besides or beyond that.

Thus a living creature's pretensions are extravagant and out- rageous. It does, nevertheless, succeed in putting these pretensions into effect to some extent. If it did not, it would not be alive; but this means that life is a *tour de force*. Even the most powerful and longest- lived living creature's successful exploitation of the rest of the Uni- verse is only local and ephemeral. Eventually the creature loses its identity, either by fission or by death; and its loss of identity signifies that it has met with its inevitable ultimate defeat. Meanwhile, during its lifetime, its locally and temporarily successful exploitation of its fellow living creatures inflicts suffering on them.

(viii) THE FAULT IN MAN: SIN AND CONSCIENCE

The world of pre-human life is a non-moral world; but it is not an immoral or sinful world. So far as we know, the self-centred be- haviour of non-human living creatures is, in human terms, morally innocent. Moral issues are not raised, either, in many of the choices that we human beings make. In the technical vocabulary of the Stoic philosophy, the alternative options in such cases are ἀδιάφορα (matters of indifference). Innumerable petty humdrum choices of this morally neutral kind are made by all of us in our daily lives. However, no human being can live out his days—however few these may be—without also being confronted with choices between good and evil, and we often choose evil in defiance of our conscience.

> Video meliora proboque,
> deteriora sequor.[1]

While all species of life are predatory, mankind is the only species that is capable of sinning. When a shark or a tiger kills and eats a fellow living creature, it is not being wicked; but when a human being deliberately injures a fellow human being, he is being wicked as well as predatory.

If this is the truth, then, at the human level, the self-centredness that sunders a human being from the rest of the Universe, including his fellow human beings, not only goes against nature and causes suffering to other living creatures; it is also a sin and is recognized as being one. Selfishness is of the essence of life itself, and human nature is not exempt from it. But in a human being the disharmony that is to be found in every kind of living creature is raised to an additional dimension. In so far as a human being gives way to his selfishness, he is sinning, is conscious of sin, and is reproached for his sin by his conscience. He may resent his conscience and defy it but he cannot easily extinguish it.

The conscious distinction between good and evil, which is an accompaniment of our human capacity to make conscious choices, is an act of thought, but it is not merely that; it is also a call to action on the moral plane. When we are confronted with a choice between doing what is morally good and right and doing what is morally wrong and evil, our conscience commands us to choose what is good and right, even if this is contrary to our own self-interest. We are free to disobey our conscience and to pursue our self-interest by

[1] 'I see what the better course is, and my conscience tells me that it is the right one, yet the worse course is the one that I follow' (Ovid, *Metamorphoses*, Book VII, lines 20–21).

making the choice that, as we see it, is wrong and evil; but we are
not free to do this with impunity. If we do disobey our conscience,
we cannot escape being reproached by it.

The reproach of conscience is formidable—and this even for a
hardened sinner—because our conscience speaks to us with an
absolute authority from which there is no appeal. The absoluteness
of conscience is something inalienable, and it is intrinsic. It needs no
authentication or validation by any authority outside conscience
itself. We may speculate about what, if any, sanction the conscience
may have behind it. We may see in it the voice of God or whatever
other name we may give to the ultimate spiritual reality behind the
Universe, supposing that we believe that there is such an ultimate
spiritual reality. Alternatively, we may interpret conscience as being
the voice of our human community. If we find this second interpretation convincing, then logically we shall also expect to find ourselves
concluding that our conscience is not morally infallible collectively,
any more than it is individually. Actually, these alternative guesses
at the source of our conscience's authority over us do not affect this
authority itself. The authority of conscience remains, for us, violable
yet absolute, in whatever way we may seek to explain conscience or
to explain it away. The inescapable absoluteness of the authority
with which conscience speaks to us is a characteristic and essential
feature of it.

I have been saying that, in my experience, all human beings consciously distinguish between good and evil, and that, if they choose
to do evil and not to do good, their consciences reproach them. But
I am not meaning to imply that the same conduct seems good and
seems bad to every human being. 'Good' and 'bad' are abstract
concepts. To be put into practice, they have to be applied to concrete situations. They have, that is to say, to be translated into a code
of rules dealing with particular cases. Each of our many human
societies has its own code, and, within each society, no two individuals take their common code in exactly the same way, while, as
between different codes, there are differences that, on some points,
are irreconcilable. For instance, slavery, polygamy, infanticide, *sati*,
and other forms of human sacrifice are in some codes permitted or
even required, while in other codes the same practices are condemned and penalized. Moreover, every sectional code is changing

all the time, and this sometimes rapidly. It would therefore, I should say, be absurd to maintain that some particular code, at some particular stage of its development, has embodied, for all time, the whole human race's intrinsic conception of what is right and what is wrong. All that is intrinsic to human nature, as I see it, is the distinction between right and wrong in the abstract. This is all, but this is much.

(ix) MAN'S STRUGGLE TO OVERCOME SELF-CENTREDNESS

Conscience tells a human being that his natural self-centredness is wrong, and it will not let him rest so long as he is not trying to overcome his self-centredness.

Since self-centredness is of the essence of life, the overcoming of self-centredness is the most difficult spiritual task that any living creature can set for itself. Conscience commands a human being to undertake this task, and it gives the command with an authority that is absolute, but this does not make the task any easier for a conscience-stricken human being than it would be for an innocently self-centred non-human creature. Conscience imposes the job, but it does not provide the tools. To provide these is the purpose and concern of philosophy and religion; and, since every human being has a conscience, he also has a religion or philosophy. Human beings who believe that they do not have one turn out to have one when their attitude to life is analysed.

One prescription for overcoming self-centredness has been to school oneself to get rid of desire. This spiritual regimen is prescribed by Buddhism, Stoicism, and Epicureanism. Of the three, Buddhism is by far the most whole-hearted in its convictions and is consequently by far the most radical in its directions for putting these convictions into effect. The Buddha recognized and proclaimed that his way was a hard way. Having found it, he was concerned to see that his followers should not flinch from it. He would not countenance their seeking escape from moral endeavour in metaphysical speculation. He held them to the performance of spiritual exercises that, if persevered in to the end, would lead, through the resolute renunciation of all other desires, to the desired goal of 'extinguishedness' (Nirvâna).

All philosophies and religions would agree that a human being ought to strive to extinguish his self-centredness. Stoicism and Epicureanism, like Buddhism, do not draw distinctions between desires of morally different kinds. There are, of course, self-seeking desires, and Christians or ex-Christian agnostics would not deny that we ought to try to extinguish these. But there are also desires that are directed towards something outside and beyond self-interest. These self-transcending desires are love, compassion, sympathy. We can include them all in the one word 'love'.

In the history of life, love may not be as old as self-centredness is. Self-centredness must be as old as life itself, whereas love is not visibly at work in the more primitive orders of living creatures. Love is, however, older than Man; for love is manifest in birds and in non-human mammals, as well as in human beings.

Love's way of dealing with us is different from conscience's way. Conscience commands; love inspires. What we do out of love, we do because we want to do it. Love is, indeed, one kind of desire; but it is a kind that takes us out of ourselves and carries us beyond ourselves, in contrast to the kind that is self-seeking—a kind that includes the desire for the 'extinguishedness' of Nirvâna. Love is freedom; conscience is constraint; yet, in two points, our relation to love is the same as our relation to conscience. We are free to reject love's appeal, as we are free to reject conscience's command; yet love, like conscience, cannot be rebuffed with impunity. Rebuffed, love will continue to importune us; and this for the reason for which a violated conscience does. Love's authority, like conscience's, is absolute. Like conscience, too, love needs no authentication or validation by any authority outside itself. Speculations about love's credentials, or lack of credentials, cannot either enhance or diminish love's absoluteness.

We may identify love with God, as is done in the First Epistle General of Saint John, as well as by an unnamed Greek philosopher who defined God as being, for a human being, the act of helping another human being (a definition that I have cited already[1] as being my own creed). Alternatively, we may interpret love as being Nature's device for counteracting an awkward consequence of her older device of endowing living creatures with self-centredness. (This attribution to Nature of a human-like purposefulness is, of

[1] On p. 146.

course, not to be taken literally; it is a piece of myth-making that is forced on us by the inadequacy of human language.)

Nature made living creatures self-centred as a means of enabling them to hold their own against the rest of the Universe. But, besides providing for the maintenance of her creatures' short lives, Nature had also to provide for the perpetuation of the various species of which her creatures are ephemeral successive specimens. When Nature went on from the reproduction of life by fission to its reproduction by sexual procreation, she saddled herself with the problem of providing for the survival of the young, while they were defenceless, in sufficient numbers to ensure the perpetuation of the species. Nature's first device for solving this problem was to endow sexual species of living creatures with a prodigal fertility; but this crude expedient was both wasteful and inefficient so long as it was not reinforced by the positive protection of parental care. The young might perish, and the species might become extinct, if the parents' built-in self-centredness were not now partially counteracted by some un-self-regarding concern for their offspring's welfare. Therefore, at a certain stage in the evolution of sexually reproduced creatures, Nature, according to this naturalistic interpretation of love, implanted love in them, to co-exist with their self-centredness and to mitigate it. Nature has cajoled them into sacrificing themselves for love by making them feel that their offspring is an extension of their selves and that their love is an indulgence of their egotism.

These two accounts of love's credentials are at opposite poles. The naturalistic account sees in love a mechanism devised *ad hoc* for perpetuating certain species of life on one minor planet; and, if this explanation hits the truth, love is a parochial phenomenon which may have no significance in the structure and working of the Universe as a whole. At the same time, even in terms of Nature, altruism will be just as 'natural' as egotism, if it is true that the psyche of a living creature on this planet is also a manifestation of a spirit that is omnipresent throughout the Universe. According to the non-naturalistic explanation which identifies love with God, the love that manifests itself on this planet in birds and beasts and human beings is not just a local *lusus Naturae* and is not just a universally present trait of Nature either; it is a manifestation of an ultimate spiritual reality that is not part of Nature but is beyond Nature and behind it.

Neither of these two accounts of love is demonstrable. Verifiable credentials of any kind and quality may be unprocurable for love. The important point is that neither the best nor the worst credentials can make any difference to our recognition of the spiritual value of love. This value remains absolute for us on all conceivable conditions and suppositions. We cannot deny it or repudiate it, for it is of the essence of love in our experience of love.

The absoluteness of love and the absoluteness of conscience are spiritual realities that are experienced directly and constantly by us in spite of ourselves. (By 'us' I mean myself together with the millions whose picture of human nature I share.) These are two certainties, and they are also two sure guides. If we follow their guidance, they will enable us, between them, to find the right way through life. In this life on Earth, and in the vast Universe that is its setting, everything else may be enigmatic, but love and conscience, together, are enough for our human needs. Both are needed by us, but the greater of the two is love.

If we follow the writer of the First Epistle General of Saint John in identifying love with God, what do we mean by this? Do we think of love in Greek terms as being *a* god—i.e. as being one member of a polytheistic pantheon? Or, alternatively, do we think of love as being the One True God of the Judaic religions? If we try to think of the divinity of love in either of these ways, we shall not be thinking of love in terms of our experience of it. The Greek god Eros and the Judaic god Yahweh differ vastly in stature, but they have one pertinent common trait. Both are conceived of as being persons, and we do not experience love as being a person like our human selves. We experience love as a supra-personal spirit that inspires a human being—and also a non-human mammal and a bird—and transfigures the self-centred creature by carrying it out of itself, so that its self-centredness is transformed into self-sacrificingness. This supra-personal manifestation of God as love in our experience is incommensurable with both the Greek and the Judaic vision of godhead in the likeness of a human person: an anthropomorphic Eros; a God the tyrant; a God the father; a God incarnate in the human being Jesus.

There is, however, another traditional vision of godhead in which this is conceived of as being a supra-personal spirit which enters into a human being and inspires him. This is how godhead is pictured, in one of three aspects of it, in the Christian version of Judaic religion. The inspiration of the Apostles by God the Spirit on the Day of Pentecost does correspond to the action of love in our experience. In this Christian vision of godhead in a supra-personal aspect, the Spirit—like love as we experience love—is actively at work on and in human souls. If we think of this Spirit which is manifestly at work in the Universe as also being the ultimate spiritual reality behind the Universe, we shall identify the Holy Spirit of Christianity with the Brahmă of Hinduism.

(x) LOVE AND CONSCIENCE MAY BE INDICATORS OF THE CHARACTER OF ULTIMATE REALITY

Love and conscience are spiritual realities. The reality of each of them is vouched for by direct spiritual experience—and the testimony is the more telling the more grudging it is. When we are confronted with these realities, we find that both of them have an absolute intrinsic value and validity for us. If this is the truth, then we human beings have our feet on firm ground, though, in other respects, life, and life's ultimate setting, may be a mystery. Human life is mysterious enough to have evoked in human minds many different explanations, some of which are mutually incompatible. We may guess that human beings will continue to speculate on these questions so long as mankind continues to exist. This seems probable because curiosity is one of the distinctive characteristics of human nature. We may also guess that the successive answers at which we arrive will continue to be unverifiable. They cannot be tested by science's method of inquiry, which has extended our knowledge and understanding of the physical universe and is beginning to throw light on the psychic universe as well. Notwithstanding science's recent achievements in these limited fields, the nature of ultimate reality seems likely still to remain beyond comprehension by our human powers of thought. But the inconclusiveness of our findings in this sphere leaves the absoluteness of love and conscience unaffected.

In India in the Buddha's time, most thinkers, including the Buddha himself, were not turning their minds towards the outer world that is revealed to a human being by his senses and that has recently been interpreted in quantitative terms by modern science; they were exploring the inner world that a human being discovers within his own psyche. One school—a school that was opposed by the Buddha—held that, if and when a human being's inward-turned contemplation penetrates to the innermost recess of his self, he finds there a spiritual presence which he will also find in and beyond the Universe as a whole. Indian thinkers of this school summed up this intuition of theirs in the aphorism 'Tat tvam asi' ('Thou art that'). A human soul is identified with ultimate spiritual reality. In opposition to this finding, the Buddha denied the existence of such a thing as a soul in the psyche of a human being; he found nothing stable or permanent there—nothing but a stream of successive psychic states that have no continuity with each other and that are strung together only by a tangle of desires which can be dissipated by spiritual exercises.

In holding that spiritual reality is all of a piece, the school of Indian thought that the Buddha opposed was in line with modern science. The uniformity of Nature is still one of modern science's fundamental postulates, though the formulation of it is perhaps less simple and less absolute today than it was a century ago. This postulate of uniformity seems a reasonable hypothesis. At any rate, it seems unlikely that the spiritual life of Man, as we experience it in ourselves and in our fellow human beings, is something that is peculiar to one species of living creature on this one planet. Why should there be a minute excrescence on the Universe which is different in nature from all the rest of the Universe? How could this exceptional patch have come into existence? We have no convincing answers to these questions, supposing that we do not believe that there is an omnipotent God who uses his omnipotence to make breaches in the uniformity of Nature—breaking the 'laws of Nature' which, if he is omnipotent, must be laws that he himself has made. A modern inquirer will therefore be inclined to endorse the sixth-century-B.C. Indian thesis 'Thou art that'. This thesis is no more than an hypothesis, and this an unverifiable one; but it is at any rate more credible than the alternative hypothesis that the spiritual constitution of one of the species of living creatures on this planet is an exception to the uniformity of Nature.

On the moral plane the hypothesis that the Universe, including Man, is all of a piece is one that cuts both ways. If human nature, as it appears to me and to those with whom I see eye to eye, is a fair sample of the Universe, love and conscience will be omnipresent, but self-centredness and sin will be omnipresent too, since these evil spiritual phenomena are as characteristic of human nature as love and conscience are. Self-centredness and sin are, in fact, inseparable from love and conscience. Here we see the obverse and the reverse of the same coin. In human life as we know it from experience there is a perpetual struggle between love and conscience on the one side and self-centredness and sin on the other side.

We believe that the struggle is going on all the time in every human soul; the fortunes of this spiritual war ebb and flow; and, while the battle may be lost or won definitively in this soul or in that, the outcome for human society has, so far, always been indecisive. We cannot guess whether there will ever be a general and definitive decision on the social plane, or, if there were to be one some day, which side would be victorious. Meanwhile, we are not in any doubt about the side that we ought to take. We know that we ought to give our unqualified allegiance to the cause of love and conscience. For us human beings, this is the right cause. It is right intrinsically, regardless of what its prospects may be. If it were to suffer decisive and conclusive defeat, it would be the right cause still, all the same; and, since the issue is in doubt, we believe that every human being is called upon to throw himself into the struggle, on the right side, with all his heart and soul and mind. In an undecided struggle, every participant counts. No one is entitled to excuse himself from playing his full part on the plea that the effect of what he does or fails to do will be too slight to make any appreciable difference.

If we hold that the Universe is all of a piece, and that the ultimate spiritual reality behind the Universe is of one substance with the spirit in the psyche of a human being, we shall conclude that our human experience and knowledge and understanding of life on this planet give us authentic information about the Universe and about what lies behind it. We shall infer, by analogy, that, in this cosmic field too, love and righteousness have the same absolute moral validity that they have in human life; that in the Universe as a whole, as well as on this planet, they are striving to prevail over evil; but that in the cosmic struggle, as in the human struggle, the forces making for goodness do not have things all their own way, and that, here too, the issue is undecided.

It is common knowledge that, in human life, every achievement has its price, and this seems to be true of the realm of non-human nature as well. Let us personify the spirits of love and righteousness for linguistic convenience, as we have personified 'Nature', without prejudice to the question whether, in truth, cosmic love and right-eousness are manifested in personality, as human love and righteous-ness are. Then the creation of life will have been a grand achievement for love and righteousness, because, without life, love could not have manifested itself, and, without human life, conscience could not have manifested itself either. But the creation of life had, for its price, the implanting of self-centredness in every living creature. This price has been high, and it will not have been paid gladly. It will have been paid because the alternative would have been to leave life uncreated, and self-centred living creatures were a more promis-ing alternative than a lifeless Universe. At this price, love has been able eventually to manifest itself in life on this planet; but love, too, has its price in the coin of bereavement. The greater a creature's love for a fellow-creature, the more grievous the pain of parting from the creature that is loved. We are parted inexorably by death, and death is the price of another achievement—the creation of living creatures high enough in the spiritual scale to be capable of loving.

The creation of a conscious living creature is perhaps the greatest achievement so far in the field of life. Human consciousness makes it possible for a human being deliberately to respond to love's appeal and to obey conscience's commands. But the price of this is that Man's freedom to choose good carries with it an equal freedom to choose evil, and human beings use their freedom in both ways. No evil, no good; no self-seeking, no love; no sin, no righteousness. The evidence that there is a price for every achievement seems over-whelming.

This is tragic, and the tragedy may be cosmic; but, if it is, there is no indication that it is due to malignity; on the analogy of our human experience, it seems more likely to be due to lack of power. All power within our experience is limited.

(xi) ULTIMATE REALITY IS NEITHER ALPHA NOR OMEGA

From the moment at which a human being awakes to consciousness until the moment at which he finally loses it, he finds himself travelling and struggling in the stream of history. He is carried along by its impetus, while at the same time his struggles have an effect—if only an infinitesimally small one—on the strength and speed and direction of the current. The history which is the flowing medium in which human life is lived is not just the history of human affairs; it is also the history of all life on this planet, and it is the history of the Universe. If it is true that every human being harbours, in the depths of his psyche, a spirit that is identical with the divine spirit, what is the divine spirit's relation to the stream of history in which every human being finds himself moving from the beginning to the end of his life? This question has exercised many human minds, and it has received almost as many mutually conflicting answers.

The Jewish-Christian-Muslim answer is that God is the creator of the stream; he set it flowing; he is going, at his own good time, to bring it to a stop; the stream is in God's power and is under his control; he himself stands outside it. 'I am Alpha and Omega, the beginning and the end, the first and the last.'[1]

This theology of history looks sublime by contrast with the view of history that is prevalent nowadays. On this modern view, history is a jostling log-jam composed of vast numbers of fortuitous events; on the classical Judaic view, history is the handiwork of God. Aesthetically, these two visions of history are at opposite poles to each other; yet morally they amount, rather surprisingly, to much the same thing. The two views agree in emptying history of its meaning. If God is the first and the last, and if God is also the ultimate spiritual reality behind the Universe, then, fundamentally, 'as things have been, they remain', and, if this is the truth, it cannot be denied that 'the struggle naught availeth', and it has to be admitted that 'the labour and the wounds are vain'. God's creation of the Universe, life, and human beings will have been pointless; for it will have resulted, at the end of the story, in God's—that is to say, ultimate reality's—being the same as he—or it—was at the beginning. We shall be reduced to accepting the desolating Indian account

[1] This affirmation is put into God's mouth in four passages of *Revelation*.

of the Universe as being a divine *jeu d'esprit*; and, if the Universe is nothing more than that, its creation has been an irresponsible and heartless practical joke; for the Universe—as the Buddha saw so clearly and felt so keenly—is a sea of toil and trouble, a mass of pain. If the Universe's travail is just God's pastime (in the literal meaning of the word), it is abominable that God should have created sentient beings to serve as his pawns for the playing of his frivolous game. But let us change the mood and tense and say, rather, that this would be abominable if it were credible. To us human beings, who are struggling in the stream of history and who are suffering—and inflicting—the labour and the wounds, it does not feel as if this travail is truly all for nothing. To believe that history has some significance and some purpose may be an unverifiable act of faith, but at any rate this is, for a participant, less difficult to believe than it is to believe that history is senseless.

The thesis that God is Alpha and Omega does not merely involve a conception of the Universe that is incredible; the thesis itself is un-verifiable. It is not founded on any data of human experience; it is an unwarranted concession to a deep and insistent craving of the human heart. The heart longs to be given its bearings in the mysteri-ous and formidable Universe in which it finds itself; and the higher religions have responded to this longing by issuing what purport to be authoritative and precise directions. The Judaic religions claim to be able to tell us just where we stand in the no-man's-land between the first year of the World and the last; the Buddha claims to be able to tell us just what we have to do in order to make our exit into Nirvâna. These unverified and unverifiable claims obtain our assent because we are eager to give it. This eagerness is a natural reaction to our awkward human condition. None the less, our deliberate credulity is an infirmity that we ought to resist. It is better to recog-nize frankly that we cannot know the unknowable. It is a mistake—and this a moral as well as an intellectual one—to take on trust, from an *ipse dixit*, confident answers to fundamental questions that human minds find themselves unable to answer for themselves, even by the utmost exertion of their inborn intellectual powers.

In reaction against the doctrine of the Judaic religions, there is a present-day school of thought which maintains, in the name of science, that the spirit which these religions identify with both

Alpha and Omega is, in reality, 'nothing but' Alpha alone, thinly disguised. The assumption underlying this counter-thesis is that, if you have succeeded in tracing the successive stages of a growth-process back to its original germ, you have exposed the process as being an illusion. The germ from which the process started is the sole reality that survives the test of your analysis. The successive stages of growth, through which the germ 'evolves', are, on this theory, 'epiphenomena' which science strips off, as a skilful picture-cleaner removes, layer by layer, the over-paintings that conceal the original work of the old master. On this view the word 'evolution' is to be taken literally. Growth is 'nothing but' the unrolling of the primal germ's package.

The fallacy in this view is that it fails to distinguish between logic and experience. Growth, by its very nature, is difficult, perhaps impossible, to express in conceptual terms, since the intellect's terms are static, whereas growth is movement and change. Yet, though growth may be illogical, growth is nevertheless a datum of experience; and, when logic conflicts with experience, it is logic that must give way. The thesis that the spirit is 'nothing but' Alpha is no more acceptable than the thesis that it is Alpha and is Omega too.

Then is the spirit perhaps exclusively Omega? Is it neither the beginning nor the beginning plus the end, but the end alone? This view, too, is unconvincing. The spirit is at work here and now; and to have arrived already at a point which has not yet been reached is surely no more possible than it is to be still standing at a point that has already been left behind.

By a process of exhaustion, we are led to adopt the only view now left open. We seem bound to conclude that the spirit is not either the beginning or the end of the Universe's history, and is not the beginning and the end of it rolled into one, but is in the movement itself.

If this location of the spirit in the stream in which we find ourselves travelling hits the truth, this means that a human being's ordeal is indeed a formidable one; for the Buddha has certainly hit the truth in equating life with pain, and, in this, Saint Paul agrees with him. 'We know that the whole creation groaneth and travaileth in pain together until now.'[1] If, in truth, this travail is the ultimate reality, can we bear it? We can, 'for we are saved by hope'.[2]

[1] Rom. viii. 22.   [2] Rom. viii. 24.

Hope on what ground? We should be deluding ourselves if we were to hope that the eventual outcome of the Universe's travail will prove to have been pre-determined, and that the scales have been weighted decisively in favour of a final victory for love and right-eousness over self-centredness and sin. We have no evidence for the truth of this consoling supposition. Our hope lies in our recognition that love and righteousness have an absolute spiritual value and therefore an absolute claim on our allegiance, whatever their pros-pects may be. We cannot silence their call, even when we refuse to follow it, or even if we believe that it is a call to volunteer on a forlorn hope. Love and righteousness set us an aim that we cannot repudiate; and, if we cannot, and if the Universe is all of a piece, we must conclude that love and righteousness set an irreversible aim for the Universe as a whole.

Here surely we have good ground for hope. Our situation is hopeful because the movement in which we are implicated is not aimless. Its prospects are uncertain and it is fraught with pain and travail, but its cost is worth while; for, at this cost, love and right-eousness are able to strive for victory. To strive on their side is a cause to which a human being can dedicate himself not only hopefully but joyfully, even if the cost for him proves to be utter self-sacrifice. In the cause of love and righteousness, life itself is expendable.

(xii) LOVE AT ALL COSTS IS AN END IN ITSELF

The consequence of unreservedly following love's lead may be crucifixion, and this may be the end of life; there may be no resur-rection. If we do not believe that Jesus, after dying on the Cross, came to life again in truth, does our disbelief in his resurrection rob the idea of resurrection of the joy and hope that has been associated with it in Christendom ever since the first Easter Day? Does our dis-belief condemn the very word resurrection to suffer disrepute as the dying name of an hallucination or a hoax? These questions were pressing themselves upon me during the last hours of Easter Satur-day night, 1966, while I was taking part in a service in the Menelik Memorial Church at Addis Ababa in Ethiopia. Though it was not yet midnight, the celebration of Jesus's resurrection in the Coptic pre-Chalcedonian liturgy was rising towards its climax. The ques-tions were thrust upon me by the joyfulness of the singing of the two choirs. The joy was less inhibited than in the corresponding celebrations in a Western church. This Ethiopian Christian joy was overflowing into merriment—as it ought to be if the resurrection that is celebrated at Easter throughout Christendom is an authentic fact. But is it authentic? And, if it is not, is not this merry Ethiopian Christian praise of God evoked by a pathetic, and indeed tragic, misunderstanding?

For those singers, Christ's resurrection was, no doubt, an unquestionable historical fact, but they were also celebrating it as an event of cosmic significance. They were, I was told, praising God for his goodness in making all things new as a consequence of Christ's rising from the dead. For my Ethiopian fellow-worshippers, the resurrection was a symbolic as well as an historical event; and, for six or seven thousand years before the first Easter Day, it had already been a symbolic event for the worshippers of the dying and rising god of the annual crops that homo agricola had been raising from his fields. 'Except the seed die . . .' I, too, believe in the reality of the resurrection in this symbolic sense, and, in this sense of it, I feel, to the full, the joy and the hope that the word inspires. Jesus did rise from the dead spiritually, though not physically. He came to life again in the souls of his disciples and in the spiritual impetus that launched the Christian Church on its still continuing career. But the resurrection has a cosmic meaning that transcends Christianity and transcends the re-birth of vegetational life at the annual return of the spring of the year. The resurrection symbolizes love's perpetually renewed endeavour to transfigure the Universe by converting all things to live and move and have their being in love's divine spirit. We do not foreknow, and we may guess that love itself does not foreknow, what the outcome of love's striving is going to be; but, knowing love, as we do, from a direct experience of it, we know that love, so long as it lives, will never cease to strive to transfigure the Universe into its own likeness. We know this because we know that this is intrinsic to love's nature.

A Greek bucolic poet has drawn a poignant contrast between the triumphant annual resurrection of humble flowers and the irrevocable death of us mighty and gifted human beings. This contrast is a genuine one on the plane of natural history, but on the plane of the spirit it is overcome. Love cannot save a human being from suffering death; but love needs no resurrection of the life that has been laid down, since self-sacrifice for the sake of love is an end in itself. Absolute love is absolute goodness, and this is self-sufficing. It is what it is, whether or not it is also omnipotent. Love gives life a purpose and meaning and value that cannot be found, in human life at any rate, so long as this is lived for its own sake. The absolute value of love makes life worth while, and so makes Man's strange and difficult situation acceptable. Love cannot save life from death; but it can fulfil life's purpose; and, in so far as life's purpose has been fulfilled, its fulfilment cannot be undone by death when death puts an end to life itself. In this sense, love is stronger than death. Death is not all-powerful, any more than love is. Death has the last word only if love is renounced, for then—but only then—life is stripped of the purpose, meaning, and value over which death has no power. If we follow love's lead at all costs, love will draw death's sting; for then 'the peace of God, which passeth all understanding' will 'keep' our 'hearts and minds',[1] even when death, or—worse than death— bereavement, is staring us in the face.

CHAPTER 9, ANNEX I: A DISCORD IN THE LORD'S PRAYER

In the Lord's Prayer we find, co-existing, two conceptions of the nature of God which are not only distinct from each other but are surely irreconcilable.

In one of these conceptions—historically, the younger of the two —God is identified with love, as he is in the First Epistle General of Saint John. We ask him to 'forgive us our trespasses as we forgive them that trespass against us' because we recognize that he is striving to extend the reign of love, and we feel a call to co-operate with him in his loving endeavour to transfigure the Universe into his own likeness. At the same time we also recognize that the Universe is recalcitrant to love's struggle to redeem it. 'Thy kingdom come, thy will be done on Earth.' In making this petition, we are acknow- ledging that, in the world in which we find ourselves, God, like us human beings, is not master of the situation. He is struggling to master it, as we are.

[1] Phil. iv. 7.

In the second of the Lord's Prayer's two irreconcilable conceptions of the nature of God, God is held to be omnipotent. His kingdom *is* established and his will *is* done in Heaven. This omnipotent God of the Lord's Prayer is no longer God the tyrant—the dominant aspect of Yahweh in the pre-prophetic books of the Old Testament. He is God the Father—an aspect of the Canaanite high god El which may also have been present, though subordinate, in the primordial Israelite vision of Yahweh. If Yahweh is, after all, our heavenly father, we can trust him, as a child would trust its human father, to provide us, day by day, with the means of life for the day ahead. So far, the omnipotent god is pictured as being benevolent and beneficent—as being, in fact, love with omnipotence added. But the addition of omnipotence makes it impossible for the role of benevolence to be sustained, for an omnipotent god is responsible for everything that is and has been and shall be. He is responsible for all that is evil, as well as for all that is good, since he is the creator of the Universe and the director of it. A god who is the omnipotent creator and director of this ailing Universe must also be the devil; and, in the last petition in the Lord's Prayer, he is addressed as the devil implicitly.

'Lead us not into temptation, but deliver us from evil.' Anyone who has been brought up in the Christian tradition will have become, since early childhood, so familiar with every word of the Lord's Prayer that he will have become insensible—if he ever was sensitive at all—to the startlingness, and indeed shockingness, of the final petition. Here God is addressed as the tempter who leads us astray but also, being omnipotent, can deliver us, if he chooses, from the evil with which he himself has afflicted us. The arch-temptation for a living creature is the one that is inherent in being alive. It is the temptation to try to make oneself into the centre and the *raison d'être* of the Universe, and consequently to exploit the Universe for one's own selfish purposes.

If anyone were to read this final petition in the Lord's Prayer out of context, without having been acquainted with it before, and were to be asked to try to identify its origin, he would probably guess that it was a passage in some Hindu prayer to Shiva. One of Hinduism's intellectual assets is its clearsightedness in recognizing, and its honesty in admitting, that, if God is omnipotent, he must be the author of evil, since he is the author of all things. He cannot be *both* good *and* omnipotent. These are mutually exclusive alternative views of God's nature. We have to choose between them, and this is a choice that the Judaic religions have been reluctant to make. In this final passage of the Lord's Prayer, God's omnipotence is vindicated by acknowledging him openly to be the author of evil. In the scriptures of the Judaic religions, this Hindu-like clarity of vision is rare.

CHAPTER 9, ANNEX II: AGNOSTICISM: FOR PARENTS A
PROBLEM, FOR CHILDREN A PUZZLE

An agnostic is under a moral obligation to have the courage of his negative convictions; a betrayal of these would be, for him, a betrayal of mankind's future, and this truth confronts him with another truth. The agnostic has arrived at his outlook by himself and for himself, yet, all the time, he has to live in society; for no human being—not even a hermit in the desert—can contract out of being a social creature; sociality is a built-in feature of human nature. The agnostic's very concern for the future binds him to fellow human beings who will be alive after he himself is dead. It binds him, in the first place, to his children, and, through them, to his grandchildren and his grandchildren's grandchildren. To bring up one's children is perhaps the most important single one of a human being's jobs in life. When the parents are agnostics, how will the children fare?

Children have to find their way about in the world into which they have been born. They have to find it quickly, and they naturally expect that their parents will give them the necessary information. All human beings, at all stages of life, hanker after a chart of the Universe that will be clear, precise, and comprehensive. Children take it for granted that a chart of this reassuring kind is in their parents' possession; and, if this expectation is disappointed, they are likely to be bewildered, perturbed, and aggrieved. Children 'programme' their questions to their parents in the binary form in which we interrogate computers: Yes or no? True or false? Right or wrong? They expect to be given answers, in these terms of binary arithmetic, not only to the practical questions of everyday life, but also to questions about ultimate reality. The dogmas of our ancestral religions offer reassuringly confident answers to 'binary' questions in this transcendental field too. An agnostic finds these answers unsatisfying and unacceptable because he judges that they are unverified and unverifiable. Rather than sacrifice his honest-mindedness, he has chosen to sacrifice his psychological sense of security. This, however, has been a personal choice, made by himself for himself. Has he a right to make this choice for his children too? And, supposing that he does, will his children be willing to accept this at his hands? Will they not feel that he is offering them a stone for bread? Will he not feel this himself?

Thus the agnostic, in his relations with his children, finds himself faced with a problem that does not arise for an unquestioningly orthodox adherent of a traditional religion. The agnostic cannot evade this problem, and his children cannot escape it. It is, indeed, a problem that besets human beings even in an age of uncritical faith; for the most comprehensively and didactically dogmatic system of theology cannot keep a human being permanently blind to the truth about our human condition; and the truth about it is that we are born into a mysterious universe, and that the mystery of it raises questions which human beings cannot forbear to ask but also cannot reasonably hope to be able to answer. This is the common human lot; and children cannot be exempted from it, since they, like their elders, are human. Kindly-meant attempts to shield a child from the impact of this experience are bound to defeat their purpose; for, the longer that a knowledge of life is artificially withheld from it, the sharper and harsher will be the shock when the artificial screen gives way to the pressure of reality, as it is bound to give way sooner or later.

If this is the truth, an agnostic parent would not be doing his children a good service if, for their sake, he were to betray his own honesty of mind. He would be wronging his children, as well as himself, if he were to give them answers in which he himself does not believe.

An honest-minded and courageous-minded agnostic's children will discover, at an early age, that, on questions about ultimate reality, and on many lesser questions too, there is no unanimity in the society into which the child has been born. Honest agnostic parents will not keep their children ignorant of the doctrines of the historic religion that looms so large in the social background that the parents and the children have in common. An agnostic's children should be brought up to be familiar with the religious beliefs and institutions with which the parent has parted company, as well as with the parent's own personal outlook. The purpose of education is to equip a child to begin to act as its own educator at the earliest possible age. The adult generation's duty towards the rising generation is to give it the moral and intellectual tools for doing the job of thinking and choosing for itself when it eventually comes of age— in so far as any human being ever does reach an age of discretion.

Mankind is groping its way, and always has been groping since before it became human. The break-through into consciousness has been mankind's greatest achievement in groping so far. Groping is a painful and alarming exercise, but it is mankind's specific lot and distinctive hope. Every human child that is born into the World has to shoulder its share of our race's special burden.

CHAPTER 9, ANNEX III: THE EFFICACY OF PRAYER TO A GOD WHO IS NOT BELIEVED TO BE OMNIPOTENT

Is it possible for a human being to pray to a god whose power he believes to be limited, as his own human power is? Prayer is one of our indispensable spiritual needs. It is a response to the ordeal of our human condition—to the uncertainties, the misfits, and the agonies with which we have to contend. We are conscious that our unaided spiritual powers are inadequate. Prayer is an appeal for help; and, in appealing for help, the suppliant is assuming that the potential helper to whom he is turning is stronger than the suppliant himself is. Can we turn to God for help with conviction if we do not believe that God's power to help us is unlimited?

The answer to this question surely is that we are also constantly asking for help, and are constantly receiving it, from our fellow human beings; and our recognition of the obvious truth that our human helpers are not omnipotent does not deter us from seeking their help, nor do the limitations of their power debar them from being able to help us effectively. Why, then, should we not look for help to a non-omnipotent god? and why should we not find in him the help that we are seeking? What we need to be sure of in a god to whom we turn in prayer is, not that he is all-powerful, but that he is all-good; for goodness is the only legitimate objective of prayer.

Power will, of course, be an important attribute of God for us if what we are praying to God for is some favour for ourselves. The greater God's power, the greater his scope for granting favours, if he chooses, to human applicants. An omnipotent god would have it in his power to grant favours that are far beyond the reach of human endeavours. Favours, however, are not the right things to pray for. In praying for them, one is praying to have the demands of self-centredness fulfilled beyond the limits within which they can be met by unaided human action. It is human to pray for favours; but, when we have prayed such prayers, our conscience counsels us to cancel them. The Gospel relates that when Jesus, in his agony in Gethsemane, had prayed 'O my Father, if it be possible, let this cup pass from me', he immediately went on to pray 'Nevertheless, not as I will, but as thou wilt'.[1]

What we ought to pray for is an increase and strengthening of spiritual dedication and endeavour—in oneself, in all creation, and in God—to help love and righteousness to prevail. If any self-regarding prayer is legitimate, this would be a prayer for closer communion with God, for more abundant grace to do his will, and for a chance of participating in his work in the infinitesimal degree that is within the compass of a human being's spiritual capacity. A god who is all-loving but not all-powerful will not spurn a human being's puny aid.

CHAPTER 9, ANNEX IV: THE UNAVOIDABLENESS AND INADEQUACY OF ANTHROPOMORPHISM

A prayer is addressed by a person to a person. This is obvious when a call for help is directed towards a fellow human being; and, when we are calling for human help, we have a palpable confrontation with the person to whom we are appealing. Prayer to God is addressed to a person by analogy; and this divine person's likeness

[1] Matt. xxvi. 39.

to a human person will appear to be closer if we do not hold that the god to whom we are praying is omnipotent.

In seeking to enter into communication with God, we are bound to imagine God in our own human image; we have nothing in our human experience that is a more adequate model for picturing God to ourselves; yet the inadequacy of this human model is glaring. The only persons with whom we are acquainted by direct experience are mortal human beings that have physical bodies as well as conscious minds and wills capable of making choices. Yet the practice of prayer implies a belief that, in or behind or beyond the Universe, there is a non-physical non-human being—or a pantheon of non-human beings—possessing personality in the human sense of the term, and this in a form like enough to the human form of personality to make communication feasible between us and him or her or them.

Within the Universe itself, if the Universe is all of a piece, and if it is also virtually infinite in extent, it is probable that, in other galaxies, there are innumerable other planets that are habitable, and are in fact inhabited, by living creatures of like passions with our human selves. If, however, this were to become a matter of verified scientific knowledge, it would not be relevant to the question of the nature of the gods or God to whom we human beings pray. Supposing that we were to succeed in establishing communication with these hypothetical anthropoid fellow living creatures of ours, and supposing that we were to appeal to them for help, this appeal would be analogous to our appeals for help to each other; it would not be analogous to our prayers for divine aid.

Indeed our picture of the gods or God has no analogy in our picture of the hypothetical anthropoid inhabitants of 'other worlds'. Our picture of these is modelled consistently on our knowledge of ourselves. We picture them as being, like ourselves, psychosomatic, non-omnipotent, and presumably also mortal. On the other hand, in picturing to ourselves the gods or God to whom we pray, we imagine a *Mischwesen* which combines some of our human traits with other traits that we have never met with, in our experience, in any living creature, human or not. We picture our gods as being human, like persons; yet at the same time we imagine them as being non-corporeal or, if corporeal, fashioned of no human clay. We also imagine them to be immortal, and to possess super-human power. If we are monotheists we imagine God to be omnipotent; if we are polytheists, we imagine the power of each of the gods to be limited, like the power of a human local sovereign, only by the rival power of the potentate's peers. In fact, we imagine the gods or God to be persons who are like ourselves in some aspects, but who are at the same time super-human, non-human, and sub-human in other aspects: super-human in power; non-human in not being incarnate in human bodies; sub-human in using their super-human powers to indulge, if they choose, in super-human crimes and follies. This is the Greek and Indian picture of the gods of the Indo-European pantheon, and it is also the Israelites' picture of Yahweh in the pre-prophetic books of the Old Testament.

On reflection, this picture of godhead is found to be so shocking morally that it has been rejected by human beings who have had the wits to criticize it and the courage to accept and declare their intellects' verdict. The Greek philosophers made the Homeric Zeus respectable by reducing him to being a barely personal 'first cause'; the eighteenth-century Western deists 'processed' Yahweh on the same lines. They recognized the intellectual untenability of the Israelite prophets' and the Christian Church's compromise, in which Yahweh had been transfigured from tyrant into father without being relieved of his omnipotence or being debarred from displaying it in arbitrary breaches of his own laws.

However, even a complete expurgation of the morally unedifying and unacceptable features of the supra-human image of the gods or God would not remove the root of the difficulty that this conception presents. The radical difficulty is that the picture combines elements which we do not find combined anywhere in our experience, while some of these incongruous elements are not only outside our experience but are incompatible with it.

This point may be illustrated by dissecting the traditional picture of an angel. Here we have an imaginary creature which, like a centaur, is portrayed as being a mammalian vertebrate with an insect's six limbs instead of a vertebrate's four. In the case of the centaur, we recognize that the addition of this extra pair of limbs makes a monster which, as Lucretius points out,[1] never has existed,

---

[1] In *De Rerum Naturâ*, Book V, lines 878–81.

and never could exist, in real life. An angel would look equally monstrous if ex-Christian eyes could divest an angel of his trailing clouds of glory.

Thus, if we open our eyes and look the truth in the face, we find ourselves unable to think of God or the gods to whom we pray as being a super-human personality or personalities. Super-human turns out to mean non-human and even sub-human. In our search for an image of the divine, we are now thrown back on human nature as we know it in our fellow mortal psychosomatic human beings on this planet. The spiritually highest human beings whom we know at first or second hand are the saints. At the western end of the Oikoumenê, we think of Socrates, Jesus, Francis of Assisi. In the saints, human personality rises to a spiritual height at which it towers above the level of the average human being. Can we find in these saintly human beings the divinity that we are seeking? We can and do turn to saints for inspiration, help, and guidance. Yet, if we ask ourselves whether we believe that human nature, even at the rare height of sainthood, is the spiritually highest presence in the Universe, we find this notion too ludicrous to be credible.

The saints, like the rest of us, are human, and our knowledge of human nature, in ourselves and in our neighbours, makes it absurd to see, in this, even at its highest, the Universe's spiritual pinnacle. It is significant that the saints are, of all people, the most painfully conscious of being miserable sinners. Their performance is, of course, vastly better than ours is; but their standards of performance are disproportionately higher than ours are; and the saints' low estimate of human nature in themselves is evidently nearer the truth than our relative self-complacency is. Human spiritual ideals—as represented, at their highest, in the aspirations of the saints—look like an indication that, in and beyond the Universe, there is a spiritual presence that, potentially at least, is spiritually far higher than Man's highest spiritual reach.

This conclusion is supported by Christian theology. Jesus's followers were so dazed by this man's spiritual sublimity that they fell to worshipping him as a god; but, when they had deified him, they found that they could no longer think of him as being no more than a human being, spiritually exalted though this saintly human being was. Jesus's manhood, being manhood, was not sufficient to contain his apparent godhead. For his worshippers, a god who was nothing but human was not enough. Their wish to worship him constrained them to see in him a man in whom a transcendent god had made himself incarnate.

How are we to picture to ourselves a god who is spiritually higher than the highest human spiritual flights, yet is at the same time, in one of his aspects, a person like enough to a human person for communication, person to person, to be possible between God and a human being? I find this incomprehensible intellectually. The nearest that I have come to understanding the mystery has been in two experiences that were not acts of thought but that felt as if they were flashes of insight or revelation. Each experience came to me at a moment of very great spiritual stress. The earlier one came when I was in a moral conflict between the better and the worse side of myself, and this at a moment when the better side was fighting with its back to the wall.[1] The second experience came at the moment of the death—a tragic death—of a fellow human being with whose life mine was intimately bound up. On the first occasion it felt as if a transcendent spiritual presence, standing for righteousness beyond my reach, had come down to my rescue and had given to my inadequate human righteousness the aid without which it could not have won its desperate battle. On the second occasion it felt as if the same transcendent spiritual presence, standing for love beyond my, or my dying fellow human being's, capacity, had pulled aside, at that awful moment, the veil that ordinarily makes us unaware of God's perpetual closeness to us. God had revealed himself for an instant to give an unmistakable assurance of his mercy and forgiveness.

Evidently these two experiences are open to more than one interpretation, and there is no possible objective test for deciding, convincingly to all minds, which of the alternative interpretations hits the truth. The visual images that these non-visual experiences have left in my mind are manifestly derived from traditional Christian mythology. In the first image of the two, God makes his epiphany in the guise of Saint George; in the second he makes it in the likeness of Michelangelo's vision of the Creator giving life to Adam. A rationalist might suggest that, in the first image, I was externalizing what was in reality a wholly internal psychic conflict, and that, in the

[1] This experience is described in Part III, section 6.

second image, I was consoling myself with a fallacious assurance of the fulfilment of a wish that I could not bear to see disappointed. I cannot disprove these demythologizations; I cannot give a different explanation of my experiences that is cogent, even to myself. All that I can say is that, in these experiences, I have come the nearest that I have ever come, so far, to what has felt to me like an immediate encounter with the godhead to whom our human prayers are addressed.

Human beings who have exercised their human spiritual faculties to the highest degree report to us that prayer, as commonly practised, is not the only or the ultimate form of communion between a human being and the spiritual presence behind the Universe that is higher than we are. When prayer—the communion between human person and divine person—has been raised to its highest degree of spiritual intensity, it is transmuted into another kind of experience. At this higher spiritual level, personality is transcended, and, with it, the separateness that is personality's limitation. At this supra-personal spiritual height, the experience is unitive. At this height, God and man do not commune with each other because, at this height, they are identical. 'Tat tvam asi' ('Thou art that'). The supra-personal ground of a human being's existence is the supra-personal ground of ultimate spiritual reality. At this height, personality is left behind, and, with it, the perhaps insoluble puzzle of divine personality.

It looks as if divine nature—and human nature too—has a number of different facets, of which personality is only one. In divine nature at any rate, the number of the facets may be infinite. Out of this possible infinity, three facets are included in the Christian presentation of the godhead as being a trinity.

To polytheists, Christianity looks like bleak monotheism; to Joachim of Fiore it looked like an allegory of the history of mankind's progress towards spiritual enlightenment; and surely Joachim was right. God the Father represents the conception of God as being a super-human personality. The tyrant has been expurgated; only the father has been left; yet, in the first person of the Christian trinity, God the super-human personality is still recognizable. God the son represents the conception of God as being a human personality of the highest human spiritual height; but, in the second person of the trinity, the humanity of Jesus has not survived unscathed. The Crucifixion symbolizes absolute self-sacrifice for the sake of love. Life is the utmost that a human being can give, and, when he gives it, the gift is irrevocable. For a human being, there is not, within our human experience, any possibility of a resurrection after death, not to speak of an ascension into another world that is free from all the ills of this world. In capping the Crucifixion with the Resurrection and the Ascension, the Christian creed has given Jesus's self-sacrificing death an anticlimax, and has tampered with his humanity in a way that diminishes his spiritual stature instead of enhancing it. Nevertheless, in the second person of the trinity, God the saintly human personality is still recognizable. In the third person of the trinity, we meet the supra-personal spirit that is identical in God and Man; and at this level the separateness of God and Man is overcome. So, too, is anthropomorphism; for, although the indwelling spirit is found in human nature, it is not man-bound; it is found in divine nature too, and in God and Man this spirit is one and the same.

PART II

Human Affairs in my Lifetime
(1889–)

THE BALANCE-SHEET AS I READ IT

1 : Human Affairs and Human Nature

ON the day, 12 January 1968, on which I started out to write the present part of this book, I was only just over three months short of having reached the age of seventy-nine, so my life had already been a long one, measured by the average expectation of length of life even in countries in which this average term has recently been extended by an amazing advance in medical science. This extension of the length of a human lifetime in part of the World has co-incided in date with a speeding-up, all over the World, of the pace of change in human affairs. The pace has been accelerating constantly since the earliest date from which any record of human affairs has survived. But in my generation this acceleration has reached a degree at which the change in the state of human affairs within the span of eighty years, dating back from the present year 1969, is not only great enough to be perceptible but is so great as to be very striking for anyone who has lived, as I have, to witness it.

'Human affairs' have to be distinguished from 'human nature'. Of course I have not lived to see any change in human nature, and I should not live to see any if I were to live as long a life as is attributed to the longest-lived of the mythical personages in the genealogies in the Book of Genesis. No doubt the nature of our authentic ancestors has changed in the past. The process by which our pre-human ancestors became human—became, that is to say, possessed of consciousness and will—was a profound change. It was of an order of magnitude which makes the most rapid and revolu-tionary of the subsequent changes in human affairs look insignificant. There is, however, no evidence that human nature has ever changed since the time at which it took a recognizably human shape. It may, for all we know, be continuing to change, but this at so slow a rate that the change is imperceptible, not merely within the span of the longest single lifetime, but also within the span of the whole period of recorded human history. On the other hand it is also possible that human nature has been static ever since it came into existence. Some of the species of living creatures that are believed to be the oldest—immeasurably older than mankind—are still in existence, yet appear, from the evidence of fossils, to have assumed at the start the form in which they exist today; so human nature, too, may have been static during the much shorter period for which mankind has been in existence so far.

If mankind were like in all respects to the rest of life on this planet, human affairs could change no faster than human nature, and, if it is true that human nature is static or virtually static, human affairs would have been static too. Most other species of living creatures known to us appear to propagate their ways of living and behaving, as well as their psychosomatic organisms, almost entirely by physical procreation, and this reproduces the same pattern faithfully from generation to generation. The human psychosomatic organism is reproduced by the same physical mechanism, and this with the same exactitude. But the psychic facet of human nature seems to be unique in being not wholly subconscious. In Man the subconscious level of the psyche is overlaid by consciousness and will; this specifically and peculiarly human psychic endowment has enabled mankind to create a culture (in the psychic or spiritual meaning of the word); and culture is transmitted, not by physical procreation, but by education in the broadest sense.

Culture and education, unlike nature and procreation, are within the realm of consciousness and will; and consequently the trans-mission of culture by education is not automatic and is not exact. A human society's cultural heritage can be modified deliberately by the transmitting generation or by the receiving generation or by both in concert. Indeed culture, unlike nature, is so flexible, unstable, and labile that, even if the transmitting and receiving generations conspire to preserve a society's culture unchanged, it will change in the process of transmission, in spite of their unanimous endeavour to keep it static.

A language, for example, will change in the course of trans-mission from one generation to another, even if each successive generation attempts, in its turn, to keep this language 'frozen' in some antique form that has come to be regarded as being 'classical', i.e. sacrosanct. A people that has been trying to preserve Sanskrit will eventually find itself speaking some kind of prakrit; a people that has been trying to preserve Latin will find itself speaking some kind of romance vernacular. Indeed, it is just as impossible for mankind to keep its culture static as it is for it (or for any other species of life) to change its nature. Man is no more able to 'freeze' his language or any of the other elements of his culture—e.g. institutions, ideas, ideals—than he is able to add a cubit to his stature or to change the colour of his skin. Phenomena in the realm of culture—phenomena which, being cultural, are perpetually on the move at various velocities—are what I am labelling 'human affairs' in this book.

Since Man is a social animal, human affairs are social affairs; since human beings are creatures endowed with consciousness and will, and since many of the more important of the choices made by a human will must affect the lives of other human beings, human beings necessarily pass moral judgements on each other's conduct. Indeed, we each pass judgement, not only on other people's acts, but on our own. Every human being is admonished by an inner voice, his conscience, to which he can turn a deaf ear but which he is not able to silence. Each of us is in some measure responsible, personally and individually, for the sum total of the social consequences of his and his contemporaries' acts; and, in my lifetime, this responsibility has come to extend beyond the limits of the individual's family and of his political and religious community to the whole living generation of mankind, since 'the annihilation of distance' through the progress of technology has now knit all mankind together, for weal or for woe, into a single world-wide society.

Every observer of contemporary human affairs is also a participant in them and is therefore involved in them morally. Indeed, each of us is involved morally in all human affairs that are within our knowledge, including those that were already accomplished facts before the observer-participant had been born and had then arrived at the age at which he had become a responsible member of society. This moral involvement makes it impossible to observe human affairs with the morally and emotionally neutral curiosity with which a scientist observes non-human nature or in the purely utilitarian spirit in which a technologist studies inanimate nature with an eye to making it serve human purposes, good or evil.

This moral involvement makes it impossible for the observer of human affairs to view these with scientific detachment and objectivity. This is true of every observer of human affairs, at whatever stage of his own life he may happen to be at the time when he is taking his observation (in the astronomer's and the navigator's usage of the phrase). At the same time, it is a well-known fact that the observer's own age does affect his judgement. It affects it, however vigilantly he may be on his guard against this age-bias. He can, and should, try to discount his age-bias for himself; but his hearers or readers would be wise not to leave this task of correction solely to him. In sizing-up his findings, they ought to do their own discounting of the observer's age-bias for themselves.

At the age at which someone has just attained an adult view of the World around him, his outlook is likely to be unduly sanguine. No doubt, he will be dissatisfied with the state in which the World has been handed down to him by his predecessors, especially those of his parents' generation. At the same time, he will feel confident that he can and will do better than they have done. The inadequacy of their performance was due, in their youthful successor's hasty judgement, to faults on their part that they need not have committed. The representative of the oncoming generation expects that he and his contemporaries will be able, at last, for the first time in history, to transform an imperfect heritage into an earthly paradise. The potency of the braking-effect of the accumulated mass of tradition, and the degree of the frustration to which this condemns any attempt to give a sharp new turn to the future, are depressing facts that are revealed only gradually by disillusioning experience.

Conversely, in old age a person's outlook is likely to be unduly pessimistic. It is difficult and painful to live in an unfamiliar world. In his youth a human being can afford to be critical of the world in which he has grown up because he takes its familiarity for granted. He will wish to make changes in it, will try to make them, and will be impatient at their slowness and be disappointed at their slightness. In old age, on the other hand, he will come to find that he is no longer running ahead of the World and failing to pull the World forward in his wake as fast and as far as he would like. On the contrary, he will now find the World forging ahead of himself—outstripping his own diminishing pace ever faster; and, as he drops farther and farther behind, the world in which he goes on living will become more and more unfamiliar.

This is one of the inevitable trials of old age in all times and places. It overtakes the old even in a phase in the history of a society in which the quantum of change in human affairs is at a minimum. In Wen-Amun's generation in the eleventh century B.C. the Egyptian culture seems to have been as nearly static as any human culture can be. Yet, if Wen-Amun lived to my age, even he will have felt, at least in some degree, the discomfort of living on into a partially unfamiliar world. My lot, in contrast to Wen-Amun's, happens to have been cast in a time and place in which the pace of change has been perhaps more rapid, and the amount of change perhaps greater, than it was in any previous time and other place from which we have any surviving records. Moreover, my personal temperament and intellectual constitution happen to be such as to put me still more out of tune than many of my contemporaries will have been put by the changes in human affairs that have been taking place in our time. In particular, I dislike machinery and am a duffer at handling it. (My distaste and my ineptitude interact to create a vicious circle.) Hence, for me particularly, but no doubt also for all my still living contemporaries to some extent, the world of the year 1969 is even more unfamiliar, and consequently more difficult and more unpleasant to live in, than the world normally is for people who have passed the age of eighty.

This increasing inability, in old age, to keep in step with a changing world produces another age-bias which has to be discounted, as youth's contrary age-bias has to be. Anything that is difficult and painful for a human being inevitably seems to him to be bad, and it may in truth be bad for him as an individual; but this individual experience of his is no evidence that the changes with which he is finding himself unable to cope are also bad for his juniors or are bad intrinsically.

Accordingly, all pessimistic judgements that I pass in this book ought to be scrutinized critically by myself and by my readers. They may be warranted; they may be confirmed by the verdict of posterity; and, if they are shared with me by people of my children's and my grandchildren's ages, this consensus between three generations will justify a presumption that these pessimistic judgements of mine do not fall very wide of the mark. At the same time, it is impossible for me, just by myself, to estimate how far my pessimism—in so far as I am now pessimistic—is truly justified and how far it has to be discounted as an illusory effect of the particular form that age-bias takes in the last phase of life.

Of course, this need to scrutinize, and perhaps rectify, pessimistic judgements of mine has its converse. My optimistic judgements may be accepted with some confidence as being likely to be valid. They will have been made by me in spite of my age-bias, not because of it, and this will be presumptive evidence that I have not made them without good cause.

2 : The Shattering of the Victorian Illusion of Stability

By the time when the First World War broke out in August 1914 I was over twenty-five years old, and for two years I had been earning my living in a professional job. (I had been a 'don' at Oxford.) Thus I can just remember the Victorian Age as a grown-up person and not merely as a child. I had already been eight years old at the time of the celebration of Queen Victoria's diamond jubilee in 1897—a celebration that had made a deep impression on children of that age. For the small minority of the World's population at that date who were British subjects of European race, the diamond jubilee had symbolized the climax of the Victorian Age. Few of them had realized at the time that this had also been the Victorian Age's ephemeral zenith.

The forebodings expressed by Kipling in the poem that he called *Recessional* were rare among Victorians of his time. On the face of it, Kipling was one of the most unlikely of all Englishmen of his generation to feel these forebodings. The intuition that moved Kipling to feel and write like this in 1897 is evidence of a vein of genius in him. Actually the outbreak of the South African War in

1899 marked the beginning of a rapid decline of the sun which, on Britain's Victorian day, had seemed, at the time of the Queen's diamond jubilee, to be standing still in the midst of Heaven, as it had once stood still there at the bidding of Joshua. The ensuing Edwardian Age was really the Victorian Age's twilight hour; but most of us who lived through it were not conscious of the fading of the light. For us, the light still seemed to be shining as brightly as ever until suddenly, in August 1914, 'the lamps' were 'going out all over Europe'. (These poignant words were uttered by Sir Edward Grey on 3 August 1914. He was a true prophet when he added: 'We shall not see them lit again in our lifetime.')

For a century ending in August 1914—a century that had opened with the British (and/or Prussian) victory at Waterloo—the World had looked stable, and life had felt secure, for the middle-class minority of the inhabitants of the United Kingdom. This was, at its largest, only a small minority, though it had risen to be a larger percentage of the total population than it was in any other country at the time or perhaps than it had been in any society at any time in the past. It was a minority, but it was large enough to constitute a self-contained society; and, if one's family's income and breeding were just high enough to qualify them for membership in this society—if, that is to say in Victorian language, they passed muster as being 'gentlefolk'—one's prospects in life were fantastically promising compared with those of any child in Britain in 1969.

A very considerable quota of the pre-1914 British middle class were 'people of independent means', or of partially independent means that had to be supplemented by some earnings if the family was to enjoy the material standard of living that it felt to be appropriate to its position in the social hierarchy. These 'independent means' had been inherited from parents or grandparents who had bequeathed them to their descendants after having accumulated them by earning them through hard work. The financial rewards of hard work had not, by then, been eroded by graduated rates of income-tax, and death-duties were a recent innovation.

The prevalence of 'independent means' in the Late-Victorian British middle class was a weakness in the life of the middle class itself and of the nation as a whole. Of course, some of the people who had inherited 'independent means' used these for doing work that was financially unremunerative but was socially and culturally valuable. In my childhood I saw something of these conscientious and public-spirited Late-Victorian British well-to-do people who had found their field in doing unpaid work for the Charity Organization Society, and in this connection, in which my knowledge is at first hand, I have something more to say, in later chapters of this book,[1] about the virtues of this minority and also about their limitations. All human beings have limitations of some sort. These voluntary British middle-class (and also aristocratic) hard-workers displayed some of the characteristic limitations of their class in their generation. Yet they were the salt of the Earth and were, incidentally, the authors of some of the best contributions that Victorian Britain made to the common cultural heritage of mankind. However, the natural human inclination is to shun work—or, at least to shun very hard work—if the possession of 'independent means' exempts one from the Pauline ruling 'that if any would not work, neither should he eat'.[2] For a human being who is not unusually ambitious or public-spirited or conscientious, 'independent means', like the damp variety of tropical climate, are inimical to leading a strenuous life, and already, before 1914, the United Kingdom was in no position to be able to afford to rest on its oars.

Already when my parents were children, Britain was losing the lucrative role, that had been hers for about a century by then, of being 'the workshop of the World'. The United States began to be a serious industrial competitor of Britain's after 1865, and Germany after 1871; and, by the time when I came to be conscious of human affairs beyond the narrow circle of my personal relations, British industry had begun to hear, at its back, 'Time's wingèd chariot hurrying near'. British industry had become disagreeably aware of German industry's competitive power, but its response to this challenge had been the wrong one.

British manufacturers ought to have been open-minded enough to face the truth that their German rivals' success was the reward of a combination of hard work with high intelligence. The Germans had been pioneers in the systematic application of science to technology. The right lesson for the British had been to study these new

[1] See Part II, chap. 5, pp. 297–300, and chap. 8 (v), pp. 335–40.
[2] 2 Thess. iii. 10.

and superior German methods and to adopt them. If the British had been alert and energetic enough to make this positive response, they might have been generous enough to admit that the Germans' success had been fairly earned and been well deserved, and to emulate it without grudging it. Unfortunately, the British manufacturers' response had been sulky and negative. Instead of countering German competition by harder work and greater efficiency on their own part, they had sought to parry it by inducing their own countrymen to pay for British industry's sluggishness. They were to buy dearer British goods in preference to cheaper German goods. British manufacturers had appealed to British nationalistic sentiment. They had procured the enactment of legislation requiring that the words 'made in Germany' must be stamped on German manufactures imported into Britain.

This British requirement had not been altogether indefensible, considering that the German people had not been simply solicited, but had been compelled, to subsidize the German manufacturers' skill and energy. German industry, and American industry too, had been built up within the shelter of a high tariff-wall which had given it an artificial advantage, in its home market, over competing British imports. The British people, for their part, could not have been persuaded at this date to abandon free trade. All the same, the branding of German imports into Britain had been offensive, and, by my time, it had also become double-edged. The quality of German goods had improved, while their prices had remained competitive. Consequently the words 'made in Germany', which had been intended to act as a political deterrent, had begun to serve as an economic incentive by coming to stand, instead, for a guarantee of excellence.

It was no wonder that the German response to the British response to German competition had been resentment sharpened by contempt. This unsatisfactory British response has to be reckoned as having been one of the contributory causes of the First World War, even if one holds that the principal causes were failings on the German people's part. Germany's sensational growth in wealth, population, and power since 1871 had turned the Germans' heads; Prussian militarism had captivated German hearts by its success, in Bismarck's deft, but steady and cautious, hands, in achieving the political unification of Germany which had opened the way for her subsequent economic advance; and, in a post-Bismarckian and un-Bismarckian mood, the German people eventually took, in 1914, the fatal step that was a moral crime as well as a gross error of political and military judgement. They sought to win by one single stroke of the sword the 'place in the sun' that, if they had kept the peace, they would have won before long by the fair and civilized means of effective economic competition—a means which, by 1914, had already demonstrated its efficacy.

I was born less than a year after the date (15 June 1888) of Kaiser Wilhelm II's accession, and one of my early memories is the concern that my parents showed when, time and again, the morning paper carried news of some provocative speech or action of 'this irresponsible young man's'. My parents were not wrong in their judgement of the Kaiser. At the same time, I doubt whether they realized that their own countrymen bore any share of the blame for the particular German hostility to Britain in which the general German arrogance and aggressiveness was now finding its principal vent.

My father had no links with the world of business. His father had been a doctor—the first ear, nose, and throat specialist in London— and his grandfather had been a farmer. When his father had died suddenly in the middle of a successful professional career (he had killed himself accidentally by experimenting on himself with anaesthetics), my father had been placed in a tea-importing firm, but he had been unable to bear the prospect of spending his working life on work that he would be doing, not for the sake of its minimal intrinsic value, but solely in order to earn the money that it would bring in. He had found work that was congenial to him by joining the salaried staff of the Charity Organization Society, a philanthropic organization whose revenue came from private subscriptions and whose salary-scale was low compared even to that of government service. By Late-Victorian British middle-class standards, my parents were poor, but, like other people of the same income-level and same social class, they were well enough off to be able to give their children the best education that was to be had in Britain at the time —though this only on two conditions: the children must have some intellectual ability and they must be willing to turn this to account by working hard. For an intellectually able child growing up in a family that was in this position, the knowledge that his future depended on his own efforts was a stimulus to endeavour.

In a previous chapter of this book I have already described my own experience of climbing, rung by rung, the Victorian middle-class English educational ladder. The climb was strenuous and pro-tracted; but, if, in the end, one had become, say, a scholar of Balliol College, Oxford, one's future in life was virtually assured, unless one were to throw it away wantonly by signal laziness or bad conduct. I have already mentioned[1] that the worst that could happen to any Balliol undergraduate before August 1914 was to win a place in the Indian Civil Service. Places in this public service, like scholarships at public schools and at Oxford and Cambridge colleges, were won by competitive examination, and the competition, in this case too, was severe; for the numerical strength of the Indian Civil Service under the British regime was astonishingly small for the administra-tion of a whole subcontinent. However, the intellectual standard required at Balliol even for 'commoners' was high enough to make the Balliol 'dons' feel reasonably confident that they could get a Balliol undergraduate into the Indian Civil Service, supposing that he had no more attractive prospect in view. Nothing less desirable than a career in the Indian Civil Service could be in store for a Balliol undergraduate before the First World War; and this was a singularly desirable fate for a boy of middle-class birth who had had to fight his way up the ladder of British higher education.

At that date the Indian Civil Service was a haven of security for a successful candidate for entry into it. When accepted, the entrant signed a contract with the Government of India which enabled him to forecast how he would find himself placed at every stage of the rest of his life, supposing that his performance in the I.C.S. came up to the average. He could now foresee that, at least at such and such an age, he would be able to afford to marry; and then, at a foresee-able later age, he and his family would retire to live at Cheltenham or Bedford on a pension that would be ample enough to provide for completing his children's education and then for maintaining his wife and himself in decent middle-class circumstances till their deaths. Of course, the Indian civil servant who distinguished him-self would end up, before retirement, as lieutenant-governor of a

---

[1] See p. 106.

province with a population of fifty million or seventy million souls.
The I.C.S. symbolized the fantastic security of middle-class life in
the United Kingdom in the Late-Victorian Age. This was the British
middle-class security that was shattered in August 1914.

I myself did not sit for the civil service examination. Before I had
taken my final examination at the University, I had been appointed
to a tutorial fellowship at my college. But by this time I had come
to understand the significance of the fact that a career in the I.C.S.
was virtually assured to any Balliol undergraduate who wanted it.
This had made me realize that I was a member of a social class in a
single country—my own—which was as greatly privileged as it was
small in numbers.

Officially any British subject was entitled to sit for the British civil
service examination, whatever might be his race and his birthplace
under the British flag. But the examination, which was for all
branches of the upper division of the civil service, including the
I.C.S., was held in London; the language in which it was conducted
was English; and Latin and Greek were among the subjects in which
the highest marks could be won. Thus an Indian British subject was
severely handicapped, and this not unintentionally, in competition
with a native of the United Kingdom. The Indian candidate must
not only be a match in intellectual prowess for his European competitors; his family must also be rich enough, not only to finance his
journey from India to London to sit for the examination there, but
also to give him a costly previous education on British lines, in order
to enable him to compete on equal terms. Moreover, if the Indian
candidate's family were Hindus, and were also of high caste, they
would be having to break a traditional religious tabu against travelling beyond the confines of India, and particularly against crossing
the sea.

The upper division of the civil service, 'home' and 'Indian' and
'colonial' and 'diplomatic' alike, was also inaccessible to any native
of the United Kingdom who was not in a position to obtain the
education, described above, that I had been so fortunate as to have
received. In other words, the upper division of the civil service was
inaccessible to the great majority of my fellow countrymen; and it
would have been inaccessible to me too if my parents' financial
resources had been slightly smaller than they were, and if I myself

had been slightly duller-witted and less industrious than I was. The diplomatic service was, in fact, inaccessible to me, since, at that date, one of the conditions required for admission to it was the possession of a 'private income' of £400 per annum, i.e. the amount of the annual income that my father was earning. I realized, in retrospect, that, if I had failed 'to make the grade', the openings for me would have been invidiously fewer and the ceiling above which I should have been unable to rise would have been invidiously lower.

I had, indeed, gradually come to perceive, at first dimly, but eventually acutely, that I had been born into a society in which the inequality in the distribution of power, wealth, and opportunity was extreme to the degree of being shockingly inequitable. As a child I had been distressed at seeing children of my own age ill-clad and, by the look of them, ill-fed. As an undergraduate I felt conscience-stricken when I met students of Ruskin College. This college for members of the industrial working class was at that date in Oxford but not of it. It was not yet a part of the University; the students had little access to the opportunities and amenities of university life. They would, I think, have felt less painfully frustrated and aggrieved if Ruskin College had been located, not in Oxford, but in, say, Warrington. I did have access to the University's amenities and opportunities; I had won this access only partly by my own ability and effort. The same ability and the same effort would not have won me the same reward if my family's income and social status had been, not 'middle-class', but 'working-class'. I was enjoying, as a privilege that I shared with a small minority of my fellow countrymen, an education of high value that ought to have been accessible to anyone with the capacity to profit by it—and a large section of the minority that was enjoying the privilege did not have this capacity; they were enjoying the privilege because their parents could afford to pay the whole financial cost and had therefore been able to send their sons to the university without the boys' having had to win scholarships.

The degree of the inequality in the distribution of a community's wealth between different sections of it can be gauged by the percentage of the population that is employed on the economically unproductive work of domestic service. By middle-class standards, my parents were poor, yet they always had a cook and a housemaid 'living in' and employed full-time. When I was born, they engaged a nurse for me in addition. In a previous chapter I have mentioned[1] that, when I reached the age of four, my father put it to my mother that my nurse was now a luxury that could be dispensed with, and that my mother persuaded my father to allow her to keep the nurse for one year longer on the understanding that my mother would earn the amount of the nurse's salary (£20 per annum) by writing a text-book. On my fifth birthday the nurse was dismissed and my mother took charge of me. I spent the next three years in close company with her, except when the housemaid was deputizing for her as part-time nursemaid, and these were blissful years for me. I not only loved my mother; I found her company intellectually fascinating. She had been a student at Newnham College, Cambridge, and had taken the history tripos with first-class honours. However, when the elder of my two sisters was born, I discovered, with a shock, that, though my mother loved me as much as I loved her, looking after me had been a tie for her (and perhaps also, I now guess, a social embarrassment for her) from which she was thankful to be relieved.

One consequence of the new baby was a new nurse, and I was now sent for walks with nurse, baby,[2] and perambulator instead of being taken for walks by my mother as before. I resented bitterly both the loss of my mother's company and my own demotion from living in congenial grown-up company back to the status of a child under a nurse's command. (At the age of five I had loved my own nanny and had wept when she had left.) When my second sister was born, the nurse was supplemented by a nursemaid. My parents could afford this now; for meanwhile my paternal grandmother had died and had left, to eight surviving children plus one surviving daughter-in-law, 'private means' bringing in £300 a year to each of them. This considerable fortune had been accumulated by my grandfather before his premature death.

Even after the First World War I myself enjoyed two servants at a minimum and sometimes three. My wife had some 'private means', yet, even so, I found myself under a severe financial strain in earning enough to cover both the servants' salaries and keep and

---

[1] See pp. 89–90.
[2] J. M. C. Toynbee, in 1969 Professor Emerita of Classical Archaeology at the University of Cambridge.

the fees for the education of my children at boarding-schools. In Britain during the inter-war period the percentage of the population that was employed in domestic service was still high. After the outbreak of the Second World War a young woman who was working with me in temporary government service told me that her grandmother (an aristocrat) had seventeen servants, and that, after the fall of France, the junior assistant scullery-maid had broken it to her employer that she felt it now to be her duty to leave domestic service in order to do war work. The girl's alert-mindedness and public spirit earned her a scolding from her antediluvian-minded 'mistress'. She was admonished that the most suitable war-work that she could do was to continue to serve in that station of life unto which it had pleased God to call her—and the house where this interview took place was in Kent, with the Battle of Britain on the point of starting just overhead and a German landing in prospect! Within a few weeks, all the seventeen servants in that household will have been compulsorily mobilized. I never heard how the unconscionable old lady reacted to this outrage, as it must have seemed to her. I suspect that she debited it to Socialism's account. The Labour Party was officially socialist, and it had now joined forces with the Conservative Party to form a war-time national government.

Stranger still, domestic service survived in Germany all through the Second World War. Hitler never mobilized Germany's womanpower, as Churchill and his colleagues mobilized Britain's. Hitler obviated, so he thought, the need for this inevitably unpopular move by subjecting the populations of countries temporarily conquered by Germany to forced labour. Throughout the War, Hitler underestimated the degree of the war-effort that Germany needed to make. After Japan had driven the United States into belligerency by her attack on the American fleet in Pearl Harbor, Japan and Germany were, of course, doomed to defeat in any case by Japan's insane act. Japan had wantonly thrown into the enemy scale of the balance the overwhelming weight of the United States' war-potential. Germany's only chance, if she still had any chance, would have lain in mobilizing her woman-power, as well as her man-power, as draconianly as Britain was mobilizing hers. Fortunately, Hitler was as blind to the realities as my war-time colleague's aristocratic English grandmother had been.

Of course it was not only the British aristocracy and middle class that were privileged before the year 1914. The same classes in the other Western countries on both sides of the Atlantic, and in Australia and New Zealand too, were privileged in an only slightly lesser degree. There were aristocrats in the United States as well as in Europe; Franklin Delano Roosevelt was one of these. Western industrial and agricultural labourers were also privileged by comparison with their counterparts in Asia, Africa, and those Latin American countries (they were a majority) in which the population was predominantly 'Indian' or Negro in blood. In these Latin American, Asian, and African indigent populations there was a handful of scandalously privileged people who were richer than all but a few Western grandees and millionaires. Latin American latifundarios and Indian rulers of 'native states' were rolling in money and were, for the most part, spending it extravagantly on luxuries for themselves and their families. The Sultan of Turkey's civil list was, I believe, larger than Victoria's, empress as well as queen though Victoria had become before her long reign was over.

Before 1914, this extreme privilege that was monopolized by a tiny minority of the World's population co-existed with a stability that seemed firmly grounded and was impressively widespread. These two aspects of the pre-1914 state of the World might have been expected to be incompatible with each other; yet they not only co-existed; they had co-existed in other societies over far longer periods of time. The most stable and longest-lived society so far had been the Egyptian; it had maintained itself for more than 3000 years. The next most stable and long-lived had been the Chinese, which was, and is, still a going concern. In both these societies the distribution of power, wealth, and opportunity had been still more unequal, and more inequitable, than it was in the Victorian world. The explanation is that, since the dawn of civilization about 5000 years ago, the exploited mass of mankind had been indoctrinated to be docile. 'As a sheep before her shearer' they had been 'dumb'.

Human nature itself, however, is not entirely docile; there is a vein of mulishness in human nature which asserts itself when people are oppressed and provoked beyond endurance. In human beings, discipline is not innate, as it is in the Prussian-like social insects. It has to be inculcated as a habit; but habits, unlike instincts, can be broken; and since 1914 the habit of docility has been broken all over the World. The Western 'working class' has become recalcitrant to earning its living by engaging in domestic service, and in industrial employment it is now chronically poised to go on strike. The non-Western majority of mankind has revolted successfully against being subject to Western rule; and it has been more drastic in deposing its native rulers, and in taxing its native plutocrats, than any Western colonial régime ever ventured to be. This has been, not a mutation in human nature, but merely the abandonment of a human habit that was probably not more than five thousand years old. This particular change of habit has had a revolutionary effect on the course of human affairs in my lifetime.

Before 1914, on the other hand, stability, not insurgency, was the salient feature in the social landscape, and this all over the World and in almost all fields of human activity. By August 1914 there had been forty-three years of relative political stability and peace which presented a striking and encouraging contrast to the immediately preceding turbulent years 1848–71. The World's political affairs were being managed (though this only precariously, as was proved in the event) by a few men in power in London, Berlin, Paris, Vienna, Rome, St. Petersburg, Washington, D.C., and Tokyo. The potentates in Washington and Tokyo took a hand in the game of international politics only when moves were made that affected the regions within which they then saw the limits of their own interests. The World's financial affairs were being managed (perhaps less precariously) by a few men in power in London, Paris, and New York.

I myself benefited by the World's temporary financial stability when I went abroad, for the second time, in 1911–12. I spent ten months of those two years in Italy and Greece; and, from the moment at which I landed at Calais till the moment at which I embarked at the Peiraeus ten months later, I was within the domain of 'the Latin monetary union'[1] all the time except for one brief excursion to Turkey, where, by contrast, the local currency was as unstable and erratic as I found it to be in China in 1929. British, French, and American gold coins were accepted all over the World at a stable rate of exchange in every country. In Britain, before the withdrawal of gold coins from circulation upon the outbreak of the

[1] See p. 26.

First World War, the only paper money that one ever saw was a five-pound note.

Moreover, freedom of travel, and the law and order without which this freedom would have been hazardous to use, prevailed in 1911–12 over the greater part of the Earth's surface. This wide extension of law and order was of recent date, and it had been brought about by the rapid expansion of the dominions of Western powers over non-Western countries. Except for the upper basin of the Nile, which had been occupied in and after 1820, and had then been lost in the eighteen-eighties, by the Turkish Viceroy of Egypt, Muhammad 'Ali, and his successors, the occupation of the interior of Africa by five European states—Britain, France, Germany, Portugal, and Italy—had been begun in the eighteen-eighties and had been virtually completed before the end of the nineteenth century. In the course of that century the Netherlands had imposed its rule on the whole of Indonesia except Achin, and Britain had imposed her rule on the whole of the Indian sub-continent. I was old enough to take note of the Anglo-Egyptian reconquest of the Sudan from the Khalifah of the Mahdi Muhammad Ahmad in 1898, and of the progressive occupation of Morocco by France from 1905 onwards.

The countries which were still unstable were some of those that were neither Western themselves nor under the rule of some Western power, but had retained their independence without having Westernized themselves more than superficially. The most conspicuous of these still unstable countries were Russia, Turkey, Iran, and China. The only still unstable Western countries were some of those in Latin America, and the most unstable of the Latin American countries were countries in which the Western civilization had never yet been more than a veneer. Of the other unstable countries, Russia had been the earliest to start Westernizing herself (she had started two centuries back, in the reign of Peter the Great), and by 1914 she had carried the process of Westernization much farther than Turkey and very much farther than either Iran or China. Yet the political régime in Russia was still arbitrarily autocratic; the country had been simmering with revolutionary opposition to the autocracy since 1825; and the Western-like efficiency that Russia had displayed in her nineteenth-century feats of conquering and pacificating the

Caucasus and Western Turkistan had revealed its limitations when Russia had been defeated in 1904–5 in Eastern Asia by Japan.

Japan was a country that was not Western and had never fallen under Western rule but that, since 1868, had deliberately Westernized herself and had demonstrated by 1904 that she had made a greater success than Russia had made of this difficult enterprise of 'acculturation'. Japan was not the only East Asian country that had Westernized in good time and had done this efficiently. On a smaller scale the same thing had been done contemporaneously by Siam (Thailand). At the turn of the nineteenth and twentieth centuries, Thailand as well as Japan was part of the stable major portion of the World, and so were one Asian and one African country that had not Westernized themselves at all so far, and one Latin American country whose population was predominantly pre-Columbian in its racial composition. Afghanistan, Abyssinia (Ethiopia), and Mexico, as well as Japan and Thailand, were parts of the stable world, not in virtue of having Westernized themselves, but thanks to having each come under the rule of an autocrat who was both intelligent and efficient, besides being masterful. These three remarkable rulers were the Amir 'Abdarrahman of Afghanistan, the Emperor Menelik of Ethiopia, and the dictator Porfirio Diaz of Mexico.

This was the state of the World at the time when I was growing up. Security and stability were in the ascendant, and it looked as if people of my age would live to see these two amenities become prevalent all over the World. It was also assumed, as a matter of course, that the framework of the coming world-order would be the Western civilization. It was taken for granted by almost all Westerners—and by many non-Westerners too, including some who did not like the apparent prospect—that the Western civilization had come to stay. Pre-1914 Westerners, and pre-1914 British Westerners above all, felt that they were not as other men were or ever had been. Westerners were 'civilized'; non-Westerners were 'natives' in the sense that they had no human rights; they merely happened to be the pre-Western inhabitants of their respective countries. Even the Chinese, who had previously been *the* civilized people *par excellence* in the eyes of half the World, had become 'natives' since China's defeat in the Opium War. Other civilizations had risen and fallen, had come and gone, but Westerners did not doubt that their own civilization was invulnerable. The house that Jack the Frank had built was a house built on the rock; the houses built by Jack's predecessors and competitors had been houses built on the sand.

The facts that the Greek civilization had come to grief and that the Roman Empire had declined and fallen were, of course, very familiar to Westerners of my generation who had received the thorough education in the Greek and Latin languages and literatures that had been a legacy to us from the fifteenth-century Italian humanists. While I had still been at school I had read Edward Gibbon's *The History of the Decline and Fall of the Roman Empire* and had taken note of his 'General Observations on the Fall of the Roman Empire in the West'. In this remarkable parenthesis in his narrative, Gibbon pauses to ask and discuss the question: 'Could the terrible catastrophe that had befallen the western half of the Roman Empire in the fifth century of the Christian Era ever overtake the modern Western World of A.D. 1781' (the probable date of the writing of this passage)? Gibbon discusses this question under a number of heads; under each head, he presents considerations—all seemingly well-founded at the time—which suggest convincingly that, in each case, the answer to his general question is in the negative; and, after allowing this series of optimistic findings to make its cumulative effect on his reader's mind, Gibbon sums up in supremely confident terms. His conclusion is that it is inconceivable that the Roman Empire's fate could be lying in wait for the modern Western World in its turn.

Before August 1914 it never occurred to me to question Gibbon's judgement. In retrospect, looking back from the present year 1969, I find myself surprised that I had not been more sceptical; for I had already noticed—and this with strong dissent and with considerable impatience and irritation—that, in the conventional curriculum of Greek and Latin studies in Britain at the time when I was *in statu pupillari*, Greek history after the date of Demosthenes' death, and Roman history after the dates at which Tacitus, Pliny Junior, and Juvenal had written their last lines, were ignored as firmly as if there had been something indecent about these 'periods'. There were, in truth, two indecent features in these passages of history from a nine-teenth-century Western scholar's point of view.

One of these indecencies was that the Greek and Latin writers who had lived and worked in these ages had no longer written in the 'classical' language and style. Their literary vulgarity set a modern Western scholar's teeth on edge. (For extraneous religious reasons, the scholar was constrained, as a Christian, to read the New Testament, in spite of its being written in a version of the post-Demosthenic Attic *koinê* that was particularly excruciating because it was shot through with Aramaic turns of speech and even with some Aramaic words.) This literary reason for ignoring 'post-classical' works of Greek and Latin literature was recognized and avowed; acquaintance with them would have menaced the purity of the present-day scholar's own style when he was composing Greek and Latin prose and verse of his own.

The second indecency was more significant because it was one that was felt subconsciously without, I think, being recognized. (It was certainly never avowed.) Modern Western scholars shrank from taking cognizance of these outlawed periods of Greek and Roman history because they were periods in which this history could not be construed as being 'a success story'; and, for modern Western scholars, there were two subconscious motives for holding that the Graeco-Roman civilization had not been a failure. In the first place, Greek and Latin literature was, for them, sacrosanct, in the way in which the Bible was for contemporary 'fundamentalist' Christians. In the second place the fact that the Graeco-Roman civilization had undeniably broken down, declined, and eventually fallen did open the door to the possibility that the modern Western civilization might eventually go the same way. Modern Western intellects might be convinced—and were convinced, as mine had been—by the speciousness of Gibbon's reasoning and by the robustness of the optimism with which his reasoning had inspired him. But 'le coeur' —i.e. the intuition that wells up from a human psyche's subconscious depths—'a ses raisons que la raison ne connait pas', and 'le coeur', in Pascal's usage of the word, was a more potent censor than even literary taste in making most modern Western scholars shy away from contemplating the periods of Greek and Roman history that had been studied and expounded by a few scholars of the intellectual stature of Droysen, Niese, Hodgkin, Bury, and Gibbon himself.

In the course of my education I had rebelled against having my horizon confined to what had seemed to me to be arbitrary excerpts from Graeco-Roman history. I had determined to try to gain a comprehensive view of it. I had broken the tabu before I had left school. Before I had finished my education at Oxford, I had come to the conclusion that, among the Greek and Roman historians whose works were extant, Polybius was the greatest of all those who had written in Greek; that Procopius had far surpassed Xenophon and had come close to being the equal of Thucydides; and that Ammianus Marcellinus's caustic character-sketches were as penetrating as Tacitus's. In fact, I had made myself at home in the forbidden territory of the decline and fall of the Graeco-Roman civilization, and I ought to have inferred that the civilization into which I myself happened to have been born was not immune against the possibility of inflicting the same catastrophe on itself.

> Haud igitur leti praeclusa est ianua . . .
> sed patet immane et vasto respectat hiatu.[1]

I already knew by heart these grim lines of Lucretius's, yet I had not taken them to heart. I had continued to concur in Gibbon's judgement till, in the first days of August 1914, the disaster, unforeseen by me, into which my own world was now rushing, suddenly opened my eyes to the truth. The illumination had caught me in a flash; my illusion that I was the privileged citizen of a stable world had been shattered by a thunderbolt. Since that moment I have seen the World with different eyes and have found that it is not the kind of world that, until then, I had naïvely imagined it to be.

---

[1] 'So the door of death is not tight shut . . . No, it stands hideously wide-open, eyeing us expectantly with an enormous gape' (Lucretius, *De Rerum Naturâ*, Book V, lines 373–5).

3 : War : The Change in its Character and in People's Attitude towards it

'IN war the forces of Europe are exercised by temperate and un-decisive contests.' This dictum of Gibbon's had been pronounced during the American Revolutionary War, and at that time it had still been valid in the physical sense that the casualties had been light and also in the political sense that the peace settlement had not been catastrophic for the defeated belligerent. But the dictum had already been invalid in terms of emotion; for this war had not been a war of the characteristic eighteenth-century kind; it had not been a war waged for limited stakes, territorial or commercial; it had been the first of the modern Western wars of Nationalism; in other words it had been a war inspired by an ideology, and ideological wars are intemperates intrinically.

Eighteenth-century Western laws of war alleviated immensely the sufferings of civilians whose habitats became war-zones. The alleviation was not complete. The most glaring exception to it was the retention of the barbarous Roman rule that the civilian popula-tion of a fortified city that had been taken by storm (as distinguished from a fortified city whose garrison had surrendered the fortress by a negotiated capitulation) was fair game for the conqueror's troops. A late, and particularly shocking, case of the abuse of this tradi-tional barbarous licence was the gross maltreatment of the civilian population of the fortified city of Badajoz in Spain when the British Army took it by storm from its French garrison on 6 April 1812. Teh presence of the French garrison had been no more welcome to the Spanish civilian population of Badajoz than it had been to the British Army. The French Army had occupied Badajoz by force, without asking the Spanish inhabitants' leave. The Spanish inhabi-tants had taken no part in the French garrison's resistance to the

British Army's assault. Yet, because the French resistance had been obstinate and the British casualties, in carrying the French defences by assault, had been heavy, the British troops had revenged themselves by committing atrocities against a non-French civilian population which had been militarily non-combatant and politically impotent, and which was officially being 'liberated' from French domination by its British tormentors.

This retention of the traditionally recognized right to sack a city that had been taken by storm was a relic of pre-eighteenth-century barbarism in the treatment of civilians in war-time. Yet the atrocities inflicted on civilians at Badajoz by British troops in 1812 seem mild today, in retrospect, by comparison with the atrocities that on 26 April 1937 were inflicted, in cold blood, by German airmen on the civilian population of another city in Spain, Guernica (the first city to be destroyed by bombing from the air), or, again, in comparison with the atrocities that were being inflicted by United States troops (not to speak of their South Vietnamese auxiliaries) in Vietnam, South as well as North, at the moment in 1968 at which I was writing these lines. The British Army, when it was engaged in the Peninsular War, did not have either the incentive or the equipment for committing atrocities that the United States Army did have in Vietnam in 1968. Though the Napoleonic Wars were already embryonic war of religion inasmuch as they were wars of Nationalism, the recrudescence of fanaticism had not yet come anywhere near to reaching the pitch that it has now reached in the current state of American, Russian, and Chinese feeling. Nor had the advance of technology then reached the point—reached only within my lifetime—at which it has put it in a belligerent's power to drop bombs from aeroplanes.

Bombing is indiscriminate by its very nature. Even if the targets of it are legitimate military objectives (e.g. enemy troops, fortifications, means of communication, and factories producing armaments or other forms of equipment and provision for the enemy forces), it is virtually impossible to bomb even a legitimate military target that is the assailant's exclusive objective bona fide without at the same time killing and wounding civilians and destroying civilian property unintentionally. Moreover, it is a standing temptation for a belligerent who is resorting to the air-arm to use it, under the pretext of aiming at military targets, for deliberately terrorizing the civilian population of the assaulted country, in the hope that this may break civilian *moral* and disorganize civilian life to a point at which the enemy forces will be paralysed and the enemy government will be brought to its knees. This is a barbarous policy which is correctly described in the German word *Schrecklichkeit*. Sophisticated technology has been prostituted not only for producing weapons for bacteriological warfare but for the production of bombs of escalating degrees of atrociousness, ranging from bombs detonating mere explosives to 'anti-personnel' bombs scattering napalm, metal pellets, and razor-sharp slivers of steel, and 'escalating' from these to atomic bombs.

In Vietnam the United States armed forces have used all these instruments of torture except atomic bombs and bacteriological weapons, and they have both these ultra-atrocious weapons in store. The United States Government has been restrained by both conscience and prudence from using the atomic weapon in Vietnam. If this weapon were ever to be used again, the increase in the annihilating power of this weapon through the perverse application of scientific ability and technological skill in the course of the last twenty-four years would make the two bombs dropped on Hiroshima and Nagasaki in 1945 seem almost as innocuous as a pair of 'Molotov cocktails' by comparison with the deadliness of the bombs that are now already in stock for possible release tomorrow. As for the bacteriological weapon, it is impossible to forecast the magnitude of the genocide that this would perpetrate if it were ever to be brought into action.

Thus, within the century and a half that has elapsed between Gibbon's generation and mine, the distinction between civilians and combatants, that had been established about two generations before Gibbon's day, has been virtually effaced. We are now back in the dark age in which entire populations—without exemption for children, women, or the agèd—are exposed, in wartime, to attack. We are also right back in the dark age of wars of religion. At the same time we are far forward in an age in which this resurgent inhumanity and fanaticism are armed with weapons that are incomparably more lethal and more fiendish than those that any pre-eighteenth-century barbarians ever had at their command.

This shameful and ominous backsliding in the conduct of warfare has been consummated in my lifetime through the cumulative effect of a series of backward steps that have been taken, one after another, since 1792. The *levée en masse* in France in that year—an event of which Gibbon lived to hear the news—re-implicated the entire population of a country in the belligerency of that country's government. The Revolutionary and Napoleonic French armies reverted to the pre-eighteenth-century practice of 'living off the country' in the foreign territories which they were enabled to invade by the general mobilization of the manpower of what was at that time the most populous of all the states of the Western World. The vehemence and animosity with which wars were waged were re-intensified by the re-injection into war of religion in the form of Nationalism in the first instance. For a century and a quarter before the outbreak of the First World War in 1914, the Gadarene swine had been rushing down the steep slope; but, till they brought the catastrophe of the First World War on themselves, all of them remained blind to the destination for which they were heading. Some of them seem to be blind to this still today, in spite of the subsequent calamity of a Second World War, ending in the invention and use of the atomic weapon.

The blindness of almost everyone in the Western World during the forty-three-years-long span of relative peace that ended in 1914 was due in part to the genius of Bismarck—a statesman who had achieved a nineteenth-century ideological objective at a minimal cost by the use of an eighteenth-century cool-headed technique. The inherent transitoriness of Bismarck's achievement, which had been augured, with the insight of genius, by Bismarck himself, and with which he had been contending during the latter part of his political career, was not recognized by his contemporaries, and least of all by his younger contemporaries in Germany, until after his dismissal by young Kaiser Wilhelm II in 1890 and after 'the reversal of alliances' in 1891, when Russia discarded her nineteenth-century friendship with Prussia and made a *rapprochement* with France.

Russia's reversal of alliances was only a symptom of the return of instability; it was not the cause of this. The cause was a change of mood in Germany—the change signified by the dismissal of Bismarck—and this change had begun to cause concern, not only to Russia and to France, but to every country that was within striking distance of Germany's formidable armed forces—as Britain, too, came to be when Germany set herself to compete with Britain in naval armaments. By the close of the nineteenth century the Germans were no longer content with the national unity that Bismarck's statesmanship had won for them. Germany was now ambitious to cap Bismarck's achievement by winning 'world-power'; she was open to persuasion that, for her, in the post-Bismarckian chapter of her history, 'world-power' was the only alternative to 'downfall'; and she was becoming inclined to take the risk on the chance of being able to snatch the prize. The outbreak of the First World War closed, abruptly, the Bismarckian half-century of peace and opened the era of instability, turmoil, crime, and suffering in which the World is still living in the year 1969— and this with no prospect of a respite in view and with the menace of irretrievable catastrophe on the horizon.

Between 1914 and 1969 mankind has suffered one shock after another: the outbreak of the First World War; Germany's violation of the neutrality of Belgium, of which she herself was one of the guarantors; the atrocities committed against civilians by German troops in their sweep through Belgium and France in a vain attempt to win victory in another seven weeks' war; the mass-slaughter, on an unprecedented scale, in a war that, instead of being over in seven weeks, dragged on for four years; the replacement of the traditional autocracy in Russia, not by a constitutional and liberal regime, but by a new autocracy dedicated to the fanatical ideology of Communism; the capture, first of inter-war Italy and then of inter-war Germany, by the equally fanatical counter-ideology of Hyper-Nationalism; Hitler's inhuman resolve to inflict a second world war on mankind, and the series of coups—all gambler's throws, not nicely calculated moves by a Bismarckian chess-player—through which Hitler brought upon Germany and the rest of the World a still more dire disaster than the First World War had been; the genocide of the Jewish diaspora in Germany and German-occupied Europe; the invention of the atomic weapon, and its use by the United States against Japan; and the subsequent persistence of the greater part of mankind in behaving as if it were still living in the Pre-Atomic Age.

This series of shocking experiences has shaken many individual

human beings, and some entire nations, out of the traditional culpable acquiescence in the institution of war and out of the fatalistic
assumption that this institution, whether respectable or criminal,
is anyway ineradicable. Unhappily, this revulsion against war—a
revulsion that ought to have been total and universal from the
moment in the year 1945 at which the World entered the Atomic
Age—is still only partial in the year 1969 even in countries in which
it has occurred, and there are still some countries in which the pre-
1945, and indeed the pre-1914, attitude towards war is being
maintained by all but a small, and so far politically powerless,
minority of the population.

I am familiar with the pre-1914 attitude towards war because I
was born and brought up in a time and place in which this attitude
was still the normal one and was still taken for granted simple-
mindedly. This was the attitude that had been prevalent in most
parts of the World for most of the time since the creation of the first
sovereign states that had the capacity for making war, and states
of this calibre had arisen in Sumeria about 5000 years before the
year A.D. 1889, which was the date of my birth in England. I myself
was jolted out of this traditional attitude, once for all, by the
slaughter, in the First World War, of about half the number of the
friends that I had made, at school and at the university, among my
contemporaries. They were of a generation and a social class in
which, in the British Army in that war, the incidence of fatal
casualties was the heaviest. They were not professional soldiers; they
had been volunteers who had been given temporary commissions
as second-lieutenants, and this, in the First World War, was tantamount to being sentenced to death. Many of them gave their lives
in the belief that they were sacrificing themselves in 'a war to end
war'. I myself am still alive in 1969 owing to an accident.[1] Thus I
have lived to be converted from the traditional acquiescence in war
to a total opposition to it. In 1914 I became convinced that war was
neither a respectable institution nor a venial sin, but was a crime.
Since 1945 I have been convinced that, if mankind still persists in
committing this crime, mankind is going, sooner or later, to commit
mass-suicide.

By contrast, during the first twenty-five years of my life, I did not

[1] See pp. 37-38.

question the age-old attitude towards war which had been part and parcel of my cultural heritage. For instance, I sympathized whole-heartedly with the peoples of Greece, Bulgaria, Serbia, and Monte-negro when, in 1912, they made war on Turkey in order to put an end to Turkish rule over the Ottoman Empire's surviving dominions in South-Eastern Europe in which the majority of the population was non-Turkish and non-Muslim. I felt that the governments of the Balkan states had been morally justified in making war with this objective; and this was consistent with my moral judgements on previous wars. I felt that Bismarck and Cavour had been justified in making wars with the objective of achieving, respectively, the political unification of Germany and of Italy. I felt that the American people had been justified in making war in order to win political independence from my own country; and that Joan of Arc had been justified in making war in order to liberate France from her English invaders. In all these cases, I judged that it had been a net gain on the right side of the moral balance-sheet when the makers of these 'just' wars had won them. My judgement on the Balkan states' victory in the First Balkan War was the same.

Looking back over the history of the last 5000 years from my present standpoint in the year 1969, I now no longer hold that any government has ever been justified in starting a war, even in the best of causes. I still believe that it is justifiable, and in some cases morally obligatory, to resist aggression (the resistance to German, Japanese, and Italian aggression in the Second World War is a case in point); but I now regard even a 'just' war in defence of one's own country or of some other country as being a tragic necessity, supposing that it is truly necessary; and I am also now on my guard against this plea, because I have become aware that right is seldom wholly on one side; that there are wars (e.g. the war in Vietnam) in which both belligerents claim, and this more or less in good faith, to be fighting in order to resist and to foil aggression; and that, in truth, either belligerent or both of them may actually be committing aggression, not opposing it.

However, in Britain when I was a child mankind's traditional attitude towards war was still almost universally prevalent there. At that time the only Westerners who regarded war as being a criminal institution, and who refused resolutely to have any part or lot in it, were the members of the Society of Friends. This stand that was taken by the Quakers was respected by people who differed from them in taking what was then still the normal view. It was recognized that the Quakers were utterly sincere in holding the moral convictions that they held; that they held some other peculiar moral convictions besides their queer notion that war is a crime; and that they were prepared to suffer for remaining true to their convictions when the test came.

The Quakers did stand up to the test. An example is the stand taken by the Quaker chocolate-manufacturer, Mr. George Cadbury, during the South African War[1]—a British war that was as controversial and as invidious as the American war in Vietnam. In taking this courageous stand on principle, Mr. Cadbury was not only voluntarily denying to himself particular contracts that would have been financially profitable; he was also incurring public odium in Britain to a degree at which this threatened to damage his business as a whole; for, in a war that the British were waging with a bad conscience, their usual respect for people who resist temptations to act against their conscience was temporarily overborne by chauvinism. The moral conflict between Mr. Cadbury and the pro-war majority of the British public was a conflict between the post-Christian Western religion of Nationalism and a small community of Christians who were peculiar in obeying the commandments that are attributed to Jesus in the Christian Gospels.

The Quakers did, and do, set a moral example to their fellow human beings. Yet the Quakers were, and are, only a handful among the English-speaking minority of the Protestant minority of the officially Christian minority of mankind. The Quakers are a yeast which has not yet leavened the lump—though human history presents some striking illustrations of the eventual triumph, contrary to all apparent likelihood, of principles held by tiny minorities who

---

[1] 'He invited . . . widespread attack by his refusal to tender for orders of chocolate and cocoa for the British army during the South African War. . . . He believed the war to be a crime, and he would have no association with it, certainly no association which involved the making of business profit out of the tragedy. It is true that when later the Queen commanded him to supply chocolate for her Christmas present to the troops in South Africa he obeyed, but he obeyed on terms which eliminated personal profit.'—A. G. Gardiner, *Life of George Cadbury* (London 1923, Cassell), p. 309.

have stood for these principles whole-heartedly and who have therefore been prepared to suffer for their principles to any extent. Time and again, martyrdom has proved more potent than the physical force that is wielded by governments.

Meanwhile, in Britain before 1914, the prevalent attitude towards war was not the Quakers' attitude; it was the traditional world-wide attitude; and this is significant, because at that time the British, like contemporary Americans, were not militaristic-minded in the sense in which contemporary Germans and Japanese were, though both nations took pride, as all other nations did, in historic military victories of theirs. Britain and the United States were unique among the great powers of the pre-1914 world in recruiting their armed forces solely by voluntary enlistment. Conscription for military service in the land-forces had never been imposed, even temporarily, in the United Kingdom, or in either England or Scotland before their union. It was imposed in the United Kingdom in 1915 for the first time in British history for service in the land-forces, though, for naval service, it had been imposed temporarily, during the Napoleonic Wars, by the villainous expedient of authorizing British naval press-gangs to kidnap civilians, not excluding American merchant-seamen. Conscription had been imposed in the United States in the course of the Civil War of 1861–5 on both sides, but it had been abrogated there as soon as that war was over.

The British people were naïve—and, no doubt, offensive to the rest of the World—in the pride that they took, and displayed, in the British Navy, after this had battled its way to world-wide supremacy in the course of the century ending in 1805, the date of the Battle of Trafalgar. The names 'Trafalgar Square' and 'Waterloo Station' stamped the memory of the two decisive British victories on the subconscious layer of the psyche of a Victorian Londoner, even if he was not consciously aware of the origin of the labels borne by these two landmarks in Victorian London's topography. Before the war of 1914–18 the people of the United Kingdom were neither war-shy nor (except for the Quakers) opposed to war on principle.

During the century ending in 1914 the United Kingdom fought more colonial wars than any of the other great powers of the day. In Britain these British colonial wars were written off as being 'little wars'—a euphemism which implied a favourable contrast with the 'big wars' waged by other powers. Of course, these wars did not seem 'little' to the victims of them, and at least two of them, the 'Opium War' of 1839–41 and the South African War of 1899–1902, were justly condemned as immoral by the World at large, and this in an age in which war itself was still generally held to be a legitimate and respectable practice. Nineteenth-century Britain's will to power was also revealed in her progressive conquest of the whole of the Indian subcontinent and in the determination with which she afterwards reconquered the districts that had been temporarily wrested out of her hands by her mutinous Indian professional troops.

Nineteenth-century Britain competed zestfully with France for still unappropriated territorial spoils in Asia and Africa. She competed less light-heartedly with Russia for political influence, control, or possession in an arena which extended from Afghanistan to the Ottoman Empire's remaining dominions in Europe inclusive. In the course of this competition with Russia during the century ending in 1907, Britain once went to war with her competitor, in the Crimean War of 1854–6, and she might have gone to war with Russia again in 1878 if Bismarck, in his concern to preserve the stability of the Bismarckian political map of Europe, had not intervened with his offer of his good offices as 'honest broker'—an exacting role to which Bismarck duly lived up.

The British people had, indeed, been straining like a bulldog on the leash.

> We don't want to fight, but, by Jingo, if we do,
> We have the ships, we have the men, we have the money too.

This music-hall song, with its refrain declaring truculently that 'the bear' should not have Constantinople, revealed the readiness of the British people in 1878 to go to war with Russia again, and the previously obscure Saint Glengulphus's queer name—arbitrarily taken in vain by the composer of the outrageous British music-hall song—has become, in consequence, a bad word in the vocabulary of the English language.

These notorious historical facts are evidence that, in its attitude towards war, the Britain into which I was born in 1889 was still unregenerate. However, in unregeneracy there are degrees—in moral practice, if not in theological theory—and Dante, had he been a

Victorian and a pacifist, would probably not have consigned the British people to the bottom-most circle of his Inferno. The prisoner in Dante's dock could have pleaded that, since the failure of Henry VIII's wanton war with France in 1512–15, England—and then the United Kingdom after England had been incorporated in it—had never again embarked on an aggressive war at the western end of the mainland of the Eurasian Continent, though she had participated in a number of wars waged to prevent the permanent subjection of the Continent's European Peninsula to the rule of some single European continental power—first Spain, then France.

This plea would have been in consonance with the truth. On the other hand, my countrymen had deceived no one except themselves when they had persuaded themselves that British sea-power was a solely and wholly beneficent force in the field of power politics: a shield against aggression for Britain's protégés as well as for Britain herself, and a menace only to slave-traders and to pirates.

An impartial judge's verdict on Britain's use of her sea-power would certainly have been that she had not been innocent of using it, when it had suited her, as an instrument of aggressive national policy. The British people had, however, perhaps been peculiar among European peoples in keeping their army, in contrast to their navy, firmly in its proper place—that is to say, under effective control by Parliament. The British Navy was the British people's idol, and it was therefore able to bring pressure to bear on Parliament by threatening to appeal, over Parliament's head, to popular senti-mentality. The British Army could not play this naval game. The British Army had been suspect ever since the New Model Army which had been created by Cromwell to fight Parliament's battle against the Crown had deposed Parliament and had subjected the English people to a military dictatorship that they had found more oppressive than absolute monarchy had been. The revulsion against being ruled by major-generals had led to the Restoration, and, since then, in constitutional theory, Britain has never had a standing army again. In practice, of course, she has had one ever since uniformed professional armies became the rule in the Western World. Indeed, Britain continued to retain an army of this eighteenth-century kind after the French *levée en masse* in 1792 had inaugurated the age of military conscription in Continental Europe. In my childhood the

British Army was composed exclusively of voluntarily enlisted men, and it is exclusively professional now, once again, in 1969.

Considering the British Army's history, it might have been expected that, in Late-Victorian Britain, soldiers would have had no glamour for boys. Yet, in my generation in Britain, playing with toy soldiers was almost every boy's absorbing passion from the age of five or six to the age of thirteen or fourteen. I can testify that it was my own absorbing passion and that, in this, I was typical of my generation at that stage of our lives. My infatuation with toy soldiers was shared by every other little boy whom I knew except one who, having been born in a High-Anglican household and intending, from an early age, to take orders, played at services instead of playing at battles. The rest of us spent our pocket-money in gradually building up armies of lead soldiers: five cavalrymen or ten infantrymen at a time, and a battery of artillery on those joyful rare occasions on which we could afford this. The prevalence of this passion for playing with toy soldiers in pre-1914 Britain—a country in which the real live Army had been rather at a discount, compared, say, to the French or the Prussian Army, for the past two hundred years and more—shows how strong a hold the institution of war then still had in the World as a whole. War's fascination for me and my contemporaries in Britain was the product of the *Zeitgeist*, and the predisposing *Zeit* was not just a span of eight or nine years of the childhood of a single generation; it was the span of five thousand years during which war had been one of mankind's master institutions. The momentum of a habit that had been holding mankind in its grip for these five millennia was the driving-force behind my generation's passion for playing with toy soldiers.

For me—and, I believe, for most of my contemporaries too—the pleasure lay in building up one's leaden army, squad by squad, and in parading the troops that one possessed in an order of battle that gradually increased in size and in splendour with the addition of each carefully chosen unit. I had to choose carefully because my budget for military expenditure was small, and sometimes the choice was agonizing; for the lead-soldier-manufacturers put on the market enticing varieties of their goods in numbers that were far beyond the reach of the young buyer's purse. I knew the uniforms of all the contemporary British Army's regiments. Their distinctive gay colours had not yet been replaced by the monotonous earth-coloured 'khaki' that came in with the South African War. As one after another of these fondly familiar uniforms made its appearance in the toy-shop window, each new display made its appeal to my cupidity.

My own choice was to concentrate on recruiting a battalion of British foot-guards. I could not be too pedantic; fusiliers had to pass muster as grenadiers, and Scots Greys troopers had to serve as guards field-officers, simply because they wore guards-like bearskins and were mounted. Before books had captured from lead soldiers the paramount claim on my resources, I had managed to assemble a battalion of foot-guards or pseudo-foot-guards which must have had at least fifty men on its strength, and the parading of this imposing force invariably gave me intense satisfaction. This opening stage of the game never palled, but then came the anticlimax. When I had set up two armies in order of battle, facing each other, I felt an obligation to produce a battle and to make one of the two opposing armies win; so I would make one army advance and the other retreat, knocking down more men on the losing side than on the winning one. I knocked them down gingerly, for fear of chipping off the paint that was the fabric of their gorgeous uniforms.

This stage of the game when I was making my armies go into action was, however, unconvincing and was therefore unrewarding. Before I had grown out of playing with toy soldiers altogether, I had taken to limiting myself to parading my troops, as before, in the morning. I would then gaze at the magnificent spectacle with undiminished rapture, but would omit the battle stage. After having taken my fill of inspecting the parade, I would spend the rest of my spare time (by then I was at school) on reading. I would then gaze, once more, for a few minutes in the evening, at the soldiers who had stood so patiently at attention throughout the livelong day, without books or other diversions to while away the time for them; and I would finally re-pack them in their boxes as carefully as I had unpacked them after breakfast.

I have described in detail the form taken by my pleasure in toy soldiers when I was a child because this does, I believe, throw light on the attitude of contemporary grown-up people towards the military establishments for which the tax-payers were willing to pay;

and this attitude, in turn, explains why the European powers allowed themselves to stumble into war in August 1914, and why they had failed to foresee the horrifying sequel. The enjoyment that my toy army gave me was, as my readers will have perceived already, precisely the enjoyment that King Frederick William I of Prussia's live army had given to this relatively harmless eighteenth-century autocrat. My army, like his, was a parade-ground pageant; it was not cannon-fodder; it was a treasure that was not expendable. It never occurred to me to associate soldiers with mortal combat—with killing and wounding and with being wounded and being killed. Even at the early stage when I was still engaging half-heartedly in the mock battles that I eventually omitted from my day's play-time programme, I was not picturing to myself, when I was knocking some of my soldiers down, that I was playing at the commission of a criminal act. It never occurred to me that, if these had been real live soldiers, they would have been shrieking as I struck them down and would then have been writhing and groaning as they lay on the stricken field, if they had not had the better fortune of being killed instantaneously instead of being left callously to die a lingering death and perhaps to be trampled by horse-hoofs or to be crushed by gun-carriage-wheels before the waning of their consciousness had gone far enough to make them insensible to pain. Being crushed, still more horribly, under the treads of tanks was not yet one of the tortures that the wounded had to fear, since tanks had not yet been invented at the time when I was playing with toy soldiers.

If, in my childhood, I had had this modicum of imagination, undoubtedly I should have been as grievously distressed as the Emperor Ashoka was when he saw, in real life, the horrors of a war which he had deliberately started, and probably, like Ashoka, I should have given up the game in disgust and contrition. Frederick William I would have been no more distressed at the spectacle of the suffering inflicted by war than were his son Frederick the Great or more recent war-makers such as Napoleon and Bismarck and Hitler. Frederick William I was, no doubt, just as callous as these war-makers were; what restrained him from going to war was not humanitarian compunction but the miserliness of the collector's mania. For Frederick William I, the 'beau spectacle' was the pageant of a living army on parade; it was not, as it was for Napoleon in his own brazen-faced indictment of himself, the sight of the young men lying dead on the battlefield on the morning after a battle had been won at that price by this inhuman war-lord.

The contrast between Frederick William I's kind of pleasure and Napoleon's kind of pleasure does, I believe, go far towards explaining the attitude of the grown-up generation in all European countries, including Germany, on the eve of the outbreak of the First World War in August 1914. Forty-three years of peace had had the same effect on people's attitude towards military establishments as the spell of peace between the end of the War of the Spanish Succession and the outbreak of the War of the Austrian Succession had had on the attitude of Frederick William I. Once again, military establishments had come to be thought of as existing for show rather than for use. They were, however, equipped and trained for use, as Frederick William I's live toy army had been. In the eighteenth-century chapter of Prussia's history the instrument that the father had created had been put to use deliberately, promptly, and ruthlessly by the son; and Napoleon and Hitler, in their turn, went to war in Frederick the Great's spirit. By contrast, the belligerents in the First World War, including Germany, stumbled into a war which even the German Government had not, I believe, either deliberately planned or seriously intended to make. All alike were caught in the wheels of their mobilization-machines, and these wheels, which had been constructed and mounted so efficiently by the general staffs, turned remorselessly when once the starting-buttons had been pressed. The wheels spun round till, in a trice, they had launched a world war, and this world war ran its course—not in a trice, but with the slow grinding of the mills of God—till it had taken millions of lives; had inflicted an incalculable amount of agony, not to speak of material losses; and had set in motion a train of disorders from which the World has not yet emerged in 1969.

The pressing of the buttons in 1914 did not merely launch a single world war (an unspeakably grievous calamity in itself); it opened Pandora's Box, and, since then, a host of demonic scourges has continued to swarm out. They are still swarming out in 1969, fifty-five years after the fateful opening act. No one knows how many more are still waiting their turn to emerge; no one knows, either, whether the true story that is being spelled out, in rapid instalments, in our time is going to have the alleviating epilogue of the Greek myth. We do not know whether, if the procession of emerging demons eventually comes to an end, the spirit of Hope will then flutter out shyly to console us; we do not know this because we do not know whether the series of man-made plagues that has been afflicting mankind since 1914 may not be going to be the death of us; and, where there is no life, there is no hope either.

The harrowing experiences that, by this year 1969, mankind has been bringing on itself for more than half a century are the bitter fruits of war, and they have affected people's attitude towards war in all countries. The general effect has been to shock people out of the traditional human attitude towards war in some degree; but, so far, the degree has not been the same in all countries. Each people's particular reaction to these common experiences has been conditioned by two factors: the relative amount of suffering that has fallen to its lot since 1914 and its particular previous history, including the attitude towards war to which this longer span of experiences has conditioned it. These two factors have not been uniform throughout the World either in their strength or in their effect. In consequence, the attitude towards war has departed from the world-wide traditional form to different extents in different countries in each successive act of the tragedy of mankind's twentieth-century history. This progressive differentiation between different nations' respective attitudes towards war is one of the most disconcerting and most ominous features of the present international situation.

The incidence of the mass-slaughter in the First World War fell chiefly on the Old-World belligerents. The United States intervened in that war late, and American casualties were relatively light in absolute figures, and were lighter still in proportion to the size of the United States' population at the time. Among the Old-World belligerents, not only the French and British and Austrian peoples, but the German people too, I believe, were cut to the heart by the bereavements that they had suffered in such appalling numbers. The Germans were also stunned by their eventual defeat through attrition after they had embarked on the war in the expectation of snatching as quick and easy and cheap a victory as Prussia had won over Austria in 1866. The Austrians were crushed by the political and economic consequences of a defeat that had been far more catastrophic for Austria and for Hungary than it had been for Germany.

The Austrians were too severely crushed to have any feelings left to spare for spending on resentment, and, for them, there was no question of Austria's ever being able even partially to recover her pre-war status in the World. In Germany the harrowing effect of huge war-casualties and the stunning effect of unforeseen defeat were offset to some extent by resentment and by a desire for revenge —the emotions that had been aroused in France by her defeat in 1870-1. Germany, however, was temporarily paralysed, as France and Britain were too, by the extreme havoc that total war had made of the complicated and delicate mechanism of these countries' highly developed economies. In Germany this havoc was aggravated enormously in 1923 by the French occupation of the Ruhr and by the concomitant devaluation of the mark to zero. The Germans' resentment, and their desire for eventual revenge, were, of course, exacerbated proportionately.

Hungary, being an economically backward agricultural country, was not hampered by the economic consequences of the war as severely as the ex-belligerent European countries to the west of her, and her thirst for revenge was not tempered, as Germany's was in the first chapter of the World's inter-war history, by a recognition that it was materially impracticable for her to try to slake this thirst by challenging the victors. The Magyars were also more backward than their western neighbours culturally as well as economically, and they were therefore perhaps less sensitive to the bereavements that they had suffered through their war-casualties.

Hungary's experience in the war and reaction to defeat had their counterparts in the experiences and reactions of the two principal belligerents to the east of her: Russia and Turkey. These two countries were, at the time, still more backward than Hungary was both economically and culturally. In the First World War their economic backwardness had made them easier to defeat than any of the other defeated belligerent countries; but this same economic backwardness also made it possible for them to recover from the economic effects of defeat more quickly. They had had little economic equipment to lose, and they therefore now had little to replace. Moreover, their cultural backwardness made them too, like the Magyars, relatively insensible to the bereavements that they had suffered through their wartime casualties. (The Russian casualties had been heavier even than the German.) Accordingly, Russia and Turkey were the first two of the countries that had been defeated in the First World War to contest its outcome and to challenge the momentary victors.

The Bolshevik Marxian Socialist (afterwards styled 'Communist') faction that had seized power in Russia had been constrained, before the war had ended on the western front, to submit to harsh peace-terms dictated by the Central Powers; but, after the peace-treaty of Brest-Litovsk had been annulled by Germany's capitulation and by the Habsburg Monarchy's dissolution, the Bolsheviks had dared to resist the 'White' Russian armies that, with the support of the victorious Western allies, had attacked the Bolsheviks from three directions. More than that, the Bolsheviks had eventually expelled their 'White' Russian adversaries and had established their own rule over the whole domain of the former Russian Empire except its western fringes together with a small parcel of Transcaucasian territory, taken from Turkey by Russia in 1878, which the Bolshevik régime in Russia now retroceded, apart from the port of Batum. The Bolsheviks had emerged victorious from Russia's war-after-the-war, partly through exploiting effectively their strategic advantage of holding the interior lines, but mainly through the energy and assurance with which they were inspired by their ideology. Like other sincere religious fanatics, the Bolsheviks were convinced that the true faith —that is to say, their own faith—was bound to triumph, while at the same time, illogically but expediently, they felt it to be their religious duty to exert themselves to the utmost, to the point of total self-sacrifice, in order to expedite the fulfilment of historical necessity's inexorable decree.

As for the Turks, they dared, for their part, to resist the Greeks, who had been unleashed against them by the victorious Western allies (Italy alone dissenting at this stage), and the Turks, like the Russians, won their war-after-the-war, in spite of the almost desperately adverse fact that the temporary victors had disarmed the Turkish Army after its capitulation and had equipped the Greeks for their invasion of Anatolia. The Turks, too, were inspired by a religious faith—in their case the religion of Nationalism—which they had embraced, with the zeal of new converts, after their defeat in the First World War had deprived them of most of the remaining dominions of the former Ottoman Empire in which the majority of the population was non-Turkish in nationality. The Turks' eventual success in routing the Greek invaders compelled the no longer victorious-minded Western allies to drop into the waste-paper basket the draft peace treaty that they had been proposing to dictate to Turkey. They had to submit, instead, to negotiating a peace settlement with Turkey as between equals who were no longer the victors and the vanquished.

It will be seen that the experience of belligerency in the First World War had not shaken the Turks and the Russians, even temporarily, out of mankind's traditional assumption that war is one of the permanent facts of normal life, whereas it had made the French and the British so war-shy that they flinched from reopening hostilities even for the purpose of imposing the ex-victors' will upon Turkey and Russia, who were the least formidable of the ex-defeated powers. The most formidable of these was Germany, and it is not surprising that, after Hitler had come into power in Germany and had started to challenge and to undo the effects of the Versailles 'Diktat', one after another, the French and British peoples should have flinched from taking up Hitler's challenge with far greater trepidation than they had felt and shown when the Turks and the Russians had called their bluff.

During the ominous years 1933–39, the two war-shy West European nations assumed different postures in recoiling from the coming Second World War that Hitler was going to force upon them on the calculation, justified by the event, that they would refrain from forestalling him. The French did not shut their eyes to the terrible truth that Hitler was resolved to condemn them to the ordeal of a Second World War; they could not abide the prospect; and, when the Second War did descend on them, they almost consciously and deliberately rode for the fall that befell them in 1940. The British did shut their eyes to the same terrible truth; when the Second War descended upon them too, they refused, even then, at first, to take this war with the seriousness with which they had taken 'the Great War'—as, until the fall of France, the British continued to call the First World War in order to avoid admitting to themselves that they were now again engaged in a war of the same magnitude. The British did, however, open their eyes wide when France collapsed, and, recognizing at last that they had allowed Hitler to push them, step by step, to the very edge of the precipice, they now began to exert themselves as perhaps they had never done before, even at the most desperate previous moments in their chequered history.

For more than a year after the fall of France, Britain fought on, virtually alone, against overwhelming odds and without any discernible prospect of ultimate victory, until she was saved, contrary to all rational expectation, by mistakes on her opponents' part which were so suicidal that, if they had been predicted, the prediction would have gained no credence. Hitler's insensate attack on the Soviet Union, followed up by Japan's insensate attack on the United States, together made it inevitable that Britain would find herself, after all, on the winning side. It remained, however, just as certain as before that in the Second World War the knock-out blow would be dealt to Germany, not by British hands, but by others. In the Second War the victory was won by the United States and the Soviet Union between them. In the First War, already, it had been the United States that had decided the issue by throwing her enormous weight into the anti-German scale.

The British people had screwed themselves up, at the thirteenth hour, to stand the ordeal of a Second World War. The French people, who had borne the brunt of the First World War on the anti-German side, had failed to stand the ordeal of the Second War. By the day in January in 1968 on which this paragraph was being written the respective positions of France and Britain after the fall of France in 1940 had been reversed. Britain was crestfallen, whereas France—or at any rate President de Gaulle—was strutting like a fighting-cock. All the same, at that date it could be predicted with assurance that if, at any future date, France and Britain were to be challenged to undergo the ordeal of becoming belligerents in a third world war—a war that would be fought with a far direr form of the atomic weapon than the bombs dropped in 1945—these two West European ex-great powers would react in an identical way. Both would avoid this ordeal at any price. This is tantamount to saying that the cumulative effect of two world wars on the French and

British peoples' attitude towards war had been to shake these two peoples out of the world-wide traditional acceptance of war as being all in the day's work.

The Russo-American victory in the Second World War had temporarily preserved or recovered for both Britain and France their pre-war colonial empires; and, when their post-war rule had been challenged by Asian and African subjects who had seen the Western colonial powers' bluff called by Japan in 1941, Britain and France had each become involved in some fresh colonial wars— Britain in Palestine, Malaya, Kenya, Cyprus, and South Arabia, and France in Vietnam and Algeria. It is significant, however, that both France and Britain gave up by far the greater part of their respective colonial empires voluntarily, before their rule had been challenged by militant insurrections; and in Palestine, Vietnam, Algeria, and South Arabia, where they were challenged and did set out to meet force with force, France and Britain were moved, in the end, either by military defeat or by war-weariness, to abandon the struggle. Colonial wars for retaining empires by force proved, after the Second World War, to be far more formidable military enterprises than the nineteenth-century colonial wars in which these empires had been won. The only two post-Second-World-War colonial wars that either Britain or France fought to a victorious finish were Britain's wars against the local Communists in Malaya and against the Mau-Mau in Kenya; and Britain followed up these two small but arduous military campaigns by voluntarily granting independence to the two countries that had been the theatres of operations.

The effect on Britain and France of their experiences from 1914 to 1969 is thus manifest. The effect on Germany of her experiences during the same fifty-five years is not so easy to gauge. Germany had been the maker of the Second World War—a war which France and Britain had sought to avoid by going to humiliating, and indeed dishonourable, lengths in practising the fruitless policy of 'appeasement'. They had 'appeased' Germany at the expense of third parties, in violation of their common general obligations under the Covenant of the League of Nations and, in France's case, also in violation of particular treaties. Yet this sacrifice of French and British honour had been foredoomed to be made in vain. Hitler had not only made the Second World War nevertheless; he had made it with premeditation and in cold blood, in contrast to the behaviour of the former Imperial German Government, which had stumbled into the First World War recklessly, but not, perhaps, with deliberate intent. In deliberately making the Second World War, was Hitler carrying out a mandate conferred on him by the German people? The answer to this question probably is that Hitler was carrying out the will of a minority of the German people who were genuine and whole-hearted adherents of the ultra-fanatical German National-Socialist version of the world-wide post-Christian religion of Nationalism. Let us imagine that it had been politically feasible in August 1939 to hold in Germany, Britain, and France simultaneous plebiscites in which the voters would have been at liberty to vote, by secret ballot, either 'aye' or 'no' to the question: 'Do you want your country to engage in a second world war?' My own guess is that, in this imaginary situation, the percentage of 'noes' would have fallen not much farther short of one hundred per cent in Germany at that date than it would have in Britain and France.

If I am right in this guess of mine about the true state of German feeling on the eve of the Second World War, I am presumably right, *a fortiori*, in guessing that the German people's experience in the Second World War will have made them, by 1969, as war-shy as the French and British peoples have become by this date. The Second World War must surely have completed the process of disillusioning the German people with war as an instrument either for achieving national ambitions or for taking revenge for defeat aggravated by injustice.

Hitler, before he made his own war, had denounced the Prussian General Staff for having gone to war in 1914 on two fronts, and he had boasted that he was not going to make the same egregious strategic mistake. Yet in 1941 Hitler did deliberately make the mistake for which he had castigated his predecessors. He attacked the Soviet Union though, on his western front, he had failed to compel Britain to follow suit to France by capitulating; and, before the year 1941 was over, his ally Japan had made, for him, the further fatal mistake of bringing the United States into the war on the opposing side—the mistake that, in the First World War, had been made by Germany herself. Indeed, the Second World War took the same course as the First World War, with the difference that in the Second War the successive reversals of fortune were more extreme.

Germany's initial military successes were more sensational in the Second War than they had been in the First War; her eventual military defeat, and its political consequences for her, were more catastrophic. After Germany's capitulation in 1918, Germany had been compelled to cede the relatively small portions of her pre-war territory in which a majority of the local population was non-German in nationality. She had also been compelled to submit to the demilitarization of the Rhineland and to the temporary military occupation of it, together with several Transrhenane bridgeheads, by the victors. After the Second World War the whole of Germany's post-First-World-War territory was occupied militarily by the victors; Germany's government was dissolved; some of its ring-leaders were put on trial; and some of these were found guilty of capital crimes and were put to death. Moreover, this time, Germany was dismembered, as Austria had been after the First World War. The territories that the Versailles Treaty had left to Germany to the east of the Oder and the Northern Neisse rivers were now partitioned between the Soviet Union and Poland. Their German inhabitants were evicted, and so was the Sudeten German minority of the population of Czechoslovakia. The rest of Germany was split into an East German state controlled by the Soviet Union and a West German state that was first controlled, and was then taken into partnership, by the Western powers. The city of Berlin was split on the same lines. Prussia, which had annexed almost all the rest of Northern Germany after her victory in 1866, was erased from the political map of Europe on which she had made so deep a scar in the course of the two centuries ending in 1945.

In terms of loss of territory the outcome, for Germany, of the Second World War thus not only confirmed the results of the First World War; it went so far beyond them that in 1969 the recovery of the reduced frontiers imposed on Germany in the Versailles 'Diktat' would seem a veritable boon to the German people if it had not passed, as it now has passed, right out of the field of practical possibilities. Hitler had predicted for his Reich a duration of one thousand years; it had lasted for a dozen years, and, when it fell, it carried away with it in its fall all the territorial gains in Eastern

Europe that the German nation had made by acculturation, coloniza-
tion, and conquest in the course of the preceding eight centuries.
The territorial consequences, for Germany, of the Second World
War must have driven home the lesson that had already been
written plain in the consequences of the First War. The lesson is that
making war seldom pays dividends; that Bismarck's feat of extract-
ing lucrative dividends from his three wars had been a *tour de force*;
and that it had been folly to expect his successors to manage to
repeat Bismarck's achievement by trying to compensate for their
inferiority to Bismarck in genius by surpassing him in wickedness.

After the Second World War, Germany can no more dream of
ever being able to recapture her pre-war status in the World than
Austria could after the First World War. The territorial consequences of the Second World War have made this unthinkable now
for Germany too. In compensation, the economic consequences of
the Second World War have been far happier for West Germany
(though not for East Germany) than those of the First War were.
West Germany now has an economic motive, which Germany
lacked in the inter-war years, for doing what she can do, for her
part, towards keeping the peace. The second inter-war collapse of
Germany's economy—a consequence of the economic crisis that
overtook the whole World in and after 1929—was the event that
carried Hitler into power; and Hitler made the Second World War.
The economic prosperity that, in West Germany, has been the
sequel to the second and more shattering of Germany's two military
defeats in our time has not been undeserved; West Germany has
earned it by her own exertions since the priming of the pump by
enlightened American generosity; but this prosperity has certainly
been something unexpected. It seems improbable that West Germany will throw her present prosperity away by attempting to
embark on any fresh military adventure. This time at any rate, it
would be obvious in advance that, for Germany, going to war
would be a forlorn hope. Not only would she have no chance whatever of winning a military victory; she would be condemning herself to annihilation; for she would be challenging the Soviet Union;
and, since the Second World War, the Soviet Union has become a
super-power, armed with the atomic weapon.

Germany's history in my lifetime lays bare the reason why, since

1914, Germany has twice inflicted a disaster on the World and, above all, on herself. Germany's share—and it is a big share—of the responsibility for the outbreak of the First World War is not confined to her Government's actions during the days between the murder of the Archduke Franz Ferdinand and his wife and the opening of hostilities. The ultimate cause of the First World War was the international tension that had been created in the course of the two pre-war decades; the cause of this tension was the German Government's provocative and truculent behaviour; in behaving in this irresponsible way, the German Government was responding to the contemporary mood of the German people; this mood was a reckless one; and it was reckless because the German people's heads had been turned by the series of three wars that Prussia had fought and won under Bismarck's masterly guidance in 1864, 1866, and 1870–1. This continuous run of military successes, half a century back, had deluded the German people into taking it to be a general rule for Germany that war-making pays. This delusion had gained so strong a hold over the Germans' minds that it has required not merely one disastrous war but a second and still more disastrous one to bring the Germans back to their senses.

This particular German story carries a general lesson for all peoples. *De te fabula narratur* is the moral for every people in the World. The general lesson is that any country which has so far been invariably victorious in a series of past wars is likely to become a menace both to itself and to the rest of the World. Within my lifetime, this intoxicating experience has been shared with Germany by three other countries: Japan, the United States, and Israel. In Japan's history, as in Germany's, the series of victorious and profitable wars has already been terminated and been negated by military disaster; and in 1969 it looks to me, after a visit (my third) to Japan towards the end of 1967, as if a disillusioning common experience had jolted the Japanese people, as well as the German people, out of the attitude towards war that was prevalent among almost all peoples throughout the five millennia ending in A.D. 1914. By contrast, a break in the run of military successes, and a consequent disillusionment with war through this reversal of fortune, had not overtaken either Israel or the United States by the time when this chapter was being written.

Japan's victorious wars were her war with China in 1894, her war with Russia in 1904–5, and the First World War, in which Japan intervened on the anti-German side. The Russo-Japanese war was as arduous for Japan as the Franco-Prussian War of 1870–1 was for Germany; but in the Japanese case, as in the German case, the outlay in effort and lives was justified, in the victorious people's judgement, by the fruits of victory. The disappointing sequels to her easy victories in 1894 and in 1914–18 offered a lesson for Japan that she might have appreciated if she had been clearer-sighted. However, the Japanese people were dazzled by the more solid-seeming gains of the harder-won Japanese victory in the Russo-Japanese War. Japanese heads, like German heads, were turned by the intoxication of past military success; and the illusion of military invincibility lured Japan, in her turn, into a military adventure which ended in a supreme catastrophe.

Japan's military adventure was relatively long-drawn out. It began in 1931 with her seizure of Manchuria by force of arms in breach of Japan's own undertakings as a party to the Covenant of the League of Nations and as a signatory of the Washington Nine-Power Treaty of 6 February 1922, and also in defiance of world opinion. This occupation of China's three Manchurian provinces was followed up by the occupation of Jehol and of the eastern end of Inner Mongolia. In 1937 Japan crossed her Rubicon. She invaded China's heartland—the provinces inside the Great Wall. At the cost of putting huge land-forces into the field, Japan then succeeded in occupying Intra-mural China's principal railroads, navigable waterways, sea-ports, river-ports, and cities. She found it, however, to be beyond her strength either to complete even her skeleton occupation of China by gaining a foothold in the South-West or—a failure that was still more ominous—to control the vast Chinese territories in her rear outside the ribbons of territory that were held by Japanese garrisons. China's size, the Chinese people's powers of endurance, and their efficiency in waging guerrilla warfare had brought this second Sino-Japanese war to a stalemate by the year 1940, in which Hitler conquered France but failed to conquer Britain.

Thereafter, in 1941, the Japanese emulated Hitler in committing a capital error. Though Japan still had on her hands, on one front, a war in which she had not succeeded in securing a military decision, she now opened up an immense new front in the Pacific and started operations here by a wanton act of aggression that was as suicidal as Hitler's assault on the Soviet Union. Instead of confining herself in the Pacific to the easy enterprise of overrunning the local British, Dutch, and French possessions, Japan also attacked the United States. This crowning act of Japanese folly is a classic example of the nemesis that lies in wait for an overweening military power which reacts to frustration by escalation.

In the Second World War the reversal of Japan's fortunes was as extreme as the reversal of Germany's. After having bombed the American fleet in Pearl Harbor and conquered the Philippines, Japan was eventually compelled by the United States to capitulate; to submit to an American military occupation of her home territory; to evacuate all the foreign territories that she had occupied progressively since 1931; and to cede all the holdings of territory on the mainland of Eastern Asia that she had acquired through her victory in the Russo-Japanese War of 1904–5, besides ceding Taiwan (Formosa), which she had acquired through her victory in the Sino-Japanese War of 1894. This was the first occasion in Japan's history on which she had been occupied militarily by a foreign power. Since the Meiji Revolution of 1868 the Japanese people had been indoctrinated with the dogma that Japan was 'the Land of the Gods', and that, in virtue of this divinely-conferred privilege, she was destined to remain inviolate and eventually to reign over the rest of the World.

The shock dealt to the Japanese people by the *dénouement* of the war of 1931–45 must have been extreme. Is there any likelihood that the Japanese people still imagine, on the strength of Japan's victory over Russia in the Russo-Japanese War of 1904–5, that war-making pays? Will Japan, like Germany, need a second and still more disastrous defeat to bring her to her senses? Having written this chapter, as I have, *en voyage* back to England from a five-weeks' visit to Japan (9 November–13 December 1967), I venture, with some confidence, to answer this question with a 'no'. I give this answer fairly confidently because my impressions on this visit, which was my third, confirm those that I formed on my second visit, which I paid in 1956. In 1967, as in 1956, I have been impressed by the contrast between Japan's post-war mood and her pre-war mood. This earlier mood made a strong impression on me during my first visit, which

I paid in 1929—on the eve of Japan's embarkation on her disastrous adventure. In 1929 I found the Japanese people still intoxicated by their previous unbroken run of victorious wars. In 1956 and in 1967 the Japanese have seemed to me to be sober-minded. Moreover, in 1967 they were enjoying a bout of economic prosperity which, like the contemporary bout in West Germany, was brilliant but precarious. In 1967 I found the Japanese people's attitude towards their post-war economic achievement reminiscent of the German people's attitude towards theirs. Like the Germans, the Japanese were justly proud of what they had now achieved in the economic field but were at the same time rather anxiously aware that their economy would need careful nursing. A false step might cause it to wane as quickly as it had waxed; and, for both Japan's and West Germany's economy, the most surely fatal false move would be to embark on a fresh military adventure. I therefore believe that a single disastrous war has been enough to teach Japan the lesson that, for her too, war does not pay.

It is true that a single military catastrophe did not suffice for the German people's re-education; but Japan's single catastrophe culminated in the dropping of the two atomic bombs on Hiroshima and Nagasaki, and this is a deterrent experience that has overtaken neither Germany nor any country so far except Japan alone. My impression is that this unique experience of war in a form whose horror has no precedent has made Japan 'allergic', not only to atomic warfare, but to war waged with weapons of any kind. This far-reaching change that I espied in the Japanese attitude towards war is rational, considering that, in the Atomic Age, any local war waged with 'conventional' weapons may escalate into a third world war waged with the atomic weapon.

The dictum that Japan is now 'allergic' to the atomic weapon is American, and it is obtuse. It implies a disturbing failure to imagine the psychological, moral, and spiritual effects of an unprecedented horror that the American people inflicted on Japan twenty-four years ago, but that the Americans themselves have not yet experienced. Japan had drawn this terrible retribution on herself. If Japanese 'conventional' bombs had not been dropped first on Pearl Harbor, American atomic bombs would not have been dropped on Japan less than four years later. An American invasion of Japan might have cost hundreds of thousands of Japanese, as well as American, lives. A case can be made for President Truman's fateful decision to use the awful new weapon that had just been put into his hands. But no case can be made for feeling, thinking, talking, or behaving as if the existence of this new weapon had become one of the familiar facts of everyday life. The invention of the atomic weapon has heightened the destructiveness and the hideousness of war to a degree that amounts to a difference in kind. So long as any atomically-armed nation shuts its eyes to the significance of this change for the worse in mankind's situation through the dropping of the two atomic bombs in 1945, mankind's survival—which till that moment had been assured ever since, in the Upper Palaeolithic Age, Man had gained his ascendancy over all other wild beasts—will continue once again to be in doubt.

The catastrophic ending of the previously unbroken Japanese and German series of victorious wars makes it reasonable to guess that the Japanese and German peoples, as well as the French and the British, have now been shaken out of mankind's traditional acquiescence in war as being a normal and a tolerable institution. On the other hand, the United States' and Israel's series of victorious wars had not been broken yet in November 1968.

In 1969 the State of Israel is only twenty-one years old; yet Israel has already fought and won four wars. Israel's first military victory was won over Britain before Britain's abdication of her mandate for Palestine in 1948 and before Israel herself had been formally constituted as a state. Israel's other three wars that she has won since then have all been won over the Arab states: the first in 1948, the moment after Israel herself had come into existence, and the other two in 1956 and in 1967. The victorious wars in the United States' hitherto unbroken series of them have been more numerous than Israel's. In this year 1969 the United States has been in existence for 193 years, as compared with Israel's twenty-one years. Like Israel, the United States came into existence through victory in a war—and this against the same opponent, Britain. The United States' first victorious war was the one that in the United States is known as the Revolutionary War and in Britain as the American War of Independence.

The United States' second victorious war, waged in 1802, was against Tripoli, a North African state, nominally under Ottoman suzerainty, whose corsairs had anticipated Japan's attack on Pearl Harbor on a miniature scale by capturing an American frigate. The United States' third victorious war was against Britain once again. It was the war of 1812–15, and it ended in the decisive defeat of a British attempt to take New Orleans. (The Battle of New Orleans was fought after a peace treaty had been signed at Ghent but before the news of this had had time to reach the war zone on the other side of the Atlantic.) The United States' fourth victorious war was won over Mexico in 1846–8, and through this war the United States made huge territorial gains. The independent republic that had been set up by settlers from the United States in the Mexican territory of Texas now became one of the states of the Union, and the United States annexed, direct from Mexico, the Mexican territories that have since become the states of New Mexico, Arizona, Nevada, and California, together with the southern fringes of the present states of Colorado and Utah. The United States' fifth victorious war was the Civil War in which the United States defeated and reconquered the seceding Confederacy. I have already noted[1] that this was the greatest war, measured by the number of the combatants and the number of their casualties, of any that were fought in the Western World during the century between the Battle of Waterloo and the First World War; the loss of life in the American Civil War was exceeded, in that century, in no wars except in the T'ai P'ing rebellion and in the Muslim rebellions in China.

The United States' sixth victorious war was the Spanish-American war of 1898, in which the United States liberated Cuba from Spain but took for herself a naval base on Cuba at Guantanamo, as well as Puerto Rico and the Philippines. The United States' seventh and eighth victorious wars were the two world wars. In both these wars the United States became a belligerent at a late stage, and in the Second World War she did not intervene of her own accord; she was drawn into the war through being attacked. In the First World War the United States dealt Germany the knock-out blow after France and Britain (above all, France) had borne the heat and burden of the day. As for the Second World War, the United States might dispute with the Soviet Union (which likewise had become a belli-

[1] See p. 46.

gerent only through being attacked) the claim to have become, before this war was over, the principal combatant on the anti-German side. The United States' ninth victorious war was the war in Korea—and here China and North Korea might perhaps contest the United States' claim to have been the victor; they might maintain that this was a drawn battle; but in any case the outcome was not an American defeat.

Thus the United States' military history has been a 'success story', as Israel's, too, has been so far and as Germany's and Japan's was till Germany's series of victorious wars was broken by her defeat in the First World War and till Japan's series was broken by her defeat in the Second World War. The citizens of a state that was brought to birth in a victorious war and that has never yet lost a war will cherish their country's unbroken record of military success and will find it hard to reconcile themselves to facing the possibility that their success story, being a story in which the actors are mortal men, may not run to an interminable number of instalments. The store set by Americans on military victory can be gauged by the apparent inability of the 'white' element in the population of the Old South to get over the defeat of the Confederacy after its brief life-term of four years. In 1969 some Southerners are still brooding over this, though 104 years have now passed since Lee capitulated at Appomattox, and though, as a result of having been forcibly re-incorporated in the United States in 1865, the Old South is in 1969 included in a country that at the present time is by far the greatest military power in the World.

If it is true that an unbroken series of victorious wars makes a nation dangerous to the rest of the World and to itself, the United States and Israel must be today the two most dangerous of the 125 sovereign states among which the land-surface of this planet is at present partitioned. They were both perhaps particularly dangerous at the moment at which I was writing; for they were both then at war and were both meeting with the experience—an unaccustomed one for them—of finding themselves being frustrated. Israel in the Third Arab-Israeli War, and the United States in the war in Vietnam, had each been as successful as before in winning battles and in occupying territory. So far, however, neither Israel nor the United States in her current war had been able to compel her opponents to sue for peace.

In November 1968, Israel in South-West Asia and the United
States in South-East Asia were each in the awkward position in which
Japan found herself in China before the end of the Sino-Japanese war
of 1931–45. It is the position that has frustrated, and has eventually
defeated, a number of successive invaders of Russia: the Poles in the
seventeenth century, the Swedes in the eighteenth, the French in
1812, and, most recently, the Germans in the Second World War
(in contrast to the Germans' ephemeral success in imposing a peace
settlement on Russia before the end of the First World War). Like
Hitler and Napoleon and Charles XII in Russia and like the Japanese
in China, the Americans in South-East Asia and the Israelis in South-
West Asia had challenged infinity. They could win battle after battle
and occupy territory after territory, but their opponents would still
stay in the field, because, though these opponents could not hold
their ground, they had at their disposal a virtually endless space into
which they could continue to retreat till their pursuers had extended
themselves over more territory than they could effectively control.

Beyond the River Jordan the Arab World stretches away eastward
to the Zagros Mountains and the Persian Gulf; beyond the Suez
Canal it stretches away westward to the Atlantic; beyond the Sinai
Peninsula it stretches away southward to Aden and to the Sudanese
Jazirah; beyond Qunaitrah it stretches away northward to the
Syrian Jazirah. In South-East Asia the Americans were confronted
with the problem that confronted the Israelis in the Arab World.
Behind the Vietcong stood North Vietnam; behind North Vietnam
lies China; and, though the population of the United States today is
about twice as big as Japan's, Japan's experience in her invasion of
China in 1931–45 indicates that even the United States' manpower
and industrial power and economic resources would be unequal to
the task of bringing a war with China to a victorious conclusion.
She would have to conquer and occupy North Vietnam before she
could begin to invade China; and here she had to reckon not only
with China but with the Soviet Union. The two major Communist
powers were at loggerheads by now over most of the issues between
them, but they still saw eye to eye in their common determination to
make it impossible for the United States to win her war in Vietnam.

In this frustrating strategic situation the United States and Israel
have both been handicapped by the inhibiting psychological effect

of their past unbroken series of victories. The mood that had been produced in the minds of both nations by this record of previously continuous military success was making it hard for them both, in 1968, to do what they had to do in order to attain their true objectives. The obstacle that has stood in their way has been an irrelevant reluctance to reconcile themselves to facing the unwelcome possibility that, this time, victory might be beyond their reach and that the renunciation of the luxury of continuing to be 'ever victorious' might be the price that they would have to pay for achieving their major objective.

Israel has one major objective that overrides all others because, if she fails to obtain this one, she will not be able permanently to survive. Israel cannot achieve security unless and until she can persuade the Arabs to accept the fact of her existence—and this bona fide, in their hearts, and not just in words typed on a scrap of paper. Israel has to persuade the Arabs to live side by side with her as friendly neighbours. She will not be able to persuade them to do this unless and until she has convinced them that she intends to reciprocate, with equal good faith, by behaving as a good neighbour towards them, and, even if she does convince them, it will be hard for the Arabs to bring themselves to make peace, since the Arabs are the injured party. To make peace will, however, be hard for the Israelis too, though in their case for a very different reason. The Israelis have been the victorious party in three successive Arab-Israeli wars; their victory in the third of these wars has been the most swift and the most sensational of the three; and victors are seldom in a mood for making concessions; a dazzling series of victories is apt to blind the victors to the truth that military victory is a wasting asset. Thus the very brilliance of Israel's military performance hitherto has become a serious psychological obstacle to her attainment of her objective. This sounds paradoxical, but it is the truth.

The United States' problem in South-East Asia is less formidable than Israel's problem in South-West Asia. It is physically impossible for Israel to disengage from geographical contact with the Arab World, just as it is for the Soviet Union to disengage from physical contact with China. The United States is more fortunately situated. It would be possible for her to withdraw totally from both continental and insular Eastern Asia, as far eastward as Hawaii, without any aggravation of her military insecurity. The United States, like the other 124 'sovereign' states of the present-day world, is totally insecure, in all circumstances, now that it has become feasible to hit a target at any point of this planet's surface with an atomic missile launched from any other point. The United States' objective in Eastern Asia is a negative one. She wants to make sure that Continental China shall not occupy—or, short of occupying, dominate—any of the other East Asian countries. It ought to be easier for the United States to attain her objective than it will be for Israel to attain hers; for Continental China's objective is the converse of the United States' objective; it, too, is a negative objective; and these two negative objectives do not conflict. Continental China's objective is that the United States should withdraw her armed forces from their present positions on China's threshold. A settlement is thus politically feasible, but there has been a psychological obstacle. The United States has been reluctant to forgo victory in the tenth of the wars that she has waged in the course of the 193 years since the date at which she came into existence.

This American mood has been alarming because, since the Japanese attack on Pearl Harbor, the United States has swung round from her traditional policy of isolationism to the antithetical policy of world-wide interventionism and, in consequence, has taken a long step towards becoming 'militaristic'.

In the history of the United States, this has been something new. Like the British people, the American people have always been war-like, but, till the United States was involved, against her will, in the Second World War, the American people—again like the British people—were never 'militaristic' in the sense in which this term applies to the Japanese people before 1945 and to the German people since their 'Prussianization' down to the same date, except for an interlude under the Weimar regime. Militarism can be identified by two symptoms. One symptom is that the armed forces are 'a state within the state'; that, instead of being firmly controlled by the civilian executive, legislature, and electorate, they are able to act as a virtually independent power in the state, and as the dominant one. The second symptom of militarism is that the bulk of the militarized country's armed forces are recruited by conscription, and that these conscripted troops are a tool in the hands of a body of professional officers which is highly organized and which has a strong *esprit de corps*. On both these tests, the United States was a non-militaristic country before the Second World War. She had fought all her previous seven victorious wars, except the Civil War and the First World War, with forces in which the rank and file, as well as the officers, were volunteers—either professional, like the officers, or volunteers *ad hoc*; and, though conscription (in American parlance, 'the draft') had been introduced as an emergency measure on those two occasions, it had been dropped, each time, as soon as the war was over. As for the officer-corps, it was never a power in American life before the Second World War. Professional service in the officer-corps of the armed forces was a career that was respected, but it was neither prestigious nor lucrative. The officers of Washington's army had advertised their dissatisfaction with their post-war treatment at their countrymen's hands by choosing the name 'Cincinnati' for the settlement that they founded for themselves in the wilderness.

By contrast, the American people was, on both tests, a militaristic people in 1968. Conscription, which was re-introduced in the United States after she had been forced into belligerency in the Second World War by the Japanese attack on Pearl Harbor, was not abolished, this time, when the emergency that had called for it passed over. Conscription has been maintained in the United States ever since. This means that every male American citizen of military age is now potential cannon-fodder for the Pentagon to consume if it so requires. So far, the conscription reintroduced in the United States in 1941 has been selective, and the selection has been made by local draft boards staffed by civilians. However, in the economic life of the United States, the Pentagon's tentacles now reach out much farther. Indeed, they have a hold on a large and increasing section of the gainfully employed part of the population. The grants voted to the armed forces by the Congress amount to a considerable quota of the American people's national income; the control exercised by the Congress over the way in which these funds are expended is apparently perfunctory; and consequently the orders for military equipment that are given by the armed forces, at their own discretion, to industrial corporations have become a major factor in the corporations' volume of business and earning of profits. This economic hold over the American business world gives the Pentagon a political hold over all Americans whose salaries and wages are earned by producing goods for which the Pentagon is the principal customer; and by handing out, not orders, but research grants, the Pentagon has secured a similar hold over the universities. Moreover, by expenditure on public relations, the Pentagon is able also to use the tax-payers' money for conditioning the tax-payers themselves to acquiesce in a servitude which their fathers and forefathers would have resented and rejected as being 'un-American'! Those Americans of an earlier generation, like their British contemporaries, would have thought of political docility as being a German failing.

The progressive 'Germanization' of the American people's attitude has proceeded *pari passu* with the escalation of the war that the United States has been waging in Vietnam, and this change in the American way of life has been a calamity for the Asian country that has been made the theatre of hostilities and has also been a menace for the rest of the World. The American people have been in a dangerous mood because 'all power corrupts, and absolute power corrupts absolutely'. The present war-making power of the United States is the mightiest that the government of any sovereign state has ever wielded yet. The defiance of this mighty American power by a small and technologically ill-equipped Asian people has been humiliating for the American people's national pride; this pride has been keyed up to a high pitch by a previously unbroken record of military success; and it has also been influenced by fanaticism. America's war in Vietnam has been a crusade, as many Americans have seen it; but it has been a crusade in which the crusaders have mistaken the identity of their adversary. In the belief that she has been tilting against Communism, America has collided with Vietnamese Nationalism, and the strength of the resistance with which America has met in Vietnam has been a local expression of a general Asian and African determination to get rid, once for all, of the West's hated ascendancy.

In this tense situation, the Administration at Washington has been under pressure from the Pentagon to bring into play the whole armoury of hideous weapons that the advance of technology has placed in the Pentagon's hands, and the American people have been inclined to endorse the Pentagon's demands, partly because Americans take delight in technological virtuosity for its own sake, and partly because they have believed—perhaps mistakenly in this case, considering the nature of the terrain in Vietnam and the spirit of their opponents there—that, in the Vietnam war, losses of American lives could be economized by making machinery do duty for man-power, as it has been made to serve so successfully in civil life inside the United States.

The words that I was writing in 1968 will not have been published till April 1969. In the meantime the negotiations that had been started in Paris in May 1968 might have resulted in agreement or might have ended in failure or might be still continuing, and in any event the American people's state of mind in April 1969 could not be predicted in 1968; but something has already happened that is ir-reversible and ineffaceable. The American people have succumbed to militarism; and, even if this lapse proves to be only temporary in the United States, as it seems already to have proved to be in Japan and Germany, it has revealed to the rest of the World an aspect of America that is as disconcerting as it has been unexpected. Even if the American people retrieve this lapse, as they did eventually retrieve their acquiescence in Senator Joseph McCarthy's tyranny, the World's 'image' of America will never again be the same as it was before.

4 : The Struggle between Human Feeling and Inhumanity

(i) THE SCHISM OVER WAR AS THE CLASSICAL CASE OF A GENERAL MORAL CONFLICT

In the last chapter before this one I have discussed the changes in the attitude towards war that I have witnessed in my lifetime and have also experienced in myself. When I was a child, the institution of war, which, by then, had been in existence for perhaps about five thousand years, was still being taken for granted by most people in the World as a normal and acceptable fact of life. One small religious community, the Society of Friends, was at that time singular in condemning war as immoral and in consequently refusing to have any part or lot in war-making. I have lived to see the Quakers' attitude to war spread to a far wider circle.

The now widespread revulsion against war has been largely due to the appalling intensification of the murderousness of war through the application of a rapidly advancing technology to the 'improvement' of weapons. The peoples of the Western World were horrified and shocked at the mutual slaughter of their physically and mentally finest young men in the trench-warfare of the First World War. This was selective human sacrifice on an unprecedented scale. It out-Aztec-ed the Aztecs. The introduction of bombing from the air during the Spanish civil war, and the invention and use of the atomic bomb in the last act of the Second World War, demonstrated that in the future the human sacrifice perpetrated in war was going to be no longer selective but indiscriminate, as it has been, in fact, in the war in Vietnam. As a result of these harrowing experiences, the necessity, for prudential reasons, of abolishing war has come, between 1918 and 1969, to be widely recognized; but simultaneously there has also been a wide recognition of the truth—declared and acted on by the Quakers for three centuries already—that the paramount argument for abolishing war is not a prudential one but is a moral one. War is wicked. Nevertheless, some people (particularly people who have not yet experienced wars in their own country) have not only continued to regard war as being normal and respectable; they have also exploited the rapidly accelerating advance of technology for making the conduct of war more and more devastating and atrocious.

Thus, within my lifetime, there has been a schism in mankind's attitude towards war as a result of the increase in the potency of weapons. Attitudes have diverged, and these divergent attitudes have both been tending, alike, to go to extremes. This polarization of feeling and opinion in my lifetime has been particularly conspicuous on the subject of war because, since 1914, the severity of the degree to which mankind has been afflicting itself with the scourge of war has been unprecedented. However, this phenomenon of polarization has not been confined to people's feelings about war; it has made its appearance within my lifetime over the whole field of human affairs. The struggle between the people who now want to abolish war and the people who now want to aggravate it by applying to it the rapidly advancing power of technology is only a particular case, though it is the most conspicuous and most momentous case, of a general struggle between human feeling and inhumanity—or, in Zoroastrian terms, between cosmic spirits of good and evil. Polarization of feelings, and of conduct too, has displayed itself in my lifetime in a number of other fields, besides the field of war.

(ii) HUMAN FEELING VERSUS GENOCIDE, EVICTION, AND APARTHEID

There has not, so far as I know, been any previous age in which the common humanity of all human beings, just in virtue of our all being human, has been so widely recognized and acted upon as it is today. The famous and moving sentiment 'homo sum, humanum nihil a me alienum puto',[1] which the Roman playwright Terence put into the mouth of one of his characters, is actually more characteristic of the present-day world than it was of the Graeco-Roman World of the second century B.C. Yet the age through which I have lived has also seen the moral implications of mankind's common humanity repudiated in outrageous doctrines that have served as excuses for atrocious acts.

Human beings have occasionally massacred each other unconstitutionally—apart from the hallowed ritual form of massacre in war—since the earliest times of which we have surviving records. But in our time we have had to coin a new word, 'genocide', to describe a new kind of massacre. The distinguishing marks of our twentieth-century genocide are that it is committed in cold-blood by the deliberate *fiat* of holders of despotic political power, and that the perpetrators of genocide employ all the resources of present-day technology and organization to make their planned massacres systematic and complete. I am old enough to remember the horror at the massacre of Armenian Ottoman subjects in the Ottoman Empire in 1896 at the instigation of the infamous Sultan 'Abd-al-Hamid II. But this act of genocide was amateur and ineffective compared with the largely successful attempt to exterminate the Ottoman Armenians that was made during the First World War,

---

[1] 'I am a human being, so there is nothing human that I do not feel to be my concern' (Terence, *Heautontimorumenus*, line 77), quoted already on p. 94.

in 1915, by the post-Hamidian régime of 'The Committee of Union and Progress', in which the principal criminals were Tala't and Enver. The Second World War was accompanied by the Nazis' genocide of the Jews both in Germany and in the other European countries that were temporarily overrun and occupied by the German military forces. Since the general level of technological and organizational efficiency in Germany during the dozen years of the Nazi régime was considerably higher than it had been in Turkey during the ten years of the C.U.P. régime, the German genocide of the European Jews was still more effective than the Turkish genocide of the Ottoman Armenians had been. The Nazi régime is estimated to have succeeded in murdering six million Jews. Since the end of the Second World War the political liberation, from European colonial rule, of the former British Indian Empire and of a large part of Africa south of the Sahara has been tragically marred by genocide, on a horrifying scale, in the Indian sub-continent, in Ruanda-Urundi, and in Nigeria. The genocide suffered by the Ibo diaspora in Northern Nigeria has led the Ibo people to fear, not without reason, that they may be in danger of being exterminated in their own homeland. This has led to the secession of Biafra from the Nigerian Federation; and this, in turn, has led to a hard-fought and devastating civil war in Nigeria. This was one of the three current wars (the other two were in the Middle East and in Vietnam) by which, in 1968, the human race was disgracing itself and was also putting its survival in jeopardy.

To be massacred is a worse fate than to be evicted from one's native land and to be robbed of one's home and property. The refugee has ransomed his life at this price, and, so long as he remains alive, he can cherish at least a forlorn hope of eventual repatriation and restitution, or alternatively of compensation and re-settlement in some new habitat that will be congenial enough to make it possible for him to strike fresh roots there. All the same, the eviction of entire populations, or even of diasporas, is a recent relapse, in the present age, into a barbarous practice that was occasionally followed in past times, but in those times less remorselessly and less thoroughly.

When the political map of Central and Eastern Europe was redrawn in the peace-settlement after the First World War, a genuine attempt was made to apply the liberal principle of political self-determination. However, the geographical intermingling of nationalities in this region worked together with the natural, yet culpable, inclination of the victors to decide in favour of countries that happened to have been on the winning side in cases in which there were rival claims to the possession of territories in which the nationality of the local population was not homogeneous. The result was that a number of minorities were placed, or were left, on the side of a newly-drawn frontier that was the wrong side from these minorities' points of view. In these circumstances it did not occur to the peace-settlement-makers on this occasion to evict these residual minorities from their homes in countries in which other nationalities were in a majority and were consequently in power. So far from that, the Principal Allied and Associated Powers compelled the newly created or newly enlarged states in Central and Eastern Europe to sign treaties for the protection of minorities of alien nationality as a condition for the award of the new frontiers to these states that had been fortunate enough to find themselves on the winning side. The implementation of these treaties for the protection of minorities was not effectively enforced. Yet the League of Nations did effectively intervene to prevent the inter-war Polish Government from evicting German agricultural colonists in Posnan (Posen) who had been planted, before the First World War, on lands in this Polish territory that had been expropriated by the Prussian Government, while Posen was still Prussian territory, as part of a policy of Germanization. This policy had been indefensible; yet, in the inter-war period, the League of Nations rightly held that the indefensible circumstances in which the German settlers had acquired their farms in Posnan did not justify their being now evicted from these, however unjustifiable their installation in them might have been. Eviction on political grounds was rightly held to be morally inadmissible, even in unusually provocative circumstances.

The first big lapse from the observance of this principle was the compulsory exchange of minority populations and their property as between Turkey and Greece and between Turkey, Greece, and Bulgaria after the débâcle of the Greek army in Anatolia in the Graeco-Turkish war after the end of the First World War. It was recognized that this compulsory migration and compulsory exchange of private property was the lesser evil in the then existing circumstances. Animosity between the nationalities concerned in this case had by then become so violent that it had ceased to be practicable for minorities to remain *in situ*. The Greek and Armenian minorities in Turkey had fled and had abandoned their property; the Turkish minority in Greece had been expelled in reprisal; the sufferings and losses of the evicted persons and of the spontaneous refugees were mitigated by the provision that the abandoned or confiscated private property in each country should be taken over by the government of that country and should then be distributed among the refugees whom that country was receiving from the other country in question. This arrangement, which was carried out under the supervision of the League of Nations, did make it possible for these Greek, Turkish, and Bulgarian refugees and evicted persons to strike fresh roots and to start a new life in new homes where their neighbours and the government were of their own nationality.

The fate of these transplanted Greeks, Turks, and Bulgarians has been happy compared with the fate of the Palestinian Arabs who have fled, or have been evicted, from their ancestral homes and have been robbed of their property since the establishment of the State of Israel on Arab-inhabited territory in Palestine in 1948. Since the Third Arab–Israeli War (the Six Days' War of 1967), the number of Palestinian Arab exiles, including children born and brought up in exile, had risen in 1968 to about one million and a half. There must also have been about one million residual Palestinian Arabs under Israeli rule in the territories on the Israeli side of the successive armistice-lines of 1949 and 1967, and this now politically subject Palestinian Arab population was suffering the 'second-class-citizen' treatment that was suffered by the Central and East European subject minorities during the inter-war years.

As for the Palestinian Arab evicted persons and refugees, those who were robbed of their homes and property by the Israelis in 1948–9 have been prevented, under pain of being shot at sight, from returning to their homes on the Israeli side of the 1949 armistice-lines, and they have received no compensation for their stolen and unrecoverable property either from the Israelis or from anyone else. They have been kept alive in exile on a pittance doled out by other nations—mainly by the United States and by Great Britain. The American and British contributions are 'conscience money' (i.e. are a tacit admission of the extent of these two countries' share in the responsibility for the Palestinian Arab exiles' present plight). This dole, insufficient though it was, was being administered efficiently and humanely by a United Nations Agency (UNRWA) till its work was dislocated and paralysed by the Israelis' military occupation of the Gaza Strip in 1967.

The governments of the Arab states have been accused of inciting the Palestinian Arabs to evacuate the war-zone in 1948 and of having, since then, deliberately refrained from re-settling the Palestinian Arab refugees in their own territories, because, so it is alleged, they have wanted to keep them for use as political pawns. The first of these two charges is unproven, while on the other hand there is evidence that, on the Israeli side, there was, in 1948, deliberate terrorization (the most flagrant single case was the massacre of the civilian population of Dayr Yasin), with the intention of stampeding the Palestinian Arabs into fleeing from their homes. The accusation that the Arab states have deliberately refrained from re-settling the Palestinian refugees in their own territories is certainly not true of Jordan or of the United Arab Republic, which, between them, have had the great majority of the Palestinian refugees on their hands. Jordan, a small and poor country, has given the refugees on her territory from Israel-occupied Palestinian Arab territory equality of rights and opportunities with her own citizens. The United Arab Republic, an over-populated country, has given intellectually promising Palestinian Arab refugee high-school children from the Gaza Strip free places in universities in Egypt and subsequent opportunities for professional careers in Egypt if the performance of these Palestinian Arab recipients of bursaries at Egyptian universities has been good.

Though the Arab World is extensive, and though some Arab states receive large revenues from oil-royalties, all Arab states except the densely populated and mountainous Lebanon are still in the stage of being 'developing' countries in which additional openings for employment are few. Nor can the Palestinian Arab refugees be re-settled forcibly against their will—and many of them are as resolutely determined to endure exile in the hope of eventually recovering their homes as the Jewish exiles were after their deportation by the Babylonians in the sixth century B.C. and their eviction by the Romans in the second century of the Christian Era.

Since the end of the Second World War the number of German evicted persons and refugees from post-war East Germany, Poland, Czechoslovakia, and the Soviet Union that have been received in West Germany has been approximately equal to the number of European Jews murdered, during that war, by the Nazis. As a result of Germany's defeat in the Second World War, the eastern frontier of Germany was set back to the Oder–Neisse line, and the whole of the former Sudeten-German minority in Czechoslovakia was expelled. Moreover, the conditions of life in East Germany and in East Berlin under the post-war Communist régime have proved so obnoxious to a large section of the population that there has been a stream of refugees from East Germany, too, to West Germany. This vast mass of Eastern German refugees—about four times the size of the present mass of Palestinian Arab refugees—has been successfully re-settled in West Germany. The moral credit for this achievement is due to the vigour and efficiency with which both the refugees and the indigenous population of West Germany have worked; but West Germany, in contrast to the Arab countries, has also had the technological and economic advantage of being a 'developed' country with a capacity for winning a large share in the world market for manufactures. West Germany's post-war industrial expansion has, indeed, been so great that, after putting to work the additional labour-force provided by the Eastern German refugees, West Germany has had to bring in non-German workers from outside her frontiers—and these not only from Italy and Spain but from as far afield as Greece and Turkey.

To be massacred is a worse fate than to be evicted and despoiled, and to be evicted and despoiled is a worse fate than being left un-uprooted at the price of being penalized. The penalization of a weaker section of a population is not a new form of inhumanity in itself. People have been penalized in the past frequently on account of their religion, their nationality, and their race. Penalization of innocent people on any ground is immoral, but the outlook is the most ominous—and this for the persecutors as well as for the persecuted—in cases in which the ground for the penalization is a differ-ence in physical race. Differences in physical race are immutable so long as their obliteration through intermarriage or through extra-marital sexual intercourse is prevented by effectively enforced legis-lation, whereas it is possible to change one's religion and one's nationality either voluntarily or under duress, and in this case the persecutor is likely, not to be obstructive, but to be gratified.

Within my lifetime I have lived to see penalization on racial grounds intensified, and the obliteration of racial differences through interbreeding obstructed by increasingly harsh legislation, by the 'white' dominant minority in South Africa. The 'white' dominant minority in Rhodesia is taking the same road. On the other hand in the United States, a century after the abolition of slavery in the Old South, the 'white' majority in the rest of the country has been mak-ing a determined effort to achieve racial 'integration', and it has succeeded in imposing its policy on the recalcitrant 'white' com-munity in the Old South. Yet 'integration' has no sooner come within sight of achieving success than it has become apparent that this is not enough to solve the United States' race-problem.

'Integration', like 'apartheid', is a matter of law, and it can achieve no more than law can achieve in any sphere. Law's weakness is that its range is not coextensive with social life. There are many kinds of social relations that cannot be regulated by legislation. The South African legislation instituting 'apartheid' would be ineffective if a majority of the 'white' dominant minority in South Africa were opposed to it. The legislation instituting 'integration' in the United States is effective only in so far as it is reflected in the feelings and behaviour of the dominant 'white' majority there; and, now that a larger and larger percentage of the Negro population of the United States is moving out of the Old South into the industrial cities of the North-East, the 'whites' of the 'blue-collar' class in these cities are showing the same antipathy to the Negro that has been shown in the South ever since the Confederacy's defeat in the Civil War and the abolition of slavery have made the dominance of the Southern 'whites' insecure. The Negro American citizen may now be the 'white' American citizen's equal in the eyes of the law, but this juridical equality does not automatically guarantee to the Negro equal pay with his 'white' fellow-worker for equal work.

It does not guarantee that he will have equal housing amenities or educational opportunities.

The Negro was promised, and this in good faith, first that emancipation, and then that integration, would spell the end of his inferiority in status and in standard of living. Each time, the hopes that the Negro was encouraged to cherish have been disappointed, and inevitably he has become disillusioned and embittered. A section of the Negro community in the United States is already inclined to revert to 'apartheid', but this time of their own volition and in a militant form. This change in the American Negro's temper and objective in the North-East threatens to make the shooting race-war that ravaged Detroit and Newark in the summer of 1967 become an annual event; and, each time that this violence recurs, it is likely to spread more widely. Endemic civil war—and this of race against race—is a formidable prospect for any nation to have to face. Since I wrote these last lines, the assassination of Dr. Martin Luther King has provoked another outbreak of violence in advance of the routine summer-time disturbances.

A Mexican, a Brazilian, or a Muslim might be justified in denouncing the race-feeling of the dominant 'whites' in the United States, Rhodesia, and South Africa. In the Islamic World, Brazil, and Mexico, race-conflict has been averted partly by the bond of common religion and partly by inter-marriage, which the religious bond makes acceptable where religion is taken seriously. On the other hand, a British observer of the tragic course of events in Rhodesia, South Africa, and the United States cannot, in 1969, have the face to be self-righteous.

In Britain down to the end of the Second World War, we plumed ourselves on being immune against race-prejudice. I remember being once gently reproved, when I was a child, by my mother for staring at some Indian students whom we were passing in the street. Curiosity, not antipathy, was the feeling that was making me gaze intently at these unfamiliar dark faces. But my mother rightly pointed out to me that to indulge my curiosity by staring was embarrassing for my fellow human beings at whom my stare was directed, and that my behaviour was therefore inconsiderate to the point of being rude. In 1969, dark faces are too familiar in Britain to excite a 'white' child's curiosity any longer, but they do excite the antipathy of a disconcertingly large number of 'white' adults. We have now realised that our previous apparent immunity against race-feeling was merely a temporary immunity from being confronted with the problem of race-relations in an inter-racial society. The symptoms that we have observed and disapproved of in South African, Rhodesian, and American 'whites' have all made their appearance among ourselves in Britain since the post-war immigration into Britain of West Indians, East Indians, and Pakistanis in appreciably large numbers.

These post-war 'non-white' immigrants have taken over work in Britain that the 'white' natives are no longer willing to do but that has to continue to be done if social life in Britain is to continue to function. Although—or, possibly, just because—the services that these 'non-white' immigrants into Britain are now performing are essential, their presence is being resented by the native 'whites'. This resentment has now risen to a pitch at which the Government of the United Kingdom has been constrained to introduce racially discriminatory legislation. First, a legal restriction has been placed on the immigration into Britain of citizens of other states members of the British Commonwealth, who previously were free to enter and reside in Britain as of right. In 1968 a discriminatory legal restriction was being placed on the entry of Indian and Pakistani inhabitants of Kenya who held valid United Kingdom passports, while 'white' inhabitants of Kenya who held identical passports were being left still free to exercise the right of entry that a United Kingdom passport legally confers. Since I wrote these lines, the race question has been made a party issue in Britain by the Conservative Party's decision to oppose a bill, laid before Parliament by the Government in office, for making illegal certain discriminatory practices with which the law can deal. Worse still, an inflammatory speech has produced an explosion of expressions of race-feeling among the 'white' natives of districts in Britain in which the settlement of 'coloured' immigrants has been relatively dense. This post-war upsurge of race-feeling among the 'white' natives of Britain puts the 'white' dissentients from it to shame. It also alarms those of us who have seen something at first hand of the consequences of race-conflict in other countries in which human beings of different race are intermingled geographically.

An alarming feature of race-feeling is its irrationality. There does not seem to be any scientific evidence that physical differences in, for example, the amount of pigmentation in the skin, or in the texture of the hair, or in the shape of the nose have any correlation with differences in intrinsic virtue and ability. In all races the percentage of geniuses, morons, criminals, and saints is probably the same. In cases in which physical differences do appear, at first sight, to be correlated with psychic differences, they usually prove, on examination, to be correlated with cultural differences in reality. Cultural differences may tally with racial differences because the members of the race in question have had a late start in civilization owing to their having been relatively isolated geographically before 'the annihilation of distance' by modern technology. Alternatively, a race may be artificially repressed or retarded culturally as a consequence of its being penalized for its physical characteristics. This adverse cultural effect of penalization on racial grounds sets up a vicious circle which it is difficult to break.

Can this vicious circle be broken? Experience tells us that, happily, it can be broken by intermarriage. Where apartheid is an established institution, the breaking of the humanity-barrier by intermarriage is an heroic act on the part of the pioneers who dare to take the lead in performing it; but, when dared, it is a sovereign remedy. This is demonstrated by the efficacy of intermarriage, illustrated in the next section of this chapter, in promoting the assimilation of diasporas. Conversely, the cases of apartheid in which intermarriage is ruled out have proved to be the most intractable and the most tragic. The classic case in point is that of the Jews.

The tragic series of conflicts between the Jews and their gentile neighbours began, on the evidence of the Books of Ezra and Nehemiah, when Ezra succeeded in forcing the members of the Jewish community in Judaea to dissolve all existing marriages with gentiles and to refrain from marrying gentiles from then onwards. This ban on intermarriage between Jews and gentiles had presumably been instituted in the Jewish diaspora in Babylonia at some date later than the return to Judaea of a fraction of this diaspora in 538 B.C.; for Ezra and Nehemiah were members of the portion of the Jewish diaspora in Babylonia that had not taken up the option to return which had been granted to this diaspora by Cyrus; and

Ezra found, when he came on his mission to Judaea, that intermarriage with gentiles was common practice among the descendants
both of the exiles who had returned in 538 B.C. and of 'the people
of the land', i.e. the Judaean peasantry, who had not been uprooted
when Nebuchadnezzar had deported the notables and the skilled
workers of the Kingdom of Judah in three successive batches which
had amounted to no more than 4600 persons in all.[1]

The tabu against intermarriage with gentiles that Ezra instituted
has become so strong in the course of twenty-three or twenty-four
centuries[2] that it has survived the emancipation of the West European Jews in the Napoleonic Age and of the Jews in the Russian
major portion of the ex-Polono-Lithuanian Jewish Pale since the
Russian Revolution of 1917. Jews who have since become assimilated
to their gentile neighbours in language and culture, and even those
assimilated Jews who have lost all belief in the Jewish religion, still
feel an inhibition against marrying gentiles, and non-Jews, on their
side, feel a corresponding prejudice, though this perhaps rather less
strongly, against marrying Jews. Nevertheless, in Germany and
Austria, as well as in Western Europe, in the course of the century ending in Hitler's coming into power in Germany in 1933,
intermarriage between Jews and non-Jews had been becoming
increasingly frequent. But on the Jewish side this progress towards
assimilation has been checked, since then, by the terrible experience
of genocide.

In the Hindu World the same inhibition persists among Western-
ised Brahmans. The extreme present case, however, of the imposition
of racial apartheid is the legislation now in force in the Union of
South Africa which forbids the dominant 'white' diaspora there
not only to marry 'non-whites' but to have extra-marital sexual
relations with them. By contrast, in 'the Old South' of the United
States, 'white' males feel no inhibition against having sexual intercourse with Negro women so long as the Negro woman's status of
social inferiority is preserved by her serving as a 'white' man's
mistress or as a prostitute. The 'white' man who can have relations
with her on these terms with impunity would incur odium among

[1] Jer. lii. 28–30.
[2] The dating of Nehemiah's and Ezra's lifetimes depends on whether Nehemiah's
Artaxerxes was the first or the second Achaemenid Persian emperor of that name.

his fellow 'whites', and would feel uneasy in his own mind, if he were to raise his Negro mistress's status by making her his wedded wife. Among Southern American 'whites' the obstacle to legal intermarriage is not any physical allergy to having sexual relations with Negroes; it is a political motive, namely the determination to keep the Southern 'white's' Negro fellow citizen in a position of social inferiority—*de jure* if possible, *de facto* if and when social integration is imposed by law. This motive is revealed in the dominant 'white' majority's tabu on legal marriage between 'white' and Negro Americans, and in the further tabu on extra-marital sexual relations between 'white' women and Negro men, in conjunction with the absence of any corresponding tabu in cases in which the male party is 'white' and the female party is Negro.

These intentionally humiliating conventions, imposed by the 'whites', on sexual relations between 'whites' and 'Negroes' are now evoking, in the American Negro community, a reaction like the European Jews' and the ex-European Israeli Jews' reaction to genocide. The injured community is retorting to compulsory re-segregation (followed, in the European Jews' case, by wholesale murder) by adopting a policy of counter-segregation on their own part. A natural and praiseworthy sense of human dignity, whatever may be a human being's physical traits, is the obverse side of the coin of Black Power whose reverse side is the threat of endemic race-war in a country in which the 'white' and Negro races are now intermingled geographically not only in 'the Old South' but throughout the United States.

These setbacks to the progress of integration as between Jews and gentiles and between 'whites' and Negroes are misfortunes for the whole of mankind—the common race of all the so-called 'races'.

(iii) DIASPORAS, PENALIZED OR DOMINANT

Diasporas are the inevitable products of local differences in the level of civilization, and these local differences have existed ever since the earliest civilization known to us emerged in Sumer about five thousand years ago. When societies that are at appreciably different levels of civilization make contact with each other, the backward society comes under pressure to try to catch up with the more advanced society, or, short of that, to try to narrow the gap between

them. The members of the backward society realize that, if they
do not now quickly acquire the arts and techniques of the more
advanced civilization, they will be in danger of going under. But it
is difficult for them to raise their cultural level rapidly without aid
from the more highly civilized society which is setting for them the
higher cultural level that has become their objective. They have
immediately to play a part in a world whose cultural level is above
their heads. They cannot afford to wait.

The remedy for their plight is to import members of the more
advanced community to perform, on their behalf, functions that
they are not yet capable of performing for themselves, but for which
they must make provision if they are to hold their own in the strange
new world into which they have been drawn. This need that the
backward society feels offers the advanced society an opportunity.
It opens up for its members a new field of enterprise. They can
staff the backward country with the skilled personnel that it requires
but cannot supply for itself. This is one of the ways in which a
diaspora comes into being. In the present-day world the local
differences in the level of civilization are great; the advance of
technology has 'annihilated distance'; cultural levelling-up has
become an urgent need for a majority of the peoples of the Earth;
diasporas are therefore now perhaps more numerous and more
important than they have ever been before; and accordingly, within
my lifetime, diasporas have become one of the World's most
intractable problems. The problem is intractable because a diaspora's
indispensability makes it unpopular.

The classical example of this crux in the Western World's history
is the indispensability and unpopularity of the Jews in mediaeval
Western Christendom. Without the services performed for it by
the Jews in its midst, mediaeval Western Christendom could not
have held its own against the superior civilizations of Eastern Orthodox Christendom and the Islamic World. The Jewish diaspora in
the West realized the value for the West of the services that it was
rendering to the West, and therefore, being human, this Jewish
diaspora priced its services high. The backward mediaeval Western
Christians realized, on their side, that the local Jews were both
performing indispensable services and taking advantage of their
monopoly and skill. The Western Christian majority retorted by

penalizing the Jewish minority so long as they could not do without them and then by evicting them as soon as they became capable of being their own Jews. They did not re-admit the Jews till they had become proficient enough in the Jews' skills to be able to hold their own against Jewish competition.

This classical example of the history of the Jews in the mediaeval West tells us that a diaspora's position is always precarious. This precariousness leads the members of a diaspora to hang together and to give each other mutual support. In the natives' eyes, this looks like a conspiracy contrived against them by an alien minority in their midst. This suspicion makes the diaspora still more unpopular, and, the more unpopular it is, the more close becomes the sectional solidarity of the members of the diaspora among themselves. This sets up a vicious circle of action and reaction that is apt to be broken in one or the other of two ways. Either the diaspora will be eliminated by massacre or eviction or, alternatively, it will become a dominant alien minority ruling over a subject native majority. The 'white' diaspora is still a dominant minority in Southern Africa today, but it has gone under already in Kenya and in North-West Africa. The Ibos have gone under in Northern Nigeria and the Chinese in Indonesia, but the Chinese are dominant at present in Malaysia.

Is there any third possible dénouement besides these two polar extremes, both of which are disastrous? Fortunately there is. The alien diaspora may acquiesce in, or may positively aim at, gradual assimilation as the 'culture-gap' between the diaspora and the natives diminishes progressively—partly as a direct result of the working of the alien yeast in the native dough.

On a visit to Ethiopia at Eastertime 1966 I was surprised, after nightfall, to see a large illuminated sky-sign, installed in a conspicuous position in the capital city, Addis Ababa, spelling out, in letters of fire, the words 'Club Italiano'. Considering what the Italians had done to Ethiopia in 1935–6, how could any Italians have ventured to remain there after the liquidation, early in the Second World War, of the brief Italian rule that had been imposed by a cynical and brutal act of military aggression? And, since some Italians evidently had remained, how could they have ventured to advertise their presence instead of discreetly lying low? On inquiry

I found that, of the three diasporas that were doing modern kinds of skilled work in Ethiopia in 1966, the Italians were the most popular, in spite of the facts that the Italians' Greek and Armenian competitors had never done the Ethiopians any wrong and that the Armenians are also the Ethiopians' co-religionists. (They are the Ethiopians' fellow members of the pre-Chalcedonian Church, commonly called 'monophysite' by Christians who are dissenters from it.) The Armenians and the Greeks were comparatively unpopular because they remitted the greater part of their earnings made in Ethiopia to their families, whose permanent domicile was somewhere abroad, and also because they married, as a rule, within their own community. By contrast, the Italians readily married Ethiopians and they kept their earnings in the country. These two Italian practices were interpreted by the Ethiopians, no doubt correctly, as evidence of an intent on the local Italians' part to make Ethiopia their permanent home. The Italians' willingness to marry Ethiopians had made the Ethiopians forgive the Italians for having massacred them in the recent past. I have already declared my conviction, based on what I have seen of the World in my time, that intermarriage is the sovereign solvent for apartheid.

Willingness, on both sides, for assimilation thus seems to be the civilized solution for the problem created by the presence of an alien diaspora among a relatively backward native majority. In Colombia in 1956 I had seen the local Lebanese and Syrian Arab Christian diaspora (known in Latin America as 'Turcos') living in much the same relation with the local creoles and mestizos as the Ethiopian Italians' relation with the Ethiopians in 1966. The 'Turcos' in Colombia, like the Italians in Ethiopia, had clubs of their own, and their level of skill, and of the income that is skill's reward, was likewise higher than the natives' level. At the same time the 'Turcos', like the Italians, did intermarry with the natives, and in Colombia, as in Ethiopia, the diaspora's freedom from race-prejudice portended their eventual assimilation and shielded them, meanwhile, from incurring the odium that their superior skill and wealth might otherwise have brought upon them.

In Argentina in 1966 I found the British diaspora opting for assimilation. More and more of them were renouncing their British citizenship and taking Argentinian citizenship. They were having their children educated in Argentina, and this at all stages, instead of continuing to send them to Britain for their secondary-school and university education. This tendency among this particular diaspora was noteworthy for several reasons. The Teutonic-speaking peoples are, in general, race-conscious and language-conscious, as has been demonstrated in Southern Africa, Australia, the United States, and Canada. Moreover in Argentina the British diaspora had been dominant economically for nearly a century ending in 1914. They had enabled Argentina to modernise herself by equipping her with modern public utilities: ports, gas-works, electrical installations and, above all, a network of railways, radiating out from Buenos Aires, which had been instrumental in opening up the pampas first for cattle-breeding and eventually for agriculture. Considering the history of the British diaspora in Argentina, its decision, after the Second World War, to merge itself in the Argentinian people was evidence of insight into the realities of its situation. If it had still struggled to maintain its separate communal identity, this would have been human, but it would also have been suicidal. The choice with which this diaspora was now confronted lay, as it recognized, between becoming assimilated and being squeezed out.

In Uruguay in 1966 I saw the process of assimilation in operation over a span of four generations. I was visiting a cattle-ranch that had been established, a hundred years or more back, by a Presbyterian Scottish settler. The ranch had prospered; the family had become local notables; and, as they had gained in wealth and status, they had identified themselves progressively with their Uruguayan neighbours. In 1966 all four living generations were already Roman Catholics in religion; the oldest generation of the four was still bilingual, though its representatives spoke English with a strong Castilian accent; the youngest generation, which was not yet grown-up, would have been taken for Uruguayans of Spanish descent if their Scottish origin had not been revealed by their surname.

Intermarriage is the key to assimilation, and community of religion facilitates intermarriage. For instance, the French Pro-testants who, after the revocation of the Edict of Nantes, had emigrated to Protestant countries—England, the Netherlands, South Africa, Württemberg, Prussia, South Carolina—had at once begun to intermarry with the local populations of the Protestant countries that had given them asylum. They had settled in their new homes in order to live among co-religionists, and they had been welcomed because they had suffered in their original homes for professing the same religion as their hosts. In these circumstances intermarriage was a foregone conclusion. Similarly in Argentina the Irish settlers had quickly started to intermarry with the Argentinians of Spanish descent because, like these, they were Roman Catholics. The English families who had settled in Argentina in the same generation as the Irish had been slower to intermarry because they had mostly been Protestants, and for them the difference in religion had been an obstacle to intermarriage and therefore to assimilation. In their case, conversions to Roman Catholicism were one of the symptoms of the living generation's decision to identify itself with its adopted country. In Colombia, many of the 'Turcos' were Uniates (either Maronites or Melchites), and for Uniate Roman Catholics it is not difficult to change over to the Latin rite when they settle in a country where Latin-rite Roman Catholicism is the religion of the land.

However, there are exceptions to the normal rule that a diaspora which is of the same religion as the natives is more inclined to intermarry with these than diasporas of other religions are. I have already mentioned that in 1966 I found that in Ethiopia the Roman Catholic Italian diaspora was intermarrying with the pre-Chalcedonian natives more readily than the pre-Chalcedonian Armenian diaspora was.

The relations between a diaspora and the native population of the country in which the diaspora is domiciled are most difficult in cases in which intermarriage is penalized or is positively banned, on the one or the other side or on both sides, either by law, whether civil or religious, or by prejudice. In 1969 the worst offenders among the now existing diasporas are the Jews, the Brahmans, and the 'white' diaspora in Southern Africa.

(iv) WEST EUROPEAN DE-COLONIZATION AND THE NEW COLONIAL EMPIRES

The struggle between human feeling and inhumanity has also been waged, in my lifetime, in the field of the political relations between the peoples of the World. I have mentioned already that I am old enough to remember vividly the celebration of Queen Victoria's

diamond jubilee in 1897 and that it can now be seen, in retrospect,
that this was really a celebration of the zenith of the British Empire.
The British was merely the largest and most potent of the empires
possessed at that date by a number of West European states: Britain,
France, the Netherlands, Belgium, Germany, and Italy. In 1897
these six West European countries, between them, were dominant,
in some degree, over almost all the rest of the World. The extent
of their empires at that date is not fully revealed by the colours on
the political map of the World in 1897, vast though this map shows
Western Europe's non-European political possessions, dependencies,
and protectorates to have been at the turn of the nineteenth and
twentieth centuries. A number of countries—some of them large
countries—that figure on the map at that date as being politically
independent were economically dependent on Western Europe,
and economic dependence, when it becomes extreme, makes
nominal political independence unreal. In 1897, Western Europe's
economic empire—invisible on the political map but palpable for
its subjects—included the Russian Empire, the Ottoman Turkish
Empire, Iran, the Chinese Empire, and all the Latin American
republics.

In 1897 the United States itself was Western Europe's debtor.
She had financed the development of her vast virgin western
territories by borrowing West European capital. The tables were
not turned till, in the First World War, the West European powers
played among themselves a suicidal game of beggar-my-European-
neighbour. In 1897 Western Europe had still seventeen years of
financial dominance ahead of her before she started, in the First
World War, to bring on herself the ruin that she consummated in
the Second World War. The tables were turned indeed when, after
the Second World War, Europe owed her economic rehabilitation
to the Marshall Plan, under which American aid was given as a free
gift, in contrast to the business terms on which the economic
development of the United States had been financed by Western
Europe in the nineteenth century.

The United States' indebtedness to Europe, heavy though this
was at its peak, did not, of course, undermine the United States'
political independence at any stage. Apart from the United States,
however, completely independent states were rare, outside Europe,

in 1897. In Asia there were, by that time, only two, namely Japan and Thailand, and in Africa there was only one, Ethiopia, after the annexation of the Orange Free State and the Transvaal to the British Empire in the South African War. Liberia, though nominally independent, was virtually a protectorate of the United States. Ethiopia—a natural fortress garrisoned by a martial people, the Amharas—had not only maintained her independence but had competed successfully with the West European powers in 'the scramble for Africa'. On the other hand, Egypt, which had started the scramble by conquering the Sudan in 1820, had not only lost her Nilotic empire to the followers of the Mahdi Muhammad Ahmad; she had herself fallen under British domination in 1882. Tunisia had fallen under French domination in 1881. Morocco was to be entered by the French army in 1905 and to become a French protectorate in 1911, and Libya was to be conquered by Italy from the Ottoman Empire in and after the latter year.

The political map of Africa in 1969, when set side by side with the map of Africa as it had been in 1897, gives the measure of the extent of the de-colonization of Africa, and of the rest of the former non-European dependencies of Western Europe, during the interval. The whole process of de-colonization has actually taken place during and since the Second World War, beginning with the liquidation, during this war, of Italy's short-lived rule over Ethiopia and culminating in Africa in France's withdrawal from Algeria. In 1968 the only surviving West European colonial empire in Africa was the oldest of them all, namely the Portuguese; and Portugal was still able to hold Angola and Mozambique only because she was being supported by one African country, South Africa, that was independent *de jure* and by another, Rhodesia, that, thanks to South Africa's and Portugal's support and Rhodesia's juridical sovereign Britain's weakness, was independent *de facto*.

Though the de-colonization movement had been started during the Second World War by the restoration of Ethiopia's independence, it was given its decisive impetus in 1947, when Britain—completing the execution of a pledge that she had given in 1917 and had been implementing progressively since then—relinquished her sovereignty over the former British Indian Empire and over Ceylon. (The liberated British Indian Empire immediately split into three separate independent states: the Indian Union, Pakistan, and Burma.) The Asian territories from which Britain withdrew in 1947 constituted so large and so important a part of Western Europe's aggregate non-European dominions that it made the liberation of the rest of these inevitable, and this in the near future.

The motives that moved the European ex-colonial powers to renounce their empires were mixed. Undoubtedly one motive was a moral one that was both genuine and disinterested. Important sections of public opinion in the West European countries that possessed colonial empires had come to feel that it was wrong for them to withhold from their non-European subjects the political independence that they claimed for themselves—and this not as a God-given European privilege but as a basic human right. There was also another motive that was not idealistic but was prudential, yet was not discreditable on that account.

By 1945—the date of the end of the Second World War— subject peoples all over the World were making insistent demands for national independence in the name of the principles of nationalism and democracy which they had learnt from their involuntary contact with their European rulers. These demands would have been made, and have been prosecuted in the last resort by violence, in any event; but the inevitable course of events had been speeded up by the effect of the two world wars—particularly by Japan's exploits in the Second World War, when she had bombed the United States fleet in Pearl Harbor and had temporarily overrun and occupied all American, British, French, and Dutch colonial possessions in Eastern Asia as far west as Malaya and Indonesia and Burma inclusive. These Japanese conquests had been ephemeral. The Second World War had ended in Japan herself having to capitulate and to submit, for the first time in her history, to being occupied militarily by a foreign power. Yet historically Japan's sensational opening victories have had more effect than her eventual defeat.

Japan has made history—irreversible history—by demonstating that the West is not invincible. In 1941 Japan called the Western powers' bluff. The reputation for invincibility that Britain had won at Plassey in 1757 and France at Imbabah in 1798 had enabled the West European powers, for the best part of two centuries, to conquer and hold vast non-European territories with small forces at slight cost. The West European empire-builders' victims had been psychologically defeated before they had joined battle physically with their West European assailants. Now that Japan had called the West's bluff, it was evident that the already rising tide of Asian and African anticolonialism was going to prove irresistible. After 1945 its irresistibility was demonstrated by French experience in Indo-china and Algeria and by British experience in Cyprus and South Arabia. After having exhausted themselves by the cumulative tribulation of two world wars, the European ex-colonial powers had neither the will nor the strength to hold by sheer force the empires that they had previously held mainly by prestige. The prudential reason for the West European powers' renunciation of their colonial empires was that they had come to the rational conclusion that the game of colonialism was no longer worth the candle.

For a brief moment it looked as if the end of European colonialism were going to be the end of colonialism itself; but, since the close of the Second World War, the Americans and Israelis have rushed in where West Europeans now fear to tread. Britain's renunciation, in 1948, of her mandate for the administration of Palestine was followed instantaneously by the proclamation of the establishment of the State of Israel on Palestinian Arab territory. The recession of the French wave of colonialism in Vietnam was followed promptly by the onset of an American wave, and the United States' war in Vietnam, like her previous war in Korea, has been part of an attempt to build an American colonial empire in Eastern Asia extending from Japan through South Korea and Taiwan and South Vietnam to Thailand, and also including Australia and New Zealand, which, in the pertinent geographical sense, are East Asian countries.

In its present first stage this American colonial empire in Eastern Asia has taken the form of an American protectorate over states that remain nominally independent but have actually become the United States' satellites. This had been the first stage in the building of the now defunct European colonial empires; so it is familiar to both the European ex-imperial peoples themselves and to their former Asian and African subjects. In the eyes of a majority of mankind, the United States in 1968 was in the act of trying, in her turn, to build up a colonial empire of the traditional kind. This foreign view of what the United States was trying to do was also held by a minority of the American public which was protesting against what their government was doing in their name. We may guess that the same view was held tacitly by some men in the Pentagon at Washington, D.C., who might be consciously and deliberately aiming at the objective that was attributed to the United States by the American dissenting minority and by the non-American world.

On the other hand, this charge was repudiated by most Americans sincerely and therefore indignantly. In this majority's eyes the Americans were not committing in 1968 the offence of empire-building which, in the past, they had justly condemned when it was being committed by their European fellow Westerners. The Americans believed themselves to be defending 'the Free World' (i.e. all countries living under non-Communist régimes of whatever kind) against 'World Communism'. In 1968 many Americans still believed, bona fide, that this monster exists and that its objective is nothing less than the conquest of the whole World. Non-American observers, on the other hand, are aware that the countries under Communist régimes are no more united among themselves than countries under other régimes are. Indeed, the quarrel between Communist Continental China and the Communist Soviet Union has been carried to extreme lengths, and the Soviet Union has retorted to liberalization in Czechoslovakia by military occupation.

The Americans see themselves waging a crusade, in the mediaeval Western meaning of the word, on behalf of World-Capitalist-Democracy against World-Communist-Tyranny. The Americans are right in thinking that the Capitalist and Communist post-Christian ideologies are religions, and these of the missionary kind, of which Buddhism, Christianity, and Islam are older representatives. President Wilson declared that the United States had intervened in the First World War 'to make the World safe for Democracy'; Trotsky, if he had been the victor in his contest with Stalin, would have expended the resources of the Soviet Union to make the World safe for Communism. The misapprehension that the Americans share with the Trotskyites is their mistaken common assumption that Capitalism and Communism are the principal— or even the sole—post-Christian ideologies that are in the running.

In reality the principal heir of Christianity and of all the other historic higher religions is, in 1969, not either of the two missionary ideologies; it is Nationalism. This is a potent religion partly because it is as old as mankind itself, and partly because, in the post-Christian Western World, the fanaticism that Christianity has inherited from Judaism has been decanted into Nationalism. The recent prestige of the West has moved the non-Western peoples to adopt this most powerful and most vicious of the three post-Christian Western ideologies. In 1969, Nationalism is about ninety per cent of the religion of about ninety per cent of the whole human race. Trotsky's defeat by Stalin is highly significant. In every country, whether Communist or Capitalist, in which the locally established ecumenical ideology has clashed with the country's particular national interests, these national interests have invariably been given precedence, and Communism or Capitalism—whichever it may happen to have been—has gone to the wall.

As I see it, the Americans have mistaken the identity of the adversary whom they have challenged in Vietnam. Their opponent there has been, not the mythical monster 'World Communism', but Vietnamese Nationalism. The military might of the United States was being frustrated in Vietnam in 1968 because Nationalism is a cause for which present-day human beings are willing to sacrifice their lives. The North Vietnamese and the Vietcong have been fighting, primarily, not to extend the domain of Communism, but to drive a foreign invader out of their country. The Soviet Union and Continental China have been giving North Vietnam and the Vietcong resistance-movement the tools to do the job, not for the idealistic reason that they are all fellow Communists, but for the practical reason that moved the United States to give the tools to Britain in 1940. The United States believed in 1940 that her own national security would be menaced by Germany if she were to allow Germany to conquer Britain. I have noted already that the Soviet Union and China, whose views of their respective national interests clash in 1969 over most issues, have been of one mind in holding that the national security of both powers would be menaced by the United States if they were to allow the United States to conquer and hold Vietnam.

In November 1968, one thing was already certain. Whatever the out-come of the war in Vietnam might be, the Vietnamese resist-ance-movement had already made history. A small 'developing' country had dared to defy the might of the strongest military power that has existed so far. The Vietnamese people had stood the ordeal of being tormented with 'conventional' weapons of unprecedented potency and atrociousness. They had prevented the invader from con-quering more than a minor part of their country, and their spirit had not been broken by enemy *Schrecklichkeit*—though this had been 'escalated' to a degree that put most previous performances in this line in the shade. Meanwhile, the heroism of the Vietnamese resistance had put a strain on the United States' economic resources that had shaken the World's confidence in the dollar. It is just conceivable that, by the time when the present book appears, the Vietnamese people will have been exterminated and Vietnam will have been made uninhabitable. The Vietnamese might suffer the fate that the Romans inflicted on the Palestinian Jewish resistance-movement in A.D. 66–70 and in A.D. 132–5. Yet in that event the Vietnamese would play the posthumous role that was played by the three hundred Spartans who were exterminated at Thermopylae in 480 B.C. They would inspire other non-Western peoples to face death and devastation rather than submit to the re-imposition on them of colonial rule by any Western power.

In any event the price for the United States of military victory in Vietnam would be likely to be the devaluation of the dollar, the human sacrifice of hundreds of thousands of American young men, and the moral condemnation of the United States by the rest of the World—a condemnation as severe and as universal as the con-demnation incurred by Germany under the Nazi regime, by Japan during the years 1931–45, and by the Soviet Union under Stalin's rule. I shall be surprised if the American people carries its interven-tion in Vietnam to these lengths, but, for several reasons, already mentioned, I do not find this possibility absolutely inconceivable.

Meanwhile, the Vietnam war's course has already vindicated both the wisdom and the virtue of the West European ex-imperial powers' renunciation of their former colonial empires. At the same time, the American people's failure to learn this lesson by salutary example is a sad illustration of human nature's recalcitrance to learning by anything short of bitter direct experience.

In November 1968 the outcome of the war in the Middle East was as unpredictable as the outcome of the war in Vietnam. In each of the three Arab-Israeli wars that had been waged so far, the Israelis had won victories whose speed and professional brilliance the men in the Pentagon at Washington, D.C., must envy. Yet, on a long view, the Israelis' military and political prospects in the Middle East were still less promising than the Americans' prospects in Eastern Asia. In 1968 the Israelis were being baffled by the same spiritual and same geographical problem that were baffling the United States. The Arabs, like the Vietnamese, were determined not to submit to being resubjected to colonial rule, and geography was in their favour. The geographical problem has been noted already. The Arab World is as extensive as Vietnam and Continental China taken together, whereas Israel's man-power is puny by comparison not only with the United States' but with North Vietnam's.

Moreover, the Palestinian Arabs, and also all other Arab peoples within Israel's reach, had a still greater incentive to resist than the Vietnamese had. While it was possible for the Americans to exterminate the Vietnamese, it was decidedly improbable that they would carry their *Schrecklichkeit* to this length. The worst that they were likely to try to do in Vietnam was to conquer the whole country and hold it down under military occupation; and, so long as a subject people survives physically, it can look forward to recovering its political independence eventually. The Vietnamese, if not exterminated, could look forward to this, because it was certain that the Americans had no intention of evicting them and replacing them by American settlers. For natives of the temperate zone the climate of Vietnam is uninviting, and the Americans have ample living-space within the United States, with a wide range of tolerable climates to choose from in different sections of this huge country.

However, the Americans had won this living-space for themselves by doing to the previous inhabitants what they were almost certainly not going to do to the Vietnamese. In what is now the United States the American settlers got rid of the Amerindian natives partly by exterminating them and partly by evicting them from all desirable land and corralling them in 'reservations'. In South Africa, Rhodesia, and Kenya, too, the African natives have been evicted by the dominant European settlers of Dutch and British origin from most land that is suitable for habitation and cultivation by incomers of European origin, and this act of robbery in these three countries has so far been reversed only in Kenya, because it is only in Kenya, so far, that political power has passed out of the 'white' minority's hands into the African majority's. I do not know whether the French settlers in North-West Africa acquired any of their land by evicting the Berber and Arab inhabitants. Some, at any rate, of these French settlers performed a valuable service for the countries in which they settled by bringing back into cultivation marginal lands, cultivated previously in Roman times, which had subsequently become derelict. The moral wrong and economic calamity that has been inflicted on African populations in South Africa, Rhodesia, and temporarily in Kenya by West European settlers has been inflicted by East European settlers, the Zionist Jews, on the Palestinian Arabs. A majority of these Arabs whose homes lie on the Israeli side of the 1949 armistice-lines have been evicted and robbed. In 1968 the Arab inhabitants of the territory between the 1949 and the 1967 armistice-lines were in danger of suffering the same outrageous ill-treatment.

Israeli colonialism since the establishment of the state of Israel is one of the two blackest cases in the whole history of colonialism in the modern age; and its blackness is thrown into relief by its date. The East European Zionists have been practising colonialism in Palestine in the extreme form of evicting and robbing the native Arab inhabitants at the very time when the West European peoples have been renouncing their temporary rule over non-European peoples. The other outstanding black case is the eviction of five agricultural Amerindian peoples—the Chickasaw, Choctaw, Creeks, Cherokees, and Seminoles—from their ancestral homes in what are now the states of Georgia, Alabama, Mississippi, and Tennessee to 'reservations' in what is now the state of Oklahoma. This eviction was started in 1820 and was completed for the most part by 1838. But the Cherokees were recalcitrant and the Seminoles resisted by force of arms. They withdrew into the swamps of Southern Florida, and their resistance there was overcome by the United States Army only in the course of the eighteen-forties. This nineteenth-century American colonialism was a crime; the Israeli colonialism, which was being carried on at the time when I was writing, was a crime that was also a moral anachronism.

(v) THE ADVENT OF THE WELFARE STATE

The traditional functions of a sovereign state have been to maintain law and order within its frontiers and to sabotage law and order outside its frontiers by going to war with other sovereign states according to its own sovereign will and pleasure. Maintaining law and order at home has meant, to a large extent, protecting the property of a rich minority against the poor majority of the state's own subjects. Going to war has meant—if the military operations have been successful enough to be conducted on foreign soil—the annexation of foreign territory and the acquisition of additional wealth at a defeated opponent's expense.

The nineteenth century saw the beginnings of a beneficent addition to the functions of a state—an addition which may eventually change this once morally unedifying institution's character for the better. In the nineteenth century some states began to use part of their financial and administrative resources for performing positive social services for their citizens, and especially for the poor and unprivileged majority of them. Even before the nineteenth century, the postal services that governments had organized to serve their own purposes had been placed at the disposal of private persons in order to make these services pay their way by increasing the volume of their business and thus reducing the overhead costs. Universal primary education was the first nineteenth-century step in the shift of the state's functions from war-making abroad and police-work at home to the promotion of human welfare. Universal social insurance was the next step.

However, in the nineteenth century the welfare state and the war-making state developed side by side. In that century the pace-maker in both spheres of activity was Prussia, and Bismarck was both a militarist and a social reformer. Indeed, as Bismarck saw it, his two roles were not incongruous but were complementary to each other. An army, to be efficient, must be composed of educated men, and a citizen who was called upon to risk his life compulsorily in war had a right, in Bismarck's eyes, to social insurance and to a voice in public affairs. In 1969, sovereign states are still playing the same morally ambivalent role that they played in Bismarck's day. They are still making wars, and are waging these wars with the more and more atrocious weapons that are being provided for them by a still rapidly advancing technology. All the same, I have witnessed within my lifetime a notable change in the balance between the state's two kinds of activities in my own country. Britain has become less of a war-and-police state and more of a welfare state. In Britain the welfare state was set going by the Liberal government that came into office in 1906; but there is some irony in the fact, which cannot be denied, that the development of the British welfare state was accelerated by Britain's calamity of being involved as a major belligerent in the two world wars.

The extent of the advance towards social justice in Britain in the course of the sixty-four years 1906–69 can be measured visually by the appearance of the people whom one passes in the street. I have already mentioned[1] that, when I went to and fro between home and a day-school in London in the years 1896–9, I was upset at passing other children who were going to school in rags. At the time, I did not realize that, when my parents had been children, large numbers of other children in Britain had never gone to school at all. (I myself had been born less than twenty years after the passing of the Education Act of 1870.) Today, when I pass children going to school on Camden Hill while I am on my way to my office at Chatham House, their clothes no longer tell me the social class or the 'income-bracket' to which their families belong. Grown-up people too, especially young women, are no longer socially distinguishable by their outward appearance. Yet it must have been less than three-quarters of a century ago that I made my mother laugh by telling her, with some excitement, that I had just discovered the difference between ladies and women. 'Well, what is the difference?'—'Why, ladies wear bonnets and women wear shawls.' To find women wearing shawls over their heads today, I should probably have to travel from Britain either eastward beyond the Euphrates or southward beyond the Ebro.

I have also described[2] the uneasiness of my conscience when I was an undergraduate at Oxford during the years 1907–11, and my distress at the unhappy plight, at that date, of the students of Ruskin

[1] See p. 193.   [2] Ibid.

College—a college for 'working men' that was located in Oxford, yet was then practically beyond the pale of the University. I had made my own way into the University partly by my own exertions. I had won a scholarship for Winchester and a pair of scholarships for Oxford, one of them awarded to me by Winchester College and the other by my college at Oxford, Balliol. At the end of my first year at Oxford, my father's health broke down and our family income declined sharply. For my remaining three years at Oxford, I forwent my allowance from my family, which had been thirty pounds per annum, and lived entirely on my pair of scholarships, which amounted to £160 together. (Of course I had free board and lodging at home during the university vacations.) To most of my fellow undergraduates I must have seemed to be hard up; yet, all the time, I was conscious that I, too, was privileged. If my mother had not received, at an opportune moment, the small legacy that had financed my three years at a preparatory boarding school, I might never have managed to get my foot on to the first rung of the scholarship-ladder, and for the climbing of that ladder—still an arduous climb in 1902–7—it was *le premier pas qui coûte*, as it had been with the martyr who was reputed to have walked for a considerable distance with his head in his hand.

In 1969, England and Wales are at least as well provided with universities as Scotland was already in 1907–11, and now even Scotland is supplementing her four ancient universities with some 'red brick'. But in England the provision for education at the university level remained so shamefully inadequate till so lately, by comparison with the contemporary provision in Scotland and in the Western Continental European countries and in the United States, that the provision is still too small and the competition for places is still considerable. However, it is no longer the cut-throat competition that it was before the two world wars, and, of the boys and girls who are intellectually capable of benefiting by a university education, the proportion who are deprived of the opportunity through lack of the financial means is at any rate much smaller than it was when I was of the age for going to the university and did get in.

Indeed, the headmaster of a grammar school in a small country-town in the North-West of England told me, several years ago, that one of his hardest tasks, and, to his mind, surely rightly, one of the most important of them, was to argue with the parents of children at his school who had the ability to win a scholarship for the university from the local education authority. He had to try to make the parents see that, if they allowed and encouraged the intellectually promising child to take this opportunity that was now open to him or her for receiving a university education, this would open up for the child the possibility of careers that would be out of the child's reach for ever if it left school at the earliest permissible age in order to start earning at once in work on which there would inevitably be a low ceiling—low in terms of the work's intrinsic value and interest, besides being low in terms of pay. Of course, this did not need saying if the father of the promising child was the local doctor or lawyer. But, in rural areas, cultivated professional people are few. The majority of the parents of the children at that country grammar school were farmers, agricultural labourers, artisans, or tradesmen for whom, in their generation, education had come to an end before arriving even at the high school stage. Rudimentarily educated parents found it difficult to see the value for their children of a higher education of which the parents themselves had had no experience.

Ought university education to be accessible, or even compulsory, for every boy and girl? Ought it to be accessible for every one of them with the intellectual ability to profit by it? Or ought the number of scholarships for the university to be just smaller enough than the number of eligible candidates to maintain at least a minimum amount of competition for places and the consequent minimum amount of practical stimulus for those able children—and they are probably a majority—who do not have enough intellectual curiosity to make intellectual work stimulating for them in itself? These are questions that the affluent minority of the peoples of the World will have to explore by trial and error.

But may one not be begging a preliminary question if one assumes that the intellectual kind of ability which can profit by a university education is the only kind of ability that there is? On some occasion during the Second World War on which I had to do some business for Ernest Bevin, this question came up (I forget how), and I listened with interest while Bevin answered it confidently in

the negative. Bevin was fully alive to the value of the higher education which he himself had not received. He had started life as a
farm-labourer, if I remember right, but he had spent the best part of
his life in doing non-manual intellectual work, first as a trades-
union organizer and then in politics, and in this career he had risen
to the top, in spite of his educational handicap. Yet, successful though
Bevin himself had been in the intellectual field, I was now hearing
him propound the thesis that only a minority of mankind was fitted
by nature for an intellectual education up to and including the
university stage. 'I know', Bevin said on this occasion, 'that many
of my colleagues in my party will not agree with me about this.
All the same, I have come to the conclusion, from a fairly wide
acquaintance with my fellow human beings, that the majority—
regardless of the individual's income-level or social class—would do
better and would feel happier if, not later than the age of sixteen,
they were allowed to give up doing purely intellectual work, in
order to take up something practical, in most cases something
manual, at a polytechnic.'

I was impressed and convinced; for my own experience told me
that Bevin was right. At school and the university, at stages of
education through which Bevin himself had not passed, I had noticed
how many boys had become frustrated, from just about the age of
sixteen onwards, by being held to an intellectual education; and they
had been held to it, not because anyone had considered whether or
not it was the best kind of education for them at this stage, but
simply because going to a 'public school' and then to Oxford or
Cambridge 'was the thing to do', and because their parents could
afford to pay the fees for children who lacked the intellectual ability
to win scholarships. Some of these unfortunate rich boys were so
allergic to a higher intellectual education that they were simply
wasting their time, and not wasting it with impunity either. They
would be lucky if, after they had been released at last from their
protracted spell of punishment-duty on the intellectual treadmill,
they succeeded in finding work, of some quite different kind, in
which their baulked non-intellectual ability could find scope. My
belief in Bevin's discernment and wisdom was confirmed when, in
1948, I was paying my fourth visit to Turkey just after the Turkish
government had set up polytechnics in the provincial capitals. In

a number of these polytechnics that I was able to inspect, I was impressed and exhilarated by the keenness of the boys who were finding there the opportunity for acquiring the manual skills for which they had a previously undeveloped natural gift. The keenness of these Turkish country-boys was in striking contrast to the listlessness of many of my own middle-class or aristocratic British contemporaries who had been starved of this educational opportunity as the penalty for the higher social rank into which they happened to have been born.

It is not surprising that the traditional Western form of higher intellectual education does not suit everyone, considering that it had originally been designed to prepare a small minority who felt a special vocation. The original purpose of our Western higher education was to provide a professional education for boys who felt a vocation for becoming clerics. The candidates might be drawn from any social class. The mediaeval Western Christian Church recruited ability wherever it found it, but the ability required was of a special kind. The cleric's education might serve well enough for the lawyer too, and to some extent also for the physician. But it was not for the knight's son who intended to be a knight in his turn, or for the peasant's son who lacked the vocation and the intellectual intelligence that would have qualified him for becoming a priest.

However, our mediaeval Western society was a hierarchical one in which the Church was exceptional in offering a career open to the talents. Our present-day society is a socially fluid one, and, in a society of this kind, educational opportunity of every kind for all who are capable of benefiting by any kind of it is the key to social justice.

5 : The Use and Abuse of Science and Technology

'By their fruits ye shall know them.' My direct knowledge of what technology has achieved by the year 1969 is slighter than that of anyone who can drive a car; my direct knowledge of what science has achieved is slighter than that of anyone in my grandchildren's generation who has had a secondary education. Yet, as a beneficiary of the use of science and technology and as a victim of the abuse of them, I am a first-hand witness for the magnitude of the enhancement of their potency, within my lifetime, both for life and good and for death and evil.

In 1909, the year in which I made my first journey beyond the bounds of Britain, the only means of conveyance from this island to any other country was by ship; in 1966 I travelled by aeroplane from London to Rio de Janeiro, and back from Santiago de Chile to London soaring over the Andes instead of climbing up and down them by train. In 1909, on the other hand, I was not in danger of being bombed from the air; for, though bombs had already been invented by then, aeroplanes were still embryonic. I have now lived to be a target, in the Second World War, not only for bombs delivered by manned aeroplanes, but for the earliest of the robot death-dealers, the German 'V-Ones' and 'V-Twos'. I have also lived to hear in 1945 the news of the blasting and blighting of Hiroshima and Nagasaki with atomic bombs. In 1956 I have visited Nagasaki and have talked there with some of the survivors of that unprecedented experience.

In 1969 a missile fitted with a super-atomic war-head can be launched from any point on the surface of the globe to hit and devastate any other point on it with precision. I do not know whether it is possible to estimate the physical devastation that the existing stockpile of up-to-date atomic bombs could achieve, but I am sure that the spiritual devastation that would result from the opening of the seventh seal[1] is unimaginable. The apocalyptic language of the author of the Book of Revelation, who was writing in the first century of the Christian Era, gives a more adequate preview of the tribulation that mankind has laid up in store for itself within my lifetime than any of the cold-blooded science-fiction that is being produced in 1969 by the team-work of experts operating in 'think tanks'.

The technological achievement of releasing the physical energy of the atom was followed immediately by the abuse of this achievement for making and using an atrocious weapon, and rocketry has now been developed with equal ardour and equal success for delivering an atomic war-head at its target. At the same time, rocketry has been extending Man's range from the surface of the Earth into outer space, and it may possibly offer Man new worlds to conquer. Atomic energy can be used for constructive as well as for destructive purposes. 'Atoms for peace' could, and perhaps will, be used on Earth one day to make the poorest human being then alive more affluent materially than the richest human being alive now. But, so far, the progress of 'atoms for peace' has been much slower than the progress of 'atoms for war'. So far, most of the ability of mankind's first generation of atomic scientists and technologists has been prostituted to serve the anti-social purpose of developing the means of abusing our recently acquired mastery over atomic energy for committing genocide. The very able men who have devoted their abilities to this devils' work must all have acquiesced. You cannot coerce a human being into making scientific discoveries, and into inventing technological devices for putting these discoveries into action, as you can flog a slave into quarrying stones and hewing wood and drawing water. The atomic scientists and technologists must have been willing tools of the governments that have been employing them and of the peoples who have been keeping these governments in power and have been financing their atomic armaments by paying taxes.

I have also lived to see a revolution in the means of conveyance on the ground. In 1969, when I travel between my home in London and Heathrow Airport, I do the whole of this rather long journey in vehicles driven, like the aeroplane, by petrol. In my earliest years,

[1] Rev. chaps. viii–ix.

when I had to make the shorter journey between my home and one of the London railway terminuses, my conveyance was horse-drawn. In 1889, the year in which I was born, neither the automobile nor the aeroplane had yet been invented. Nowadays, I am both a beneficiary and a victim of each of these two products of technology's cumulative achievement and accelerating advance. As a passenger in planes and cars, I have travelled far more extensively over the surface of the globe than was feasible, within the span of one lifetime, in my parents' generation. I have, however, seen less than the travellers who did their travelling in the pre-steamship and pre-railway age—an age that ended only in my grandparents' generation. The lifetime mileage of those antique travellers was a far smaller figure than my mileage has been within these last twenty-four years. Each of those earlier travellers explored no more than a tiny fraction of this planet's land and water surface; but the primitiveness of the means of conveyance that limited their range also compelled them to enter into intimate relations with the local landscape and its inhabitants.

'He saw the towns of many men and came to know their minds.'[1] The last half of this verse is the significant half; and, though the *Odyssey* is mainly, and perhaps wholly, a fairy-tale, the truth to life of this fascinating piece of poetic fiction is vindicated by surviving authentic first-hand records of travels ranging in date from the eleventh century B.C. to the eve of the invention of steam-traction. The records that come first to my mind are Wen-Amun's account of his mission in the eleventh century B.C. to buy timber in the Lebanon for the Egyptian Government; William of Rubruck's and John of Piano Carpini's and Marco Polo's accounts of their travels from Europe to Eastern Asia and back in the thirteenth century of the Christian Era; James Bruce's account of his even more hazardous journey from Scotland to the source of the Blue Nile and back (he was in Ethiopia in the years 1769-72); and the shelf-full of narratives of the journeys of Western travellers during the last half-century before the invention of steam-traction started the progressive spoiling of travel, which has now reached a climax in the invention of supersonic aircraft. This classic last half-century of travels in the rewarding archaic style begins in the seventeen-eighties with

[1] *Odyssey*, Book 1, line 3.

Goethe's *Italienische Reise* and closes in the eighteen-thirties with Kinglake's *Eothen*.

Each successive technical improvement in the means of convey-ance has been a victory for the traveller whose purpose is the sense-less one of getting himself catapulted as rapidly as possible from point to point, but each has been a defeat for the bona fide traveller who wishes to see the world of men in the way in which Odysseus saw it according to the author of the *Odyssey*.

Since civilian air-services were started during the interval between the two world-wars, progressive technical improvements have made air-travel progressively unrewarding. My first extensive air-journey was round the United States, from coast to coast, in 1942. It was wartime, and the windows were blinded by 'security curtains' for the first few minutes after taking off and for the last few minutes before landing; but this frustration was far more than compensated by the lowness of the planes' ceilings. I do not know whether this low flying was a deliberate military precaution or was an undesired effect of technological incompetence at this early stage in the development of civil aviation. Whatever the cause, the result was a bonus for the curious-minded traveller. Flying low over Iowa, I could see not only the chequer-board lay-out of the roads; I could see the corn (maize) standing in the fields and the hogs (today they would be black Angus cattle) huddled in their pens. Skimming (not yet soaring) over the Rocky Mountains, I could see the criss-cross cattle-trails and the dark mouths of the deserted gold-mines. Of course I also saw 'the towns of many men', though it was only during the brief intervals between flights that I 'came to know their minds'.

In a previous chapter, in which I have given thanks for my three Greek educations, I have described how, in 1911–12, I spent nine months in hiking over Greece, and how I was rewarded by receiving an unexpected education there in current international affairs. I received it, thanks to spending evening after evening in one village shop after another, listening to the Greek peasants' conversation and eventually taking part in it. On 19–20 February 1960, I flew from London to New Delhi. Within less than twenty-four hours I made on this flight at least twice the mileage that I had made in Greece in 1911–12 in nine months' travelling on foot; but, in 1960 I did not come to know anything of the minds of the inhabitants of the western half of the Eurasian Continent, and, though I was passing over the scenes of the principal events in the history of one-half of mankind, the only thing on Earth that I saw between dawn and murky eve was Lake Avernus, which was revealed to me by a momentary rift in the monotonous blanket of cloud that deprived me of the vision of the rest of the variegated landscape and animated world of men concealed beneath.

Thus, in my own life, I have practised all the successive forms of travelling that have been superseded, one after another, by technology's frustrating advance. In Greece in 1911–12, I travelled on foot like Philippides and I consequently saw and learnt almost as much as Odysseus did. Between London and New Delhi in 1960, I travelled by plane and consequently travelled blind and deaf. I suppose my plane must have been a technological masterpiece. I do not know what make it was. Anyway, it was a giant. If you do have to travel by plane and are given a choice of makes (you seldom are), be sure to choose a Cessna. Even in a Cessna you will see less than you would have seen on foot, but you will see almost as much as you would have seen on muleback. The better, in the technical sense, that a mechanized conveyance is, the more frustratingly it works as a social insulator, cutting the traveller off from intercourse with fellow human beings of his over whose countries he is making his way.

In an earlier chapter of this book, I have mentioned my debt to F. W. Hasluck, who was librarian of the British Archaeological School at Athens in 1911–12, when I was a student there. I remember Hasluck's telling me that he had once picked up somewhere an eighteenth-century English–Magyar or French–Magyar conversation-book (I forget which of the two the West European language was), and that the opening phrase had been 'My postilion has been struck by lightning'. Bizarre? No, prosaically practical.

The French or English grandee who kept this conversation-book in his pocket would have been making the grand tour in his private coach. He would have been travelling from palace to palace as, in 1969, his American counterpart travels in his private cadillac from Hilton to Hilton. The palaces at which the eighteenth-century grand-tourist spent his nights would have been the homes of fellow aristocrats with whom he was connected personally by a network of intermarriages and who spoke, as fluently as the traveller did, the 'polite' languages—French, English, Italian, Spanish—which they had learnt to speak in early childhood from governesses of these nationalities. (The present-day American who spends his nights in the World's Hilton hotels can likewise be sure of making himself understood; for he will be served there by a staff that speaks the traveller's sole language, namely English.) Thus the eighteenth-century West European aristocratic traveller, like the twentieth-century American plutocratic traveller, had no need to talk to the ordinary natives of the countries through which he was passing in the local vernacular that was the only language that the natives spoke and understood.

The traveller had no need of the vernacular so long as his means of conveyance functioned according to design. However, no man-made vehicular contraption is proof against 'acts of God' (in the actuary's usage of the term). A drop of rain-water penetrates one's carburetter; one's postillion is struck by lightning; and then one finds oneself stranded in the wilderness and thrown upon one's own resources. The traveller now has to alight and to apply for help to the first native whom he meets; and in this emergency the eight-eenth-century grand-tourist, suddenly marooned on the Hungarian *puszta*, will have congratulated himself on his foresight in having taken the precaution of carrying with him that French–Magyar or English–Magyar conversation-book. The first phrase in this efficiently compiled vade-mecum was the necessary opening gambit. The stranded grandee must begin his unexpected converse with the native by describing to him the contretemps that has compelled the grandee to enter into communication with him.

The traveller who is brought to a halt by postilion-trouble or engine-trouble is, of course, fortunate by comparison with the traveller whose journey is abruptly terminated by one of the engines of his private plane catching fire or dropping off. A coach and a cadillac have one valuable safety-asset in common. They both do their business of conveying human beings by keeping on the ground; so the wheels on which they move can stop moving without danger to the passenger's life and limb. For the travellers de luxe by air it would be as idle to carry conversation-books in local vernaculars as it would be for a fisherman on Lake Titicaca to learn to swim. When some contretemps capsizes the fisherman's balsa-raft or puts the air-traveller's plane out of action, this is likely to be the end of the story. The fisherman who falls into Lake Titicaca's ice-cold water (the lake's altitude is 12,500 feet above sea-level) will be paralysed with cramp before he is released from this physical agony by being drowned. The air-traveller, if he is lucky, will be killed instantaneously by his crashing plane's impact on the ground before he has been half burnt-alive in the course of his fall. In nine seconds, between fastening the safety-belt and hitting the ground, the falling human traveller may suffer worse torments—'hurled headlong flaming from th' ethereal sky, with hideous ruin and combustion'— than were suffered by Satan and his horrid crew in their nine-days-long fall from Heaven to Hell.

Nowadays my wife and I risk this unpleasant death each time we travel by air (and our air-journeys have become frequent). We have the consolation of knowing that, if one day death does overtake us in this physically painful way, we shall neither of us be condemned to suffer the spiritual pain of bereavement.[1] Unfortunately, our simultaneous deaths would not bring with them for our heirs the financial benefit of having to pay only a single round of death-duties on our estates. The United Kingdom Inland Revenue authorities would deem that one of us had died just long enough after the other, even if only by one millionth of a second, to have had time to inherit the other casualty's estate, and, on this ruling, the authorities would levy death-duties on our heirs twice over.

In the meantime, while still alive, we are beneficiaries of petrol-driven conveyances on the ground during the month or two out of the year that we spend in the country, but we are victims of these recent products of technology during the greater part of the year, which we spend in London. Since neither of us is a driver (and, in London, even the most expert driver may be baffled by failing to find a place for parking his car), we can afford, while we are in the country, to hire a car with a congenial driver whenever required. In London we are bus-riders and pedestrians, and, in both these forms of locomotion, we are technology's victims. The congestion of petrol-driven traffic in the World's great cities now makes the timing

[1] For this consolation, see p. 123.

of urban journeys impossible to estimate, whether one is travelling by omnibus or by taxi or on foot; and in London today the pedestrian is being more and more vexatiously penalized for being less of a nuisance than the congested wheeled-traffic is. The pedestrian is being made to wait longer and longer for the green light, and, in crossing Pall Mall, he has to run if he is to reach the farther shore alive before the light turns red again and the piled-up flood of impatient drivers roars forward, like the unleashed Red-Sea water, to submerge any loitering pharaoh whom the flood overtakes between curb and curb.

'By their fruits ye shall know them.' Automobiles and aeroplanes and atomic weapons are not the only achievements of science and technology within my lifetime that I know, in my ignorance, by their fruits. I also know by their fruits the discoveries within my lifetime that have been made in the sciences of bacteriology and chemistry and in the technique of surgery. The advance in bacteriology has been applied to the technique of exterminating bacteria and of fostering them. The advance in chemistry has been applied to the invention of drugs that are unprecedently potent and effective. The advance in surgery has made it feasible to perform operations that would have been inconceivable when I was a child, and bacteriology has co-operated with surgery to cheat bacteria of their human prey by making wounds aseptic, whether these wounds have been inflicted benevolently by the surgeon's knife or malevolently by anti-personnel bombs and napalm. I know these achievements by their fruits because I myself have been a beneficiary of all three of them.

In my family's household in London when I was a child, we did not venture to drink water from the main without having first passed it through a filter. This was probably an ineffective precaution, but it had the psychological value of setting my parents' minds at rest. In 1911, the year in which I paid my first visit to Italy, there was an epidemic of cholera in the Mezzogiorno, and I did not drink a drop of water that had not previously been boiled. I drank vast quantities of this beverage; for hiking on foot in Central Italy in the early autumn is thirsty work, and wine is no thirst-quencher. In 1911 I discovered by trial and error that a litre of wine is not enough to allay one's thirst though it is more than enough to make one drunk. Nowadays I drink water straight from the main both in Italy and in England, and I do this with a confidence that is justified by subsequent impunity.

At Palmyra on 3 May 1957, my temperature suddenly shot up from normal to 103 Fahrenheit. If the date had been 1911, I should probably have left my bones in one of those inviting Palmyrene tower-sepulchres that still have room to accommodate additional human carcasses. However, the local doctor was a young man who had only lately qualified and had therefore had an up-to-date education in the properties and uses of the most recently invented drugs. I lost count of the number of these that he injected into me, but I am lastingly grateful for the effects of his professional skill. After one day's convalescence, I was *en route* on 5 May by car from Palmyra, heading across the desert for Rusafah, with my temperature now slightly below normal.

As for surgery, I was, so I have been told, the first child in London to have its tonsils removed. I suffered from being a pioneer guinea-pig. I have not forgotten how sore the operation left my throat, and how long the soreness lasted. When two of my grandchildren had their tonsils removed, they were romping in high spirits before they were released from hospital on the third day. Twelve years ago, in my sixty-ninth year, I had a hernia successfully mended and my pros-tate gland successfully removed in rapid succession, and, though the cumulative physical exhaustion prostrated me for the next few weeks, I am in good health today thanks to the skill of the two surgeons who operated on me.

By then I had already lived to see brain-surgery started in the course of the Second World War. I have now lived on to read the news of greater feats of surgery than those by which I myself have benefited, but which were not practicable for human beings who were in need of them in my parents' generation. I have lived to see a damaged human heart successfully replaced by the sound human heart of another human being who had met with a sudden death through an accident. At the first few attempts, the human being into whose body an alien heart has been grafted has survived the operation for only a few days. However, the most recent case on the day on which I was writing, namely 12 April 1968, was faring better, and I may perhaps live to see this novel operation carried to a degree of expertise at which it will give the beneficiary a fair expectation of living out his life to its natural term.

This surgical triumph that has been pioneered in South Africa is a triumph for the whole World, and it is therefore a precious moral link between the dominant 'white' minority in South Africa and the rest of mankind, from which this minority has otherwise done its worst to sever itself morally by the policy of apartheid that it is imposing on its 'non-white' compatriots. When, on 8 January 1968, I passed the hospital in Cape Town in which a dead 'non-white' man's heart had been transplanted into a living 'white' body, I felt a glow of admiration and gratitude that was a welcome change from my feeling during much of the rest of the brief time that I spent on South African soil when my ship touched at Durban and at Cape Town *en route* from Hong Kong to London.

If the successful transplantation of hearts, the most vital of all organs, were to become part of the regular practice of surgery, we could look forward to a day at which any and every defective or damaged or worn-out organ will be replaceable. For the present they will have to be replaced by healthy natural organs taken from the bodies of other human beings who have died by accident or who, whatever the cause and circumstances of their deaths, have had the forethought and the human feeling to bequeath, by will, to an international 'organic replacements bank', any of their organs that may be judged to be serviceable for transplanting when their own bodies have been dissected the moment after they have died. Such bequests, supplemented by the mounting toll of sudden deaths on roads infested with ever denser and ever faster-moving mechanized traffic, might perhaps keep this beneficent bank tolerably well supplied pending the at present unforeseeable date at which the science of organic chemistry, and its application to surgical technology, will have reached the point at which it will be possible to manufacture artificial living organs for insertion into living bodies in any quantities that may be required. In this not improbable event, organic chemistry and surgery, working in co-operation with each other, will be able to reduce still further the toll of premature deaths that has already been reduced so notably by preventive medicine administered by public health authorities.

It is unlikely that I shall live to see chemical technology produce

artificial living organs, but, within my lifetime, it has already produced not only all manner of new drugs but also fertilizers and
insecticides. Applied in the practice of medicine, the new drugs perform splendid services for life and good when they are used as antibiotics or as anaesthetics. They can, however, also be used as noxious
narcotics, and mankind's inventory of these has been augmented
pari passu with the augmentation of its inventory of curative chemical
products.

The use and abuse of intoxicants is, of course, not one of mankind's newest self-inflicted evils. Intoxicants have been known and
used before the invention of agriculture. The Aryas' sacred haoma
(soma) drink is said to have been brewed from a wild plant. However, the domestication of cereals, rice, sugar-cane, cabbage, and
potatoes has been exploited, in each case, for the production of
alcoholic intoxicants as well as for the production of foods. Poppies
have been cultivated to produce opium, and hemp to produce
hashish; and alcoholic intoxicants of an enhanced degree of alcoholic content have vied with opium in working havoc since the
invention of distilling. Today, however, even the strongest and
most poisonous alcoholic intoxicants and even opium itself have
come to seem as innocuous as coca cola by comparison with the
drugs that are now at a drug-addict's disposal.

Nor are drugs the only products of chemical technology that can
be used, and are being used, for death and evil as well as for life and
good. A maker of the housewife's cooking-gas and the dentist's
anaesthetising-gas could also make the soldier's poison-gas. A maker
of fertilizers could also make defoliants. A maker of algipan could
also make napalm. The bacteriologist who can make water drink-
able and wounds aseptic by killing bacteria that are inimical to the
human form of life can foster bacteria to serve mankind as yeast or
to put vim into kumis and yoghurt; but he could also foster the
bacteria that are Man's deadliest enemies to serve as weapons for
human beings to use against each other in bacteriological warfare.
At this very moment, bacteriologists are credibly reported to be
secretly at work, on behalf of the governments of some of the
World's still sovereign local states, on making provision for the
deliberate propagation of deadly diseases which our physicians and
our public health authorities are striving to stamp out. The

war-bacteriologists are even reported to be 'improving' the lethal germs by breeding new strains that are more virulent, and are nearer being proof against antibiotics, than the natural strains that are the war-bacteriologists' raw material and are the public health authorities' present adversaries. Like the production of ever more devastating atomic bombs, this preparation for bacteriological warfare (if it is an authentic fact) is scientific and technological devil's work.

Within my lifetime the scientific exploration of Man's psychosomatic structure has advanced beyond the frontiers of the visible, tangible aspect of human nature to reconnoitre its psychic aspect. Freud's and Jung's pioneer plumbing of the psyche's perhaps bottomless subconscious abyss did not start till after the date of my birth, and, as recently as 1908, medical practice in this field was still groping helplessly in the dark.[1]

Psychological theory has now been translated into practical curative treatment. Yet, in this newly-won domain of science and technology, as in so many others, the self-same arts can be used for good or for evil at will. They can be used to 're-condition' a patient's ailing psyche for the patient's own benefit; they can also be used to 'condition' a psychically healthy person's psyche in the conditioners' interests.

In the art of 'conditioning' there are a number of degrees, but even the first degree is sinister. This first degree—propaganda—is as old as the oldest missionary religions and political parties. The word itself is derived from the title of the Papal *Congregatio de Propagandâ Fidê*, which was established in 1622. However, commercial propaganda did not become intensive until the Industrial Revolution in the Western World at the turn of the eighteenth and nineteenth centuries, when the promotion of sales by forced draught was found to be needed in order to unload on a reluctant World the voluminous product of big capital investments in elaborate and costly plant which could be made remunerative only if the wheels were kept turning for twenty-four hours in the day so as to achieve the maximum output. As for political propaganda, this was conducted with a previously unheard-of vehemence by both sets of belligerents in the First World War. But First-World-War political propaganda and nineteenth-century commercial advertising were crude com-

[1] See p. 121.

pared to the sophisticated technique of present-day Madison Avenue.

Propaganda of all kinds is an affront to the dignity of human nature and a menace to the honesty and the rationality that are indispensable moral requisites for social life. Yet even the most insidious propaganda is innocent by comparison with the 'brain-washing' that is effected by various methods of mental and physical torture, and it is conceivable that 'conditioning' may be carried to still further lengths. The psychological technique that can be used to re-integrate a psyche can perhaps also be used to disintegrate it. It is even conceivable that, one day, psychological and surgical techniques may be devised for permanently dehumanizing a human being's hereditary human nature, and perhaps even for conditioning the victim's genes to transmit this artificially induced psychic deformity to his or her descendants.

The foregoing survey of the achievements of science and technology in my lifetime will perhaps have sufficed—brief, superficial, and ill-informed though it has been—to make the point that science and technology are morally neutral forces. They are exertions of Man's amoral intellectual ability, and they reward Man for his success in this sector of human activity by endowing him with power that he can use at will either for life and good or for death and evil.

'By their fruits ye shall know them', and we can now also see who 'they' are. 'They' turn out not to be the 'trees', science and technology, themselves. The good fruit and the bad fruit alike is brought forth by the self-same trees; and these trees bear this disconcerting medley of good and evil fruits according to the use or misuse, by us human beings, of the power with which science and technology have equipped us. The fruits of science and technology are never to be found raw and fresh; they are 'processed', for consumption, by our use and misuse of them; they come on to the market as fruits of human action; and the knowledge that the fruits of our actions give us is the knowledge of our own human nature.

The moral diversity of our human fruits tells us that we are morally ambivalent beings. Each one of us is both a good tree and a corrupt one, so each of us can, and does, bring forth both evil fruits and good fruits promiscuously. In every human soul throughout its life on Earth there is a perpetual moral struggle between the good and the evil in human nature.[1] Science and technology merely give us the tools to do the job that we choose to do with them; and our intellectual prowess equips us, with a morally blind impartiality, for doing devils' work or doing angels' work according to our human will and pleasure.

Man is, of course, a social animal, and sociality is impossible without some minimal moral code that is accepted by a decisive majority of the members of a human society; but the codes of different societies differ profoundly—in some cases, almost *in toto*. Their one common feature—and this is, of course, a cardinal one—is that they all draw the distinction between good and evil, however greatly their notions of what is good and what is evil may vary.

All judgements on the relative merits of different moral codes are inevitably subjective; for the maker of any such judgement is bound to be a member of some society with a code of its own; so his judgement will be influenced by his native society's code, and this whether he accepts his ancestral code or is in revolt against it. The one feature of these diverse codes that is demonstrated by our knowledge of history to be an objective fact is that the authority of every code is precarious. The morally highest-seeming codes may be disestablished by a moral relapse; the morally lowest-seeming codes may be improved by the spontaneous efforts of their adherents or may be superseded by morally higher-seeming codes introduced from abroad.

Thus, in the moral sector of human activity, we can observe an unceasing ebb and flow both in the lives of human beings and in the histories of human societies, but we cannot discern any long-term ('secular') curve of change either for better or for worse. So far as we can make out, the moral stature of the living generation in the present 'advanced' (i.e. scientifically and technologically advanced) minority of the human race is no different from the moral stature of the first of our ancestors who became human. We are powerless to add a cubit to the moral stature with which Nature endowed mankind in the act of evolving it out of some pre-human species of mammalian life. On the other hand, some affluent communities (e.g. the people of the United States) have succeeded within my lifetime

[1] For the Zoroastrian origin of this insight into the ambivalence of human nature, see p. 137.

in adding an inch or two to the average physical stature of a privileged section of their population by improvements in diet, in medical care, and in sanitation.

This remarkable demonstration of Man's power to make an impact on the physiology of the human body illustrates the difference in kind between the moral and the intellectual aspect of human nature and sector of human activity. These two components of human-ness must have come into existence simultaneously and must also be coeval with human nature itself. The distinctive feature of human nature is its consciousness and the consequent reasoning power that enables a human being to draw distinctions and to make choices, some of which are inevitably choices between good and evil. Consciousness is the mother of conscience and of science alike, and science is the mother of technology. Our first humanized ancestors demonstrated that they had become human by chipping stones to turn them into more effective tools than these stones had been in the natural shape in which the ancestors of the first generation of human beings will have used them, as some extant species of non-human animals do use unworked natural objects as tools in the present geological age. The first stone-chippers were the first human beings and, *ex officio humanitatis*, they were also both the first scientists and technicians and the first living creatures on this planet to be haunted by 'the knowledge of good and evil'.

The moral and the intellectual facet of human nature must have come into existence simultaneously; but, unfortunately for every human being and for mankind collectively, human nature is so constituted that its moral and its intellectual performance have been, and are bound to be, incommensurate with each other. Its moral performance is inevitably handicapped by the built-in self-centredness which is another name for life itself, and which is consequently implanted in each specimen of Man as ineradicably as it is in each specimen of every other species of living creatures. By contrast, human nature's intellectual ability has a free run for thinking scientifically and for putting such thought into action in technology. Accordingly there will have been, from the beginning, a gap between Man's respective performances in the moral and in the intellectual field. Morality will have been outstripped by technology from the start.

This 'morality gap' (as we may label it by analogy with the 'credibility gap' that sunders present-day politicians from their constituents) is certainly a 'fixed' gulf, but it will not have been a 'great' gulf during the first million years of human history. It is not a great gulf in the life of the now fast dwindling remnant of mankind that has remained in the food-gathering stage of science and technology down to the present day. From the beginning, no doubt, science and technology have been advancing while morals have been static; but, for the duration of those first million years, a period that we label 'the Lower Palaeolithic Age', the advance of science and technology, as registered in successive types of artificial tools, was so slow that the 'morality gap' remained narrow enough to be negotiable. In the Lower Palaeolithic Age, Man's moral performance was, we may feel sure, just as poor as it is today; but, happily for Lower Palaeolithic Man, his technological performance was likewise so feeble that, when he chose to use his technology for death and evil and not for life and good, the damage that he could inflict on his fellow human beings and on himself was, by present-day standards, slight. His bad intentions will have been no less bad than ours are, but his power to put his evil designs into effect was incomparably feebler than ours is. Lower Palaeolithic Man's technological incompetence protected him efficaciously against himself, and this was a precious compensation for the discomfort of living in the Garden of Eden.

Adam and Eve were destitute of all the material amenities of 'the American way of life'. They had to make their living, as the surviving Australian natives still make theirs today, by gathering whatever food, vegetable or animal, was provided for them by undomesticated Nature. Man's material condition during the Lower Palaeolithic Age was indeed even less rosy than it is depicted in the first two chapters of the Book of Genesis; for in this age, which has been by far the longest age of human history so far, Man did not in truth have the dominion over all other forms of animal life on this planet that the authors of these chapters ascribe to him. In Eden, other food-gathering and hunting species of animals besides Man were on the prowl, and we may guess that, in the course of Man's first million years, when his technological talents were still lying buried in a napkin, more human beings were caught and devoured by sabre-toothed tigers than sabre-toothed tigers by human beings.

A sabre-toothed tiger's natural equipment for making his living as a predator was far superior to Man's so long as the intellectual element in Man's natural equipment was not yet effectively exploiting its technological potentialities.

It was not till the dawn of the Upper Palaeolithic Age, perhaps no more than about thirty thousand years ago, that Man developed his technology to the point at which he did acquire dominion over sabre-toothed tigers, mammoths, mastodons, and such big deer. It was not till my grandparents' generation that Man began to acquire dominion over bacteria, alias bacilli, alias microbes. Till then, bacteria had exercised dominion over Man, thanks to Man's having, so far, remained unaware of their existence. In the catalogue of Man's non-human animal slaves in the Book of Genesis, bacteria are conspicuous by their absence. The man who first identified and named them was not Adam; he was Pasteur. For the bacteria, their eventual detection by Man has been a fatality. In my lifetime the bacteria have been fighting a rearguard action which looks like a losing battle, in spite of the resourcefulness of this fellow living creature of ours in responding to Man's escalating challenge to its survival by contriving to render itself immune to one man-made antibiotic after another.

Probably the bacteria are doomed—though their prospects might improve dramatically overnight if Man were ever to wage bacteriological warfare against himself. Since there is no conceivable crime or folly that Man can be guaranteed never to be going to commit, the bacteria can still live in hope. Yet, even if Man does not deliberately retrocede to the bacteria the dominion that they have exercised for so long over Man, the bacteria are not Man's only enemy that is still in the field. Antibiotics may be ineffective weapons against viruses if viruses prove not to be animate; and a present-day politician who, by pressing a button in his war-room, could have launched hundreds of rockets fitted with atomic war-heads, will be as impotent as one of his Lower Palaeolithic progenitors would have been to save himself, by technological apparatus, from being devoured by a shark if he has the bad luck to find himself 'man overboard', from ship or plane, in tropical waters. Viruses and sharks are still defying human technology, and these are not the last enemy either.

In Saint Paul's vision the last enemy is death,[1] but an observer of human affairs who has lived from 1889 into 1969 cannot share Paul's certainty that death is going to suffer the fate of mankind's other enemies. The twentieth-century observer may entertain, as a rational expectation, a prospect that, for Saint Paul, would have been an impiously presumptuous fantasy. In our day we can envisage the possibility that, without waiting expectantly but passively for Christ's second coming, human chemical and surgical technology, between them, may succeed in making human beings immortal (a dubious blessing) by discovering how to replace any damaged or worn-out organs by spare parts for an unlimited number of times in succession. In our day, however, we can also envisage the counter-possibility that atomic technology and rocketry, between them, may frustrate both God's and Man's beneficent power to destroy death by discovering how to give the human race the power to commit mass-suicide at the very moment when chemical and surgical technology will have succeeded in making human beings potentially immortal. This second twentieth-century possibility, which would have been dismissed by Saint Paul in its turn as a fantastic nightmare, compels us to revise Saint Paul's identification of the last enemy, and to question Saint Paul's assurance that what for him was the last enemy will be destroyed too. Through the lens with which science and technology have equipped us in propelling us into the Atomic Age, we can see, not darkly, but in the lethal glare of the explosions at Hiroshima and Nagasaki, that Man's last enemy is, not death, but Man himself. Man is his last enemy and his worst one—worse than death, worse than viruses, worse than bacteria, worse than sabre-toothed tigers.

This is another way of saying that, between the date at which our ancestors first became human and the year 1969 of the Christian Era, the 'morality gap' has widened portentously. It has widened to the dimensions of a 'door of death' that 'stands hideously wide-open, eyeing us expectantly with an enormous gape'.[2]

If we now look back from the present year A.D. 1969 over the course of Man's scientific and technological advance up to date, we shall discern in this course two 'secular' tendencies. In the course of

---

[1] 1 Cor. xv. 26.
[2] Lucretius, *De Rerum Naturâ*, Book V, lines 373–5, quoted on p. 202.

these first million or so plus thirty thousand or so years, the advance has been cumulative and its pace has been accelerating. These are manifestly the long-term tendencies, but of course neither the curve of accumulation nor the curve of acceleration has been regular. The accumulation has been interrupted from time to time by losses that have had to be recouped. In the Aegean basin, for example, the technique of writing seems to have been lost in the twelfth century B.C. and not to have been re-acquired before the ninth century B.C. As for the acceleration, this seems to have occurred by fits and starts.

The earliest fit of acceleration known to us was at the beginning of the Upper Palaeolithic Age, when, perhaps about thirty thousand years ago, there was a sudden refinement of the technique of chipping stone tools—sudden, that is to say, by contrast with the hardly perceptible advance registered in the series of tools manufactured during the preceding million years. The second fit of acceleration was at the beginning of the Neolithic Age, when, ten or eight thousand years ago, chipped stone tools were superseded by ground stone tools; when, more or less simultaneously, agriculture and spinning and weaving and pottery were invented; and when the already achieved domestication of the dog was supplemented by the domestication of a number of other animals. The third fit was the invention of metallurgy and of writing at, or on the verge of, the dawn of civilization about five thousand years ago. The fourth fit of acceleration was long delayed, but the impetus of the pent-up ability, then tardily released, was proportionately vehement.

This fourth fit was the Industrial Revolution that began approximately two hundred years ago. The distinctive feature of this fourth fit has been the harnessing of inanimate forces of nature to supplement, and eventually to replace, the physical work previously performed by muscle-power, human and animal. (This revolution in the source and character of man's supply of physical power has not been an innovation in principle. Wind-power had been harnessed with sails at the dawn of civilization, and water-power with mill-wheels before the beginning of the Christian Era.) In 1969 this fourth fit of acceleration is still in full swing, and there are not yet any signs of its slowing down, as each of its predecessors has slowed down sooner or later. So far from that, my generation has seen this fit keyed up to the demonic intensity of a paroxysm. The symbol of this present paroxysm in the acceleration of the advance of science and technology is the discovery of the structure of the atom and the technological exploitation of this scientific discovery in the harnessing of atomic energy. This is the most dramatic, most awe-inspiring, and most menacing of the signs of the times, yet it is only a single sign out of a multitude of many different kinds.

Thus I have lived to see an acceleration in the advance of science and technology such as there has never been before within the span of a single human lifetime; and within this same span I have seen the most advanced devices of science and technology misused for the cold-blooded well-organized commission of crimes that have surpassed all previous crimes of which we have surviving records.

Poison-gas fortunately proved to be a two-edged weapon when it was used on the battlefield. The wind that once veered round in Joan of Arc's favour could change as capriciously for the discomfiture of soldiers who had defiled its pure wings by lading gas on them to poison the gas-launchers' opponents. The wind could turn about to gas the gassers. We may guess that it was this deterrent experience, not a newly awakened feeling of humanity, that restrained both sets of belligerents from using poison-gas in the Second World War; for, while this war was being waged, the lethal product of chemical science and technology that had been found unsatisfactory for use in the field was being employed with monstrous effectiveness in the gas-chamber. Poison-gas was the Nazis' handiest instrument for their genocide of the European Jews; and, since the end of the Second World War and the liquidation of the Nazi regime in Germany, science and technology, forging ahead impenitently, have invented, in napalm, a chemical weapon that is still more atrocious than poison-gas and that, unlike gas, has the further demerit of being capable of being broadcast over town and country from aeroplanes.

These atrocities that I have lived to see perpetrated with devices that science and technology have now placed in human hands might have made me and other survivors of my generation despair of mankind's future—the future of our grandchildren and their descendants to the seventy-seven-millionth generation. Happily I have lived on to see the beginnings of a recognition of the perilous breadth to which the 'morality gap' has now expanded. Better still, I have lived on to see this recognition begin to cause concern. At my age, I can hardly expect to live to see this concern put into action by the mobilization of the spiritual forces of education and religion.

If these forces are to be mobilized effectively, they must be mobilized on the institutional as well as on the personal plane; and, like all other institutions, these two can be operated, at will, either for good or for evil. Institutionalization is inimical to spirituality, and it is only in the strength of the immortal but not omnipotent spirit of love that the 'morality gap' can be reduced until, if love triumphs, the gap is eventually closed. Institutions are morally ambivalent; but, in any society that has burst the narrow bounds of a network of direct personal relations, institutions are necessary instruments for social action. We shall therefore have, at our peril, to enlist the services of institutional religion and institutional education to help us to close 'the door of death' that now stands so 'hideously wide-open'.

In espying a recognition of the present breadth of the 'morality gap', and in taking some comfort in seeing this being recognized at last with trepidation, I am not indulging in uncorroborated wishful thinking. I am comparing the attitude of the scientists and of the cultivated intelligent public, as I observe their attitude in 1969, with the attitude of an eminent man of science of my parents' generation as I observed this in 1903.

At the end of my first 'half' at Winchester I came home to London for Christmas 1902 in the grip of pneumonia and fell seriously ill. (The drugs that would have rallied me quickly in 1969 were not yet at the doctor's disposal two-thirds of a century ago.) By the time when I was convalescent, I was not well enough to go back to school for the tail-end of 'Common Time', 1903, but I was well enough to go out of London for a change, and my Aunt Grace Frankland and her husband my Uncle Percy came to my sorely-tried parents' aid by inviting me to stay with them.

My Aunt Grace was the eighth of my Toynbee grandparents' nine children (my father was the youngest); my Uncle Percy Faraday Frankland (1858–1946) had, as his second name proclaimed, been dedicated since baptism (Faraday was his godfather) to become a successor of the founding fathers of modern chemical science. He

had indeed been 'born in the purple'; for his father, Sir Edward
Frankland (1825–1899), had been as eminent a chemical scientist as
his son duly became.[1] Both Sir Edward Frankland and Percy Frankland made distinguished contributions to the advancement of organic
chemistry. Percy Frankland distinguished himself in bacteriology as
well. Here he had the advantage over his father in age, for Pasteur
was Sir Edward Frankland's contemporary, so bacteriology had just
become a going concern by the time when Percy Frankland got to
work. In entering fields of research which, in their day, had only
recently been opened up, both men showed that their intellectual
ability was mated with originality and with adventurousness; and
their merits were appreciated by their confrères. Father and son were

[1] In the Frankland family, as in the Darwin and Huxley families, outstanding mental
ability has been persistent, and, in the Franklands too, this gift has displayed itself
in other fields besides science. My Uncle Percy Frankland's son, my first cousin
Edward Frankland, gave proof of an ability in chemical science that was on a par
with his father's and his grandfather's. If Edward had not been prevented by ill-
health from making his career in his ancestral field, he would unquestionably have
become the third eminent chemist in three successive generations of Franklands.
When Nature intervened to prevent Edward from winning these hereditary
laurels, she compensated him by giving his ability the opportunity to flower in a
variety of fields. Edward fulfilled himself as a novelist, an artist, a gardener, a
farmer, a forester, and a deservedly much beloved father. He struck root in the
Ravenstonedale district of Westmorland, where, in his youth, his parents had
acquired a holiday home. He linked himself with Ravenstonedale in the most
intimate way possible. He married a member of the Metcalfe-Gibson family. He
became wedded to the local landscape too. The sensitiveness of his feeling for it
comes out in his water-colours and in his drawings. Each tree and leaf, each wall
and stone, is rendered in these with a faithfulness that is a reflection of love.

Through Edward, the Frankland family's abiding scientific ability has descended to a fourth generation—in this case in combination with Edward Frankland's love and understanding of Nature. His daughter, my cousin Helga Frankland, is now an officer of the Nature Conservancy. From her headquarters at
Grange-over-Sands, she administers a region that is approximately conterminous
with the Archdiocese of York and with the former Kingdom of Northumbria.
The Government of the United Kingdom has shown foresight and imaginative-
ness in setting up, in the nick of time, a public body to protect, in order to study
scientifically, what remains of Man's natural environment in the country that has
been the first in the field in the reckless game of overwhelming and obliterating
Nature by the imposition on her of an artificial environment created by technology.
My cousin has managed, by leading a strenuous life, to give herself an education
in science (biology) all the way to the post-graduate stage, while keeping her hand
in as a practical farmer. She thus has the essential qualifications for the post that
she now holds, while her gifts and her training make the work highly congenial
for her.

elected presidents of both the Royal Institute of Chemistry and the Chemical Society.

At the time of my visit to my aunt and uncle in 1903, my Uncle Percy was Professor of Chemistry in the University of Birmingham (England)—a great modern university in which the value and importance of chemistry were recognized as a matter of course at a date at which chemistry was still receiving no more than a grudging recognition at Winchester and at Oxford. My uncle held his chair at Birmingham—it was one of the key chairs in the university there —from 1894 to 1919. In 1903, when I went to stay with him and my aunt, they were living on the outskirts of Birmingham at Northfield, in what was then still almost open country.

My visit was not a long one—if I remember right, it ran to no more than about three weeks—yet it has made a life-long impression on me. This was my first acquaintance with a huge industrial city, and I became aware of the links between industry, technology, and science. No doubt, this highly significant feature of modern life would have been impressed on me still more strongly if my uncle's professorial chair had been not at Birmingham but, say, at Würzburg, as it might have been, since my uncle had studied organic chemistry there for two years and he also had some German blood in his veins. What impressed me most, however, was not anything public or impersonal; it was my Uncle Percy Frankland himself— his personality and his outlook on life. His personality was dynamic. He was dynamically masterful, arbitrary, and dogmatic; but, beneath his intimidating *persona,* he was dynamically benevolent too; and on this occasion he went out of his way, busy man though he was, to be kind to me.

One act of kindness that still touches me whenever I recall it was that he took me on a special expedition to buy an historical atlas for me at a bookshop in Birmingham. This was the first historical atlas that I ever possessed, and I learnt volumes from it. The gift was all the kinder, considering that my uncle's professed faith was that science was all the World. Actually, he was a widely cultivated man —more widely cultivated, I should guess, than many present-day men of science who have attained comparable eminence in some narrower professional field. For instance, he is said to have been the best classical scholar but one in Birmingham in his time. The way in which he liked to express himself was emphatic to the point of hyperbole, and I think he expected his audience to let him have the best of both worlds. They were to gratify him by being shocked, but they were also to take his more extravagant and provocative pronouncements *cum grano*. However, there could be no mistake about my uncle's benevolence. He had taken the trouble to draw me out, to discover what my intellectual interests were, and to give me timely help in pursuing them.

In Uncle Percy's company my eyes were opened to a vision of science and to an attitude towards life that, for me, were new and exciting. My own recent start at school in elementary chemistry had been damping. Half-way through my first 'half' at Winchester I had been 'hotted up' into a higher division, and consequently I had had to break into my new division's course of chemistry lectures midway, and had been left to pick up the unfamiliar threads for myself as best I could. The exposition had not been inspiring, and the 'don' who had been giving the course could not have been expected to recapitulate, for my sole benefit, the opening lectures in which presumably he had given the key to the sequel. Consequently this sequel had been, for me, unintelligible and therefore repulsive.

Now, however, I was watching Uncle Percy analysing samples of water that were being sent to him for analysis, once a month, by the municipal authorities of a number of the most famous industrial cities in Britain. The authorities were taking no risks over the purity of their water-supply, and they had therefore retained the services of one of the most eminent chemists in the country to report to them, at monthly intervals, on their municipal water's composition. I have mentioned that my uncle was in the forefront of the rapidly advancing science of bacteriology. Legions of bacteria, including, if I remember right, some of those that afflict mankind with the deadliest of our diseases, were housed in jars in the attics of my aunt's and uncle's house. My Aunt Grace shared her husband's scientific interests and activities. One of the jobs that she had taken on was to tend and feed the domestic bacteria. It gave me a thrill when I was allowed by her to watch her feeding, let us say, typhoid, dysentery, tetanus, and yellow fever. She fed them on brews conveyed in the medium of gelatine.

But what fascinated me most was to listen to my uncle holding forth on the sovereign virtues of science as a panacea for all the age-old ills that mankind had had to endure in the pre-scientific age. Uncle Percy was not content with lauding science's material benefits. Science could 'fix' (in the American sense of the word) all manner of bacteria. That was indisputable. But Uncle Percy claimed for science a great deal more than that. He claimed, and this with an aggressive show of confidence, that science could, and would, cure all social evils and settle all political and religious questions. I am not caricaturing his claims; I am not exaggerating them, incredibly excessive though they may sound in 1969 to readers of the present book. I have mentioned that he talked in superlatives which were probably intended to be discounted. Yet, when these have been scaled down, the residue is still portentous. As Uncle Percy saw things in 1903, the World was on the move—it was moving quite fast towards the attainment of an earthly paradise—and, in this triumphant march of mankind, science was the prime mover. In Uncle Percy's vision, science was the irresistible force that predestination was in Calvin's vision, and historical necessity in Marx's. But Uncle Percy, too, was an activist, and an impatient one. The irresistible force's votary did not feel it impertinent on his part, or derogatory to the irresistible force's dignity, to keep omnipotence moving by the push of a human policeman's hand.

This was a very different picture of the World from the one with which I was familiar, namely my father's. My father, Harry Valpy Toynbee, was not a scientist; he was a social worker. In his picture, the central feature was not the triumph of science; it was the problem of poverty. Moreover, my father's outlook on life was not promethean, as Uncle Percy's was. Uncle Percy was looking forward, and pressing forward, to a future in which science would have made all things new. My father was looking back like Epimetheus to an event in the past: the passage, in 1834, of an Act of Parliament embodying a new version of the Poor Law.

For my father, the Act of 1834 was a law of the Medes and Persians. For him, it was an article of faith that the Poor Law of 1834 was immutable, but he did not also hold that its provisions were, by themselves, an adequate solution for the persisting problem of poverty, and his attitude was no more passive than his brother-in-law's attitude was. Indeed, my father spent himself on the arduous and painful task of wrestling with the problem of poverty on the adverse terms to which he was committed by his principles. My father held that the Poor Law needed to be supplemented by private charity, and that the fund provided by charity needed to be judiciously and painstakingly administered with two objects in view: to ensure that the money should be spent only on provenly deserving 'cases', and further to ensure that, when a candidate for financial aid from private charity did pass muster, the extent of the aid, and the conditions on which it was given, should be kept within limits within which the charity would not undermine the recipient's self-reliance and self-respect. These principles were not, of course, peculiar to my father; they were the principles of the Charity Organization Society. The 'C.O.S.' had been founded in 1869, and my father worked in its service from 1881 to 1908.

The C.O.S. had been founded, and was supported financially, by well-to-do people belonging to the upper and the middle class who took for granted, as being both immutable and morally acceptable, the contemporary division of the community into sharply demarcated classes and the accompanying inequality of incomes, which was much more extreme in my father's generation than it is in 1969. Within the limits imposed by this postulate, the sponsors and officers of the C.O.S. were charitable-minded, public-spirited, and conscientious. The standard of social behaviour that they set for themselves was exacting. A middle-class father of a family who had no 'private means', or not much of them, was expected to work diligently enough and competently enough to pay for the education of his children and at the same time to save enough to provide for his wife's and his own maintenance after his retirement. He would expect this of himself. His self-respect required him to live up to this standard of self-reliance. He was, in fact, practising what the C.O.S. officer was preaching to the 'cases' which came before him for judgement. The C.O.S. was surely right in holding that self-reliance and self-respect are virtues on which no human being can default with moral impunity.

The point on which the C.O.S. was, I daresay, open to criticism was its failure to recognize that circumstances alter cases. The 'cases' with which the C.O.S. had to deal were poverty-stricken human beings of the 'working class'; and, in that chapter of the history of

Britain, the circumstances in which members of the 'working class' were condemned to live were so very much more adverse than the circumstances of even the lowest-paid members of the middle class— the income-group in which my father's salary placed him—that a rigid application of middle-class standards to working-class 'cases' might give more than their due to logic and method at the expense of uninhibited compassion. It is clearly right to foster self-reliance and self-respect in one's neighbour as well as in oneself. It is also clearly right to be businesslike in detecting imposture and declining to reward it. But it is surely also right sometimes, at the risk of being taken in, to act on one's impulse to give a suppliant a cup of water to drink in Christ's name, without waiting to ascertain whether his 'case' is or is not 'deserving'. The spontaneous call of love that this unaccredited suppliant has evoked in one's heart may be a signal that the suppliant is Christ himself appearing *in formâ pauperis* to judge his judge.[1]

Comparing my father's and my uncle's outlooks in 1903, I was conscious that my uncle's outlook was highly optimistic and that my father's was relatively sombre. At the time, I found my uncle's outlook exhilarating, and my father's outlook seemed to me rather melancholy now that I could set it against this flamboyant foil. Comparing the two outlooks again in 1969, after the passage of two-thirds of a century, I judge that my uncle's outlook was relatively naïve and that my father's was, by comparison, realistic.

The difference between the two outlooks was, no doubt, partly due to a difference in personal temperament, but it was also due, it

---

[1] For the history of the C.O.S., see Charles Loch Mowat, *The Charity Organisation Society, 1863-1913, its Ideas and Work* (London 1961, Methuen). The author is singularly well qualified for writing this book. He is an historian and the son of an historian, while, on his mother's side, he is the grandson of Sir Charles Loch, whose name he bears. Loch was appointed Secretary of the C.O.S. in 1875, and, though at that date he was only twenty-six years old, he quickly became, and thereafter remained, the Society's moving spirit till he retired in 1913. Loch's grandson records (op. cit., p. 63) that 'before long Loch and the C.O.S. were almost interchangeable terms, and his long years of service made him the embodiment of the C.O.S. idea for friend and foe alike'. He certainly was the embodiment of it for my family when I was a child. In the book cited in the present footnote, C. L. Mowat has given an account of a controversial movement that is sympathetic and at the same time critical. His objectivity makes his study of the C.O.S. illuminating.

now seems to me, to the difference between my father's and my uncle's respective fields of work. My uncle's field was science and technology; in this field human history has been a brilliant 'success story'; and it has never been so successful-seeming as it was in the pre-atomic phase of the current fit of acceleration—the phase before this fit escalated into its present paroxysm. On the other hand, my father's field was human nature: the social relations between one human being and another and a human being's relation with himself. This field is the forum of conscience, self-respect, self-reliance, public spirit, and charitable-mindedness—the virtues that were all-important in the eyes of the sponsors and the officers of the C.O.S. and that therefore determined the Society's principles and governed its policy.

These virtues are truly all-important; for mankind is one of the social animals; sociality requires co-operation; and co-operation is impracticable without the acceptance, by the parties concerned, of at least a minimum common moral standard. Thus morality is infinitely more important for mankind than science and technology are. No morality, no society; and, no society, no science and technology either; for science and technology call for more pairs of hands than one, as Robinson Crusoe discovered when he found that his work on the first boat that he built was labour lost, because he had built it so big and so far from the water's edge that, single-handed as he was, he lacked the man-power required for shifting and launching it. This signifies that the history of science and technology has been a 'success story' only on sufferance. The cumulative growth and accelerating advance of these performances of the intellect could not have been achieved in the past, and could not continue to be achieved in the future, if social relations had become, or were to become, so bad that society dissolved. Moreover, the advance achieved by science and technology within these last thirty thousand years is a luxury with which mankind could have dispensed, considering that, for the first million years of its existence, this species managed to survive on the strength of its primaeval Lower Palaeolithic scientific and technological equipment.

It is unfortunate for mankind that its success has been scored in its scientific and technological side-show, and that its performance on the stage of human relations—the stage on which the issues of th drama are life and good versus death and evil—has been a tragic failure. This inequality between the respective levels of Man's performance in the less important and in the more important of the two fields of human activity has become more than just unfortunate since the beginning of the present fit of acceleration in the advance of science and technology. The consequent widening of the 'morality gap' was already a cause for concern before the invention and use of the atomic weapon. Since that epoch-making event the spectacle of the gaping 'door of death' has become terrifying.

The current widening of the 'morality gap' was causing concern to Tennyson at as early a date as 1849. His concern is expressed in the seventh quatrain of the opening invocation, written in that year, of his poem *In Memoriam*, and this invocation is the last word in a sixteen-years-long dialogue between the poet and his own soul in which he had gradually worked through the spiritual travail into which he had been plunged by the sudden and unexpected death of a bosom friend.

> Let knowledge grow from more to more,
>   But more of reverence in us dwell,
>   That mind and soul, according well,
> May make one music as before,
> But vaster.

Tennyson was masterly in his choice of words, and, if I interpret this quatrain correctly, the two short words 'grow' and 'dwell' are evidence that Tennyson was aware in 1849 of the widening of the 'morality gap' and was praying, not merely that it should be closed, but that it should actually be converted into a 'science gap', in order to restore to mankind a lost margin of safety. In the first of these four lines, Tennyson is recognising the current acceleration of science's advance as a fact and as one that is to be welcomed conditionally; but in the one word 'grow' the poet puts his finger on the character of the intellect's achievement. Knowledge grows cumulatively because it is collective, impersonal, and therefore external. By contrast, reverence 'dwells' in a human soul because it is a human being's inward personal approach to ultimate spiritual reality. The increase in reverence therefore cannot be quantitative; it must be qualitative if it is to be real. Increase in reverence and increase in knowledge take place in two different psychic dimensions; and the increase of reverence must more than keep pace, in its own dimension, with the increase of knowledge in its different one.

I think it is clear that in 1849 Tennyson was concerned at the widening of the 'morality gap', but I also have the impression that he did not appreciate the radicalness of human nature's 'fault' (in the geological sense of the word). Tennyson was aware, as stanzas lv and lvi of *In Memoriam* reveal, that the advance of geological science has lengthened immensely our vista of past time; but, if I am not mistaken, he was thinking, in the seventh quatrain of the invocation, in terms of a far shorter time-span than in those stanzas. 'Before' in this quatrain means, I think, 'before the recent beginning of the current fit of acceleration in science's advance'; and Tennyson is assuming that, before that, Man's mind and soul had been in harmony with each other. An inquirer of my generation whose unaided insight is myopic compared to Tennyson's has the advantage over Tennyson of being able to read the signs of the times in the new light of further experience of the course of current human affairs and of additional knowledge of the descent of Man, thanks to the advance of a number of branches of science: psychology, anthropology, palaeontology; and, in this light, Tennyson's word 'before' acquires a new magnitude.

From the observation-date 1969, the word 'before' can only mean 'before our ancestors became human'; and we have sorrowfully to dissent from Tennyson's assumption that 'mind and soul' have formerly made 'one music'. We find mind and soul always in disharmony with each other as we trace their relations back, aeon behind aeon, to the date at which mind and soul came simultaneously into existence and our ancestors simultaneously became human. The genesis of mind and soul was also the genesis of the discord between them. Our forebears' nature has never made one music since, in the course of its evolution, it ascended—or descended—to the level at which it became human nature. The price of becoming human has been the forfeiture of the harmony of innocence—the amoral pre-moral psychic harmony that still reigns in the nature of the shark, the tiger, and the microbe.

The quatrain of Tennyson's on which I have been commenting did not come up for discussion between my Uncle Percy and me in 1903. If we had considered these lines together at that date, I am sure

that Uncle Percy would have endorsed the first line. '"Let knowledge grow from more to more": full marks.' But I guess that a
recitation of the other three lines would have made Uncle Percy
grow restive. He might have dismissed these later lines rather
impatiently as being at best irrelevant and at worst obstructive.
Uncle Percy's impulse would have been to demand the prompt
utilisation of all increases in scientific knowledge for all the corresponding increases in technological action which the new knowledge would have made practicable, and it would not have occurred
to him to doubt that any and every technological application of
science would be beneficial. I can fancy him in 1903 tossing Tennyson's collected works aside, pulling Goethe's out of the shelf, and
pointing gleefully to *Faust*, Part I, lines 1236–7:

> Mir hilft der Geist! Auf einmal seh' ich rat
> Und schreibe getrost: 'Im Anfang war die Tat'.[1]

When I was ruminating on the writing of the passage of the
present chapter that I am writing now, I found myself condoning
Uncle Percy's optimistic estimate of the consequences of the indiscriminate conversion of scientific knowledge into technological
power. His optimism, I was saying to myself, was warranted by his
own experience within his working lifetime; and no one can be held
to account for not having learnt the lesson of experiences that he
has not lived to undergo. Uncle Percy had been an eminent bacteriologist, and he had put into action his scientific knowledge in this
field by helping a number of municipal authorities to safeguard the
purity of their water-supplies. What application of science could be
more beneficial than that? No wonder that Uncle Percy's view of
the effects of science was sanguine, considering what the period was
in which he himself was putting his own scientific knowledge to
such beneficent practical use.

I was still thinking of the Uncle Percy with whom I had been
in intimate contact during those memorable weeks in 1903, and I
therefore got a shock when I looked up the notice of him in the
supplementary volume of *The Dictionary of National Biography* that
commemorates eminent British men and women who died in the

---

[1] 'The Spirit succours me! All at once I see light and write confidently: "In the
beginning was the deed".'

course of the years 1941–50. My purpose had been merely to verify the dates of my uncle's tenure of his chair at Birmingham; but, reading on, I read here that in 1914–18 'he carried out much research for the chemical warfare committee on synthetic drugs, on explosives intermediates, and on mustard-gas, and he was responsible with (Sir) W. J. Pope for the adoption of Guthrie's method for the manufacture of mustard-gas'.

So chemical warfare, not the analysis of drinking-water, had been the practical application of his scientific knowledge on which my uncle had employed himself during the closing years of his professional career. (He retired in 1919.) This was news to me. It came to me as a complete surprise. I had continued to keep in touch personally with my uncle and aunt till their deaths; and their descendants, in three successive generations, had been, and are, among my closest relatives and dearest friends. My uncle's and aunt's great-grandson is my godson. I had not, however, kept myself *au fait* with my uncle's work. Its field was one of which I was ignorant; during the First World War, I had been as busy as I now know that my uncle then was with noxious war-work. During part of the duration of that war, I had been employed on the production of British government propaganda, and propaganda is as poisonous in its way as mustard-gas is. Accordingly, I did not know till the other day that my uncle had ever used his knowledge (as I used mine, for my sins, during those same years) for death and evil, besides having used it for life and good. Till the other day, my Uncle Percy, the eminent scientist, was still for me the scientist of 1903—the scientist who was benefiting mankind by making war, not on his fellow human beings, but on Man's mortal enemies the bacteria. Today, I know that he took a hand in the invention of mustard-gas, and I feel thankful that he was *hors de combat* before the date at which, had he been still in harness, the Pentagon might have appealed to him, in a Transatlantic telephone-call: 'Come over into California and help us' to plan for bacteriological warfare.

What did Uncle Percy think of his war-work in retrospect? Well, what do I think, today, of mine? I have come to think that, in the First World War, almost all of us, in both camps, were not only whole-heartedly belligerent; we were also naïvely sure that our cause—whichever of the two it happened to be—was one hundred per cent righteous; and, besides, we behaved irresponsibly in shutting our eyes to the possible long-term consequences of our hand-to-mouth wartime acts. But Uncle Percy's case also raises a wider question. What did he come to think about the use and misuse of scientific knowledge in general and in principle? He had time to think about all this, for he lived through the inter-war period and through the Second World War too. He lived to hear the news of the dropping of the two atomic bombs in 1945. By that late date in an unusually long life, his powerful mind may have begun to lose its grip; but, while he was fully *compos mentis*, had his mind mellowed? Had he become less dogmatically sure that science was an infallible talisman than he had been in 1903, the year in which I had come to know his outlook of that date at first hand? I guess that his dogmatism will have been toned down by growing age and by disillusioning experience; but I can only guess; I shall never learn the answer to this question. I should have been shy of putting it to my uncle himself if it had been in my mind on the last occasion (this was in some year between the wars) on which I saw my uncle and aunt at Letterawe, on Loch Awe, where they lived after their retirement. My cousin Edward could have told me the answer, and would have spoken frankly, but he too is no longer alive.

Another question that exercises me is how a man of my uncle's immense ability could have been so naïvely optimistic even during those halcyon forty-three years 1871–1914 within which he received the latter half of his education and which saw him through his professional career, save for those last five disconcerting years of it. Considering that Tennyson was aware of the 'morality gap' in 1849, why was my Uncle Percy not aware of it in 1903? And I am certain that, at that date at any rate, this sombre fact of life was not taken into account by my uncle and therefore did not temper his sanguine mood.

I find what I think may be a key to my uncle's attitude, as I knew it, in the attitude of a contemporary of my uncle's father who was connected with my uncle himself by marriage. I am thinking of my own great-uncle Captain Henry Toynbee (1819–99),[1] one of whose nieces, my Aunt Grace, was my Uncle Percy's wife.

At first sight, Uncle Harry and Uncle Percy might appear to have

[1] See *Acquaintances*, pp. 1–20.

belonged to two entirely different worlds. Uncle Percy was an eminent scientist's son; Uncle Harry was a successful farmer's son. Uncle Percy had had a formal education in science as well as in the humanities before he had made science his life-work and had risen to eminence in it; Uncle Harry made his mark in science too, though in quite a different branch of it, namely navigation. Uncle Harry could study navigation with professional help only during the intervals between his voyages, before he got a command;[1] he was self-taught in mathematics and in astronomy,[2] which are the scientific bases of the navigator's skill; yet he distinguished himself by working out an accurate method of taking lunar observations to serve as a check on the time-keeping of the chronometers which were a nineteenth-century navigator's primary means of ascertaining his longitude but which, like less sophisticated clock-work, were not infallible.[3] Uncle Harry's contributions to the technique of navigation were notable enough to gain for him, in 1866, the post of Marine Superintendent at the Meteorological Office.[4] However, his science was not the thing in which Uncle Harry put his treasure, and here the difference between his outlook and Uncle Percy's might appear to be extreme; for Uncle Percy certainly did put his treasure in his science. Uncle Harry put his treasure in his religion, and this is the point in which he is the key to Uncle Percy; for Uncle Percy's science *was* his religion, and his attitude towards this newfangled secular religion of his was, as I now see it, essentially the same as Uncle Harry's attitude towards the old-fashioned form of Low Church Episcopalian Protestant Christianity that was his religion in the conventional sense of the word.

What strikes me now is that Uncle Percy's belief in science was psychologically a replica of Uncle Harry's belief in his particular school of Christian theology. Both these uncles of mine lived by faith. Their faith in their respective religions was absolute. Each of them felt quite certain that his religion was one-hundred-per-cent true and was therefore one-hundred-per-cent efficacious. It was the talisman that could open all doors, solve all problems, and cure all ills. Uncle Harry was an Early Victorian; Uncle Percy was a Late

---

[1] Captain H. Toynbee, *Reminiscences of my Life* (London 1901, privately printed), p. 11.
[2] op. cit., p. 13.   [3] op. cit., pp. 15–16.   [4] op. cit., p. 20.

Victorian; but Uncle Percy, too, was not a Victorian for nothing. As I now read the riddle that he presents to me, he had merely discarded the old bottle but had kept the old wine; and, in the new bottle into which he had defiantly decanted it, this old wine was the same stuff that Uncle Harry had continued to keep in its traditional container.

My two uncles' fundamental common characteristic was their certainty that they had the facsimile of truth and the blueprint for salvation in their pockets. Both of them were, in fact, fundamentalists, in the sense that they held beliefs which they took to be fundamental and which they never called in question. The Age of Faith outlasted the loss of faith in Christianity. The terminal date of the Age of Faith in the Western World is not 1859, the year in which Darwin published *The Origin of Species*; it is 1914–45, a time of tribulation that began with the outbreak of the First World War and ended in the dropping of the two atomic bombs.

When I talk to scientists nowadays and compare their state of mind with my Uncle Percy's in 1903, I realize that, within my lifetime, the scientists' *Weltanschauung* has changed as greatly as so many other features of human affairs have also changed within the same time-span. Present-day scientists, if I read their minds aright, are no longer fundamentalists, such as my Uncle Percy was in 1903. They appear to me to be, like me, agnostics, and this in two senses.

As professionals, these present-day scientists do not, I believe, feel the Victorian scientists' assurance that the truth, as they see it, is the whole truth or even nothing but the truth. If I am correctly informed, the investigation, since my Uncle Percy Frankland's day, of the minimally minute constituents of so-called 'inanimate' Nature has shown that these display some of the waywardness and elusiveness with which we are familiar in human beings. These minute 'quanta' move erratically, and they can be observed behaving as particles or behaving as waves, but they can never be observed behaving as both at once. If this is the truth, it means that the so-called 'laws of Nature' are statistical regularities only; they are functions of quantity, not intrinsic properties of each of the units singly that present themselves in quantities which are vast. Conversely, the behaviour of human nature, which is unpredictable in a single person, becomes predictable in a crowd with a margin of error that decreases in proportion to the number of persons under observation.

Neither anyone else nor I myself can predict how many times within the next twelve months I shall take the round-trip flight between London and New York or shall take a meal at a Lyons' corner-shop; but the airlines and the caterers will be able to predict approximately how many people will be purchasing their services and their goods within the same twelve months. These statistical predictions of theirs will be less exact than the scientists' corresponding predictions about the behaviour of the 'inanimate' sector of Nature; yet the predictions about human behaviour in the mass will be accurate enough to enable the purveyors of food and of transport to earn frequent enough profits, and suffer rare enough losses, to make it worth their while financially to do business. As for the scientists, my impression is that, in their non-professional capacity as human beings, they are agnostics in the sense that they do not feel the Victorian scientists' assurance that 'all things work together for good' to them who apply science to technology indiscriminately. This Victorian assumption may have survived the invention and use of mustard-gas, but it certainly has not survived the explosion of the atomic bombs that have been dropped on Nagasaki and Hiroshima.

6 : The Tug-o'-War in Education

I HAVE described my own education in an earlier chapter of this book. My education in the conventional sense of the word was the first of my three Greek educations, on the third of which I am still eagerly engaged. I began learning Ancient Greek at the age of ten, after an overture in learning Latin, which I had begun at the age of seven.

At Winchester, when I was 'in College' from 1902 to 1907, only two subjects were taken completely seriously at that time. The subject that was on a par with Greek and Latin was mathematics.[1]

[1] See p. 12.

The mathematics taught at Winchester were advanced, and the teaching was good, but the subject was 'pure', and its application to science and technology was ignored—at least as far as I climbed—and, unfortunately for me, I was allowed to dismount from the mathematics ladder when I had reached the rung just below the calculus.[1] At Winchester, mathematics were genuinely esteemed. In the scholarship examination at Winchester in 1902, I, with my classics, gained the third place on the Election Roll, but the second place was gained by a mathematician, Ralph Fowler.[2] Our generation was just young enough for its eminent pure mathematicians to become eminent mathematical physicists at the university stage. Ralph Fowler and the Charles Darwin of his and my generation became stars in this firmament at Cambridge. At Winchester, however, mathematics in our time were, like classics, insulated from practical life, and I suspect that it was their 'purity' that won them the remarkable honour of being held in equal esteem with the two 'classical' languages and literatures.

At Winchester in 1902–7 we were still living in the mental world of the fifteenth-century Italian humanists, and we were hardly aware that science and technology were on the march; that they had joined hands with each other; and that mathematics had stooped to lend efficacious services to them both. Yet, in the age in which the classical education that we were receiving at Winchester in 1902–7 had been instituted in Italy, one of the greatest of Renaissance Italy's geniuses, the 'universal man' Leonardo da Vinci, had declared that 'mechanics is the paradise of the mathematical sciences because, with mechanics, we reach the fruit that mathematics can be made to bear'.[3] In these words Leonardo had expressed his gusto for this coming event with a gluttony in which, with the genius's gift of being ahead of his time whether for good or for evil, he had been anticipating the spirit that was to become prevalent in the Western World in the nineteenth century.

In the seventeenth century, Francis Bacon had criticised the unpracticality of contemporary science and the unsystematicness of

[1] See p. 12.   [2] See p. 5.
[3] 'La meccanica è il paradiso delle sciētie matematiche, perchè cō quella si viene al frutto matematico' (*The Literary Works of Leonardo da Vinci*, compiled and edited from the original mss. by J. P. Richter, 2nd ed. (London 1939 Oxford University Press, 2 vols.), vol. ii, p. 241, No. 1155).

contemporary technology, and had deplored the lack of cross-fertilization between them.¹ In the middle decades of the seventeenth century the founders of the Royal Society in England had set themselves to achieve this cross-fertilization. A hundred years later, the Industrial Revolution had broken out in Britain in a haphazard way. A hundred years later again, the Industrial Revolution had been carried a further stage forward in Germany by a systematic application of science to technology that was the earliest approximation to a fulfilment of seventeenth-century English aspirations. In London by 1884, H. G. Wells had found his opportunity for getting his start in life by being accepted as a 'teacher in training', with a maintenance-allowance of one guinea a week, at the Normal School (the embryo of the present Imperial College of Science and Technology).² Most of this was unknown to me when I was receiving my classical education at Winchester and then at Oxford.

In the last quarter of the nineteenth century the parsimony of the United Kingdom Government was at its acme. What, then, moved the 'Establishment' of that day to spend even a pittance of public funds on technological education and even to go to the length of providing a maintenance-allowance for teachers in training for work in this field? The date is revealing. It is the date of the deliberate initiation (not, in this case, haphazard outbreak) of the second phase of the Industrial Revolution. British industry was already feeling the breeze of German competition. British public opinion had become dimly aware that human affairs had reached a stage at which scientifically instructed technological skill had become the key to wealth and power, and the Government had therefore been allowed, or constrained, to make a minimum provision for higher technological education. Wells's bitter comment is, I should guess, justified.

The powers in possession conceded the practical necessity for technical and scientific instruction long before they would admit the might and value of the new scientific knowledge. Just as these conservative forces

¹ See the passages of Bacon's works quoted in M. Purver, *The Royal Society* (London 1967 Routledge and Kegan Paul), on pp. 27–28 and 34.
² See H. G. Wells, *Experiment in Autobiography*, vol. i (London 1934 Gollancz), chap. 5, especially pp. 205 and 208–9.

permitted elementary education to appear only on the understanding
that it was to be a useful training of inferiors and no more, so they
sanctioned the growth of science colleges only on condition that their
technical usefulness was recognised as their sole justification.[1]

In the course of the eighty-five years that have passed between
the date of Wells's admission to the Normal School and 1969, the
potency of scientifically 'programmed' technology has been demonstrated sensationally, during each of the two world wars, in successive trials of military strength between Germany and Russia.

On both occasions Germany was a dwarf, by comparison with
Russia, in area and population, but in the First War she was relatively a giant in the size of her technologically skilled population—
particularly in the abundance of her skilled mechanics in the lower
ranges. A community's technological and scientific task-force has a
pyramidal structure, and, for its effective working, the breadth of
the base counts for more than the height of the apex. On this test,
Germany in 1914–18 was overwhelmingly superior to Russia, and
the Russian army's superiority in numbers was stultified by its
inferiority in equipment and, still more, by its inferiority in
technological training.

Between the two wars, the Government of the Soviet Union
showed that it had taken the lesson of the First War to heart. It
used its breathing-space to put in hand a 'crash' programme of
mass-education in technology. Even so, those twenty years 1921–41
were not enough to make the Russians a match for the Germans in
technological efficiency, and this time the German invaders penetrated farther into Russian territory than in the First War. But in
the Second War they were unable to force the Russians to capitulate; and it seems probable that the Russians would have turned the
tables on the Germans eventually, as in fact they did, even if the
product of their own armaments industries had not been reinforced
by additional supplies from the United States and Britain. The
previous twenty years of educational effort in the Soviet Union did
tell when Russia was compelled to pit her strength against Germany's
for the second time.

By 1969, all the peoples of the World have been converted by
events to the belief that scientific technology is the key to wealth and

[1] Op. cit., p. 208.

power, and that therefore public expenditure on scientific and technological education is not only justified but is imperative. The material equipment required for education in this field has, from the start, been more expensive than the equipment required for education in the humanities. Even the simplest laboratory or engineering school costs far more than the pens, paper, books, and lecture-rooms that suffice for the teacher of the humanities and for his students. Moreover, science and technology have been becoming more and more sophisticated and elaborate, and the cost of education in these fields has been rising proportionately. Yet this has not deterred the World's 125 governments and their respective tax-payers. In 1969 they are pouring out public money on scientific and technological education almost as lavishly as on material armaments; and this is logical; for highly educated scientists and technologists are armaments in themselves. Indeed, material armaments are useless without human hands that can manipulate them, and they would not be there for the soldier-technician to use if the soldier-scientist had not provided the knowledge that has been applied to their invention.

Thus today scientific and technological education has virtually unlimited resources at its disposal as far as money goes, but in this sphere there are limits to what money can buy. It cannot buy scientific and technological ability for a student whose natural gifts are poor or, if good, are good for other uses. Nor can money buy an enthusiasm for science and technology, and a consequent willingness to make his career in them, even in a student who does possess a natural gift for them. Man's nature, fortunately for mankind, has in it something of the intractability of the camel's, goat's, and mule's. Government and big business may bribe or coerce their country's higher educational institutions into making ample provision for the teaching of science and technology. They may bribe students into entering these fields of study by offering scholarships in them in quantities with which the old-established endowments for scholarships in the humanities cannot compete. Industrial corporations may further tempt students to opt for education in science and technology, in preference to the humanities, by dangling before them the prospect of secure and remunerative jobs after they have graduated. But suppose that the students do not take to science and

technology and do not choose to spend their lives on them, and
suppose that a revulsion from science and technology were to become a mass-movement in the rising generation, what could the
educational authorities or the industrial magnates or the politicians
or the electorate do about it?

You can flog a slave into digging a trench or building a wall, or
perhaps even into hoeing a field; but you cannot flog a student into
educating himself in science and technology against his will; and,
even if you could force him, by giving him no alternative choice,
to go through the motions, you could not turn him into a scientist
or technologist who would be of any use to you. The only effective
maker of a scientist or technologist is the man himself; and he will
not make himself into one if he does not want to be one. Even if,
for the sake of filthy lucre or of drab security, he were to try
against the grain, he would not succeed. At this level of activity,
opportunity is not enough, and ability is not enough either. These
are only enabling conditions; the congeniality of the career is the
sine qua non for succeeding in it; and it is only the successful scientist
or technologist who serves society's purpose by augmenting its
wealth and power.

No doubt, a large percentage of the human race does find congenial openings in this field. I have already cited Ernest Bevin's
belief that this is so, and I have also mentioned my own experience
of subsequently seeing Bevin's opinion corroborated by the spectacle
of the zest with which Turkish country-boys were educating themselves in recently established provincial polytechnics.[1] On the other
hand, Wells's career shows that governments cannot mould a human
being to suit governmental purposes if the human being's own
inclination does not coincide with his government's policy. Wells
did not spend his working life as the teacher of science-classes which
the United Kingdom Government had trained him to become,
though Wells had been given his training gratis with the bonus of a
maintenance-allowance of one guinea a week thrown in.

At the Normal School, Wells had luck. By inadvertence the public
authorities had admitted on to the School's teaching staff an eminent
scientist, T. H. Huxley, who studied and taught science for its own
sake, with no utilitarian *arrière pensée*. Wells spent his first year at

[1] See pp. 270–2.

the Normal School as Huxley's pupil, and he testifies[1] that 'that year I spent in Huxley's class was, beyond all question, the most educational year of my life'. Of course, Wells had greater freedom of manœuvre than most of us have, because he had genius. Yet, in spite of Nature's exceptional generosity in endowing him, Wells had a hard struggle to extricate himself from doing punishment duty 'in that state of life unto which it' had pleased, not Nature and not God, but Her Majesty's Government, to call him. Many less able men and women have struggled, and will struggle, still harder and longer but less successfully than Wells for the sake of following their own bent.

An eye to the main chance is not the inner directive in the hearts and minds of most of those students who take their education seriously. Their choice of subject for their education, and of field for their subsequent work, is governed more powerfully by the intrinsic interest and value that the subject has for them. In our day, when the pursuit of science and technology has become as remunerative as the pursuit of Greek and Latin was in the West in its pre-industrial age, students have been demonstrating, by their deliberate choices, the compelling power of the passage in the Book of Deuteronomy that Jesus is said to have quoted in one of his answers to the tempter: 'Man doth not live by bread only'.[2]

I came across a remarkable exhibition of this disinterested quest of knowledge and understanding at a temporary university, with a six-weeks' course, that the United States Army had set up in the West of England for the benefit of American soldiers who, after the final collapse of German resistance at the close of the Second World War, were waiting their turn to be ferried home across the Atlantic in order to be demobilized. The commandant told me that, when he and his colleagues had been planning the courses and deciding how many lecturers to assign to each of them, they had assumed that a majority of the students would opt for subjects that would be useful to them for obtaining lucrative jobs in the civilian life to which they were now going to return. The authorities had therefore provided faculty, in strength, for courses in such 'practical' subjects as business administration, accountancy, dentistry, engineering, and agricultural science. When, however, the students

---

[1] In op. cit., p. 201.   [2] Deut. viii. 3; Matt. iv. 4; Luke iv. 4.

had begun to arrive and to make their choices, the authorities had been taken by surprise. The most numerous applications had been for the philosophy course, and the next most numerous for the course in classical music. These unexpected preferences had sprung an academic crisis. The staff of instructors in dentistry, accountancy, and the other well-staffed 'practical' subjects had had quickly to be reduced, and the staff for the 'unremunerative' subjects had had as quickly to be reinforced. This quick-time reconstruction of the Army's temporary teaching-staff had been quite a difficult emergency operation.

The commandant's explanation of his students' preferences was, and is, convincing to me. The commandant had come to the conclusion that the majority of these men were not thinking, at this stage, in terms of their future careers; they were thinking in terms of eternity and of ultimate reality. They had just been released from months or years of active military service during which they had been facing death and had been inflicting it. This experience had been apocalyptic. They had met their 'moment of truth'. At least for a spell of time, they had been moved, by the events that had overtaken them, to live on the spiritual level of their fully human selves —the selves that, in counter-Buddhist Indian philosophical doctrine, are identified with the ultimate spiritual reality behind and beyond the phenomena of the Universe. What they wanted now was to digest their harrowing and illuminating experience and to orient themselves spiritually by taking their bearings in the Universe and beyond it. This was the first call that they felt, now that they had a brief interval of leisure. Till they had satisfied this spiritual need, their concern for their future mundane prospects was suspended.

I then recollected that I myself had been surprised at the commandant's choice between the alternative subjects that I had offered for the lecture that he had invited me to give. If I remember right, I had offered both a talk on current international affairs and a talk on the so-called 'philosophy of history', and the second subject had been the one that the commandant had preferred.

Twenty-four years later, in the academic year 1968–9, the business corporations are finding it difficult to recruit ex-university students in the numbers that they need. The students are turning away from industry and trade to what used to be called 'the liberal professions', in spite of their awareness that, in these, the openings are far fewer and the remuneration is also lower on the average. This time, as in 1945, the state of the World goes far towards accounting for the orientation of the students' interests and aspirations. In 1968, wars were being fought with inhuman weapons, and with spiritually and materially devastating effects, in Vietnam, the Middle East, and Nigeria. In the United States, race-riots are threatening to become chronic. In Britain, a sudden explosion of race-feeling has opened up the alarming prospect that Britain might go America's way. British 'whites', too, might run amok to the point of provoking 'non-white' counter-violence, though the percentage of 'non-whites' in the population of Britain is not of anything like the order of magnitude of the percentage in the United States. In these once again apocalyptic circumstances, it is not surprising that the rising generation should feel that the first call on them is to work for raising the standard of human conduct, and that meanwhile the further advance of science and technology can well be left to take care of itself.

This reaction is reasonable, considering that the application of science and technology is a matter of human choice. The more potent science and technology become, the greater become their potential effects for evil as well as for good; and, if they continue to advance while the standard of human conduct remains stationary or declines, this advance of Man's power over Nature will be a curse for Man instead of being the blessing that it is assumed to be by the promoters of it. Our current experiences warn us that we do need to give priority to the study of the nature of the human psyche, and that we need to study it not only for the sake of its intrinsic interestingness as an object of intellectual curiosity. We also need to study human nature for the further purpose of applying our findings about it to the practical enterprise of mastering it, as we have already learnt to apply science to the practical mastering of non-human nature through technology.

This task whose field is the humanities is the most urgent because in this field we are comparatively backward, and this in both theory and practice. In the intellectual history of the Hellenic World, Thales, the father of physics, made his appearance nearly a century and a half earlier than Socrates, the father of ethics. Socrates' deliberate transfer of his attention to ethics from the physics that had fascinated him in his youth was an epoch-making event; but throughout Hellenic history, and throughout Western history thereafter till within living memory, the study of human nature was virtually confined to a charting of the human psyche's conscious and volitional surface, and a great gulf stayed fixed between epistemology and self-discipline, notwithstanding the efforts of the Stoic and Epicurean schools to bring philosophy down to Earth.

In the West, at any rate, it is only within my lifetime that we have begun to explore the subconscious abyss of the human psyche, layer below layer, and it is only since this recent new departure that theory and practice have joined hands for the simultaneous study and mastering of human nature, as they joined hands for the simultaneous study and mastering of non-human nature at the earlier date at which science and technology were consciously brought into partnership with each other. The effectiveness of the partnership in the non-human field holds out hope that, in the human field, it may likewise prove fruitful. The history of the relations between Western science and Western technology during the last three centuries indicates that theory and practice both advance by leaps and bounds when they interact reciprocally.

Meanwhile, we are barely in the second generation of the new age that has inaugurated the exploration of the subconscious layers of the human psyche, and our application of our findings in this unfamiliar field to the practice of human affairs is consequently still in its infancy. In fact, our study and mastery of the subconscious is in 1969 at about the same stage that the study of physics had reached in the generation of Thales' *diadochi* Anaximander and Anaximenes. We have no time to lose in travelling the long and arduous road from childishness to spiritual maturity now that the advance of science has placed potentially annihilating weapons in our still childish hands.

Fortunately the very backwardness of the study of human nature and the proportionate backwardness of our clinical use of this new knowledge provide a twofold inducement for able minds to enter this field. One of these two inducements is the sheer attractiveness of the unknown. The other inducement is the fact that, in entering a new field of study and action, we all start at scratch, with equal

Experiences

opportunities, irrespective of the differences between our various social and cultural backgrounds.

The headmaster of a grammar school in the North-West of England, whose testimony I have already cited in another context,[1] told me a few years ago that able boys and girls who came to his school from relatively uncultivated families tended to take up science rather than the humanities, not necessarily because they had a personal gift or bent for science, but for the social reason that, in science, they could compete on equal terms with children from more cultivated families, whereas in the humanities they would have found themselves handicapped. In the humanities the doctor's daughter or the lawyer's son would be receiving all the time a supplementary informal education at home which would give her or him a signal advantage in school-work. At home this child would hear talk at mealtimes about public affairs and perhaps also about literature and art; and there would be educative books in the house on which an able and alert child would browse. On the other hand, this informal education in the home would not extend from the humanities to science. This is a subject that can be studied only systematically and with the aid of apparatus, and that therefore can be studied only at school. In science the professional man's child and the artisan's child start on a level with each other. In science, therefore, individual ability tells, without being either fostered or frustrated by the personal accident of the social and cultural milieu into which a child happens to have been born.

The humanities that were being taught at this North-Western grammar school in the nineteen-fifties were, of course, the humanities on which I myself had been educated in the years 1896–1911, so I was able to see the point of the observation that the headmaster of the grammar school had made. I myself had been fortunate in having fallen in love with the humanities in their traditional form and in having turned out to have, in this field, an aptitude that I did not have in mathematics. My devotion to the study of the humanities was fostered during the years of my formal education by a succession of first-rate teachers who were themselves devoted to the humanities for the sake of their intrinsic merits. These teachers have inspired me by their example. All the same, I agree with Ernest

[1] See pp. 269–70.

Bevin's criticism of the traditional system of education as a social institution—and this criticism applies not only to an education in the Greek and Latin classics but to an education in 'pure' mathematics as well.

An abstract intellectual education, carried on beyond the age of fifteen or sixteen, appears to be uncongenial to a majority of young people, irrespective of the social class into which they happen to have been born. The reason why this uncongenial form of higher education has been imposed, until recently, on children born into the 'upper middle' and 'upper' class in Britain and in other Western countries is that it is both expensive and non-utilitarian. As a 'gentleman's education', it serves to distinguish its numerous reluctant victims, as well as its rare devotees, socially from the majority of people who have had either only a primary education, or, at the secondary stage, only a technological one. In the examination for the British civil service (home, Indian, and colonial), for which a number of my contemporaries at school and college sat, the knack of translating a passage of Emerson's works into plausible-seeming Platonic Greek prose was rewarded with as generous a quota of marks as the corresponding knack of writing an essay in the style of *the Analects* or a poem in the style of *the Book of Songs* had been rewarded in the examination for the Chinese civil service during the thirteen centuries ending in A.D. 1905, the year in which this historic examination was held for the last time.

If I and my British classmates had been born Chinese, we should have been unlucky in our generation. Half way through our laborious old-style education, the bottom would have been knocked out of it through its being suddenly deprived of its objective, and we should have had to start educating ourselves all over again— and this in the alien material of Western science and technology. This would have been a nuisance for those of us to whom the Greek and Latin classics were uncongenial; it would have been a tragedy for the minority for whom the Graeco-Roman World had become their dearly beloved adopted country.

Something like the break in Chinese education in 1905 has been happening in Western education too in the course of my lifetime. The gulf between a traditional Western education in the Greek and Latin humanities and a present-day Western education in the latterday humanities—sociology, anthropology, economics, and above all, psychology—is surely no less wide, in spite of the fact that, in the West, these new lines of human studies are native growths, not alien imports. The new lines cannot be denied the title 'humanities'. They are at least as intimately concerned with human affairs as Plato's dialogues or Thucydides' and Polybius's histories or Virgil's poems are; and, though sociology, anthropology, and economics, as hitherto cultivated, 'smell of the lamp' as strongly as my Greek and Latin verses that are printed in Part III of this book, their younger sister, psychology, does have her feet firmly on the ground, or, if this is not the right metaphor, psychology, we may say, has her feet treading water vigorously on the upper levels of the human psyche's unplumbed sub-conscious abyss (Greek *abyssos*: Sumerian *abzu*).

As I try to peer into the future, I seem to see psychology becoming the queen of the humanities; and, in my vision, she becomes their queen because, in contrast to the Greek and Latin classics, psychology is equipped for giving timely practical aid to Man in an age in which Man needs all the aid that he can obtain, whether from God or from himself, to save him from committing the crime and folly of liquidating his own species. Today we are still only on the threshold of this new realm of knowledge that may perhaps help to save us if we succeed in applying it in practice. We have each to learn how to master himself (a discipline that, in India, the Buddha was already teaching in the sixth century B.C.), and, having mastered ourselves, we have to learn how to master our relations with each other.

It is an inescapable law of human life that all knowledge can, at will, either be used for good or be misused for evil. An understanding of the human psyche is being misused for evil in so far as it is being turned to account for propaganda, for advertising, for bamboozling. This is a pernicious misuse of our new-found psychological understanding. This understanding can, however, be used, just as readily, for an honest searching of our hearts and mending of our ways and an honest endeavour to raise the standard of our relations with our fellow human beings to a level that, hitherto, has been attained only by the saints.

Are not the humanities, in this new guise, at least as stimulating a field for action as science and technology are? And are not these 'new humanities' likely to minister far more effectively than science and technology ever can to Man's present need to save himself from himself? The sinister feature of science and technology is their moral neutrality. The 'new humanities' are morally committed. *Ex officio* they are on Ahuramazda's side against Angramainyush, to speak in Zoroastrian language. I do hope that, in my grandchildren's generation, this is going to be the field that will prove the most attractive to human ability of every kind.

7 : The Wind of Change in Religion

In the realm of religion I have now lived to see the wind veer round twice. I am just old enough to have seen, with grown-up eyes, the melancholy spectacle of the historic higher religions apparently foundering, in a final irretrievable plunge, after a long-drawn-out process of settling lower and lower. In the Western World, this process had started more than two centuries before the date of my birth, and, like many of my contemporaries, I took the disappearance of the historic religions complacently; I saw no reason why the places that they had vacated should be re-filled; and I was therefore taken by surprise when an ancient and supposedly extinct religion promptly sprang up again like a jack-in-the-box, and this in three different styles of modern dress in which it has masqueraded as three rival ideologies. I have been still more surprised at the cheering spectacle of the historic religions unexpectedly looming up again above the horizon since the end of the Second World War.

In re-emerging, these old religions have proved that, after all, their disappearance from view at the turn of the century did not mean that they had foundered. The wind that had originally filled their sails had not sent them to the bottom. So far from rising to the pitch of a fatal hurricane, this once favouring wind had, of course, been gradually dying down. It had not sunk the ships; it had eventually left them temporarily becalmed, but this not before it had carried them out of sight. The temporary calm had indeed been swiftly broken by a wind, blowing from quite a different quarter, which had been of full hurricane strength—the wind that had brought the ideologies crashing into a world whose inhabitants had come to assume that their world's structure was now stable and secure. For a time, the ideologies filled the whole seascape, but in 1969 they seem to be receding as boisterously as they advanced from 1914 until the nineteen-fifties. In 1969 a third wind is blowing, and this in the diametrically opposite direction to the wind that was dying down, but was still prevalent, when I was a child; and this third wind is blowing the traditional religions back towards the central position in the seascape that they occupied for so long a tale of centuries in the past.

Thus the vicissitudes of mankind's religious history have twice taken me by surprise; and now I can see in retrospect that, on both occasions, my astonishment was naïve.

It was naïve of me, in the first instance, to suppose that the sea-scape could remain untenanted for long, or indeed for a moment. I have now come to believe that religion is an inseparable accompaniment of the consciousness and the power of choice that are the distinguishing characteristics of the human psyche. In my belief, every human being has a personal religion, and every human community has a collective religion, whether the person or community is aware of this or not. Each of us does, I believe, have a religion even if he denies that he has one and denies this in good faith. Spiritual nature, like physical nature, abhors a vacuum. If we succeed in repudiating the religion that we have inherited, we shall inevitably acquire a substitute for it, and this substitute may be both more evil and more archaic. This point has been put in a classical form in one of the most awe-inspiring of all the parables in the Gospels.

> When the unclean spirit is gone out of a man, he walketh through dry places, seeking rest, and findeth none. Then he saith: 'I will return into my house from whence I came out'; and, when he is come, he findeth it empty, swept, and garnished. Then goeth he and taketh with himself seven other spirits more wicked than himself, and they enter in and dwell there; and the last state of that man is worse than the first.[1]

[1] Matt. xii. 43–5. Cp. Luke xi. 24–6.

The man in the parable is modern Western Man in our day. The parable fits, like a glove, Western Man's experience within my lifetime. The original unclean spirit with which modern Western Man was once possessed is the spirit of fanaticism that has been part of Christianity's and Islam's heritage from their parent religion, Judaism. In Western Christendom this endemic fanaticism boiled over into the hideous sixteenth-century and seventeenth-century Catholic-Protestant wars of religion. The atrocities that had been committed in the name of religion shocked the most sensitive and most enlightened souls in the contemporary Western World so deeply that, before the close of the seventeenth century, some of them were beginning to repudiate Christianity and indeed religion itself in any form. 'Tantum religio potuit suadere malorum.'[1] From Pierre Bayle's generation down to mine, this scepticism, born of moral revulsion, spread progressively, from its origins among a small and at first unrepresentative intellectual and moral élite, till it came to be accepted, to the extent of being almost taken for granted, by the masses.

Pre-Voltairean Christian fanaticism died hard. I was born not too late for my lifetime to overlap with a Christian's who was so fanatical that he would have found himself at home in the age of Western history in which Christians of conflicting persuasions burned each other at the stake. I have given a sketch of my evangelical great-uncle Captain Henry Toynbee in a previously published book.[2] However, my great-uncle, though he was a skilful professional navigator, was fated in his religion to play the role of the captain who goes down with his sinking ship. He was a rare surviving specimen of a species that, since his death, has become virtually extinct. Christianity paid the extreme penalty for its persistent fanaticism and factiousness. It was cast off; and, since, at the time when Western Man was repudiating Christianity, he was simultaneously imposing his domination on the rest of the human race, Western scepticism followed the Western naval, commercial, and colonial flags. The Westernizing non-Western intelligentsia followed suit to the Western intellectuals. They repudiated their own respective ancestral religions: Hinduism, Buddhism, Zoroastrianism,

[1] 'So great were the enormities that religion could induce human beings to perpetrate' (Lucretius, Book I, line 101).   [2] See *Acquaintances*, pp. 1-20.

and even Islam, which had previously had the reputation of being invulnerable.

The dry places through which emancipated Western Man and his emancipated non-Western disciples now walked, seeking rest, were the spiritual vacuum that they had created in their own souls, and they were bound to find no rest in this state, considering that it is a state which is contrary to human nature. Their house was empty. It had been swept by rationalism and it had been garnished by science—garnished superbly, but not made hospitable for human habitation, for it still remained empty of religion, and to offer Man science as a substitute for religion is as unsatisfactory as it is to offer a stone to a child who is asking for bread. Modern Western Man and his non-Western fellow-travellers had perforce to replace their ancestral religions by some authentic other religion; and the authentic religions with which they did fill the spiritual vacuum in their souls were certainly more wicked than Christianity had ever been even in those passages of its history in which the temperature of its fanaticism had reached and passed boiling-point. The parable speaks of seven other more wicked spirits. In real life in my generation I can identify three, namely Nationalism, Individualism, and Communism. The enormities that have been perpetrated in the name of each of these three post-Christian ideologies have been, if possible, still more wicked than the worst that have ever been perpetrated in the name of Christianity. Modern Man's state in the age of agony and atrocity that dawned in 1914 has been even worse than modern Western Man's state was in the age of the Catholic-Protestant wars of religion.

Happily, however, this worse state has now turned out not to be the last. The historic higher religions have inaugurated a new chapter in the history of religion by re-emerging unexpectedly, and this in a new mood that presents an encouraging contrast to their traditional mood of mutual envy, hatred, and uncharitableness. The resurgence of the historic religions began, in the interlude between the two world wars, when some of the Protestant Christian churches started the Ecumenical Movement and led some of the Eastern Orthodox churches to join in. This rejuvenescence of Christianity was given a potent fresh impetus when Pope John XXIII was elected to sit in Saint Peter's chair and when, during his brief tenure of it, he began the *aggiornamento* (the 'bringing up to date') of the Roman Catholic Church and carried this movement, before his untimely death, beyond 'the point of no return'. The Ecumenical Movement and the *aggiornamento* stand for the mutual charity, esteem, and love that make possible, and call for, reconciliation and co-operation without prejudice to the question whether eventual reunion is also practicable and desirable. This change of heart among the adherents of Christianity has spread to the adherents of other historic religions as rapidly as the repudiation of Christianity spread to them towards the close of the three centuries that ended in the nineteen-fifties. Since the end of the Second World War, the Northern and Southern sects of Buddhism have made peace with each other, and Hinduism has made peace with Buddhism of both denominations. In the Arabic-speaking World, Islam has simultaneously made peace with Christianity.

Meanwhile, the post-Christian ideologies have had free rein and have done the worst that they could do within the short span of a single generation during which they have been disastrously paramount. I give them only a short span because I believe that these substitute-religions are incapable of helping human beings to preserve their personalities, and this is the most elemental need that every human being has in an age in which the triumph of technology is threatening to dehumanize personalities by demoting them into being mere 'things'—identified, not by a 'proper name', but by a serial number punched on a card that has been designed to travel through the entrails of a computer.

Competitive Individualism, bee-like or ant-like Communism, and tribal-minded Nationalism all resemble each other and resemble technology in being impersonal. An impersonal social dispensation is at variance with the essence of human nature. It is therefore a dispensation against which human nature is bound to rebel; and, when human nature's well-justified protest is answered either on a stock official 'form' or by sheer silence, a human being is driven to the conclusion that no action on his part, short of physical violence, will extort attention to him as a person from the impalpable, elusive, Boyg-like smog of impersonal relations in which he finds himself caught.[1] A human being will insist on being treated as a person,

---

[1] For the Boyg, see Henrik Ibsen, *Peer Gynt*, Act II, scene 7.

even if the only way in which he can secure personal attention is to get himself knocked on the head by a policeman's truncheon and had up next day before a magistrate as a 'case'. This I believe, is the underlying cause of the demonstrations, foaming over into acts of violence, which are now rearing their crests, in waves, above the dead-level surface of modern Man's dehumanized world.

Modern Man has indeed brought an ironical fate upon himself in our time. Since the moment when his ancestors became human by taking their first short feeble step towards the control of their natural environment, Man's dream has been to make himself master of non-human nature instead of remaining at its mercy. After a million years of effort that seemed to have been out of all proportion to the results that it had achieved, Man's perennial dream was still an unfulfilled dream in Francis Bacon's generation, which was little more than three centuries ago. Within these latest three centuries, the dream has at last been fulfilled to a fullness that has been beyond all previous expectation. Man has not only subdued his natural environment; he has obliterated it by conjuring up around him an artificial environment of his own making. This artificial environment is the product of modern Man's technology, which has made more progress within these last few centuries than in the whole previous span of human history, and more progress in the lifetime of my generation than in the previous quarter of a millennium. Man has now decisively overcome Nature by his technology; but the victor has been technology, not Man himself. Man has merely exchanged one master for another, and his new master is more overbearing than his former one. Man is still the slave of his environment; but this is now the environment that he has created for himself, not the environment with which Nature originally endowed him. Nature used to chastise Man with whips; Man's own technology is now chastizing Man with scorpions.

Man's present plight is not just ironical; it is tragic. His enslavement to technology and his vain rebellion against this enslavement have both been moving towards some unforeseeable menacing climax since 1914, and, *crescendo*, since 1945. Among all the evil that Man has been doing and has been suffering during the post-war years, the re-emergence of the historic religions above our horizon has been the one auspicious event. This is a piece of good news that has taken mankind by surprise. Yet perhaps it is no accident that these old religions have made their unexpected comeback just at this juncture; for these old religions have always been strong in the point in which the ideologies and technology have been weak. They have offered effective guidance and help to a human being in his rough passage through life—and the passage is rough because being human means having consciousness and having the power to make choices, and the possession of these god-like powers is an ordeal for a mortal mundane creature such as Man is.

A drowning man clutches at straws, and to pin hopes on the re-emergence of the historic religions might have been written off as a futile exercise in wishful thinking if these religions had made their re-entry in the same spirit in which they made their exit at the turn of the century. Their re-entry gives reasonable grounds for hope because, at the nadir of their fortunes, they have reacted to adversity by changing their spirit, and the change has been all-important. The evil genius of the higher religions, which has debased them below their in other respects lower predecessors, has been their inveterate factiousness and the unbridled rancour with which they have pursued their quarrels. The adherents of each religion have quarrelled with the adherents of every other one; and, within the bosom of each religion, the adherents of differing sects have quarrelled still more bitterly with each other. Jew has contended against Christian, Christian against Muslim, Muslim against Hindu; and, within the several religions' respective folds, Pharisee has contended with Sadducee, Trinitarian with Arian, Catholic with Dyophysite and Monophysite, Eastern Orthodox Catholic with Roman Catholic, Roman Catholic with Protestant, Shi'i with Sunni. This factiousness, and the malice, hatred, and uncharitableness into which it rankled, brought Western Christianity into the disrepute that has alienated Western Man from his ancestral religion progressively since the seventeenth century. This was the spirit in which, at the turn of the nineteenth and twentieth centuries, the historic religions sank below mankind's horizon. In the years 1907–11, when I was an undergraduate at Oxford, it was these religions that seemed to have no future. Their factiousness seemed to be incurable. Yet I have now lived to see the unlooked-for all-important change of heart come over them.

The historic religions have now reappeared above our horizon in a spirit of mutual charity, and this change of heart has removed the age-old stumbling-block. It has opened the way for these religions to perform the spiritual services for a human being which they have always had it in their power to perform, if only they had not stultified themselves, as they have, persistently, in the past, by exhibitions of spitefulness and intolerance that have justly brought them into discredit. Their service is one that they alone can provide, and it is a service of superlative value. The historic religions can give a human being the help that he needs for gaining direct touch with the ultimate spiritual reality behind and beyond the phenomena of the Universe. Along their different paths towards an identical spiritual summit, these religions can give a human being the spiritual power to break out of his servitude to human technology and to human society into a true spiritual freedom. A human being who has entered into communion with ultimate spiritual reality, and has made it his paramount concern to live in harmony with this reality, will have fulfilled Man's *raison d'être*, and his personality will then be proof against the assaults of the impersonal forces of a once human world that the progress of technology has been transforming into a termitary.

This is the fruit that can be borne by the historic religions' recent change of heart. Is this change going to prove permanent or to prove ephemeral? All depends on its being permanent, and, at this early stage of the new era, we cannot be sure that the change will last. There are, however, at least two good auguries. The change is such a fundamental one—so complete a new departure—that it is hard to imagine how it could now be reversed; and it is also a new departure that responds to a new need. The present threat to human personality is the greatest peril to which mankind has exposed itself at any time so far since our ancestors became human; the threat to the physical survival of the human race is merely an incidental consequence of this spiritual crisis. The higher religions alone can help mankind to save itself from itself by helping it to regain contact with the ultimate spiritual reality which is the ground of being and the source of salvation.

The change of heart is the heart of the matter. If this change has truly been achieved and if the achievement is going to be permanent, it will bring with it a change of conduct for the better, not only in the relations between human beings in their role as adherents of their respective religions, but in all human relations on every plane of human activity. The union of hearts is primary. Questions of doctrine and of administration are secondary to this. The union of hearts has been manifested already in numerous personal meetings. Two of these may be picked out for recall as being fair, though striking, examples.

When Pope Paul VI landed at 'Amman airport in the course of his pilgrimage to the Christian holy places in Jerusalem, he was met and greeted by a welcoming crowd which must have been about ninety per cent Muslim. When, on a later journey, he arrived at Bombay to take part in a Catholic Christian eucharistic congress, he received another warm-hearted welcome from a crowd that must have been about ninety-nine per cent Hindu. The reason, we may guess, why the Pope touched the hearts of crowds whose religion was not his own was that they recognised that the Pope's concern was not limited to the members of his own flock but embraced all human beings of all religions—as Pope Paul had shown, and has continued to show, in his untiring labours on behalf of world peace. When Muslims and Christians, and Hindus and Christians, have attained to this degree of spiritual unison, there is already 'one fold and one shepherd'.[1] The fold is not any single one of the historic religious communities; it embraces them all. The shepherd is not some fallible ecclesiastical authority; it is the ultimate spiritual reality which, being ineffable for human lips, is called, in different religions and philosophies, by different names that veil the identity of the reality that eludes them.

Peering into the future, we cannot foresee whether this or that religious community, which has a separate existence today, is or is not going to unite with this or that other religious community tomorrow. We cannot foresee, either, whether this or that doctrine is going to be maintained in its present form or is going to be modified, and, if it is going to be modified, what the direction and the extent of the modification is going to be. We do know that everything that is man-made is subject to change, and ecclesiastical institutions and theological doctrines are man-made. This will be

[1] John x. 16.

acknowledged not only by agnostics who hold that the ecclesiastical paraphernalia are man-made and are nothing more than that; it will also be acknowledged by people who believe that these are man-made expressions of something trans-human or supra-human or, in theistic terms, divine. The essence may be eternal, but the human expressions of it, being human, are bound to be no more than provisional and ephemeral accommodations to particular times and places. Change is of the essence of life, and human life is changing in our time *accelerando* under the relentless drive of technology's quickening advance.

The problem presented by the inexorable fact of mutability has confronted the ecclesiastical authorities always and everywhere, but it is particularly acute in an age in which the pace of change in all human affairs is unprecedentedly swift, and it is most acute of all for the responsible heads of ecclesiastical institutions that have been allergic to change for some time past. In this situation, only a hero will dare to open the long-closed door, and only a statesman will have the judgement to decide how far and how fast the process of *aggiornamento* is to be carried. Pope John XXIII played the pioneer's *beau rôle*. The problem inherited from him by Pope Paul VI is a challenge whose dimensions are those of Pope John's spiritual stature.

We cannot foresee how each of the historic religions is going to change, or what changes there are going to be in these religions' relations with each other. If, however, I am right in believing that their common new spirit of mutual charity and appreciation has come to stay, we can be sure that each of them will be accessible, as never before, to the adherents of the others; and, for human beings who are truly in quest of ultimate spiritual reality, this is going to be an inestimable boon. It will be a boon for them because it will open up for them a choice between different paths leading to the identical goal that each of them is seeking to reach, and the opportunity to choose is precious because different paths fit the feet of people of different temperaments.

In the past, before the so-called 'annihilation of distance' through the recent astonishing progress of technology, a person's religion was virtually predetermined for him, and this for life, by the accident of his having been born and been brought up in this or that time and place. He inherited his ancestors' religion automatically, and the possibility of embracing some other religion was virtually closed for him by ignorance of any but his own, and by the prejudice that ignorance creates. In the Western World, however, for about a hundred years by now, it has been possible for a Protestant-born or a Catholic-born Western Christian to make himself familiar enough with the alternative form of Western Christianity to enable him, at the age of mental maturity, to make the choice between abiding by his ancestral form of the Christian religion and adopting the alternative form. As a third choice, he has been able to reject both forms by becoming an agnostic.

We are now moving into an age in which the range of choice will be wider and the exercise of the freedom to choose will become more frequent. We can look forward to a coming stage in mankind's religious history at which a person's religion will normally be, not the one that he has inherited, but the religion that he has chosen for himself when he has come of age—a religion which may or may not be the one in which he has been born and brought up. This is a spiritual gain for future generations of mankind that has already been brought within sight by the change of heart which has over-taken the adherents of the diverse historic religions in our time.

8 : Unintended Consequences

(i) THE HYDRA'S HEADS

IN the world of time and change there is no last chapter. The story never ends in a full stop. Life is like Herakles' contest with the Lernaean Hydra. When the human combatant has smitten off one of the serpent's heads, a cluster of fresh heads springs up in the severed head's place. The solution of one problem creates other prob-lems which have not been foreseen and certainly have not been pro-duced intentionally. The poet George Herbert was right in saying that rest is the last and best of God's blessings, and that God has with-held it from Man, His creature. For the living there is no rest on this side of death.

(ii) THE BACKLASH OF BENEFICENT DRUGS

The unintended and, in some cases, disconcerting consequences of achievements that are good in themselves are ironical facts, but they are inescapable. A typical case, which may serve as a symbol for the whole genre, is the unintended side-effects of some of those wonder-working drugs with which the physicians' pharmacopoeia has been immeasurably enlarged and enriched within my lifetime. Let us assume that one of these newly-invented potent drugs has been used beneficently and also with success in the sense that it has cured the malady to which it has been applied. It may still exact a price for its good service by producing some untoward effect. If the physician who has prescribed the drug has foreseen the unwanted effect, he will have acted on the calculation that this is the lesser evil in a situation in which his choice lies between tolerating this effect and forgoing the use of the drug to cure the major malady. This situation is actually occurring in real life all the time nowadays. It is a parable of what is happening in our generation in many departments of the artificial man-made environment to which we have subjected ourselves.

(iii) THE SOCIAL PRICE OF THE NEW TECHNOLOGY OF
FARMING IN IOWA

For instance, the systematic application of science to agriculture on the most fertile soil in the technologically foremost countries since the end of the Second World War has made possible a vast increase in the amount of the product per acre and per worker. In Iowa today one farmer, with his family, can cultivate as many as 450 to 600 acres, in contrast to his father's 260 acres; and from each acre he can produce, let us say, four times as much as his father could. The new-style farmer achieves his *tour de force* by making a massive capital investment in machinery and chemicals. He preserves the whole product for consumption by its intended consumers—beef cattle and human kind—by ploughing weed-killers and insecticides in with his seed; and, since his investment has been too great to allow him to afford any pause in his task of earning returns on it, he ploughs in fertilizers as well, as a substitute for the old-style farmer's periodical fallow years.

This has been a paying business so far, but has it been an economically sound one? The farmer's ultimate capital is the soil, and he has been snatching year-to-year profits from this without providing the equivalent of a depreciation and replacement fund. Thus in present-day Iowa the soil is a possible future sufferer from the application of agricultural science, but Man has been a victim of the new-style farming already. Today the Iowan countryside maintains only about half the number of families that it used to maintain in pre-war days. As you travel, you admire the richness of the fertilizer-fed corn and the profusion of the power-driven plant. Byre and barn have been transformed into workshop and factory, and the operator is a mechanic, chemist, manufacturer, and dealer rather than a farmer of the traditional kind. However, you also cannot avoid being distressed by the eye-sore with which this industrialized farm-land is now disfigured. For every farm-house that is still in occupation, you see another that is deserted and decaying. These are the abandoned homes of those former two-hundred-and-sixty-acre farmers who have failed to 'make the grade' to becoming an operator of one of the 'king-size' farms of today. These losers have given up the struggle and have migrated to a city. What kind of an alternative life have they found for themselves there, and what kind for their children? For a child, to grow up in the country is a happy lot compared to growing up in a city, and this happiness was enjoyed by a majority of American children during the first century of the history of the United States.

In 1783, the nuclear United States was a farmers' country, and most of the urban minority was still living in small country towns. Moreover, the farming population was already surging westward over the Appalachians and the Alleghanies, and, from the western foot of the mountains, fabulously vast untouched reserves of potential farmland stretched away westwards to a line half-way between the Mississippi and the Rockies. The American agricultural 'frontier' did not stop moving on westward till about 1890. Even as recently as the time of the Second World War, if a Londoner fell into conversation with an American soldier in one of the London parks, it was surprising to find in how many cases the American turned out to be a country boy for whom his passage through London was his first experience of city life. Even in 1969, some now utterly urbanized

American office-workers or professors' wives turn out to have grown up on a farm. However, today a mere five per cent of the population of the United States produces enough food to feed itself and the rest of the population of the country, with a surplus to spare. Only one rural product has fallen off, but this is the most important product of all: it is country-bred children. In the United States in 1969 to grow up on a farm has come to be a rare piece of good fortune.

(iv) POLITICAL AND ECONOMIC NEO-COLONIALISM

In another continent and in another dimension of life, one can see in Africa today an unintended untoward effect of political de-colonization. In a number of African countries the abdication of the former European rulers has spelled, for the majority of the population, merely a change of masters. Britain's loss of her grip on Southern Africa has opened the way for the hegemony there of the local white settlers, who treat their African fellow-countrymen as the Spartans treated their helots. In Kenya the handful of white settlers has now gone under or gone away, but the vacated seat of power has been occupied by one of the local African peoples, the Kikuyu. This efficient agricultural people has come to the top because it has had the ability to adapt itself to the modern way of life. The pastoral Masai and Somalis have been less successful, and it may be doubted whether they have benefited by the change of régime. Nor are the Kikuyu the only indigenous African neo-colonialists. In Ethiopia the Amhara are a master race; in the post-British Sudan the Muslim Northerners are trying to subjugate the pagan and Christian South. In Nigeria the ablest constituent of a mixed population is the Ibo people; but the Ibo are a minority; their superior ability has made them as unpopular as the Chinese diaspora is in South-East Asia and as the Jewish diaspora was in mediaeval Western Europe and in the former Russian Empire's ex-Polono-Lithuanian 'pale'; and accordingly today the Ibo, in their turn, have their backs to the wall.

Moreover, the European ex-colonial powers who have given up their former conspicuous political empires have retained their surreptitious economic empires, which were, and are, more extensive. Today, most of Africa north of the Zambesi, most of Asia south of Continental China and the Soviet Union, and almost the whole of

Latin America are still being dominated economically by the West European countries or by the United States or by both. An unexpected sequel to the world-wide process of political emancipation has been that the politically liberated countries have been growing relatively poorer, while the ex-imperial countries have been growing relatively richer. The officially liberated countries have discovered that it is easier to change flags than it is to change terms of trade, and that a change in the terms of trade to the disadvantage of the producers of primary products can more than offset the 'foreign aid' that the affluent industrialized countries dole out to them.

(v) THE DEBIT COLUMN OF THE BRITISH WELFARE STATE'S ACCOUNT

A particularly puzzling problem is presented by the present-day 'welfare state'—for example, in Britain. The revolutionary re-distribution of the British people's national income during my lifetime has been a long stride forward in the direction of social justice. The allocation of income has become less unfair, and surely this change is unquestionably good. Moreover, national education, financed out of public revenues since 1870, has been followed up since 1906 by publicly financed national health and unemployment insurance, a national health service, and national pensions. As a result, the security, the health, the average amount of a family's real income, and the general condition of the people as a whole have improved visibly, and at first sight this outcome of the series of social reforms, on socialist lines, that were started by a Liberal Government in 1906 looks like a decisive confutation of the principles of the Charity Organization Society. The items on the credit side of the welfare state are in fact indisputable, but time has now shown that the C.O.S.'s forebodings have to some extent been justified by the event. Like Iowa's new-style farming, the British welfare state evidently has a catch in it.

The C.O.S. ignored both the inequality of the nineteenth-century distribution of the national income in Britain and the potency of the play of impersonal economic forces in the functioning of a modern industrial society. The C.O.S. knew that the middle-class Victorian Englishman was in a position to fend for himself. He could do this, by self-discipline and effort, even if he were in the lowest of the middle-class income-brackets. The C.O.S. expected the industrial worker to rise to the middle-class standard of self-reliance. The members of the middle and upper class whose voluntary contributions supplied the C.O.S. with its funds were blind to the truth that even the most virtuous cloth-capped industrial worker —one who did not drink or smoke or bet or swear but did toil and save to the maximum of his power—might, through no fault of his own, come to end his days in the workhouse, a fate with which an equally virtuous top-hatted office-worker would seldom be faced.

When my father's health suddenly broke down just as he was approaching the climax of his career, members of the C.O.S., who had appreciated his devoted hard work for twenty-seven years as their salaried employee, realized that this was a family catastrophe for which he could not have been expected to make provision, and they raised by subscription among themselves a capital fund which provided enough income to save the situation. Yet these self-same good, kind, and generous people took no account of the insecurity of the industrial worker's weekly wage or of the impossibility of saving enough out of this slender and precarious wage to provide against unemployment, sickness, and old age. In fact, they hardly thought at all in terms of working-class economic realities; they thought almost entirely in terms of middle-class moral ideals that were practicable for the British middle class but not for the British working class of their generation.

This sounds preposterous, and it was. Yet posthumously the C.O.S. has been partially vindicated. The social reforms that have been put into effect from 1906 onwards have succeeded in raising the standard of living of a majority of the industrial workers in Britain to a level which, before 1906, would have been reckoned as being at least 'lower' middle-class. But the industrial workers have not taken to behaving in a middle-class way. They have been given social benefits without having been schooled in the middle-class virtues, and this has had some unfortunate effects now that the practice of these virtues has been brought within their reach, and therefore within their field of moral obligation, by the improvement in their economic position. This is, at any rate, how I see it today; but of course I am not a detached observer. Though I am a

dissenter from the nineteenth-century middle-class creed, I am looking at things, as my father and his colleagues in the C.O.S. looked at
them, with middle-class eyes.

Subject to these doubts of mine about my own objectivity, my
impression is that the average British industrial worker is still
childish-minded and irresponsible-minded if judged by average
British middle-class standards. In my judgment, this working-class
attitude of mind was inevitable before the social revolution that
began in 1906. In that bygone era, the fault was not the industrial
worker's own; it was the fault of a middle-class and upper-class
'establishment' that appropriated a fantastically excessive share of
the national income and withheld from the industrial worker the
margin of income, security, and leisure which are the indispensable
enabling conditions for practising the middle-class virtues. Today,
the lion's share of the national income is being received by the
industrial working class. It is they, not the diminished (though by no
means yet extinguished) 'establishment' who now have the biggest
stake in the nation's productivity and solvency; so, if Britain were to
go bankrupt, the industrial workers would be the biggest losers.

The industrial workers do not seem yet to have taken the point
that they now have a major interest in maintaining the national
income and, if possible, increasing it. They seem still to be more
intent on contending with their employers for a larger share in the
annual cake than they are on holding their own in the world-
market against their competitors there—for instance, the industrial
workers of Germany and Hong Kong and Japan. They are still
acting on the assumption that the cake, all but a few crumbs of it, is
being appropriated by their employers, and that therefore the pre-
servation of the cake itself is their employers' concern and responsibility, not theirs. In short, two-thirds of the way through the
twentieth century, the British industrial workers are still fighting the
nineteenth-century battle on the home front that began to become
out of date when, a century ago by now, Britain lost her brief
monopoly of being the unchallengeable 'workshop of the World'.
In the industrial workers' continuing struggle with their employers,
the workers have now gained the upper hand. The development of
trades union organization has given them the power to maintain and
extend the restrictive practices that were their nineteenth-century

defence against overwork and unemployment. They can also now expect to be able to enforce their demands for shorter hours of work and for higher pay. Yet these are pyrrhic victories. The price of them is a depreciation of the currency in which the British workers are paid, and a progressive loss of the foreign markets in which their livelihood is earned.

Am I asking too much of my fellow-countrymen in expecting them to show a more intelligent understanding of their own present interests? I do not think I am calling for something unreasonable; for I have been in post-war Germany, Hong Kong, and Japan, and I have the impression that in these countries the industrial workers are more wide-awake and enlightened.

If this impression of mine is correct, what is the explanation? I fear it may be that the provision of social services, not accompanied by an education in the middle-class standard of foresight and responsibility, has fostered the childish-minded short-sightedness that was the British industrial workers' inevitable attitude in the pre-welfare-state age. Even the best-paid and most virtuous industrial worker then had no choice but to spend the whole of each of his weekly wage-packets on the current week's necessities of life, and, as often as not, he and his family began to feel the pinch before the next weekly wage-packet fell due. Habits die hard—especially habits that have been inculcated by bitter want. The 'establishment' whose injustice drove the industrial workers into forming the habit of fecklessness is to blame. In 1969 an industrial worker and his family are still inclined to spend the whole of one wage-packet before receiving the next; but, since the advent of the welfare state, they have come to think of this wage-packet as being primarily pocket-money that they can afford to spend on superfluities because some of the family's chief basic needs—for instance, education, health and unemployment insurance, medical care, and old-age pensions—are now being provided for them out of public funds.

In truth, of course, the wage-earners are paying for these services indirectly. The sole source of income is productive work; and, if the funds applied to public services were not herded into the public sector of the national budget by taxation but were distributed in wages, each wage-earning family's income would be increased sub-stantially. Then, however, the wage-earner would have to pay for the services that he now receives apparently, though not really, gratis. The middle-class salary-earner has always had to pay for these services, and it has been this direct obligation that has implanted in him his sense of personal responsibility. The acquisition of a sense of responsibility is the crucial qualification for becoming an adult human being. This is one of the fundamental truths about human nature and human life.

The backlash of the tardy achievement of social justice through the institution of the welfare state is, for me, the most disconcerting of all the unintended consequences, within my experience, of deeds that have unquestionably produced intended good results as well as their undesired and undesirable aftermath. To my mind, the crucial question is: is it practicable to provide social welfare and to inculcate a sense of personal responsibility simultaneously? Is it equitable, or, if equitable, politically feasible, to exact financial contributions towards the cost of social services that are provided compulsorily? In 1870, when universal primary education was made compulsory in Britain by an Act of Parliament, the wage-earning industrial workers whose children were the beneficiaries could not have contributed, even fractionally, towards the cost. This Act was an early harbinger of the welfare legislation that eventually followed it from 1906 onwards; and, in the course of the intervening thirty-six years, a certain presumption had been created that a compulsorily imposed service ought to be provided gratis. However, this presumption has not, so far, been allowed in Britain to set hard into a principle. The compulsory insurance against various contingencies that has been introduced since 1906 has been partly financed by a contribution to the cost from the beneficiary and a larger one from his employer, though these private contributions have had to be supplemented out of the public funds raised by taxation. Yet it is still an open question—for instance, in the financing of the National Health Service—whether the beneficiary should or should not be required to contribute, and, if he should, what the extent of his contribution ought to be.

In the light of experience, it seems desirable that, for some, at any rate, of the social services, some contribution should be payable by the beneficiary. This seems desirable on the moral grounds on which the C.O.S. would have advocated it, and on political and social grounds as well. The treatment of an issue, not as a question of principle, but as a question of more or less, is usually expedient, since, when once a vexed question has been shepherded into quantitative terms, it becomes both negotiable and re-negotiable; and, in a rapidly changing society, it is imperative that the door should be kept ever open for reconsideration and readjustment in every department of mankind's life and activity.

(vi) SOME PITFALLS IN THE PATH OF EGALITARIANISM

The re-distribution of the national income in Britain within my lifetime has been made on two moral grounds that are distinct from each other. The more conspicuous but shallower of these two grounds has been the recognition that the previous distribution was unjust in the economic sense. The deeper ground—a fundamental ground—for this (happily non-violent) social·revolution in Britain has been the echo, in the conscience of every human being, of God's rejection of Cain's claim that he was not his brother's keeper. At all times and all places, every human being has been, and is, aware that a human being has certain inalienable basic rights. He has these rights intrinsically, *ex officio humanitatis*, whatever may be his race, his nationality, or his religion.

In the mythical case in point, Abel had an intrinsic right not to be murdered by Cain; and this myth is a presentation of an historical truth. An appalling consequence of our pre-human ancestors' achievement of becoming human has been a lapse, in human beings, from the standard of behaviour of non-human mammals towards fellow-members of their own species. Non-human mammals compete and contend with each other, but apparently they do not go to the length of fighting each other to the death. By contrast, in human society, killing is tabu, is morally reprobated, and is punished only if it has been committed without sanction. Human communities have always made a distinction between murder and killing which is 'no murder'. Anthropologists tell us that this is one of the very few universal applications, in social practice, of the universal human distinction, in the abstract, between right and wrong. The morally dubious distinction between 'unlawful' and 'lawful' killing of fellow human beings seems to have been common to all human societies of which we have any knowledge.

All societies have, in the past, put to death human beings who have been convicted of offences for which the legal penalty has been capital punishment. So far, the death-penalty has been abolished in only a few of the World's 125 states, and this only recently and in the teeth of vigorous opposition. (The abolition of the death-penalty in Russia under the pre-1917 Imperial regime was made virtually a dead letter, in cases of political offences against the régime, by resort to martial law.) The genocide committed against the Armenians in the Ottoman Empire in 1915 and against the Jews in Germany and in the German-occupied non-German parts of Europe during the Second World War was carried out, in both cases, under the cloak of legality, by cold-blooded governmental action. These were not mass-murders committed spontaneously by mobs of private people. The responsibility of the private citizens of the Committee of Union and Progress's Turkey and Hitler's Germany was, of course, grave, but it was a sin of omission. Private citizens in general did not summon up in themselves the public spirit and the readiness for self-sacrifice that are required of a human being by his conscience (a daunting requirement) when his conscience condemns the acts of people in power who are acting in his name as representatives of the government of the country of which he is a citizen.

The other action, besides the execution of the death-penalty, in which killing has been almost universally sanctioned as being 'no murder'—and has indeed been commended as a social duty and been glorified as a patriotic deed—has been killing in war. In a previous chapter, I have noted[1] that, in the modern Western World, the Quakers have been unique in condemning the institution of war as being wicked, and in consequently refusing to take any part in war. The Quakers are a small private society. The only state that has ever yet renounced resort to war in all circumstances is, as far as I know, post-1945 Japan in the terms of her present constitution. In our generation we are only just beginning to recognize that one of the basic rights of a human being is that he should not be killed deliberately in any circumstances, and that the killing, by public authority, of enemy combatants in war and of convicted criminals (including murderers) is as unwarrantable as the killing by private enterprise which, so far, is the only form of killing that most human societies have stigmatized as being 'murder'.

[1] See pp. 209–11.

The right not to be killed deliberately is the primary right. If one has been killed, one has been deprived, in the act, of the possibility of benefiting by other rights. However, the other basic human rights, which the right to life brings into play, are hardly less precious than the right to life itself is. There is, for instance, a right not to be allowed to die of starvation or of exposure to the elements. Short of these extremes, there is a right not to go hungry, and not to be driven to dwell in housing that is not weatherproof and not sanitary, or that is over-crowded. There is also a right not to be parted forcibly from other members of one's family. These rights are all negative, but there is also the positive right to be given full opportunity for cultivating personal ability of any kind, in order that it may be used for society's benefit as well as for one's own. In practical terms, everyone has the right to the best education from which his ability will enable him to profit, and the right to be given the best kind of work for which he is qualified by his ability and his education.

In the Britain of 1969, in contrast to the Britain of 1889, few people go hungry, but many people's housing is still not weatherproof and is also insanitary and over-crowded. Moreover, some families are being broken up because they cannot find any housing at all at the maximum cost that they can afford at the current rate of real wages. This is a continuing violation of the basic right of the members of a family to live together which, in the past, was frequently violated, under the Poor Law, in the workhouses.

Considering that the value of money can be measured only by what the money can buy, the contrast, in present-day Britain, between the average standard of housing for a still well-to-do minority and the majority indicates that the re-distribution of the national income, far though this has gone, has still not gone far enough. On the crucial test of housing, the Britain of 1969 is still, as Victorian Britain was, a house divided against itself into 'two nations'.

On the still more crucial test of the relations between inhabitants of Britain who are of different physical races, we have now to confess to ourselves that Britain's house is also divided against itself today. In April 1968, while the present part of this book was being written, one public speech made in Britain by one politician touched off, like a lighted match thrown into a powder-magazine, an explosion of race-feeling which is evil in itself and is also alarming on account of the extent and of the violence of its animosity.

In deploring and condemning this evil spirit, I am conscious that I am in no position to preach. I am a member of the well-to-do minority, and members of this minority are seldom confronted personally with the problem of a direct encounter with neighbours or colleagues of a different race. It is this experience that has now got on the nerves of the 'white' wage-earners in Wolverhampton and in Birmingham and in Notting Hill.

Race-feeling is now tense among the 'white' population of these and other districts in which members of the 'coloured' minority that has settled in Britain since the Second World War happen, for economic reasons, to be concentrated. In the country as a whole, this immigrant minority is a minute fraction of the total population. Indeed it is infinitesimal, measured by the relative size of the overwhelmingly huge percentage of 'non-whites' in the populations of South Africa and Rhodesia. In Britain the problem of race-relations will be manageable in numerical terms if the 'coloured' minority is not appreciably reinforced and is distributed, as it could be, more evenly. At present there is discrimination against the 'coloured' minority in housing, in the terms on which they can finance the purchase of houses by loans, in insurance-rates, and in openings for employment. Some aspects of this discrimination can be dealt with by anti-discrimination legislation, but legislation alone can only mitigate the evil. This can be cured only by a change of heart in the racialist-minded section of the 'white' majority.

On the issue of race, which is a new issue for her, Britain now stands at a parting of the ways. She can take the road of racialism that has been taken by the 'whites' in Southern Africa and in the United States, or she can take the road of racial reconciliation and eventual fusion that has been taken in the Islamic World and in some of the Latin American countries—in Mexico, for instance, and in Brazil. Manifestly the way to salvation for Britain lies along the Islamic and Latin American road, not along the Southern African and North American road.

Britain is still free to choose, but she has not much time for taking the momentous decision. In Britain the race-issue has exploded at the moment when, all over the World, the great 'non-white' majority of mankind has come to the end of its patience with the hitherto dominant 'white' minority. Everywhere the 'non-whites' are now turning savage and militant. In Britain, too, anti-'colour' animus among the 'whites' will evoke, if its temperature is not quickly reduced, a counter-animus among the 'coloured' minority.

Every fact so far examined in the present section of this chapter seems to tell in favour of thorough-going egalitarianism. Basic human rights are sacrosanct; when we see them violated, our consciences revolt; and is not egalitarianism the only approach to the conduct of human affairs that promises to vindicate basic human rights in full good faith? I myself believe that it is; but I also believe that, when once we have made up our minds to follow this path, we ought to keep our eyes open for pitfalls. My survey of the facts, brief and superficial though it has been, has revealed a number of them. As illustrations, I will pick out two—from the fields of housing and of education.

I think it is widely agreed that the amount of new housing built by municipal authorities and financed by them on non-profit-making terms has been inadequate. Therefore, prima facie, it looks like one step farther towards equality in housing when a wage-earning family is moved out of a jerry-built house in a slum into a new block of municipal flats. Is not the transferred family being raised to something nearer the level of the housing that is at the disposal of the middle class? Its level is, in fact, being raised in the literal, as well as in the metaphorical, sense if the flat allocated to it in the new block is, say, on the eleventh floor. And what is wrong with physical elevation? There is an electrically-powered lift, and 'high rise' liberates space on ground-level out of doors for making a playground for the children. However, there are pitfalls here both for the children and for their parents.

A mother will be tied to her flat on the eleventh floor by her household duties, and perhaps also by a baby in the cradle; and then how, from that altitude up aloft, can she keep an eye on children playing on ground level out of doors? She may not dare to let the children out of her sight, because she is aware that an increase in crime has been keeping pace with the modest increase of prosperity that has hoisted her up to the height at which she now finds herself.

Her children of pre-school age will then have to stay immured with her, and their only opportunity for getting a breath of fresh air and a glimpse of the World will be when their mother takes them with her on one of her shopping expeditions.

The move that has immobilized the children will also have frustrated the parents; for the tenants in a block of flats are physically juxtaposed without having much chance of becoming each other's neighbours in the traditional human sense. Each household is likely to feel lonely, and this will give them a nostalgia for their former house, now demolished. They will forget that the roof used to let the rain in, that the plumbing was defective, and that the landlord was never willing to carry out even essential repairs. They will remember only the jerry-built house's amenities. They had that little house all to themselves, so it was a home. It was two storeys, or perhaps only a single storey, high, so the mother could keep an eye on her children playing on the pavement just outside. There was also a tiny backyard, in which the father could coax a few flowers into life. Wife and husband could lean over the yard-wall and chat with the people next door. So in that vanished home they did have real neighbours.

These pitfalls are genuine and unavoidable consequences of slum-clearance and large-scale standardized municipal housing. They are unfortunate consequences; yet who would be prepared, on that account, to pronounce that municipal re-housing is a social evil? We are left with a puzzle on our hands. A good move has had some unintended bad results that are disconcerting.

In the field of education, egalitarianism sometimes runs to a fanatical extreme at which its devotees wreak private injustice and public damage.

There are egalitarians who regard it as an infringement of equality if an old-established grammar school which has been incorporated in the national educational system still maintains a higher standard of teaching than younger national schools of a new type. If they can, these doctrinaires will reduce this exceptional school, whose offence is its persistent superiority, right down to the standard level. (The Nazis had a name for this levelling-down operation; they called it *Gleichschaltung*.) Meanwhile, the egalitarians will not be able to prevent enterprising parents from sending their children to such a school, but they may try to prevent even painstaking parents from getting to know that this particular school has special merit. For instance, the headmaster of the former grammar school may be forbidden by the local school board to display his school's original name at its gate.

An even more perverse aberration of fanatical egalitarianism is to regard it as an infringement of equality if a child has unusual mental ability. In the egalitarians' eyes this child is a mental rentier whom Nature has inequitably over-endowed, and he ought, like the grammar school, to be *gleichgeschaltet*. (I am not drawing a caricature; I have heard of actual cases of the attitude and policy that I have been delineating.)

Carried to this excessive length, egalitarianism becomes blind to the fact that true equality is equality of opportunity for all human beings each to make the fullest use of his natural endowments. Human beings are born with unequal endowments, and injustice is committed if an unusually gifted child is deliberately held down under a ceiling set by the average level of ability of children of his or her age. A gifted person who is thwarted so unjustly in childhood may be ruined for life by this.

The egalitarian who quashes an unusually gifted child or an unusually good school is also doing the greatest injury to the public interest. The only capital with which mankind has been supplied by Nature is the mental ability of unusually gifted specimens of our species. Nature has deprived Man of the built-in tools, weapons, and clothes with which she has furnished non-human living creatures, including Man's own pre-human ancestors. Nature has stripped off from Man's skin all but a few patches of his ancestral fur and has turned him out into the World all but naked. She has whittled down his claws into fragile finger-nails and toe-nails, and has filed down his teeth till they are not a match even for a rat's teeth. Man's wits are the sole capital that Nature has doled out to Man, in compensation for all the assets of which she has deprived him. The average standard of human wits is far higher than the average standard in any other species of life on this planet; but, in endowing human beings with wits, Nature is not egalitarian; she produces occasional mental defectives and occasional geniuses.

Genius can be spiritual, artistic, or intellectual. It is the intellectual geniuses, working in co-operation with their far more numerous averagely intelligent contemporaries, who have made mankind's material fortune. Intelligence is mankind's only true capital. The inanimate natural objects and natural forces that we mis-call 'capital' —mineral oil and natural gas, coal, water-power, electricity, and the titanic force latent in atoms—have been valueless to Man till some human being of unusual ability has discovered how to make them serve Man's purposes.

Thus the doctrinaire egalitarian who quashes the unusually gifted child or the unusually good school is striking an assassin's blow at the heart of the public interest. He ought to be sternly restrained from preventing that school and that child from doing their best. This is surely indisputable, but it is also not the last word that has to be said. A person who has been generously endowed by Nature is under an uncovenanted moral obligation to use his gifts, not in Napoleon's way, just for his own selfish advantage, at his less gifted fellow men's expense, but, if he can rise to this height, in a bodhisattva's way— that is to say, at his own expense for the benefit of all other sentient beings. Moreover, if the gifted person has been given, in his child-hood, the opportunity to cultivate his natural gifts by being given the best education accessible to him at the time and place at which he happens to have been born, he will have incurred a social obligation —though this, too, will not be a contractual one—to use his gifts for society's benefit. If, in benefiting society, he benefits himself as well, he may be forgiven for not having risen to a bodhisattva's height of self-transcendence.

(vii) SOME PARADOXICAL CONSEQUENCES OF THE AMAZING RECENT PROGRESS OF MEDICINE AND SURGERY

Compared to the progress of medicine in my lifetime, the progress of other branches of applied science has been paltry, immense though this too has been. My paternal grandfather was the first specialist in London in throat, nose, and ears. If he could rise from the dead in this year 1969, he would find, I expect, that medicine had made as much progress since 1866, the year of his death, as it had made between the generation of Hippocrates in the fifth century B.C. and A.D. 1815, which was the year in which my grandfather was born. My grandfather would, however, also find that this unforeseeably rapid progress of medicine had created problems for physicians, for surgeons, and for mankind which, in my grandfather's generation, were still beyond both the professional's and the layman's horizon.

The innumerable particular achievements of medicine and surgery and public hygiene within these last 103 years add up to one general achievement. The average expectation of life has been lengthened appreciably, and this all over the World, in the 'developing' countries, in which the birth-rate still continues to be high today, as well as in the 'developed' countries. This lengthening of the average expectation of life has, in itself, been a magnificently beneficial achievement. As the price of this immense benefaction, the recent progress of medicine has produced a population explosion in the 'developing' countries and—at any rate in the 'developed' countries—at least one technical problem for physicians and surgeons, together with a growing number of moral problems for the physicians and surgeons and for their patients and their patients' relatives and legal representatives.

The cause of the population explosion is well known. The rate of premature deaths can be reduced sensationally, even in 'backward' countries, by simple measures taken by a small staff of public health officers, whereas the birth-rate can be reduced only by the free choice of innumerable husbands and wives. Unregulated breeding has already given way to family planning in almost all the 'developed' countries. But the population of this group of countries is only a minority of the total human population of our planet. In the 'developing' countries the ancient habit of unregulated breeding is dying hard. Meanwhile, the net natural increase in the population of these countries is nearly offsetting, and in some countries is more than offsetting, the rise in the population's general standard of material living that the governments and peoples of so many of the 'developing' countries are now striving to achieve.

In the 'developed' countries within the last few years the medical profession has acquired a previously undreamed-of freedom of manœuvre in disposing of life and death; and in this field of human action, as in every other, an enhancement of the distinctively human power to choose has brought with it a corresponding increase in the number and the difficulty of the problems that freedom of choice inevitably creates. In the 'developed' countries today, physicians and surgeons are confronted with the novel intellectual problem of defining death, and, though this problem is a technical one, it is not academic; it concerns not only the professionals but the public and consequently the public authorities.

Until only the other day, death was assumed to be both inexorable and unmistakable, and so indeed it was before the recent astonishing advance in medical and surgical knowledge and skill. In the past, when a few minutes had passed after a human being's heart had ceased to beat, medical practitioners could certify with assurance that the patient was dead because, at this stage, it was unquestionably beyond their power to bring him back to life again. Now that hearts have been transplanted from the bodies of dead persons to the bodies of still living persons whose own hearts have become incapable of continuing to function well enough to go on keeping them alive, the old definition of death has lost its meaning. If death can now no longer be diagnosed by the traditional criteria— the heart's ceasing to beat, the blood's ceasing to circulate, the lungs' ceasing to breathe, and so on—what new criteria can we find? And, if we do find some, how can we be sure that these, too, are not going quickly to be put out of date by medical and surgical science's still accelerating advance?

Nature allows Man's vital organs to run down in course of time, without providing for their replacement, and thus ensures his eventual death so long as human physicians and surgeons cannot replace these organs. Now, however, human practitioners have made a start in replacing the most vital of all organs, namely the heart; and the advance of the science of organic chemistry may reach a point at which it will be feasible to manufacture live organs, instead of taking an organ from another body. Then a man will be able to order a new foot as readily as a new shoe, and a new heart as readily as a new suit of clothes. This flight of my imagination, on which I have ventured in an earlier chapter of this Part,[1] is 'science fiction' today, but it may well be overtaken by events in real life the day after tomorrow.

This sudden increase in Man's power over life and death has raised some previously non-existent questions. Hitherto the life of

[1] See p. 282.

any specimen of any species of living creature has been a limited liability both for Nature and for the specimen itself. Nature has been committed for only a limited time-span to the existence of a physically or mentally or morally defective human being, and conversely a sick or sad or conscience-stricken human being has been committed for only a limited time-span to his suffering. Sooner or later, death has been bound to save the situation, and we can now see that the inexorability of eventual death may have been a boon for Mortal Man as well as a relief for Nature.

However, Man has always been unreconciled to the fact that he has been created mortal. He has repined against this fact ever since our ancestors became aware that they were going to die by becoming conscious in the act of becoming human. In the past, Man has spent on the quest for immortality much of his surplus energy and resources. Egyptian pharaohs in the Age of the Old Kingdom mobilised Egypt's labour-force, year after year, in the agricultural year's dead season, for winning immortality for the pharaohs by building pyramids; some Chinese emperors squandered the product of their subjects' labours on their alchemists' quests for the elixir of life, and shortened their lives, instead of prolonging them, by confidingly drinking the potions that their alchemists served up to them. Human beings desired immortality even when they believed that they were going to experience it only as an eternity in the wretched shadow-world of Hades or Sheol, or, worse still, in the fire of Hell (a more likely destiny for sinful Man than the bliss of Heaven). Almost always and everywhere, with the notable exception of countries in which the Indian attitude to life has prevailed, immortality has been Man's heart's desire.

Ironical minds have recognized that these frantic labours have been in vain. The branch of the tree of immortality that the Sumerian hero Gilgamesh had acquired through herculean exertions slipped out of his hand into the mouth of a snake; and a snake (the same snake?) caused Adam and Eve to be expelled by Yahweh from the Garden of Eden lest they should eat the fruit of the Tree of Life after having eaten, at the serpent's suggestion, the forbidden fruit of the Tree of Knowledge. In the Western World before the close of the seventeenth century, at the dawn of the age of rationalism, modern Western Man had come to dismiss his predecessors' pursuit of immortality as being a misapplication of human ability that was both unprofitable and silly; and now, suddenly, the progress of rationalism's offspring, medical and surgical science and technique, has confronted Man with the prospect of a prolongation of human life beyond its natural term. The postponement of death, for however long a span of time, is not the same thing as the achievement of immortality, but the present prospect does put Man's age-old thirst for immortality to the test. Is this novel prospect of unnatural longevity attractive? If it is not, then the hope of immortality will lose the traditional charm that it has had, in the past, for most of mankind.

In matter-of-fact terms, would I, for instance, relish the prospect of having to make out an annual income-tax return *in saecula saeculorum*, with no chance of escape from this *corvée* short of my being overtaken by senility? Should not I prefer to die still in effective enough possession of my wits to be aware that my income-tax inspector and collector were becoming powerless to serve demands on me any longer?

I can, of course, speak only for myself. I should plead to be allowed to die if I found myself being condemned to endure an unnatural longevity by a *fiat* of the medical profession or of the public authorities. I should also make the same plea on behalf of any human being who, like me, shrank from the prospect of an inordinate prolongation of life in this World. I should make this plea, particularly, for those whom I love most and whose companionship gives my own life its meaning and value. I should make it even at the risk to myself of suffering the long-drawn-out torment of bereavement that I should be condemned to suffer if they were absolved from prolongation of life while I was not.

Up to this point I have been assuming that, if it were to become feasible to keep a human being alive for an indefinite length of time, the decision whether to accept this unnatural longevity or to reject it would rest, in each case, with the person concerned. This assumption, however, is unwarrantably optimistic. It seems quite possible that the decision would be taken over his head, either by members of the medical profession or by public authorities or be a consensus between the two. This seems possible even in the case of someone who was *compos mentis* at the time; and it would be a certainty in the case of someone who was already senile. In the latter case the fateful decision would have to be taken for the patient without his even being consulted. These possibilities are the most disturbing of all the features of the new presentation, now looming up into view, of the perennial question of life and death.

At an earlier point in this chapter I have suggested that the primary basic human right is a person's right to life as against the hitherto customarily recognized prerogatives of other human beings to cut his life short by violence through putting him to death either judicially or in war. My formulation of this right needs now to be made more precise. In view of the greatly increased freedom of manœuvre that medicine and surgery have recently acquired, the right to life must now be defined as a person's right to have his life neither cut short nor prolonged by other people against his own will. This new formula implies a right to death, as well as a right to life. In other words, it implies a right to choose for oneself, at any stage of grown-up life between childhood and senility, whether to go on living or not; and this choice of 'to be or not to be' gives everyone the option of committing suicide either by his own hand or by commissioning a physician to give him the quietus.

This right to decide for oneself whether or not to go on living is a precious right. Anyone might, for example, choose to exercise his right to cease to remain alive if he became permanently incapacitated physically or if he were suffering from some agonizing disease that medical skill had proved unable to cure or if he were suffering grief from bereavement, or from remorse for sin, which he found unbearable, or if he preferred to die rather than remain alive under some political régime that he felt to be wicked but had not the power to overthrow, or if he felt that by committing suicide as a public protest against this evil régime he would be performing a public service by helping to bring the régime into disrepute and to undermine its foundations. Anyone might also choose to put an end to his own life if he felt that his physical or mental powers, or both, were beginning to fail.

Suicide, for any or all of these reasons, has always been recognized as a basic human right in Eastern Asia and in India. Within the last few years, Buddhist monks and nuns in South Vietnam have burnt themselves to death publicly as a protest against some of the successive régimes that have been maintained, by American military support, in those parts of the country that are not under the control of the Vietcong resistance movement. Suicide was also regarded as being legitimate, and in certain circumstances noble, in the Graeco-Roman World before its conversion to Christianity. The philosopher Democritus is said to have put an end to his own life when he felt a decline in his mental powers, and this was regarded as being an admirable exhibition of a strength of mind that was one facet of Democritus's spiritual greatness.[1] Cato's suicide made Cato redoubtable for Caesar. These are only two out of a number of Greeks and Romans who were venerated as heroes by posterity for the spirit that they had shown in putting an end to their own lives. They were even more admired for having chosen this dénouement than they were for any of their previous acts.

This general consensus in regarding the commission of suicide as a legitimate and, in some circumstances, a sublime act has not received the assent of the Christian and the post-Christian World since the date at which Christianity became the established religion of the north-western extremity of the Old World. Before that date, some of the Christian martyrs had committed suicide morally by forcing the hand of Roman public officers who were doing their utmost to avoid having to pass the death-sentence on the Christian prisoners in the dock. Yet the very verb 'commit', with which the word 'suicide' is coupled in Western languages, indicates that in post-Constantinian Christendom suicide has been condemned as a crime, because it has been held to be for God, and not for the mortal himself, to decide the moment at which he is to die. This doctrine is illogical, considering that Christians have not thought that God's prerogative has been infringed when a physician has postponed his patient's death by applying his human professional skill, or when a soldier or an executioner has inflicted a premature death by violence on a fellow human being. It is also illogical that the Christian tabu on suicide should have been inherited by post-Christian Western agnostics who do not believe in divine prerogatives because they do not believe in the existence of God. All the same, it is a fact that, in the post-Christian Western World, a human being's right to put an end to his own life is not admitted. In Western countries the medical

[1] See Lucretius, *De Rerum Naturâ*, Book III, lines 1039–41.

profession and the public authorities will conspire with each other to try to prevent anyone from exercising this right.

The medical profession also has two professional motives for keeping patients alive, even against their clearly expressed will. Physicians have always regarded it as being their mission to fight death; and it has been a point of honour with them to postpone death's inevitable ultimate victory to the latest moment to which their skill can delay it. Today, when physicians have acquired the power to revive bodies that formerly would have been certified as being dead, they may be moved to override a patient's wish to die by a second professional motive—namely, the inner urge to exercise their virtuosity and at the same time to indulge their curiosity by discovering how far their increasing skill will enable them to circumvent Nature.

Conversely, professional curiosity might conceivably tempt a specialist, in search of spare healthy organs to transplant into one patient who is *in articulo mortis*, to allow another patient to die or, short of that, to forbear from trying to revive this second patient if and when he has died in the traditional meaning of the word. In this case the physician might be overriding the wishes of a patient whose desire was to go on living or, should he die, to be brought back to life again by the new medical and surgical techniques.

However, this risk would seem to be little more than theoretical, since a physician who was under this temptation would be inhibited by his profession's tradition of trying to prolong life in all circumstances, by the tabu against taking human life if one is not either a public executioner or a uniformed soldier, and by a fear of finding himself on the wrong side of the law. Moreover, it seems unlikely that the temptation will present itself. Eventually, I have already guessed, artificially manufactured human organs will be on the market. Meanwhile, a sufficient supply of organs seems likely to be assured by voluntary *prae-mortem* donations. We may now expect to see the establishment, all over the World, of 'organic replacements banks'.[1] Perhaps we may also see a clause, donating the testator's body, after his death, to this chain of banks, become one of the stock clauses in a will—a clause that the legal draftsman will include as a matter of course, unless his client asks to have it struck

[1] See p. 282.

out. For these reasons it seems probable that the basic human right which is now under the direst threat owing to the recent progress of medicine and surgery is not the right to life but is the right to death— a right that is enjoyed by non-human domesticated animals, for whom it is exercised mercifully by human proxies.

Up to this point I have been discussing problems created by novel prospects of its becoming possible to prolong life far beyond its natural term. In 1969 it is still impossible to see the limits, if there are going to be any, of the vista that these prospects have now opened up. It is, however, already an indisputable fact that a human being's expectation of life has already been lengthened appreciably in almost all the countries of the World, though most signally in the 'developed' minority of them.

It is an undesigned and unhappy coincidence that, at the moment at which the expectation of life has suddenly been lengthened considerably in the Western World, an apparently chronic inflation of currencies has set in there, and at the same time the hitherto worldwide institution of a household embracing all living generations of a family has broken up in the West. The comfort of this traditional dispensation was great for the agèd, and the burden of it was not intolerable for the middle-aged generation, since the oldest generation's expectation of life was appreciably shorter than it has now come to be. Today, however, the typical Western household consists only of a married couple and their not yet grown-up children. The grown-up children and the grandparents now have to fend for themselves.

In this situation, the grown-up children do not fare badly; for, though prices are constantly rising, wages and salaries are also rising to match, and the workers can look after their own interests by striking. By contrast, the retired ex-worker has been disarmed, by his retirement, of the strike-weapon, so he cannot bring any pressure to bear on society to halt the inflation that is melting away his savings and is reducing the real value of his pension—which is in any case incommensurate with the remuneration that he was earning while he was still at work. If this pension comes from public funds, it will no doubt be increased, in terms of money, from time to time, but it will not keep pace with the galloping progress of inflation. In these adverse social circumstances the longevity conferred by the progress of medical science may be not a blessing but a curse. More-over, the word 'conferred' is a euphemism when it is applied to the lengthening of the expectation of life in Western countries. In these countries, longevity is not conferred; it is imposed.

These consequences of the amazing recent progress of medicine and surgery are indeed paradoxical. In Arthur Hugh Clough's poem *The Latest Decalogue* the sixth couplet runs:

> Thou shalt not kill, but need'st not strive
> Officiously to keep alive.

In this couplet Clough was satirizing the hypocrisy and callousness of a rich man who would certainly disapprove of murder, and perhaps also of capital punishment and of war, but who would probably allow his poverty-stricken neighbour to die of starvation or exposure to the elements. To bring *The Latest Decalogue* up to date, we have now to transmute it, by changing one key word, from satire into an official instruction addressed to the medical and surgical professions and intended to be taken literally. The revised couplet will run:

> Thou shalt not kill, but *must* not strive
> Officiously to keep alive.

I should like to see this revised couplet quickly written into the legislation of all the sovereign states on the habitable surface of our planet.

(viii) MAN'S SELF-ENSLAVEMENT TO HIS MAN-MADE
ARTIFICIAL ENVIRONMENT

The most ironical of all the unintended consequences of Man's achievements during the first million years of his existence is that his struggle to become the master of his situation, instead of continuing to be its slave, has resulted merely in his exchanging one servitude for another. In the act of becoming human, our ancestors were taking the first step in modifying, to suit their liking, the environ-ment in which they found themselves parked when they awoke to consciousness. The earliest material evidence of this awakening is the stones that they chipped in order to make them into more serviceable tools than they had been in their natural form. Since then, Man's original natural environment, typified in his pre-human ancestor's unchipped stone tool, has been progressively overlaid and been finally obliterated by a man-made artificial environment. This has in truth been a triumph for Man over Nature. But the price of Man's self-liberation from servitude to Nature has been his self-subjection to the artificial environment which he has created by the development of the technology through which his conquest of Nature has been achieved.

Today Man finds himself genuinely in danger of being destroyed by a Frankenstein's monster which is the work of his own hands. He has now inflicted on himself magnitudes, quantities, and speeds which may be more than a match for the human nature which, so far, Man has not been able to modify to offset his revolutionary modification of Nature's non-human sector. I will now take a rapid glance at Man's new inhuman man-made adversaries.

The most conspicuous of the menacing man-made magnitudes is Ecumenopolis: the coming world-city is which all the present local mammoth cities—the megalopolises—are going to coalesce with each other. This urban magnitude is three-dimensional; besides encompassing the habitable surface of the Earth, it is rising sky-high as well.[1] Life in Ecumenopolis threatens to afflict the world-city's inhabitants with mass-claustrophobia; and all but a tiny and ever dwindling percentage of the planet's rapidly increasing population is going to be condemned to live in Ecumenopolis. The current diminution of the World's rural population which I have already noted,[2] working together with the current population explosion, is going to pour a torrent of immigrants into Ecumenopolis. However fast and far the coming world-city may expand, it will always be packed as full with human beings as a beehive is with bees and a termitary with termites.

The second menacing magnitude is not constructional but is operational. The advance of technology is constantly increasing the minimum size of economic and political operational units. (Economics and politics have now become inseparable and hardly distinguishable from each other.) Today the smallest effective economic and political units are 'super-powers' on the scale of the Soviet Union and the United States, and it looks as if even units of this magnitude were now doomed rapidly to become obsolete. The

[1] See pp. 344–45.   [2] See pp. 333–34.

source of supply, the workshop, the market, the state are all increasing in magnitude *pari passu* with the city. They too are expanding to world-wide dimensions, and the coming world-organization of economic and political affairs is going to have the same effect on life as the coming world-city. It is going to depersonalize human relations.

Already, popular reactions to public affairs in the United States, now a country with a population of two hundred millions, are appreciably slower than they are in countries of the fifty-million class, such as Britain, France, and West Germany, even though the United States today is ahead of all other countries in the development of material means of communication. In organizations even on the present-day scale, personal relations are already being stultified, and consequently the participating persons are being frustrated. They are feeling what Peer Gynt felt in his encounter with the Boyg.[1] They are finding themselves confronted with an impalpable but impenetrable obstacle that they can neither surmount nor by-pass nor ignore. Human beings are persons or nothing, and therefore depersonalization provokes them into revolt.

The effacement of personality is the common underlying *primum mobile* of many world-wide current movements: demonstrations that boil over into violence; revolts of students; revolts of 'back-bencher' members of parliament; 'wild-cat' strikes led by local shop-stewards in defiance of instructions from the central administrative offices of trades unions of national dimensions; the tendency for ever smaller communities—French-speaking Canadians, Flemish-speaking Belgians, Scots, Welsh, Ibos—to assert claims to political autonomy or to outright political independence on the strength of the principle of national self-determination; the rise, among intellectuals, of the philosophy of Existentialism. Superficially, these various kinds of movement might appear to be disparate, but they resemble each other in all being protests highly charged with emotion—Existentialism is an exceptionally emotional philosophy. They are all expressions of exasperation, loss of patience, and a conviction, based on a long course of disillusioning experience, that nothing short of violence is ever going to win attention and consideration from a dehumanized repository of power. Persons who have claims or grievances which, in their opinion, deserve to be con-

[1] See p. 325.

sidered have a human right to receive consideration, even if it is not going to lead to satisfaction or redress.

Perhaps the most significant of all the symptoms of unrest in 1969 are the world-wide disturbances among university students. Some of these student insurrections are directed against the authoritarian structure of university administrations, some against sins of commission or omission that are being committed by the governments of the students' own countries or of others. It is also significant that the occasions of these upheavals turn out in many cases not to be their true cause, even though the indignation over the occasions may be genuine. The true cause is an only half-conscious feeling that the students' social duty calls upon them to spring, prematurely, into the arena of adult life because their elders, who ought to be managing mankind's affairs properly, have shown themselves to be incompetent or perverse or both.

This is the feeling that drove the Burschen into political activism in post-Napoleonic Germany and also their counterparts in Russia during the last phase of the Imperial regime there.

> The time is out of joint. O cursèd spite
> That ever I was born to set it right.

When the Danish students Hamlet and Horatio play truant from the East German university of Wittenberg, this bodes no good either for the two young men or for King Claudius or for Queen Gertrude either. The criminal pair's doom has been sealed when Hamlet accepts their advice to renounce his intention of 'going back to school in Wittenberg'. Hamlet's murdered father's ghost has been given his chance to reveal the truth, and Hamlet has been confronted with the challenge to which he will respond with such catastrophic consequences.

In putting the time out of joint, quantities are as baneful as magnitudes. Quantities are in fact the self-same Boyg in another of his many metamorphoses. The provocative depersonalizing of present-day administration of all kinds is not the work of malice. 'In tragic life, God wot, no villain need be'; numbers 'spin the plot', and numbers are therefore the ultimate generators of the 'passion' for which I have substituted the word 'numbers' in this parody of George Meredith's lines.

Numbers are a menace because, in human affairs, the difficult business of living and working together—a business out of which human social animals cannot contract—goes most smoothly when it is done, face to face, by word of mouth, not by exchanging lawyers' letters or by filling in forms. Unfortunately, the number of persons who can be in continuous personal relations with each other is infinitesimal by comparison with the number with whom we may have to do business through some channel or other.

What is the maximum number of persons whom the hall-porter of a club or the headmaster of a school can distinguish by sight sufficiently well to be able to address each of them by his right name? There are people who have this sixth sense, but I should guess that even they cannot know, even just by sight, as many as one thousand of their fellow human beings. How many Christmas cards do I send to friends and acquaintances? The number falls considerably short of two hundred, and in some of these cases an annual exchange of Christmas cards is the only regular communication that my friends and I have with each other. Our personal relations are confined to this minimum by the pressure of modern life. What is the largest local community in which it is possible for all the inhabitants to know each other personally? I should judge that the limit is reached in a village and that it is already passed in even the smallest city: in, say, Abraham's Ur or Goethe's Weimar or Thomas Hardy's 'Casterbridge'. In the struggle to preserve personality, one person in ten thousand is, for practical purposes, facing as 'fearful odds' as one person in three thousand million.

The depersonalizing effect of numbers is the hard core of the problem of administration. I have served as an administrator for only seven years of my life, but this was long enough to teach me that the administrator's prime duty, and prime interest too, is to be accessible. His fellow human beings who are under his authority are at his mercy in their work and perhaps even in their private affairs too to some extent. As far as possible, therefore, the administrator's time must be at their disposal for prompt discussion of any questions to be settled that require a decision by him. They cannot, of course, be given assurance that the administrator's eventual decision is going to be the one that they want, but they will be readier to accept an unpalatable decision if it is taken, not over their heads, but after they have had the opportunity of putting their case to the administrator and of hearing his view of it.

My short and modest stint of administration was fairly straight-forward—luckily for me, for I came to it as an inexperienced novice. The numerical strength of the temporary wartime organization of which I was the head from 1939 to 1946 was less than that of the population of a hamlet. It was therefore possible for me to do business personally with all my war-time colleagues.

A village, too, can be administered by way of direct personal relations. At the village of Lalibela in Ethiopia on 21–22 March 1964 I found the whole population assembled, under the chairmanship of one of the village priests, to inquire into the cause of a fire that had occurred in the village the night before. Had it been accidental or had it been a case of arson? Even in a small-sized city-state it was possible for justice to be administered by the king or by the council of elders or of notables, sitting in the market-place or at one of the gates in the city's wall. The judicial authorities could hold open court, in the presence of the whole community, for any citizen— and perhaps for any stranger too—who had a petition to make or a case to bring. The scene that I saw with my own eyes at Lalibela was already familiar to me at second hand. It is depicted in the representation of city life in peace-time on the shield that was made for Achilles by Hephaestus.[1]

The dominions of the Samanid dynasty, which ruled large tracts of what are now Soviet Central Asia and North-Eastern Iran and North-Western Afghanistan from A.D. 874 to A.D. 999, were vastly larger and more populous than those of the largest city-state in Sumer or in the Graeco-Roman World or in mediaeval Western Europe. Yet Isma'il b. Ahmad, the second of the princes of the House of Saman, used to make a regular practice of sitting on horseback in the open, before the hour of morning prayer, to listen to personal representations from any of his subjects who might wish to have an audience with him. In these sessions the Samanid ruler presented himself in full panoply of war, as a visible indication that he had the power as well as the will to do justice. The Nizam-al-Mulk has given a vivid description of this scene in his *Siyaset Nameh*.[2]

---

[1] *Iliad*, Book XVIII, lines 497–508.
[2] See Ch. Schefer's French translation, *Siasset Nameh* (Paris 1893 Leroux), pp. 12 and 26.

The Samanid ruler braved even the frost and snow of a Central Asian winter in order to be perpetually accessible to his subjects. He voluntarily endured this severe physical ordeal because, in his and his subjects' eyes alike, accessibility was of the essence of a ruler's duty.

This deservedly lauded Samanid practice survived the Samanid dynasty's fall. It reappears as recently as the eighteenth century of the Christian Era in Georgia, a Transcaucasian Christian country that was under age-old Iranian influence until the incorporation of Georgia in the Russian Empire in the nineteenth century. A modern Western publicist, J. de Maistre, has made a contemptuous reference[1] to the King's slow progress on horseback through the streets of Tiflis, dispensing justice impromptu *en route*. This Frank, for whom the scene stands for a ridiculous exhibition of administrative inefficiency, is obtusely unaware that the Western World of his day might have a lesson to learn from contemporary Georgian practice.

I, for my part, was impressed when, on 6 November 1948, I sat in the office of my host the governor of the Turkish province of Yozgad and watched him giving audience, Samanid-fashion, to one person after another from among his flock. Some of the petitioners were people in the humblest walks of life and were inarticulate, but all of them received a courteous and careful hearing and a prompt—and, of course, therefore unavoidably impromptu—decision on their case. The governor was sitting behind a Frankish-style desk, but he was not burying himself in impersonal deskwork. He was doing business face to face with anyone under his jurisdiction who had business to bring before him.

This admirable direct method of administration is feasible only when the population is small and when public business is simple. It would not work in a state in which the public revenue depended on the annual compilation, presentation, and scrutinizing of several million individuals' returns of income, and on the subsequent assessment and collection of income-tax. At this degree of numbers and of complexity, the administrator's transaction of his business takes the dreary form of a procession of files across his desk in lieu of the traditional lively procession of persons ambling past his stirrup.

[1] J. de Maistre, *Lettres et Opuscules Inédits*, vol. i, (Paris 1851 Vaton), p. 215.

In 1969 the files are being superseded in their turn by computer-cards, and these make the relations between the governors and the governed still more jejune.

At Yozgad in 1948 it was still practicable for the provincial governor to hold open court, but already before that date, in Washington, D.C., President Franklin D. Roosevelt's children's only means of getting access to their father was, so I have been told, to make an appointment with him through the White House secretariat. Before long, I suppose, computers will have replaced most of the human secretariat in the White House, and appointments with the President will have to be made by inserting a petitionary card and awaiting the computer's verdict. 'The quality of mercy' is not built into the computer's electronic brain. The computerization of personal relations is inhuman; but what alternative way is there of transacting public business in a country with a population of two hundred millions and with a president whose diary is filled chock-full with engagements for months and years ahead?

Within my own working lifetime, I have lived to see revolutionary changes in the quantity of official documents and in the format in which these are presented. When I was serving as a 'temporary Foreign Office clerk' during the First World War, Sir Eyre Crowe, who had induced the Office to institute a registry and to let it be operated by women, had not yet reached retirement age; he was then Permanent Under-Secretary of State. 'Ladies', meaning women secretaries versed in shorthand and in typing, were a still more recent novelty. However, the Foreign Office in 1918 was at least one length ahead of the adjoining India Office, where copies of telegrams and other current documents were produced in the form of purple jellygraphs culled from a matrix on which the document had been written out with a pen in copper-plate handwriting. This method of multiplying copies of a document was familiar to me, because, as child, I had been fascinated by watching my mother pull off one sheet after another for distribution to her fellow members of the Newnham College, Cambridge, Old Students Association, of which she was honorary secretary for several years.

By this present year 1969 the increase in the quantity of documents to be copied has long since put the jellygraph technique out of commission. The increase has been on a fantastic scale. The cubic content of the documentation produced by government departments of the United Kingdom during the Second World War—a time-span of six years—was equal to the cubic content of all the surviving archives of the United Kingdom and of its predecessors the Kingdoms of England and Scotland down to the outbreak of war in 1939. I heard this fact stated in a post-war lecture delivered by Sir Keith Hancock, the eminent Australian historian who was editor-in-chief of the set of histories of the U.K. government departments' transactions during the Second World War.

Administration, public and private, is only one of many fields in which human beings are now suffering from the pressure of the inordinate current increase in numbers. This pressure is now being felt in every department of life. I will glance at only two further samples of it: the pressure of correspondence and the pressure of traffic.

In 1969 there are about three thousand million people alive simultaneously on the face of this planet, and, though the coming world-government is still beyond our horizon, a world-society is already a reality. On the plane of communications it is indeed a century old by now; it dates from the creation of the International Telegraphic Union in 1864 and of the International Postal Union in 1875. In the course of these last hundred years the volume of correspondence conducted by letter, telegraph, telephone, and radio has been increasing at more than the breakneck pace of the contemporaneous increase in the number of the World's inhabitants. There has been a formidable increase, not only in the number of potential correspondents, but in the percentage of these who make active use of the present-day material facilities for communication to get into touch with contemporaries of theirs all over the World.

This increase in correspondence is to be welcomed. Correspondence is an effective means of knitting our incipient world-society together more and more closely, and in the Atomic Age we are faced with the choice between social unification on a world-wide scale and self-destruction. But, to judge by my own experience, this mounting flood of correspondence has now become overwhelming. Since the end of the Second World War, dealing with necessary correspondence has been taking up more and more of my working time and has been becoming more and more expensive for me. I have passed the point at which I could cope with my correspondence without the help of an energetic secretary (this is, I guess, 'a point of no return'), and the cost of postage to all parts of the World continues to rise. This is, as far as I can see, the inevitable price of the constant widening of my range of communication with my fellow human beings—a development in the social side of my life which, in itself, is something that I prize.

The pressure of traffic in the streets of the cities that are now fast coalescing into Ecumenopolis is an aggravation of the ordeal to which human nature is being subjected by the progress of urbanization. While the fixtures, in the shape of buildings, are increasing in magnitude vertically as well as horizontally, traffic is increasing in volume; and, the more massive the scale of building-construction, the less feasible it becomes to face the cost of widening the traffic-lanes. The first casualty of this increase in traffic has been the pedestrian; but the obstinate and powerful resistance to any drastic curtailment of mechanized wheeled traffic in built-up areas promises, if it is not overcome, eventually to turn the tables in the pedestrian's favour. Already he occasionally has the pleasure of walking slowly but surely towards his destination past a miles-long line of stationary vehicles that have been caught, head to tail, in a traffic-jam.

Speed has defeated itself in a traffic-jam, but it has free rein on radio, along telephone and telegraph wires, and along air-lanes. In the present-day World, speed of communications is indispensable. The area that our systems of communication have to cover is the entire land and water surface and entire air envelope of the globe, and, in the Atomic Age, Man's global habitat is not only vast, it is also dangerous. A hot wire between Moscow and Washington, D.C., has now come to be mankind's life-line. We could not afford to see this line cut. Yet I find my teeth chattering whenever I recall that decisions which are fateful for mankind's future are now constantly being taken in conversations at opposite ends of a telephone-wire or, if face to face, at journey's end of two trans-time-zone flights that have brought the decision-makers to their meeting-place from opposite quarters. If only one of the two parties has flown while the other has remained stationary, the result is even worse. The stationary party will have an unfair advantage; the traveller's nerves will be on edge.

While personal meetings are, in themselves, the best of all ways of doing business, they may become hazardous if one or both of the parties has just had his psychosomatic organism temporarily deranged by its having been catapulted through several time-zones. A long-distance telephone-conversation may be preferable, but this has its own hazards. It allows the user no time to deliberate and no chance of gracefully procrastinating, which he can do in a face-to-face talk, and it limits the possibility of keeping a record of what has passed. Without a record, a telephone-conversation may leave, in the minds of the parties to it, two different and possibly irreconcilable impressions of what they have said to each other.

Correspondence by air-mailed letter is better than any way of communicating except a personal meeting at the end of two long sea-voyages. Unfortunately, human affairs move too fast nowadays, as well as too dangerously, for the responsible heads of state of two atomically-armed super-powers to be able to indulge in the refreshment of sea-voyages or even to take the time needed for brooding over the contents of a letter and thinking out a reply. While the air-letters are shuttling to and fro or while the ships are creeping over the ocean towards their rendezvous, the fatal button may be pressed and Man and all his works may be incinerated. Speed in transactions between heads of states holding clutches of atomic weapons in their hands is a hazard besides being a safeguard; but, if we cling to the safeguard, as we must, we have to accept the incidental hazard as well.

The present mounting pressure of speed is not just an occupational affliction of the relatively small number of human beings who, in the present-day world, wield power in its various forms—political, economic, educational, religious, and the rest. No doubt the pressure bears most heavily on this minority that now holds the fate of the rest of mankind in its hands—or seems to hold it; for these tycoons may turn out to be in truth technology's marionettes. But in some degree all of us are victims today of the accelerating speed of the current advance of science and technology. An end to this advance and its acceleration is not yet in sight; and therefore we cannot foresee any limit to the increase of the pressure on human life.

Science and technology have not only substituted a man-made artificial environment for the natural environment in which mankind started its career, and they have not only enslaved their maker Man to themselves as imperiously as Man was once enslaved by Nature. Unlike Nature, science and technology are not static; they are restlessly on the move; and, at each further move that they make, they produce disturbing and bewildering changes in the alien environment that they have imposed on us. We have to adapt and re-adapt ourselves to these ever-changing conditions of life as best we can; but the rate of this perpetual transformation of Man's artificial environment has now reached a degree at which the amount of adaptation that is demanded of a human being in the course of his lifetime is straining human nature almost to breaking-point. Like the rest of Nature, human nature is virtually static; but the intellect, which is one of the constituents of Man's nature, has shown itself capable, by applying science in technology, of 'processing' almost everything in the realm of Nature except human nature itself. Can human nature stand the pace? Are there limits to its adaptibility, or, short of that, to its patience? Are we going to submit to being kept perpetually on the run at an ever faster speed and to being demoted from being 'persons' who are at least partly masters of their own fate into becoming 'things' that are 'pushed about', like parts of a machine, by implacable inhuman forces? These are the issues in the Third World War in which mankind finds itself engaged in this year 1969.

This Third World War is a war of a different kind from the first two world wars, or indeed from any previous war, international or civil, of which we have a record. This is a mercy; for a third world war of the traditional kind would be fought with the atomic weapon, and it is impossible to forecast the extent of the physical and spiritual devastation that mankind would inflict on itself in an atomic world war. The current world war is not a fratricidal war between conflicting human armies. It is a war of human nature against technology—a revolt of persons against the effacement of personality—and this revolt is being conducted as a 'resistance movement' of 'freedom-fighters' against 'Brave New World'. Unhappily it is not being conducted without violence. Its operations range from orderly protest-demonstrations to street-fighting behind barricades. However, so far, the number and the seriousness of the casualties and the material losses that have been incurred in this world-wide upheaval have been slight compared to the toll of life and wealth that was being taken in any single one of the local wars of the traditional kind that were being waged in 1968 with so-called 'conventional' weapons.

We cannot forsee the outcome of the present new-style world war. Can persons reassert themselves against technology without wrecking the artificial environment to which technology has subjected Man? And, if this is the price of a victory for personality, can mankind afford to win a spiritual victory at this material cost, or shall we come to the dismal conclusion that the lesser evil will be to resign ourselves to living for evermore in 'Brave New World' as slaves of an impersonal master? In 1969 the answers to these questions still lie on the knees of the gods. But what gods? An unknown god? If unknown, let us pray that he may reveal himself to be love.

9 : Posthumous Agenda

Am I called upon to write this chapter? In the preceding eight chapters of the present Part of this book, I have chalked up a row of problems that are confronting mankind in this year 1969. I am now over eighty years old. Have I not now discharged my obligations? Am I not now at liberty to bow myself out and leave it to my juniors to find and apply solutions for problems of which they are just as well aware as I am? My expectation of life is now short compared to theirs. Has not my stake in the future diminished proportionately? Am I not now entitled to 'pass the buck'? No, I am not; and, if I were to feel tempted to do that, I should be put to shame by an affirmation of faith that is attributed—I believe correctly—to Lord Russell.[1] At an age that was old in terms of my present age, but young in terms of his, Bertrand Russell declared, so it is said: 'It is very important to care intensely about what is going to happen after one is dead.' I cannot vouch for the accuracy, *verbatim*, of this citation, but these words convey the sense of what Bertrand Russell said, as I have heard this reported. In a more general form, which covers the past as well as the future, Russell's

[1] See p. 106.

affirmation has been made by the Roman dramatist Terence in a memorable line that I have quoted already: 'Homo sum, humanum nihil a me alienum puto.'[1] This line comes home to me because I am an inquisitive historian besides being an enthralled spectator of current human affairs and an eager participant in them as far as my puny power extends.

I am indeed involved in human affairs totally and without reservations. I am involved immediately because I care intensely about the future of my children, my grandchildren, and my great-grandchild. This concern of mine for them is, in the first instance, personal and direct, but it is also symbolic. These sixteen persons (I am including my sons and my daughters-in-law) represent, for me, all other human beings of their three generations, and also all those still unborn, who, if mankind refrains from liquidating itself, will come and go in their turn, long after my great-grandchild is dead. Moreover, if mankind does liquidate itself, or if it permits itself to survive on this planet for as long as this planet continues to be habitable, or if it prolongs its existence by having made a lodgement on some other planet in some other solar system or some other galaxy, I, here and now, am involved in mankind's future, whatever its future may prove to be; and I am also involved in what will happen to the Universe after mankind has become extinct, supposing that extinction is mankind's eventual fate.

I am still involved, because my concern with mankind is a concern for the spiritual facet of the psychosomatic presence that a human being displays to his fellow human beings and to himself. I believe in the truth of the Indian intuition 'tat tvam asi'—'thou art identical with that'.[2] The truth (as I believe it to be) that is expressed verbally in these lapidary three words has been expressed visually by the Victorian English painter Watts in a picture that he has called 'The Dweller in the Innermost'. I believe that the dweller in the innermost spiritual sanctum of a human being is identical with the spiritual presence behind and beyond the Universe, and I believe that this ultimate spiritual reality is love. I have already declared my two beliefs about love. I believe that love is not omnipotent and I

[1] 'I am a human being, so there is nothing human that I do not feel to be my concern' (Terence, *Heautontimorumenos*, line 77, quoted on pp. 94 and 241).
[2] Cited already on pp. 124, 140, 159, and 177.

believe that love 'endureth all things'[1] and 'never faileth'.[2] If I am committed to humanity, I am thereby committed to love; and it is of the nature of love that a commitment to love is unlimited.

This unlimited commitment to love carries a human being beyond the bounds of his own brief lifetime. It gives him the freedom of the city of infinity. Meanwhile, for the rest of the time, however short or long this may be, during which I shall continue to be alive with my wits still intact, the call of love will, for me, be accompanied by the prod of curiosity. I am curious to see what is going to be the *dénouement* of the current act of the drama of human history. My curiosity is lively enough to make me willing to put up with the discomfort of an exceptionally long extension of my life, if this were to be my lot.

The discomfort of living on beyond the term of the average expectation of life is considerable, and it is at its maximum when the current of history is gathering speed, as, in 1969, it is gathering it as fearsomely as the waters of the Great Lakes in the last lap of their race towards the Niagara Falls. If one lives on beyond the average length of life, one has to pay for this, even in relatively tranquil and sluggish times, by finding oneself being carried into an ever less familiar and more alien world. In estimating the discomfort of longevity, I am reckoning with mere discomfort; I am leaving out of account the pain of bereavement—a pain that is agony. However, discomfort is the occupational risk of an observer of current human affairs. The discomfort of serving as a war-correspondent in Vietnam at this moment is merely a third-degree enhancement of what the ageing arm-chair observer, too, has to suffer in a milder measure. For the sake of living to witness the *dénouement* of the present act, I should be prepared to face the prospect of having to make, say, twenty—but not more than twenty—further annual returns of income for the United Kingdom Inland Revenue authorities.

What are my prospects of living on actually to see, and not just to forecast, 'the shape of things to come'? In Western Christendom till within living memory, there were still some *croyants* who believed that they, in their generation, might live to see the *dénouement*, not just of the current act, but of the play itself. Zarathustra seems to have been the originator of the dogma that human history

---

[1] I Cor. xiii. 7.   [2] ibid., 8.

is destined to come to an abrupt end on a Day of Judgment on which one generation will be caught alive, while all previous generations will be raised instantaneously from the dead to share in the ordeal. From this Iranian source the dogma has been transmitted to Pharisaic Judaism, to Christianity,[1] and to Islam. I have lived to see this traditional belief in the certainty of the coming of 'the Last Things' fade out in the Western World, and have lived on to see the ending of human history become a mundane possibility that would be translated into fact by an act, not of God, but of Man. However, if the present generation of mankind did, one day, commit the supreme crime and folly of liquidating the human race, it is obvious that the generation which committed self-genocide would not be able also to register its experience of instantaneous annihilation. This is, indeed, a truism for anyone who envisages 'the Last Things' in terms, not of Zoroastrian theology, but of the potentialities of the misuse of atomic power for death and evil.

Granting that it will be impossible for any human spectator to witness the end of the whole play, can a spectator ever reasonably look forward to seeing the end of an act? This is not only possible; it has happened already in a number of cases that are within our knowledge. There have even been cases in which it has been possible for a spectator to have witnessed, within the span of his lifetime between childhood and senility or death, the end of a chapter of which he has also witnessed the beginning. I myself was already twenty-five years old when the current act of the drama of mankind's history opened in August 1914. A German born in 1846 who lived to be seventy-two (an age eight years younger than my age now) would have witnessed, at the age of twenty-five, the establishment of the Second German Reich in 1871 and would have lived on to witness the Second Reich's fall in 1918. A German born in 1781 who lived to be ninety (an age eleven years older than my age on 24 May 1968, but six years younger than Lord Russell's on that date) would have witnessed, at the age of twenty-five, the formal liquidation in 1806 of the First German Reich—the Roman Empire of the German People—and would have lived on to see the establishment of the Second German Reich in 1871. It would need a qualified actuary

[1] See Matt. 16. 28; Mark ix. 1; Luke ix. 27; and, for details, 1 Thess. iv. 15–17.

endowed with the gift of prophecy to guess whether I am going to live on to witness the end of the act of which I have witnessed the beginning in 1914. I myself am neither a prophet nor a mathematician, so my own guess is a sheer shot in the dark, but I will declare it for what it is worth. I guess that I am unlikely to see the end of mankind's current dithering over the answer that it is going to give to the question 'to be or not to be'. As a student of human affairs, I find this prospect tantalizing; as a human being, I find it consoling.

Meanwhile, *noblesse oblige*. I am speaking of my generic moral obligations in virtue of my being human: the intrinsic *grandeurs* that are mated with the intrinsic *misères* of human nature. Every human spectator of the drama of human affairs is also an actor in the play, and his inescapable concern with the weal and woe of all his fellow human beings calls upon him to leave his comfortable seat in the auditorium and intervene, at his peril, in the action on the stage at a moment's notice if the cause of life and good is visibly falling into jeopardy. Every human being is morally bound, and is also psychologically constrained, to have feelings, to pass judgements, and to take action about human affairs. By watching the play, he is committing himself to taking part in it as well.

In action, what is practicable depends, of course, on the actor's own situation. In our concern about what is going to happen after we ourselves are dead, our action cannot go beyond suggesting in advance, while we are still alive and in possession of our wits, some of the steps that seem to us, as we peer into the future, to be possible and desirable steps for our survivors and our successors to take. I will conclude the present Part of this book by jotting down my posthumous agenda for dealing with some of the current problems on my list. I will propose first some superficial adjustments and then a change of heart that would be less facile but would also, for that very reason, be more promising—at least, as I see it with my feeble powers of spiritual vision.

I will start my superficial prescriptions by coming down, not to earth, but to the sea, and drawing attention to the sea's hitherto virtually unexploited potentialities as a source of food-supply for mankind. In the preceding chapter I have mentioned an unintended consequence of the recent advance in preventive medicine and in public health administration. This has produced a population explosion whose duration cannot be forecast, since it is impossible to predict the length of time that the 'backward' majority of mankind is going to take in educating itself in family planning. If this process were to take a century, the size at which this planet's human population will eventually stabilize may be ten times as great as the present figure. Moreover, at the present day, only one-third of the planet's human population is adequately nourished. We may therefore have to reckon with a need to increase our production of adequately nourishing food thirty-fold within the next hundred years; and, for achieving this huge increase, we cannot count on the food-producing capacity of those patches of the planet's surface that are not submerged under salt water. In describing the post-Second-World-War increase in the production of food in Iowa, I have taken note of the doubt whether even Iowa's fertile soil can stand for long the strain that is now being put upon it. *A fortiori*, we cannot expect to be able to work miracles with the poorer soils of the tropical regions in which the population explosion is erupting the most vigorously. The future of agriculture and animal-husbandry lies, not on the land, but in the sea.

Up till now we have been content to win food from the sea by the Palaeolithic method of gathering or catching the foodstuffs that Nature supplies. On land, this primitive method survives only in outlying parts of the planet's land-surface—for instance, among the natives of Australia in the 'out-back'. The greater part of mankind moved forward, on land, from food-gathering and hunting to agriculture and animal-husbandry eight or ten thousand years ago, but it is only lately, and this, so far, only in Japan, that a beginning has been made with farming the sea, and consequently the land-farmers have resented the sea's occupation of the greater part of the surface of the globe. In the Homeric poems the stock synonym for the sea is 'the salt', and the stock epithet for it is 'unharvested' ($\dot{\alpha}\tau\rho\acute{\upsilon}\gamma\epsilon\tau\sigma\varsigma$); and, when the writer of *The Revelation of Saint John the Divine* 'saw a new heaven and a new earth', he observed with satisfaction that 'there was no more sea'. Today, some eighteen or nineteen centuries after the publication of *Revelation*, technology has furnished mankind with a new heaven and a new earth which might not have been to the early Christian apocalyptic writer's liking. Our new heaven hums with aeroplanes in its air-envelope and with telstars and space-capsules above its stratosphere. In 'Brave New World', however, there is still the sea; and we should thank our telstars that our technology has not been able to abolish the sea, as it might have done improvidently if it could have found some empty container with the necessary capacity on some other planet. We should be thankful for technology's failure to abolish the sea because the sea is mankind's still unrifled treasure-chest.

Even now, our antediluvian method of skimming food from the sea by catching some of the sea's wild-life provides an appreciable quota of mankind's hitherto insufficient food-ration. When the Japanese pioneer-work of cultivating seaweed and breeding domesticated fish has been followed up, the sea's productivity will have been increased to a hardly imaginable degree.

On 11 December 1967 I visited the place in Japan—it is Shirahama —where the yellowtail fish is being bred. Just before my visit, the breeders had made a 'break-through'. For many years they had been able to fertilize yellowtail eggs artificially, but invariably the brood had died before reaching maturity. Now, for the first time, they had just succeeded in nursing a female and a male yellowtail to the adult stage at which the pair had respectively laid eggs and had secreted semen that could be used for a fresh round of artificial fertilization. In other words, a complete life-cycle of yellowtail procreation had been produced for the first time artificially; presumably any number of further rounds of this artificially engineered cycle can now be achieved; and this is a major victory over the menace of future world-famine; for the superiority of thrifty artifice over prodigal Nature is enormous. In the state of Nature a yellowtail female lays (if I have got my figures right) about one million eggs in the course of her lifetime, and the toll taken of these million eggs by the inefficiency of natural fertilization and the efficiency of unhampered non-human predators is so high that, out of those one million eggs, only three survive, on an average, to grow into mature fish that will lay eggs or will secrete semen in their turn. By contrast, when the eggs are fertilized artificially and when predators are barred out, the average number of eggs that will grow into mature fish is, not three, but about one hundred thousand!

A second problem has to be solved before the breeding of yellowtail becomes economic. So far, the fish, which are penned in large crates moored in sheltered waters, are being fed on wild fish; so fish-breeding, in this pioneer stage of the new industry, is parasitic on the Palaeolithic practice of fishing. Research is now being made into the possibility of finding some artificial alternative diet for yellowtail which will make the breeding of fish independent of the catching of wild fish for feeding them. An amateur can imagine plankton being collected by some mechanical device and then being processed. Technology might find its clue for mechanizing this operation in the outfit for performing it that Nature has given to whales. Amateur though I am, I feel confident that the Japanese experts who have already solved their first major problem are going to solve their second one too.

The sea is indeed a treasure-chest. Its waters promise to solve the problem of providing the increase in the supply of food edible by Man that will be required for feeding the planet's exploding population; but this is not all. Below the sea's food-producing waters there is a solid bottom that is vastly more extensive than the high and dry patches of the solid surface of the globe, and presumably there lies buried, below the bottom of the sea, as much mineral wealth per square mile, on the average, as the prospectors have found below the exposed patches of the globe's solid surface in the course of these first five or six thousand years of the history of the mining industry. For the submarine miner as well as for the marine livestock-breeder, the sea promises to be an eldorado. Best of all, nearly the whole of this eldorado is outside the territorial waters of the planet's local sovereign states. It is a patrimony that is waiting to be appropriated, as mankind's common property, by the coming world state; and, even if the world state has to appease the greed of its local constituents by extending the limit of their territorial waters from Britain's three-miles claim to Peru's two-hundred-miles claim, this will leave the government of the world state in possession of the major part of the planet's still intact material resources. This will be enough to equip the world state with a larger stock of material capital and a larger annual revenue than the aggregate capital and revenue of all the local states added together.

This prospect is cheering because, if the world-state is to be effective, it will need to be muscled-up with the sinews of peace, and the establishment of an effective world state is the positive act that is required for enforcing the abolition of the institution of war—an institution that has to be abolished now that technology has carried mankind into the Atomic Age. The negative condition that has to be fulfilled if war is to be abolished is the provision of alternative outlets for human pugnacity. Since an organism is a fragment of the Universe that has defiantly declared its independence of the rest of the Universe and is seeking to make the rest of the Universe centre upon it and serve its purposes, pugnacity is synonymous with life. At the same time it is obvious that the institution of war is not the only outlet that human pugnacity can find for itself. Human pugnacity must have found other outlets before war was invented; it needs to find others again now that the advance of technology has made war prohibitively destructive.

Mankind has done without war for by far the greater part of the time that has passed since our ancestors became human. Mankind may be as much as a million years old by now, but war cannot be much more than five thousand years old. Making war requires organization, discipline, and a surplus of material resources over and above the amount of these that is consumed in meeting the bare needs of hand-to-mouth subsistence. This set of requirements was not forthcoming until the alluvial soil of the lower basin of the Rivers Tigris and Euphrates had been won for cultivation and had been occupied by a mosaic of local sovereign independent city-states. War must have been invented by the Sumerians; the abolition of this pernicious Sumerian institution is on my generation's post-humous agenda; and, though, since 1945, war has manifestly become suicidal, it may be difficult to persuade mankind to give war up unless we can offer, as substitutes for it, some alternative outlets for pugnacity that, like war, are competitive, exciting, and hazardous but that, unlike war, are neither wicked nor destructive.

Possible substitutes for war that occur to present-day minds are sport, mountaineering, spacemanship, and deepseamanship. Of these four, deepseamanship has, so far, been the least in the news, though it is the only one of the four that promises to be rewarding materially as well as psychologically. We may expect that deepseamanship, too, will be taken up, sooner or later, as obsessively as the three already popular pursuits. We may also expect, however, that the obsession with these suggested substitutes for war will fail to produce the effect that is demanded of it. Unfortunately it is possible for a human mind to be the victim of more than one obsession at a time. It seems likely that the obsessions with deepseamanship, spacemanship, mountaineering, and sport will merely coexist with the obsession with war, and will not displace it.

However, human pugnacity is now being offered a target that may attract it more strongly than space, sea, mountains, an opposing team, or a hostile army, This new target is 'Brave New World'; the man-made artificial environment, conjured up round human beings by the advance of science and technology, which has been enslaving its human makers and has been effacing their personalities. In the preceding chapter I have suggested that the revolt of human beings at being demoted from being 'persons' into becoming 'things', and then from being 'things' into becoming 'ciphers', is the common underlying cause of nearly all the unrest that, in 1969, is erupting all over the World in a multitude of diverse outward forms. Man's current struggle to save his personality from being ironed out by his technology is something more than a substitute for war; it is a form of war itself, but a form that is unfamiliar because it is novel. In the present world war—and we are living through our third world war in this year 1969—the combatants are not armies of human beings fighting, to kill, on behalf of contending local states; the combatants are human personality versus human technology.

How is human personality to maintain itself in 'Brave New World'? On my posthumous agenda this is, as I see it, by far the most important piece of business. Here, too, I can think of a number of superficial adjustments through which the present pressure on persons could be partially relieved.

For instance, the pressure of the world state—an institution that is part of the price of the abolition of war—is a pressure that can be eased by devolution. In order to be made tolerable, the world state will have to be given a federal constitution. The existing sovereign states can be partially compensated for the necessary sacrifice of their sovereignty by being made the world state's direct constituents. They, in their turn, will need to be articulated into regional subunits. These exist already in those now sovereign states that have federal constitutions in which devolution is effective. In other states which are at present unitary there is a widespread tendency today for the inhabitants of regional units to demand devolution in degrees ranging from local self-government to independence. The Scots, the Welsh, the Flemings, the Ibos, the Southern Sudanese are all now making this demand, and Canada's federal constitution, as this now stands, does not satisfy the French-speaking Canadians. Moreover, political devolution will, I should guess, have to be carried at least one rung farther down the devolutionary ladder than the regional unit. Devolution will not relieve the pressure on persons perceptibly unless it is carried down to units with so small an area and population that the demesmen (to use an Attic term of political art) will all be able to know each other personally and to transact local public business with each other direct.

This basic constituent unit of the coming world state will be identical with the basic constituent unit of the world city; for world-state and world city will be conterminous. They will be the political and the structural facets of the self-same world society. A pre-view of the structure of the coming world city can already be seen in Brasilia, the new capital of Brazil which has been built according to plan because it has been laid out in what was a virgin wilderness. The designer of Brasilia, Senhor Lucio Costa, has articulated this van-guard of Ecumenopolis into quadros. These are sections which are small enough to make it possible for the inhabitants of each quadro to know each other personally. A quadro is self-contained in the sense that it is not intersected by any roads open for mechanized wheeled traffic. The children can therefore walk between home and school inside their quadro, and the women can do their shopping and their washing inside it, without risk of being run over.

The men are less fortunate; most of them have to travel beyond the bounds of their own quadros in order to do the work by which they earn a living for their families. The problem of the congestion of traffic is a serious one for them; and, as I see it, this problem can be solved only by the drastic measures by which it was once solved in Ancient Rome and has been solved in present-day Venice. At Venice nowadays an arriving motorist has to park his car in a public garage on the outskirts of the city. Inside the city he has the choice of walking along the alley-ways and over the bridges or boarding a steamer (i.e. a water-bus) or hiring a gondola (i.e. a water-taxi). In

Ancient Rome, wheeled traffic of all kinds, commercial as well as private, was forbidden to circulate during daylight hours. In Ecumenopolis a combination of the Venetian and the Ancient Roman traffic-regulations will have to be introduced in order to make any kind of locomotion possible. In daylight hours, traffic in the world city's ganglions will have to be the monopoly of public conveyances, and, once given this monopoly, a public transport-service will have no excuse for not being first-rate.

We have still to find superficial devices for easing the pressure, on a worker's personality, of mechanized work in factories and in offices. Automation is going to turn the factory-worker and the office-worker into a cipher, or alternatively it is going to make him or her redundant. When automation has been carried to the limit, the only form of remunerative work within the economic system in which it will still be possible for a worker to be a person is 'self-employment' in one of the 'liberal' professions; but the openings for this will be relatively few even in the most highly cultivated and sophisticated society. For the great majority, the only possible relief from unemployment on a financially lavish but psychologically impoverishing dole will be non-economic 'self-employment' either on 'doing it oneself' (e.g. re-soling one's own shoes or mending one's own watch) or on some entirely 'unpractical' activity (e.g. the arts and sciences or religion).

Superficial adjustments, of the kind that I have just been sketching, are assuredly worth making. We ought to make them with all our might. But my foreboding is that, when we have done our utmost at this superficial level, we shall find that we have not yet won the victory for personality over technology—a victory that we have to win because, should we fail to win it, life would become unendurable for human beings.

The indispensable victory cannot, I am convinced, be won solely by superficial adjustments of externals, imperative though such adjustments are. The pressure of 'Brave New World' on a human being's personality can be met victoriously only by a change of heart. In the Computer Age, the only salvation for persons is the inward spiritual grace of serenity, and serenity cannot be attained either by taking to drugs or by capitulating to fatalism. Man, the social animal, cannot contract out of society, however oppressive spiritually may be the society in which he finds himself implicated by the accident of the time and place in which he happens to have been born; 'for none of us liveth to himself and no man dieth to himself'.[1] The serenity that has to be achieved henceforth by a human being who is striving to preserve his personality is a serenity that is exposed to the pressure of 'Brave New World' and that withstands it.

Serenity in the midst of toil and trouble can be of one or the other of two kinds. There is the defensive serenity of the garrison of an impregnable fortress, and there is the suffering serenity of the citizens of a city that has deliberately been left open. The negative form of serenity has been the objective of the Greek philosophies of Epicureanism and Stoicism and of the Indian philosophy of Buddhism. In the pursuit of this austere objective, the two Greek philosophers did not go to all lengths; the Indian philosopher did; and the revulsion from primitive Buddhism which has taken the form of the Mahayana indicates that the whole-heartedness of the primitive Buddhists' pursuit of their negative objective is not enough—noble though the pursuit of this austere objective is. The serenity that can give a human being the spiritual strength to live in 'Brave New World' as an uneffaced person is the serenity that does not seek to barricade itself against the assaults of suffering but embraces suffering for the sake of following the lead of love. In the serenity of love I will fear no evil, though I walk through the valley of the shadow of death.[2]

[1] Rom. xiv. 7.   [2] Psalm xxiii. 4.

PART III

Reflections

1 : ΕΛΛΗΝΙΚΑ

ΑΛΕΞΑΝΔΡΟΥ ΑΝΑΒΑΣΙΣ

Ἄνδρες Ἀλεξάνδροιο παρασπισταὶ βασιλῆος,
οἳ πάλαι εὐρείης λὰξ ἐπέβητ' Ἀσίης,
εἴθ' ἤγειρα σὺν ὔμμιν ἀϋτήν τε πτόλεμόν τε·
εἴχετε γὰρ χάρμην—εἴχετε—θεσπεσίην.

4 July 1911

ΜΑΚΕΔΟΝΩΝ ΚΑΤΑΣΤΡΟΦΗ

Αἴλινον αἴλινον εἰπέ· κατήριπε δῶμα Φιλίππου·
αἴλινον· ἐξ ἐδάφους ὤλετο γῆ Μακεδών.
ἡ δὲ φάλαγξ ἔστρωται ἀνὰ στίχας, ὡς ὅτ' ἀμητὴρ
ἐστόρεσεν δρεπάνῳ Θεσσαλικὰς στάχυας·
ὣς ὄγμος κατὰ κόσμον ἐλήλαται αἰχμητάων,
οὐδ' αὐτὸς κείνων τάξιν ἔλυσ' Ἀΐδης.
ἴσχει χεὶρ ἀμενηνὸς ἑῆς ἔτι θραῦμα σαρίσης,
ἀσπίδα δ' ἀργυρέην λύθρος ἔβαψε μέλας.
τῶνδ' Ἀσίην πρόγονοι μὲν ἐπικρατέως ἐρατεινὴν
εἷλον, ὑπερφιάλοις κῆρες Ἀχαιμενίδαις·
νῦν δ' αὐτοῖς ἀτηρὸς ἀπὸ ζόφου ἦλθε τριακτήρ,
αἰετὸς αἰπολίοις, Ὀσκὸς ἀμαιμάχετος.
ἡ δ' Ἑλλὰς τρὶς ὄλωλ', αὐτόχθονος οὐκέτι χειρὶ
κοιράνου ὀψομένη σκῆπτρον ἀνασσόμενον.

1909 or 1910

IN LUCRETIO NULLA SALUS?

LUCRETI, φιλόμουσε διδάσκαλε, καρτερόθυμε,
νύχθ' οἵην, φάος ὢν οἷον, ἀπεσκέδασας.
Ζηνὶ γὰρ αὐτῷ πρῶτος ἐναντίος ἐλθέμεν ἔτλης,
αἶψα δ' ἀμαυρώθη τὰ ψολόεντα βέλη·
ἡμῖν δ' αὖ μετόπισθε θεῶν κακὰ δείματ' ἔλυες,
ἄτλητόν τι βροτοῖς ἄχθος ἐπισμυγεροῖς.

χαῖρε, σοὶ αὐτῷ γὰρ σὺ μέγα σθένος ηὗρες, ἐγὼ δὲ
φαῦλος ἀνήρ · τί ἐμοὶ σὸν σθένος ηὗρ' ὄφελος;

1907

OPTIMAS ROMANUS LOQUITUR

Imperium nostrae libertas addidit urbi,
sed libertatem perdidit imperium.

1907

ΑΙΘΙΟΠΕΣ ΑΓΩΝΙΣΤΑΙ

Κεῖνοι μέν, γυμνοὶ καὶ βάρβαροι ἄνδρες ἐόντες,
ὄργανα φρικώδους οὐκ ἐφοβοῦντ' Ἄρεως,
ἀλλ' αὐτοσχεδίῃ, ἔτ' ἐλεύθεροι, οὔ τι τρέσαντες,
εἰς Ἀΐδην καλῶς μαρνάμενοι κάτεβαν.
ἡμεῖς δ' οἱ μεγάλοι καὶ καρτεροί, οἱ σοφοί; ἡμῖν
τῶν αὐτῶν ὀδυνῶν γευσαμένοισι θανεῖν
μοῖρ' · ἀλλ' οὐ θάνατον τὸν Ἀρήϊον · οὔποτε τοῖον
τοῖς ἐπιορκοῦσιν δῶρον ἔδωκε θεός.

April 1936

Without our arms or art, these men could dare
War's utmost frightfulness, since men they were,
And, in close fight, to death untrembling passed,
Still freemen, battling nobly to the last.
But we, whose science makes us strong and great,
Are doomed to share the tortures of their fate,
Yet not their soldier's grave; the gods in scorn
Withhold that privilege from men forsworn.

Translation of the preceding Greek epigram by G. M. Gathorne-Hardy.

AN UNFULFILLED INTENT

VERSÛS CONSTANTINI PORPHYROGENITI OPERUM OMNIUM EDITIONI MIHI PROPOSITAE PRAESTRUENDI

Χαῖρέ μοι, ὦ μεγάλου μεγάλη πόλι Κωνσταντίνου,
τοὺς Κωνσταντίνου χαῖρ' ἐφέποντι λόγους,
οὐ κτίστου γ', ἑτέρου δέ, σοφοῦ σοφὸς ὅς ῥα Λέοντος
υἱὸς ἐγεννήθη πορφυρέῳ 'ν θαλάμῳ.

καὶ Δάναπριν περάτης τε καὶ ἠοῦς ἱστορεῖ ἔθνη,
ἐσθλά τε 'Ρωμαίων ἐξέτασεν Θέματα.
νῦν δ' ἐγὼ ἐκ γῆς ὀψὲ Βαράγγων ἐξανέτειλα
τερπνὰ διορθώσων τοῖο γέροστος ἔπη.

TO A. D. GILLESPIE, ΕΙΡΕΛΑΝΔΟΝΙΚΗΙ

'Ησσήθην τ' ἀλγέω θ' ἡσσημένος· ἀλλὰ σὺ χαῖρε,
ὦ φίλ' ὁ νικήσας, ξὺν δὲ σοὶ αὐτὸς ἐγώ.

18 December 1910

2 : ΕΡΩΤΙΚΑ

ΕΠΙΦΑΝΕΙΑ

'Εκθύμως πονέοντι κατὰ σκότον ἐξαπιναίως
οὐράνιον φαίνεις, ὦ 'Ροσάλινδα, φάος.
ἐργάσομαι μεγάλ' ἔργα· δι' ἔργων σοῦ πελάσαιμ' ἄν·
κἂν ἄρα λείψωμαι, μείζον' ἔτ' ἐργάσομαι.

November 1910[1]

ΕΡΩΤΟΜΟΥΣΟΜΑΧΙΑ

Μουσάων θεράποντα καθ' ἵμερος ἔσχε γυναικός
—οὐ γάρ, Μοῦσαι, ἄπαντ', οὐ γάρ, ἐν ὕμμιν ἔφυ—
ἵμερος ἔσχε γυναικός· ὃ δ' αἰνῶς λῆμα ταραχθεὶς
θερμὸς ἀθήρατον παῖς ἐδίωκεν ἄγραν—
ἄλλως· οὐ Μοῦσαι δ' ἔτι γ' ἵλεῳ, ἀχθόμεναι δὲ
ἄλλοσ' ἀποστείχουσ', οὐδαμόθεν δὲ φάος.

April 1911

ΠΟΘΟΥ ΚΕΝΤΡΟΝ

Τί χρήσωμαι ἔρωτι; τὸν ἐν φρεσὶ βαλλόμενός τε
ἠσχύνθην, ἱλαρῇ τ' αὖτις εὐφροσύνη
ἔνδοθεν ἦτορ ἐπάλλετ'· ἐπὴν παρὰ σοὶ γὰρ ὁμιλῶ,
εὔδιον, ἄπληστος δ' ἔσπετ' ἀπόντι πόθος·

---

[1] Comment, September 1965: εἰ δὲ ἐξ ἔργων, οὐκ ἔτι ἐστὶ χάρις : 'If it be of works, then it is no more grace.'—Rom. xi. 6.

κοὐκ οἶδ᾽ εἴ με φιλεῖς τι ἢ οὐδ᾽ ὅσον—ἓν τόδε μοῦνον
οἶδα σάφ᾽· ἐκθύμως σοῦ, 'Ροσάλινδ', ἔραμαι.

4 July 1911

ΟΥΚ ΕΧΩ ΠΡΟΣΕΙΚΑΣΑΙ

Θυμέ, πανόπτης μοι καὶ πάσσοφος εἴθε γένοιο·
θυμέ, φυὴ κούρης πᾶσι πρόχειρον ἰδεῖν,
ἢν δ᾽ ἄρ᾽ ὁμιλήσῃς ὅσον οὖν χρόνον αὖτε, μαθήσει
καὶ νόον· ἀλλ᾽ αὐτῆς ἀρά ποτε στοχάσει;

8 July 1911

ΕΜΠΟΔΟΝ ΗΛΘ᾽ ΟΣΙΗ

'Αλλὰ παρῆν ἐπιδεῖν σὲ καὶ ἅψασθαι καὶ ὁμιλεῖν—
κεῖνο παρῆν· κείνῳ δ᾽ ἔμποδον ἦλθ᾽ ὁσίη.
οὐχ ὁσίη γὰρ μήτερ᾽ ἐρήμην ἐγκαταλείπειν,
αὐτὸν δ᾽ ἀκράτου γεῦσαι ἐϋφροσύνης.
νῦν δ᾽, ὦ Ζεῦ, ἡγοῦ μοι ἀλωμένῳ ἂμ πεδί᾽ 'Οσκῶν
τηλόθι τ᾽ Αἰγαῖον ποντοποροῦντι σάλον,
δαρὸν ὅπως καλὰ πολλὰ μαθὼν δαρόν τε μογήσας
δή ποτ᾽ ἄτερ κακίας ὄψομαι ἢν ποθέω.

30 August 1911

3 : ΕΠΙΤΑΦΙΟΙ

BOB GIBSON

Spring riots heedlessly through France,
 Drunk with tempestuous light.
Across the plain her white beams dance,
 And my friend's face is white.

His body parts the rising wheat,
 A torn, discarded thing
God strove more fiercely to complete
 Than all the works of spring.

27 March 1925

GUY LEONARD CHEESEMAN AND
JAMES ELROY FLECKER

Εὕδουσιν κεῖνοι μέν, ἐγρήγορε δ', ὡς πάρος, ἡμῖν
πράγματ'—ἔτι ζώντων μοῖρα—μέριμνα, πόθος·
κεῖνοι δ' ἄτρεμα κεῖνται, ἐπεὶ 'θέτο μόρσιμον ἦμαρ
ἥρωας, βιότου παῦσαν ἐπιχθονίου.[1]

GILBERT MURRAY

ποῖός τις ὡνήρ; εὖ νιν ἐγνωκὼς φράσω.
τόνδ', εἴ τιν' ἄλλον, χρῆν φιλάνθρωπον καλεῖν
εἰ μὴ φιλόφρων πᾶσι καὶ ζῴοισιν ἦν,
πᾶσίν τ' ἀρωγός. αὐτὸς εὔκολος τρόπῳ,
κακοῖσιν οὔτ' ἄθικτος οὔθ' ἡττημένος,
πρᾶος μέν, ἀστεμφὴς δέ· τῆς οἰκουμένης
ὁμοῦ πολίτης τῆς τε τῶν Μουσῶν πόλεως·
σοφός, φιλόκαλος, λόγιος, ἀργυρόστομος.
τοῖος βιώσας ἐννεάδας ἐτῶν δέκα,
γέρων ἐπέπνυτ' ἐν γέρουσιν ὡς νέος.
νικηφόρος δὴ τοῦδ' ἀπηλλάχθη βίου,
φίλοις ποθεινός, θεῖος ἐν τεθνηκόσιν.

31 December 1958

4 : ΦΙΛΙΚΑ

FLORENCE LAMONT

Alma viatori portarum hera semper hiantum
dat mihi inauditae pignus amicitiae

[1] Amicorum manibus. At some date before August 1914, James Elroy Flecker gave to his friend G. L. Cheeseman, who was my friend too and my schoolfellow, a copy of an English translation, published in 1899, of *Also sprach Zarathustra*. On one of the blank pages before the title-page, Flecker had written |ames to en| and

> The melancholy feature
> About the life of Nietzsche
> Is that the poor creature
> Thought he was a teacher.

Flecker died on 3 January 1915. Cheesman was killed in landing on the Gallipoli Peninsula in August 1915. I inherited this book of Cheesman's among others, and wrote my four lines on the blank page opposite Flecker's four.

scriptori: tot tanta volumina quanta quot edo
improbus, illa acri femina mente legit.
Musa, dehinc nunquam cessabis gignere libros
ingentes. quotvis haec domus accipiet.

20 October 1942

EDWARD FRANKLAND

When Wild Boar rises to my eye,
Clean-cut against an eastern sky,
And bends in symmetry to swell
Into his yoke-fellow Swarth Fell;
When, tossed together at my feet,
Swift Lune and swifter Rawthey meet;
The sounding waters sing 'Neat Dale',
The silent hills take up the tale,
And hills and waters, fair before,
Grow fairer, opening Memory's door,
Yet fairer still fond Memory holds
A house that such true friends enfolds.

3 September 1948

5 : ΣΥΝΕΡΓΑΤΙΚΑ

CUIUS MANUS?

Haec mea conscripsit—verum est—manus, adfuit autem
(nesciat hoc quamvis lector) ubique tua.

July 1925

CUIUS OPUS?

'Templum construxit Salamo.'—'Quis saxa, quis aurum
contulit?'—'Haec David.'—'Aedificavit uter?'

July 1925

6 : ΑΓΩΝΙΑ

ΓΡΑΜΜΑΤΙΚΟΣ ΜΙΝΟΤΑΥΡΟΣ

Γραμματικός, νωθρός τι νόημ' ἕξιν τ' ἐπιεικὴς
σώφρων τ' αὖτε τρόπον κἂν πόνῳ ἐργατικός—
φαίνομαι ἆρ' ἐφορῶντι φυὴν τοῖός τις; ἀληθῶς;
ἦ μὴν δαιδάλλων Δημιοεργὸς ἐμὲ
ἐξείργασται, ἐς ᾠὸν ἀκήρατον οὐρανίωνα
δαίμονά θ' ἱδρύσας κῆρά θ' ὑποχθόνιον—
δαίμονα μὲν ψυχὴν βροτοῦ ἀνέρος, ἰσόθεόν τι,
κῆρα δέ τοι ταῦρον γηγενῆ ὠγύγιον.
κείνοιν δ' αὐξομένοιν περιτελλομένων ἐνιαυτῶν,
τοῖν βασίλευεν ἀνὴρ θῆρά θ' ὑπερφίαλον
αἰεὶ χειρὶ κατεῖχε κραταιοτέρῃ, καὶ ἀκηδής,
ἄτην οὐ προορῶν, αὐτόνομος προάγει.

κλῦθι, θεός· τί πέπονθας ἐνὶ φρεσίν; ἦ στυγέεις σὺ
ἤδη σὸν χρόνιον δαίδαλον ἔργον—ἐμέ;
ἔπλασας οὖν θνητόν περ ἀρείονά μ' ἀθανάτου σοῦ;
ἦ σὺ μέδοντι κακοῦ θηρὸς ὅμως φθονέεις;
ἦ σὺ μανεὶς πλήξας με; τόδ' οἶδα σάφ'· ἐξ Ἀφροδίτης
ἔκπαγλον πληχθεὶς μαίνομαι αὐτὸς ἐγώ.
γυῖα δέ μοι πρὸς γυῖ' ὀλοὴν ἔριν ἐντὸς ἐρίζει,
βουλὴ δ' ἐκ κραδίης ἔνδοθεν οὐδεμία
ἐξεφάνη· γυμνὸς δὲ καὶ ὀρφανὸς ἀντιτέταγμαι
γηγενεῖ ὠγυγίῳ ταύρῳ ἐπερχομένῳ.

'A man of letters, slow, sedate,
Industrious, affectionate'—
Is that the image that you see?
O then indeed most cunningly
The Demiurge hath fashioned me.
Within that smooth and seamless shell
He planted Heaven and planted Hell:
Seeds of the godlike human soul,
Seeds of the black primaeval bull.

Yet, as the germs fulfilled their nature
And beast and man increased in stature,
The man was lord, and ever faster
He held the bull—unchallenged master—
And went his way, nor feared disaster.

O God, what ails thee? Doth it irk—
Thy cunning long-wrought handiwork?
Didst better than thyself create?
Dost envy me my lordly state?
Hast struck in madness? This I know:
I reel beneath a maddening blow.
My members war with oneanother;
Dumb oracle is Life my mother;
Alone, I face, with naked breast,
The rampant black primaeval beast.

22 December 1929, at sea between Wei-hai-wai and Shanghai

GOMORRAH

You Smyrna weeping London's tears,
You London racked by Smyrna's fears,
Busy detestable Shanghai:
Our anchor's up, thank God: goodbye.

3 January 1930

ΑΓΝΩΣΤΩΙ ΘΕΩΙ

Χαίρετέ μοι σωθέντι παρ' ἐλπίδα, χαίρεθ', ἑταῖροι·
ἥκω νικήσας, ἀντίπαλος δ' ὀλοὸς
κεῖται τεθνηώς. ὑποδεξόμενον γὰρ ἐρωὴν
κείνου πατρῷοι προύδίδοσάν με θεοὶ
πάντες ὁμῶς, ἀμενηνοί· ἀνέλπιστος δὲ παραστὰς
εἰς ἄγνωστος Ἄρη δῶκε δεκαπλάσιον.
καὶ τότε δὴ πλήσσω γυμνῇ χερί· θὴρ δ' ὑπὸ πληγῇ
πρηνὴς θαρσαλέη κάππεσε—θαῦμα—μιᾷ·
αὐτὸς δ' αὐτόνομος προάγω ταχύ, γηθόσυνος κῆρ,
ὡς πάρος, ἀγνώστου γνοὺς ἐν ἀγῶνι θεοῦ
ἵλαα ἔργ', εἴδους δ' ἀγνὼς πάνυ. ἀλλὰ φάνητι
ἀντιπρόσωπος ἰδεῖν δὴ τότ', ἐπευχομένῳ.

22 January 1930, in the train in Siberia, near Achinsk

Rejoice with me returned again—
The battle won. The foe lies slain.
For, as I faced those fearful odds,
Left desolate by all my gods,
A god unknown stood by me. Then
My strength was as the strength of ten.
With naked hand I smote; and, lo,
The beast fell prone at one brave blow;
And, where he fell, there still he lay.
With singing heart I went my way.
O unknown god, I feel thy grace.
When shall I see thee face to face?

ΠΑΝΤΑ ΕΙΣΩ

I girdled Asia, bore her blows,
Her summer suns, her winter snows,
Trod plain and hill from Rum to Ch'in:
Yet all I learnt I found within.

December 1929, in China

7 : ΣΥΓΓΡΑΦΕΩΣ ΒΙΟΣ ΕΣΦΑΛΜΕΝΟΣ

Κῆρες ὅσαι θανάτοιο πιέζετέ μ', οὐ γὰρ ἔτ' ὕμμιν
  εἴξας ὀφλήσω αὐτὸς ἑκὼν κακίην,
οὔ, μὰ θεοῦ μέγαν ὅρκον, ὃς ὤμοσε μή με ματαίως
  οἰχήσεσθαι, ἅπαξ καλὸν ἰδόντα φάος
ἠελίου, ῥέξαντα δ' ἐν ἀνθρώποισιν ἀέθλους·
  τῷ πίσυνος κείναις οὐκέτι δοῦλος ἐγώ.
ἀλλ' ἔρξω, καιρὸς γάρ· ἀλάστορες ὦ σκιόεντες,
  ἔρρετε· σωτείρας ηὗρον· ὑποτρέσατε.

Μοῦσαι μειλιχίαι ἐλεήμονες, ἤλθετε κἀμοί,
  χειμερίῳ 'ν πόντῳ νηΐ τινασσομένῃ—
πένθεος ἐν χειμῶνι· καὶ αἰνῶς μ' ἐστυφέλιξεν
  ἲς ἀνέμων, κοὐδὲν τέρμ' ἐπέφαντο κακοῦ,

αἰανὴς δ᾽ ἔπι μόχθος, ἐφίκετο δ᾽ ὅσσον ὀπωπὴ
ἀήρ τ᾽ ἄξενά τ᾽ ἦν κύματα παλλόμενα.
τῶν μ᾽ ἄπο, σώτειραι, τότ᾽ ἐλύσατε, καὶ πάλιν ὀρθῇ
στείρῃ λευγαλέης ποντοπορῶ δι᾽ ἁλός.
Μούσας ὑμνήσω νόος ἔμπεδος εἰς ὅ κ᾽ ἔπηται,
Μούσαις λατρεύσω παντὶ χερὸς σθένεϊ,
Μούσας ἂν δὲ προδῶ, τῷ γ᾽ ἤματι κἀμὲ προδοίης,
φιλτάτη ὠκυμόρων—μηδ᾽ ἐλεοῖς με—βροτῶν.

Ἀλλ᾽ ἔραμαι· Μοῦσαι δὲ καλοῦσί με. τηλόθι, Μοῦσαι,
στρωφᾶσθ᾽ ἀνθρώπων, τῆλ᾽, Ἑλικωνιάδες.
πίδακες ὕμμιν ἐκεῖ καὶ τέμπεα δενδρήεντα,
τρηχὺς ὁ δ᾽ οἶμος ἐὼν ζῆλον ἐνῆκε ποδί,
τέρμα δ᾽ ὁδοῦ προὔστηκε μέγα ῥίον αἰθερίη τε
στίλβουσ᾽ εὐαγής—εἴθε θίγοιμι—νιφάς.
οὐκέτ᾽ Ἔρως ἔταρος δέ· τὰ μείλιχα ἔργ᾽ ἀνθρώπων
κεῖνος δὴ νέμεται· τὸν δ᾽ ἄρα θελγόμενος
καλλείπω στρεφθεὶς πρὸς τὦρεα· ἀλλ᾽ ἔραμαί σου.
ἴσχε, φίλη, μ᾽, ὤμοις χεῖρα βαλοῦσα πέρι.

Ἔσχες ἀδημονέοντά μ᾽, ὑπέστρεψεν δ᾽, ἀπιών περ,
σῇ χερὶ θελγόμενος, κοὐκ ἄρα φροῦδος, Ἔρως·
ἀλλ᾽ ἔπεται τρίτος αὐτὸς ὁδοιπόρος—οὐ τρίτος οἶος,
Μουσῶν γὰρ θιάσου κεῖνος ἅμ᾽ ἡγέεται.
"Χαίρετέ μοι, στίλβουσαν ἕδρην Ἑλίκωνα λιποῦσαι
πότνιαι"· ἡ δὲ γελῶσ᾽ ἵλα Καλλιόπη
"Τέκνω," ἔφη, "στείχωμεν ὁμὴν ὁδόν, ἧς ῥα πέφανται
τέρμ᾽ οὐ δῆθ᾽ Ἑλίκων, οὐ ῥίον οὐδὲ νιφάς·
τῆλε γὰρ οὐ στρεφώμεθ᾽—ἔπος φύγεν ἕρκος ὀδόντων
κεῖνό τοι εἰκαῖον—κοινὸς ὁδηγὸς ὅδε."

Ἐρχόμενον γὰρ ὁρῶ σε, τελεσφόρε, παυσιμέριμνε
πᾶσι βροτοῖς, κἀμοὶ καίριε νῦν, Θάνατε—
χαῖρέ μοι οὔ ῥα μάτην βεβιωκότι, ὦ Ῥοσαλίνδη
σύζυγος, ὀργεῶνες Μοῦσαι, ὁδηγὸς Ἔρως.

October 1910—September 1927

8 : CAESURA

GANTHORPE: AN ELEGY AND DEDICATION

I

When work, my kind task-master,
Loosens his guardian grip and bids me stand at ease,
My will lets slip the bow-string of desire
And my spirit—sped with demonic archery—
    Flies straight to Ganthorpe
With the timeless speed of pain-driven thought,
Far swifter than the flight of homing pigeons
    Eager to nestle
In the grey stone pigeon-cot tower—
    Ganthorpe's rugged core.

    Longing and lingering,
    My eyes embrace the house,
    Caress it stone by stone,
Follow the mouldings round each door and window:
    The broken lintel
(The split stone bowed and yet still bearing its burden);
    Tony's window;
The empty gun-rack in the room behind:
    Each window a face,
Each room a life bound up with mine.

Spell-bound, like a sleep-walker,
    I beat the bounds:
The path between the apple-trees and the lawn
Haunted by print of Tony's melancholy play—
    The day-long practice of his tennis-service,
    The day-long shooting at little cardboard targets;
The corner of the garden by Freer's barn,
Where a glimpse of the plain is framed between hillsides
In a V like the nick of a rifle-sight.

Old Freer too was drawn by this magnet.
At the gate of his field how often have I seen him
On October evenings in the autumn of his life
Gazing at that blue distance with sad patient eyes.
    The undying vision of Nature's beauty,
    Seen day by day since his days of promise,
    Gave solace to the old man's soul
    In the last stand of his losing battle.

II

    Setting my course as desire drives me,
I take the hollow way below the garden wall,
Past Fosdyke's cottage, past the chain of pools—
A watery staircase, dappled with light and shadow
By overarching boughs of elm and beech—
Then out into the sunlight on Freersmoor
    And over the sky-line
Till suddenly breaks into view, familiar yet ever surprising,
A landscape conjured up by Vanbrough's art.
    The feather-crowned pines overtopping Ray Wood—
For all the world like palms on Treasure Island—
Are mirrored on the North Lake at my feet,
But not the Wolds, though they seem but a stone's-throw away,
    So clear up their flank climbs the road
Travelled by Tony taking ship for Holland.

Past Owlës Wood and across Bell Bottom,
    Ploughed by snouts of rooting pigs,
And through the gloomy pine-plantation,
Where jays scream and squirrels chatter,
    I thread my way to Slingsby Moor
And throw myself down on the old man's barrow,
    Musing, while Tilda chases the rabbits,
On other times of trouble which the lord of the barrow has
      witnessed.
'Old Man, give me an oracle!' But the lord of the barrow is silent
    And silent the dark brow of Slingsby Banks.

III

At my desk in the attic window
I lift my pen from the page
As I rise from the depths of thought to the surface of awareness
    To hear flies droning on the window-pane,
    Sheep bleating homeward over Ventris' field,
    And young owls snoring in the hollow trunks,
Filling the air with the rhythmic mysterious sound
Like the murmur of planes lost to view in the stratosphere.

    Lifting my eyes to the window,
I catch the shimmer of birches down in the hollow
And think of Laurence walking there once at my side,
Clutching his gun in the dusk, aglow like Tilda
    With unquenched ardour,
Dreaming of unimaginable achievements,
Unaware of the signs of the times—an open book to me
Who, thrusting forebodings aside, now give myself up to the
       moment,
    Tasting the joy of companionship,
    As once when, through the dark plantation,
Heedless of chattering squirrels and screaming jays,
A robin, hopping beside me from bough to bough,
    Warmed my heart with his gift of friendship.

    Lifting my eyes to the hills,
I gaze at the bare green prow of the Morpeth Plantation,
And measure the length of the fence from the point where the
       trees break off
To the bows of the bank, clear-cut like a destroyer's,
Falling away to disclose, uncurtained by Hovingham Woods,
    The far-away acropolis of Hawnsby Hump,
    Moated, like Veii, by forking streams,
    Skirted by Bilsdale, whose long ascent
    Leads to a Pisgah sight of Tees-side:
    Ingleby Greenhowe, Rosebery Topping,
    Smoke-spuming chimneys and high-level bridge
Built by jinns to delight Child Laurence.

IV

Built by monks in the hidden valley,
Unseen from the window yet transfiguring the landscape—
Revealing God's presence in the beauty of His works—
Lies Ampleforth, where once the gates of Heaven's mercy opened
    to me
    As I stood on the threshold in distress for my son
Flung off the path of life,
    And Father Paul,
Who cheerfully bears on his shoulders the burden of Atlas,
Took Philip into his fold and sped him again on his way
    For the glory of God by the power of Saint Benedict.

    This inexhaustible fountain of charity
    Has its well-spring in the choir
Where, clinging to the feet of the Crucifix over the altar,
My soul is swept by the impetus of the Office
Chanted by Benedict's sons through fourteen hundred years
    In a golden chain of indomitable worship
    Whose links are forged on the anvil of tribulation.
Silenced on Monte Cassino, the song wells up at Westminster;
Silenced at Westminster, it wells up at Dieulouard;
Silenced at Dieulouard, it wells up at Ampleforth.
    Echoing down the ages from land to land,
    Their sound has gone forth throughout the World.

V

Lowering my eyes from the window to the unpenned page on my
    desk,
    I dream that one day, in this attic,
Hearing, as now, in my ears the bleat of Ventris' sheep,
Listening, as now, in my soul to the chanting of the Office,
I shall lay down my pen as I end the last line of my book,
And walk out, like Gibbon, into the quiet of the garden,
Rejoicing to have reached the goal of my endeavours,
Bewildered to find myself free from the task that has held me in
    thrall,

As once, lying under the stars at a wayside station in Thrace,
    We marvelled to have reached our journey's end
On the arduous road to Ístanbul from Calais.

    Then I let my mind savour the foretaste
Of pleasures hanging ever ripe on the bough
But never plucked by me in these years of toil,
When the puritan's anxious conscience and the artist's demonic
      drive—
    Strange partnership of censors—
    Kept me bent, like a bow, to my task,
    In a trough between waves of war,
    Running my strenuous race with the titans Time and Fate.

To-morrow evening I shall take my ease,
Absolved from wearily climbing the attic stair,
And next year I shall learn how Ganthorpe looks in May,
A sight I have longed to see these twenty years,
    Since that first Easter-tide
When, standing at gaze on the crown of Freersmoor,
We drank in the fresh beauty of Owlës Wood:
Green splash of awakening larch, white foam of blossoming
      cherry,
    Broidering the purple depths
    Where the slower trees still slumbered.
If this (I dream) was Ganthorpe's April promise,
How radiant must her May-time fullness be.

I dream again: When I have written my book,
    When I have launched my sons,
    When I have seen Ganthorpe in May,
    Then, death, come when thou wilt.
One day at dawn, in the moment of silence
Between crow of cock and chorus of song-birds,
Stretched on my bed with my eyes on the sky-line,
    I shall see thee appearing
    Over Coneysthorpe Banks, over Raysmoor,
Bringing thy gracious gifts of peace and fulfilment.

And, when thou hast done thy friendly office,
I shall be laid to rest in Ganthorpe earth
Like the old man under his barrow on Slingsby Moor.
I have been sure of this since that first summer
    When in this magic countryside
    I lost my olive stave
    Close-grained, knotted, twisted,
Carved with mysterious symbols round the butt,
Given me by a Cretan aghoyiát
Riding from Cnossos to the Mesará,
Carried by me in wanderings round the World,
To Ístanbul from Calais, from Baghdad
To Shan-hai-kwan, from Nara to Ostend,
Not lost on the retreat from Inönü,
Lost and recovered on a Bosporan tram,
    Treasured Palladium,
Now gone to earth in Yorkshire.

    Grieved at my loss—
Being ignorant then of deeper griefs than this—
I made an omen to console myself:
    'My stave, old wanderer,
'Has found at last the haven where it would be;
    'Here is my haven too;
'I have lost my staff to find my abiding place;
'Here, 'tis now certain, I shall end my days.'

VI

    The pitcher is broken at the well:
I shall not finish my book at the attic window;
I shall not see how Ganthorpe looks in May;
I shall not greet death striding over Raysmoor;
I shall not be buried in Ganthorpe earth to sleep by the side of my
        olive stave.
                Nothing is left
But the trap of memory, gripping my soul in fangs
That rive her with anguish at every quiver of thought.

Still, Ganthorpe, I possess you.
Others—de Vaux, de Multon, Dacre, Howard—
    Have conquered you with swords,
    Held you with title-deeds,
    And charmed you with their presence—
Kindly, commanding, casual, capricious—
But I possess you as Wordsworth possesses his Lakes,
Thoreau his Walden, Tolstoi his Clear Glade.
My joys and griefs have melted into your landscape,
Your lineaments are written into my book,
And readers who have never heard your name—
In Pasadena, Birmingham, Bombay—
    Will be touched, unawares, by your spell.

    Who else has possessed you as I do?
Who else, with his ear to the ground on the old man's barrow,
Has heard, across sixteen miles of moor and wood and fell,
    The voice of a river flowing through York—
Not the muddy Ouse, but the living waters of history—
Shouting round Constantine raised on the shield,
Whispering round Severus on his death-bed?
    Who else has possessed you as I do?
It is *my* ghost that will walk through Owlës Wood,
It is *my* ghost that will sit at the attic window,
    Holding you against all comers,
Invincible in his demonic power.

VII

    All things are bought at a price.
The power in which my ghost holds Ganthorpe,
    Is dark desire,
    On which I nourish him
    As, in a twilight land
    By the foggy shore of Ocean Stream,
Odysseus, with a sop of ram's blood,
Gave a ghoulish glimmer of life to the feeble shades of the dead.
Through bondage to desire my ghost holds Ganthorpe:
I will not be the bondsman of desire.

How shall I break my bondage to desire?
Shall I listen to Zeno and Gautama
    Crying: 'Annihilate desire;
    'You cannot parley with a tyrant;
'You must slay him or still be his slave;
'Annihilate desire, your implacable tyrant;
'Annihilate desire and set your self free;
'Free from desire, you are a king,
    'In consciousness invulnerable,
    'Insensible in Nirvâna;
    'Annihilate desire.'

    Insensible in Nirvâna,
I cannot feel pain and cannot praise God.
    In consciousness invulnerable,
I am proof against adversity and proof against God's love,
    For whom the Lord loveth He chasteneth,
And scourgeth every son whom He receiveth.
    Making myself a king,
I make myself God's peer and not God's subject.
    Annihilating desire,
I thwart God's purpose and desecrate His work,
For the arrow and its target are alike God's creatures.
    I will not be a king,
    I will not be invulnerable,
    I will not be insensible,
    I will not slay desire,
I will not follow the counsels of the philosophers.

How shall I break my bondage to desire?
The demon archer who speeds my spirit to Ganthorpe
    To long and linger and suffer anguish there—
Desire, my tyrant—is also God's servant:
    I will wear desire's yoke in the service of God,
Feeling through stabs of memory the workings of God's will,
Forging my pangs into acts in the furnace of God's love,
Gathering fruits from my acts to offer to God for His harvest,
Teaching the demon desire to serve God as an angel of light.

Thou shalt worship the Lord thy God and Him only shalt thou
    serve.
Belovèd works of the Lord: Bell Bottom, Owlës Wood,
Bull Inns, Coneysthorpe Banks, sheer prow of the Morpeth
    Plantation,
Barrow on Slingsby Moor, dim summit of Hawnsby Hump,
Sound of many waters from Time's ever-rolling stream,
    Flitting dryad, sleeping hero,
    Urgent muse, elusive goddess,
    I have loved you beyond measure;
    I shall love you always;
I will dedicate my love for you to God.

The beauty with which you kindle my love
Is the light of God's countenance shining through His creatures.
Mistaking in you God's beauty for yours,
    Loving you beyond measure,
Worshipping you instead of your Creator,
    I have shrouded God's light in my darkness,
I have changed the veils through which God reveals His face
Into palls eclipsing the Beatific Vision.
Belovèd works of God, I shall love you always,
But henceforth I will love you for your Creator's sake,
    Seeing you with Columba's eyes—
    Seeing God in you through a glass darkly,
    Seeing God with you face to face.

                       1943

ΤΟΙΣ ΑΝΑΣΠΑΣΤΟΙΣ ΧΑΙΡΕΙΝ

    ῎Ανδρες ἀνασπαστοί, φῦλον τάλαν, αἰνὰ παθόντες,
    οὓς πάρος ἐκ ῥιζῶν Μῆδος ὑπερφίαλος
   ᾿Ασσύριός τ᾿ ἀγέρωχος ἀνέσπασε νηλέϊ θυμῷ,
    χαίρετ᾿· ἐγὼ δ᾿ ὑμῖν ὀψιγενὴς ἕταρος.
   κἀμὲ κατέπληξεν τοῖος μόρος· ἀλλὰ χαρῶμεν,
    ἡμεῖς γὰρ μεγαλοῦ φίλτατα τέκνα θεοῦ.
   ἡμεῖς τοῖο προφῆται· ἀπήμονας οὐκ ἐμύησεν·
    μάρτυρας ἀνθρώποις εἵλετο τοὺς τάλανας.

                    May 1947

9 : SCRIPTORIS VITA NOVA

ΠΙΟΜΑΙ ΕΞ ΑΛΛΗΣ ΠΙΔΑΚΟΣ Η ΠΟΤΑΜΟΥ
(Loquitur, prima, vox quotidiana ; secunda, vox ab imo
surgens pectore)

O silvae, silvae, raptae mihi, non revidendae,
    O mea, Silvani filia, musa dryas,
non dolet: hoc Paeto dictum immortale profata
    Arria procudit mi quoque robur et aes—
mi quoque, non solus tamen exsulo: nonne priores
    clara creaverunt tristi opera exsilio?
exsul—et immeritus—divom, Florentia, carmen
    edidit, alma intra moenia tale tua
nil orsus, vates. non iuste expulsus Athenis,
    Pangaei clivis advena Threïciis,
scripsit postnatis in perpetuom relegendam
    vir, bello infelix dux prius, historiam.
his ego par fato: par sim virtute. fovetur
    acrius aerumnis magnanimum ingenium.
me patriae excidium stimulat nova quaerere regna.
    Troia, vale! Latium per maria atra peto.
silvae, musa dryas, praesens Silvane, penates,
    'non' mihi clamanti, 'non' reboate 'dolet'.

Quae sibi nil quaerens quaerenti tanta ministrat,
    quae nil accipiens omnia suppeditat,
quae constanter amat non tali robore amata,
    quae dare—et hoc totis viribus—ardet opem,
nonne haec digna suo Beronice nomine sancto?
    quod patet ante oculos, improbe, nonne vides?

Cui tam cara comes, non exsulat exsul: ubique
    patria quâ praesens coniugis adsit amor.

Caece diu, tandem vidisti clarius. audi:
    perdita mortali gaudia flere nefas.

non datur humanis in perpetuom esse beatos:
  mox marcent vitae praemia: segnities
Elysii pretiumst: hebetat dulcedo: doloris
  sopitam recreant volnera viva animam.
haec non quaesitae tibi ianua aperta salutis:
  tu fato felix: te nova vita vocat.

Gavisus iuvenis vitae describere metas
  ausus eram fatum prospicere ipse meum.
prospexi triplicem—fauste ducentis Amoris,
  Musarum comitum, coniugis—harmoniam,
amens, qui, vasti peragrans vagus aequora ponti,
  non cavi fulmen, saeva procella, tuom.
non iterum de me dictabo oracula: nosti
  qui me servasti tu mea fata, Deus.

1944

10 : SCRIPTORIS RELIGIO

ΤΑ ΑΙΩΝΙΑ

Save love and loyalty and truth
All things are unsubstantial: youth
Has dreams, and weaves of these its bower,
Till harsh life shatters it; and power
Is unsubstantial—strain and stress
Of fingers grasping emptiness;
And grown men's wisdom, bought with sorrow,
Proves foolishness upon the morrow;
And age is sluggish, not serene:
Life ends as if it had not been:
But truth and loyalty and love
Part Hell beneath from Heaven above.

Some date later than 8 October 1918

A PRAYER

O Lord who, in thy mercy, hast taken from me a familiar and seemingly secure resting-place, and hast set me on an unknown path in life in order to prepare me for the unknown path of death which sooner or later I must follow: grant me to gain a little courage and a little wisdom now in this lesser ordeal, that so I may become a little less unfit to meet thee face to face in the greater ordeal that awaiteth me hereafter.

25 January 1924

AN ACT OF FAITH

'Νικήτῃ τίνι δὴ νίκην ἔφερεν Βερονίκη;'—
'Νικήτης ὅδ' Ἔρως.'—'τίς δ' ἄρ' ὅδ' ἐστι;'—'Θεός.'

7 August 1965

ΑΛΗΘΗΣ ΛΟΓΟΣ

Ἔρως, ἀνίκητόν σ' ὁ ποιητὴς καλῶν
ἥμαρτεν· οὐ γὰρ αὐτός οἶσθα, κοὐ θεῶν
ἄλλος τις οἶδεν, ἥντιν' οἴσεται χρόνος
τυχήν. βροτοῖς τὸ μέλλον ἄγνωστον πέλει
θεοῖς θ' ὁμοίως. εἶεν· οὐκ ἐμοὶ μέλει.
ἔρως ἐρῶσιν ἁγνὸν αὐτάρκες τέλος,
ἔρως ὁδηγός. τῷδ' ἄοκνος ἕψομαι—
νικῶντι, χαίρων· ἂν δ' ἰδῶ νικώμενον,
ἄοκνος αἰὲν οὐδὲν ἧττον ἕψομαι.

18 March 1966

ΑΘΑΝΑΤΟΣ ΠΟΤΕΡΟΣ;

'Θανὼν ἀνέστη Χριστός.'—'Οὐκ, ἄνθρωπος ὤν.'—
'Θεὸς γὰρ ἦν.'—'Θεῶν τίς;'—'Ἆρ' οὐκ οἶσθ'; Ἔρώς.'
'Ὁ θεὸς ἀθάνατος, θνητὸς οὔνθεος βροτός.'

21 March 1966

INDEX

BY V. M. TOYNBEE

Genesis, Book of, 288, 289, 350
Genius, 346–7
Genocide, 36, 205, 207, 241–2, 251,
252, 274, 292, 341
Geology, 302
George, Saint, 176
Georgia, Transcaucasian, 362
Geraneia, Mount, 26
German language, the, 11, 12
Germany: absence of, from Paris Peace
Conferences, 51; aggressive policy of,
before 1914, 17, 189–90, 227; atroci-
ties committed by, 204, 207, 242, 264;
Bismarckian policy in, 189–90, 206–7,
209, 226, 267–8; colonies of, 198, 258;
defeat of, in 1918 and 1945, effects of,
51, 218, 222, 224, 225, 226, 230, 231,
246; devaluation of currency in, after
First World War, 219; economic
prosperity of, after Second World
War, 226, 230, 246; education in, 310,
311; in First World War, 190, 207,
217, 218, 224, 225, 234, 311; in Second
World War, 195, 207, 222, 224–5,
234, 311, 314, 341; industry in, 188–9,
310, 337, 338; Jews, treatment of, 207,
242, 251, 341; militarism in, 189–90,
207, 211, 217, 236; political changes
in, during a single lifetime, 371; political unification of, 189–90, 206, 209;
population of, 189, 358; public
opinion regarding war in, 224–7, 231;
refugees in West Germany, 246;
revenge, desire for, after 1918, 219,
221; student revolts in, 359; technological efficiency of, 242, 246, 311;
Third Reich, actions and policy of,
before 1939, 59, 207, 221, 223, 264
(*see also* HITLER, NAZIS); welfare
state's origin in, 267; *see also* EAST
GERMANY
Ghana, 43
Gibbon, Edward, 109, 203, 205; *The
History of the Decline and Fall of the
Roman Empire*, 5, 110, 200, 201
Gibson, Robert, 69, 386
Gillespie, A. D., 8, 9
Giotto, 23
Gleichschaltung, 345–6
Goethe, Johann Wolfgang von: *Faust*,
11, 12, 303; *Italienische Reise*, 23–4, 53,
276
Graeco–Roman Civilization, the, 14,
200–2
—— World, the: as A. J. T.'s spiritual

home, 17–20, 28, 107–8; city-states in,
28; 14, suicide in, 353; topography
of, 18–19, 28
Graeco–Turkish exchange of populations, 58, 243–4
—— War in Anatolia, 58, 72, 83, 101,
220–1, 243–4
Great Britain: August 1914 as break in
history of, 45–6, 106, 371; defeat of, in
wars with United States, 231, 233; economic effects of First World War on,
219; education in, 3–19, 21, 40, 91–2,
107, 268–72, 295, 296, 308–11, 313–14,
318, 335, 339, 345–6; French Protestant refugees in, 256–7; housing in,
342, 343; in Second World War, 195,
222, 232, 263, 311; industrial workers
in, 298–9, 336–9; industry, foreign
competition in, 188–9, 295, 310, 337,
338, invincibility, reputation for, 260;
mandate of, for Palestine, 231, 245,
261; middle class in, 187–94, 298–9,
335–9; national income of, distribution of, 190, 193, 268, 298–9, 335, 337,
338, 340, 342; Nature Conservancy in,
294; population of, 358; position and
policy of, after 1945, 222–3, 259; race-
prejudice in, 248–9, 316, 342–4; revulsion of, from war, after 1918, 221–2;
social conditions in, before 1914, 187–
188, 190–4, 268, 298–9, 335–6; welfare
state in, 33, 268–71, 335–40; will to
power of, in nineteenth century, 211–
212; *see also entries under* BRITISH
Greece, 4, 18–45 *passim*, 197, 209, 246,
276, 277
Greek emigrants to United States, 30–1
— history, 18, 93–4, 96, 106–7, 200–2
— language and literature: classical,
11–18, 28, 93–5, 98, 106–7, 192, 200–
201, 308–9, 320; post-classical, 200–
202
— language, modern, 11, 29, 34
— Orthodox Church, the, 11, 30–1
— peasants, interest of in current international affairs, 28–9, 32–3
— railways, 34–5
— religion, 157, 174
— residents in Ethiopia, 255
— roads, 28, 29, 38
— shepherds, as amateur brigands,
26–7
Grey, Sir Edward (Viscount Grey of
Fallodon), 25, 32–3, 51, 187
Grocyn, William, 14

missionary religions, 262, 284; non-essential accretions in faith and practice, 144; orthodoxy in, 117–18, 127, 129–45, 147, 169–70; physical science in relation to, 297, 306–7, 324; reconciliation and co-operation between religions, 325–30; re-emergence of traditional religions since 1945, 321–2, 324–7; sectarianism in, 110, 327; spiritual vacuum created by loss of belief in, 322, 324; uniqueness, claim to, 129, 131; wars of, 205, 323, 324

Renaissance, the Italian, 14–16, 106, 108, 200, 309

Rendall, M. J., 9, 17

Resurrection, 132–5, 141, 147, 165–7, 178

Revelation of St. John the Divine, 162, 274, 373

Reverence, 301–2

Rhineland, the, 225

Rhodesia, 247–9, 254–7, 259, 265, 266, 334, 343

Rocky Mountains, the, 276

Roman Catholic Church, the, 11, 117–118, 130, 256, 257, 272, 324–5, 329, 330

— Empire, the, 5, 11, 16, 17, 107, 200, 246, 264

— governing class, the, 115–16

— history, 18, 93–4, 106–7

Romano–Carthaginian Wars, the, 104

Rome, 18, 22, 23, 378, 379

Roosevelt, President Franklin Delano, 196, 363

Royal Society, the, 310

Ruanda-Urundi, 242

Rubruck, William of, 275

Ruhr, the, 219

Rumania, 25

Ruskin College, Oxford, 193, 268

Russell, Bertrand (Earl Russell), 106, 368–9, 371

Russia, 25, 51, 58, 86, 197–9, 204, 206, 212, 219, 220, 221, 234, 251, 258, 311, 341, 359; *see also* UNION OF SOVIET SOCIALIST REPUBLICS

Russian diplomacy, 52–3

— Imperial family, the, 55

— language, the, 52

— Revolution (1917), the, 207, 220, 251

Russo-Japanese War (1904–5), the, 17, 199, 227–9

— -Turkish War (1878), the, 220

St. Hugh's College, Oxford, 39

St. Jean de Maurienne, Secret Treaty of, 58

Saints, 175, 320

Salamis, 19, 20, 104

Samanid dynasty, the, 361–2

Samos, 37

Samuel, first Viscount, 122

San Francisco, 100

Sanskrit language, the, 183

Sarajevo, 47, 48

Saronic Gulf, the, 19

Scheldt, the, 102

Science, physical, 107, 108, 131–3, 139, 158, 159, 273–321 *passim*

Scientists, *Weltanschauung* of, 293–7, 299–300, 303–8

Scotland, 269, 358, 378

Scottish settlers in Uruguay, 256

Sea, the: as source of food supply, 372–5; mineral wealth beneath, 375

Self-centredness, 125, 136–8, 149–52, 154–6, 161, 165–8, 172, 287

Self-discipline, 317, 320

Self-employment, 379

Self-observation, 126, 127

Self-respect and self-reliance, 298–300

Self-sacrifice, 130, 135, 146, 157, 165, 167, 177, 178, 341

Serbia, 209

Servius Sulpicius Rufus, 19

Senility, 121–2, 352

Serenity, 379–80

Sèvres, Treaty of, 73, 221

Sin, 123, 124, 131, 149, 152, 160, 165, 352; original, 36, 138

Sino-Japanese Wars: (1894), 227, 229; (1931–45), 228, 234

Slavery, 83, 153, 247, 274

Smith, A. L., 68, 69, 70–1

— Mrs. A. L., 71

Smuts, General Jan, 108, 109

Smyrna, 58, 72

Social insurance, 267, 335

Social justice, 267–72, 335–40

Sociology, 320

Socrates, 175, 316–17

Some Problems of Greek History, A. J. T.'s book on, 96, 112

Sophocles, 16; *Antigone*, 101

South Africa, Union of, 247–9, 251, 254, 256, 257, 259, 266, 282, 334, 343

— African War, the, 186–7, 210, 212, 215, 259

Sovereignty, local, 84

Spain, 203-4, 213
Spanish-American War, the, 232
— Civil War, the, 204, 240
— language, the, 278
— Succession, War of the, 217
Sparta, 16, 17, 96, 264, 334
Specialization, 94-5, 108, 110, 111
Speed, pressure of, 366-7
Spello, 23, 24
Spengler, Oswald, 13
Spercheius, River, 34
Spooner, W. A., 69
Spy, arrest of A. J. T. as, 34-5
Stainton, Sir John, 119-20
Stalin (Djugushvili), J. V., 262, 263, 264
States, sovereign: devolution in, 377-8; functions of, 267-8; origin of, 208
Stevenson, Sir Daniel, 74, 76
Stoicism, 111, 152, 154-5, 317, 380
Stone tools, 287, 291, 356-7
Strachan-Davidson, J. L., 68-71
Strikes, industrial, 197, 355, 358
Study of History, A, A. J. T.'s book, 80, 85, 87, 100-1, 108, 112
Subconscious, the, 127, 182, 211, 317, 320
Sudan, the, 198, 259, 334, 378
Suez Canal, the, 234
Suicide: individual, 123, 352-4: mass, 290, 320, 369, 371, 372
Sumer, 208, 252, 350, 361, 376
Sumerian language and script, the, 109
Superstition, 123
Surgery, advance in, 280-2, 290, 347-56
Survey of International Affairs, the, 29, 37, 40, 65, 73-6, 78-81, 83, 85, 87, 100-2, 111, 112
Sweden, 234
Switzerland, 11

Tacitus, C. Cornelius, 200, 202
T'ai P'ing rebellion, the, 46, 232
Taiwan (Formosa), 229, 261
Tala't Bey, 242
Technology: advance in, 183, 204, 205, 238, 240, 241, 253, 273-321 *passim*, 326, 330, 357; application of science to, 310-16, 317; artificial environment created by, 357, 366-7, 374, 377; dehumanizing effect of, 325, 326, 328; moral neutrality of, 316, 321; revolt against, 367-8, 377, 379
Temperley, H. W. V., 73
Temple, Archbishop William, 138

Temptation, 36, 168
Tennyson, Alfred, Lord, 302, 303, 305; *In Memoriam*, 147, 148, 301-2
Terence, quoted, 94, 241, 369
Territorial waters, 375
Texas, 232
Thailand, 199, 259, 261
Thales, 316, 317
Thebes (Greece), 16
Theology, history in relation to, 90
Thermopylae, 34, 264
Thompson, M. S., 22, 23, 24
Thor, the god, 95
Thucydides, 96, 202, 320
Tiflis, 362
Tigers, sabre-toothed, 288-90
Tirol, South, 58-9
Titicaca, Lake, 279
Tobruk, 100
Toy soldiers, 82, 214-17
Toynbee, Arnold (A. J. T.'s uncle), 39, 119, 144
— Charlotte, 48
— George (A. J. T.'s great-grandfather), 190
— George (A. J. T.'s great-uncle), 119, 144
— Gertrude, 119
— Grace (Mrs. Percy Frankland), 293, 296, 304, 305
— Harriet, 194
— Harry Valpy, 3, 6, 26, 76-7, 88, 127, 144, 188, 190, 192, 193, 194, 269, 297-300, 336
— Captain Henry, 117-18, 144, 145, 305-6, 323
— Jason, 3
— Jocelyn M. C., 194
— Joseph, 83, 127, 144, 190, 194, 347-8
— Margaret R., 194
— Paget, 94
— Philip, 4-5, 113-14
— Rosalind, 4, 70, 141, 194
— Sally, 3
— Sarah Edith, 3, 4, 6, 18, 89-90, 127, 132, 188, 190, 192, 194, 248, 268, 363
— Veronica M., 3, 24, 29, 72, 78-80, 85, 100, 101, 104, 112, 279
Trafalgar, Battle of, 211
Traffic, speed and congestion of, 365, 378-9
Transition, times of, 145
Trans-Siberian Railway, the, 101
Travel: A. J. T.'s zest for, 99, 113; freedom of, before 1914, 198; methods of,

22, 24–5, 28, 29, 99–100, 273–80, 365, 366
Tribal life, at Winchester College, 8, 9, 10, 14, 79
Trieste, 35, 39
Trinity, Christian doctrine of the, 177–8
Tripoli War, the, 37, 232
Trotsky, Leon, 262, 263
Truman, President Harry, 231
Tunisia, 259
Turkey, 25, 34, 58, 73, 196–8, 219–21, 242, 244, 246, 271–2, 313, 341, 362; *see also* OTTOMAN EMPIRE
Turkish language, the, 11, 95, 98–9
— Revolution (1908), the, 107
Turner, E. J., 11, 12

Uniate Roman Catholics, 257
Union of Soviet Socialist Republics, 59, 111, 222, 224–6, 229, 232–5, 246, 262–264, 311, 334, 357
United Arab Republic, the, 245
United Nations, the, 245
United States of America: air bombardment not experienced in own territory by, 230–1; air travel in, 276; Amerindians, treatment of, 265, 266; as a 'super-power', 357; as Western Europe's former debtor, 258; climatic variations in, 265; colonialism of, 259–266; communications in, 358; Communism, attitude of American public towards, 86, 262, 263; conscription in, 237; contribution of, to UNRWA funds, 245; depersonalization of human relations in, 358; dollar, possible devaluation of, 264; economic empire of, 335; education in, 20–1, 269, 314–316; effect on, of victory in wars, 227, 231–9; farming in, 332–5; foreign aid by, 226, 258, 335; French Protestant settlers in, 256–7; Greek immigrants in, 29–32; 'image' of, 239; in First World War, 218, 222, 224, 232, 237, 262; in Second World War, 195, 207, 224, 228–32, 236, 237, 260, 263, 311, 315; industry in, 188–9, 195; isolationism in, 236; material amenities in, 288; Middle West of, 29, 32; militaristic tendency in, since 1945, 236–9; non-militaristic attitude of, before 1914, 211, 237; north-eastern industrial cities in, 247–8; objectives of, in South-East Asia, 235–6; physical stature of affluent members of society

in, 286–7; population of, 234, 358, 363; political docility in, 237–8; power politics in, 59, 197; race-problem in, 247–9, 251–2, 256, 316, 343; South, the Old, 233, 247, 248, 251–2; urbanization in, 333–4; Vietnam War, 86, 204, 205, 209, 210, 233–4, 238–40, 242, 261, 263–5, 316, 353, 370; war-making power of, 234, 238, 264
Universe, the: misfits in, 121, 131, 148, 150–1; nature of, 90–1, 116, 117, 120–1, 130, 132, 142, 170; recurrences in, 49–50; transformation of, by love and righteousness, 160–1, 165–7
Ur, 360
Urbanization, 42–4, 333–4, 357, 365
Uruguay, 256

Venizelos, Elevtherios, 58, 72
Venice, 378–9
Versailles, 55, 56; Treaty of, 51, 221, 225, 242–3
Vico, Giambattista, 109
Victoria, Queen of England, 186, 187, 196, 210, 257–8
Vietnam, 86, 204, 205, 209, 210, 223, 233–4, 238, 240, 242, 261, 263–5, 316, 352–3, 370
Villages, 360–1
Violence, prevalence of, 248, 316, 325–6, 358, 367–8, 377
Virgil, 16, 320
Virgin Birth, the, 127, 132, 133, 134, 135
Viruses, 289, 290
Visio Beatifica, the, 91
Vlachs, the, 22
Voltaire, François Marie Arouet de, 323

Wace, A. J. B., 22–4
Wales, 358, 378
Wanderjahr, A. J. T.'s, 18–39, 75, 79, 93, 197
War: abolition of, 82–5, 208, 240, 376; air bombardment, 204–5, 230–1, 240, 273; as legalized murder, 241, 341, 354; as repudiation of love, 148; atomic weapons, 37, 50, 60, 84, 205–7, 222, 226, 230–1, 236, 240, 273–4, 289–290, 301, 305, 307–8, 364, 366, 367; bacteriological weapons, 205, 283–4, 289, 304; casualties among fighting for ces, 10, 37, 40, 81–4, 105, 118–20, 124, 203, 207, 208, 216–20, 231, 232, 239, 240, 264, 368; chemical weapons,